MW00718285

COMPREHENSIVE TRAVEL GUIDE

SEATTLE &
PORTLAND '94-'95

by Karl Samson

PRENTICE HALL TRAVEL

NEW YORK • LONDON • TORONTO • SYDNEY • TOKYO • SINGAPORE

*For my wife, Jane, who followed me
down the Oregon trail.*

FROMMER BOOKS
Published by Prentice Hall General Reference
15 Columbus Circle
New York, NY 10023

Copyright © 1990, 1992, 1994 by Simon & Schuster, Inc.

PRENTICE HALL is a registered trademark and colophon is a trademark
of Prentice-Hall, Inc.

ISBN 0-671-86659-1
ISSN 1045-9308

Design by Robert Bull Design
Maps by Ortelius Design

FROMMER'S EDITORIAL STAFF
Editorial Director: Marilyn Wood
Editorial Manager/Senior Editor: Alice Fellows
Senior Editors: Sara Hinsey Raveret, Lisa Renaud
Editors: Charlotte Allstrom, Thomas F. Hirsch, Peter Katucki, Theodore
Stavrou
Assistant Editors: Margaret Bowen, Christopher Hollander, Alice Thompson, Ian Wilker
Editorial Assistants: Gretchen Henderson, Bethany Jewett
Managing Editor: Leanne Coupe

Special Sales
Bulk purchases (10+ copies) of Frommer's Travel Guides are available to
corporations at special discounts. The Special Sales Department can produce
custom editions to be used as premiums and/or for sales promotion to suit
individual needs. Existing editions can be produced with custom cover
imprints such as a corporate logo. For more information write to: Special
Sales, Prentice Hall Travel, 15 Columbus Circle, New York, New York 10023.

Manufactured in the United States of America

CONTENTS

20 EASY EXCURSIONS FROM PORTLAND 246

APPENDIX   256

INDEX   266

LIST OF MAPS

by Arthur Frommer

My own first trip to Seattle was made in a state of constant wonderment. How in the world could I have delayed visiting this remarkable town for so long?

For Seattle is an unexpected combination of San Francisco, Boston, and New York, of Europe and a bit of Asia—it is a sophisticated city of well-educated and well-read people who none-theless save great chunks of their time for outdoor recreation and consider themselves laid-back and "cool."

The brainy Seattleites from Microsoft, Boeing, and other high-tech firms go hiking in the mountains (Mt. Rainier hovers nearby), skiing year around, fishing, boating, bicycling, kayaking, and rafting, just as tourists can so easily do here. They enjoy excursions to excellent beaches, old-growth forests, and hot springs. But within the city, they savor bookstores, a highly intellectual cafe life, and—especially—coffee taken from more than 150 streetside espresso carts (more than in any other city) and almost as many attractive coffeehouses devoted to conversation and exotic brands of the bean. They also patronize the single greatest food-and-crafts market of the nation (Pike Place Market), a chaotic jumble of shops and stands that evolved quite naturally, over decades, and is today a place of battered old floors, dark nooks and crannies, real fishmongers, produce vendors, and moderate prices. Knowing nothing about it at the time of my first visit, I wandered its colorful arcades in a happy daze, past fresh salmon and dungeness crabs selling at remarkably low rates, past the almost unbelievably fresh vegetables more attractive than any you've seen. Though the reference to a city as "surprising" is the most overworked cliche of travel writing, I can't desist from using it here: Wait until you see surprising Seattle!

Portland is of course different, but still unusual: A big city yet with a small-town flavor and attitudes to match; sparkling and clean; and linked to the great outdoors by the ever-present sight of Mt. Hood and Mt. St. Helens. For visitors, its chief utility is as a base for exploring the underrated, undervisited Oregon Coast and its charm-ing Cannon Beach and Village, looking as if they had been lifted unchanged from a New England whaling port of the 1790s. Two summers ago, I vacationed for half-a-month along those rugged and largely underdeveloped shores, and reveled in the experience. From a coastal town with the unlikely name of Yachats, we darted periodi-cally to Portland and the nearby university city of Eugene, and made a particular point of visiting the two open-air Saturday crafts markets of both. The Saturday Market in Portland is now the world's largest.

To evaluate the touring facilities of Seattle and Portland, we've gone to the best possible observer: a resident of the Pacific North-west and an inveterate traveler. Karl Samson, of the Portland area, is a widely published guidebook writer who gravitated toward the profession after a childhood of moving about from one capital of southeast Asia to another as the son of a U.S. State Department official. In the course of his many writing assignments, including several stints as an author of Frommer Guides, he discovered the Pacific Northwest, and quickly decided to make it his home.

For this 1994–95 edition of *Frommer's Seattle & Portland,* Karl Samson has updated and supplemented the text as only a resident could. In addition to revising hundreds of prices and other details, he alerts readers to the brand-new Seattle Art Museum (with its important exhibits of native American art, among other collections) and just-as-new Oregon Museum of Science and Industry in Portland and much more.

I should note that many visitors to Seattle decide, upon concluding their stays, to add a trip to the Canadian city of Victoria, on Vancouver Island, and to the important city of Vancouver as well; the latter is three hours (including time for border-crossing) from Seattle by car. If you're among that group, we invite you to equip yourself with a copy of *Frommer's Vancouver & Victoria '94-'95,* in a format similar to this book.

We wish you the very best of trips, and thank you for your support of Frommer travel guides. We'll do our best to continue deserving your trust.

INVITATION TO THE READERS

In researching this book, I have come across many wonderful establishments, the best of which I have included here. I am sure that many of you will also discover appealing hotels, inns, restaurants, guest houses, shops, and attractions. Please don't keep them to yourself. Share your experiences, especially if you want to comment on places that have been included in this edition that have changed for the worse. You can address your letters to:

Karl Samson
Frommer's Seattle & Portland '94–'95
c/o Prentice Hall Travel
15 Columbus Circle
New York, NY 10023

A DISCLAIMER

Readers are advised that prices fluctuate in the course of time and travel information changes under the impact of the varied and volatile factors that affect the travel industry. Neither the author nor the publisher can be held responsible for the experiences of readers while traveling. Readers are invited to write to the publisher with ideas, comments, and suggestions for future editions.

SAFETY ADVISORY

Whenever you're traveling in an unfamiliar city or country, stay alert. Be aware of your immediate surroundings. Wear a money belt and keep a close eye on your possessions. Be particularly careful with cameras, purses, and wallets, all favorite targets of thieves and pickpockets.

INTRODUCING SEATTLE

I t is the Emerald City of the Northwest—the jewel in the crown of a land of natural beauty. The sparkling waters of Elliott Bay, Lake Union, and Lake Washington surround this city of shimmering skyscrapers. Forests of evergreens crowd the city limits. Everywhere you look, another breathtaking vista unfolds. Once a sleepy backwoods town, Seattle has become one of the key cities of the Pacific Rim, forging new trading links with Japan and the rest of Asia. In many ways, the city is similar to San Francisco: It is surrounded by water, was built on hills, and has a Chinatown, a large gay community, and even a trolley. What makes Seattle different are its people and their pace of life.

Things move more slowly up here, and although Seattle is growing more cosmopolitan by the minute, it is the wildness of the Northwest that has attracted many of the city's residents. With endless boating opportunities and beaches and mountains within a few hours' drive, Seattle is ideally situated for the active life-style that is so much a part of life in the Northwest. The city's rainy weather may be infamous, but the people of Seattle have ways of forgetting about the clouds. They either put on their rain gear or retreat to the city's hundreds of excellent restaurants, its dozens of theaters and performance halls, and its outstanding museums. They never let the weather stand in the way of having a good time—and neither should you. Although summer is the best time to visit Seattle, the city offers year-round diversions and entertainment.

1. CULTURE, HISTORY & BACKGROUND

GEOGRAPHY/PEOPLE

Seattle is located on Puget Sound in northwestern Washington State. To the east are Lake Washington, the communities of Kirkland and Bellevue, and Mercer Island; to the south are Renton, Kent, Auburn, Tacoma, and other communities; and to the north are Edmonds, Lynwood, Everett, and other communities. Within Seattle's city limits are Elliott Bay of Puget Sound, the Lake Washington Ship Canal (which passes through Lake Union), and Green Lake. Many of the region's bodies of water were formed by glaciers during the last ice age. When the glaciers receded, the valleys left behind were flooded. The Cascade Range, a large series of volcanic peaks that

WHAT'S SPECIAL ABOUT SEATTLE

Beaches
- ☐ Alki Beach stretches for 2½ miles down West Seattle.

Architectural Highlight
- ☐ The Space Needle is a futuristic-looking tower with observation deck and two restaurants.

Museums
- ☐ The Museum of Flight, next to Boeing Field, is one of the best such museums in the world.
- ☐ At The Seattle Aquarium you can watch salmon returning to spawn if you happen to be here at the right time of year.

Festival
- ☐ Seafair, Seattle's summer extravaganza, features all manner of public spectacles, from starlight parades to powerboat races.

For the Kids
- ☐ Seattle Center, a little amusement park in the middle of Seattle, has rides, arcade games, and a children's museum.
- ☐ Ye Olde Curiosity Shop is part museum of the bizarre and part tacky gift shop.

Natural Spectacles
- ☐ Mount Rainier, only 90 miles away, is the tallest mountain in the Northwest.
- ☐ Olympic National Park is home not only of the Olympic Mountains but of an extensive rain forest.

- ☐ The San Juan Islands make an idyllic summer getaway for urban Seattleites.

Regional Food & Drink
- ☐ Smoked seafood, salmon in particular, is a popular Seattle delicacy.
- ☐ Washington State wines rank high in international wine competitions.

Activities
- ☐ Sailing, sailboarding, and sea kayaking on any of the waters surrounding Seattle are favorites.

Shopping
- ☐ Pike Place Market is filled with hundreds of shops and vendors selling everything from fresh produce to fine arts and crafts.

Great Neighborhood
- ☐ International District, which would be called Chinatown anywhere else, has lots of interesting shops and good restaurants.

Offbeat
- ☐ The Seattle Underground Tour takes the curious under the city's streets to see the remains of old Seattle, which burned to the ground in 1889.
- ☐ The Bus Tunnel, under downtown Seattle, provides electric bus service. All terminals have interesting works of art.

includes Mount St. Helens (which erupted explosively in 1980), is some 50 miles east; Mount Rainier (14,410 feet high), the tallest peak in Washington and visible from Seattle on clear days, is about 90 miles southeast. The Olympic Mountains of the Olympic Peninsula are about 60 miles west. Beyond the Olympic Mountains is the Pacific coast, with its rugged headlands and long stretches of empty beaches.

Life in Seattle has been changing in recent years. Not long ago, it was considered the most livable city in America, with a cultural and natural diversity unrivaled in the USA. With the development of Seattle as a major business hub of the Northwest, the cityscape and population has changed a bit. Jeans and down jackets have been replaced by high fashion from Europe; and if you walk into a downtown bar, you are more likely to hear financial gossip than tales of mountain climbing. No longer is the populace as laid-back as it once was. However, Seattleites are still as proud of their cultural offerings as they are of "their" mountain (Mount Rainier). They are still an active lot, with water sports (sailing and sea kayaking) and skiing dominating athletic agendas. This isn't surprising, considering how much water surrounds the city and how close the ski slopes are. In the early 1990s Seattle proper had about 520,000 inhabitants. About 2.6 million people lived in the metropolitan area.

HISTORY

EARLY DAYS   Seattle got a late start in U.S. history, and to this day the city has been trying to make up for it. The first settlers didn't arrive until 1851, although explorers had visited the region much earlier. Captain George Vancouver of the British Royal Navy—who lent his name to both Vancouver, British Columbia, and Vancouver, Washington—had explored Puget Sound as early as 1792. However, there was little to attract anyone permanently to this remote region. Unlike Oregon to the south, Washington had little rich farmland, only acres and acres of forest. It was this seemingly endless supply of wood that finally enticed the first settlers.

The first settlement was on Alki Point, in the area now known as West Seattle. Because this location was exposed to storms, within a few years the settlers moved across Elliott Bay to a more protected spot, the present downtown Seattle. The new location for the village was a tiny island surrounded by mud flats. Although some early settlers wanted to name the town New York—even then Seattle had grand aspirations—the name Seattle was chosen as a tribute to Chief Sealth, a local Native American who had befriended the newcomers.

In the middle of town, on the waterfront, the first steam-powered lumber mill on Puget Sound was built by Henry Yesler. It stood at the foot of what is now Yesler Way—but what for many years was simply referred to as Skid Road, a reference to the

DATELINE

- **1792**   Capt. George Vancouver of the British Royal Navy explores Puget Sound.
- **1841**   Lt. Charles Wilkes surveys Puget Sound and names Elliott Bay.
- **1851**   The first white settlers arrive in what will become West Seattle's Alki Point.
- **1852**   These same settlers move to the east side of Elliott Bay from Alki Point, which is subject to storms.
- **1853**   Washington Territory is formed.
- **1864**   The transcontinental telegraph reaches Seattle, connecting it with the rest of the country.
- **1866**   Chief Sealth, for whom Seattle is named, dies and is buried across Puget Sound at Suquamish.

(continues)

way logs were skidded down from the slopes behind town to the sawmill. Over the years Skid Road developed a reputation for its bars and brothels. Some say that after an East Coast journalist incorrectly referred to it as Skid Row in his newspaper, the name stuck and was subsequently applied to derelict neighborhoods all over the country. But only Seattle can lay claim to the very first Skid Row. To this day, despite attempts to revamp the neighborhood, Yesler Way attracts the sort of visitors one would expect, but it is also in the center of the Pioneer Historic District, one of Seattle's main tourist attractions.

By 1889 the city had more than 25,000 inhabitants and was well on its way to becoming the most important city in the Northwest. On June 6 of that year, however, 25 blocks in the center of town burned to the ground. By that time the city—which had spread out to low-lying land reclaimed from the mud flats—had begun experiencing problems with mud and sewage disposal. The fire gave citizens the opportunity they needed to rebuild Seattle. The solution to the drainage and sewage problems was to regrade the steep slopes to the east of the town and raise the streets above their previous levels. Because the regrading lagged behind the rebuilding, the ground floor of many new buildings wound up below street level. Eventually these lower-level shops and entrances were abandoned when elevated sidewalks bridged the space between roadways and buildings. Today sections of several abandoned streets that are now underground can be toured (see Section 4 of Chapter 6 for details).

One of the most amazing engineering feats that took place after the fire was the regrading of Denny Hill. Seattle once had seven hills, but today has only six—nothing is left of Denny Hill. Hydraulic mining techniques, with high-powered water jets digging into hillsides, were used to level the hill, of which only a name remains—Denny Regrade, a neighborhood just south of Seattle Center.

The new buildings went up quickly after the fire, and eight years later another event occurred that changed the city almost as much. The steamship *Portland* arrived in Seattle from Alaska, carrying a ton of gold from the recently discovered Klondike goldfields. Within the year Seattle's population swelled with prospectors ultimately headed north. Few of them ever struck it rich, but they all stopped in Seattle to purchase supplies and equipment, thus lining the pockets of Seattle merchants and spreading far and wide the name of this obscure Northwest city. When the prospectors came south again with their hard-earned gold, much of it never left Seattle, sidetracked by beer halls and brothels.

20TH CENTURY A very important event in Seattle history took place on Lake Union in 1916. William Boeing and Clyde Esterveld launched their first airplane, a floatplane, with the intention of flying mail to Canada. Their enterprise eventually became the Boeing Company, which has since grown to become the single largest employer in the area. Unfortunately, until recently Seattle's fortunes were so inextricably bound to those of Boeing that hard times for the aircraft manufacturer meant hard times for the whole city. In recent years, however, industry in the Seattle region has begun to diversify. There are now many computer-related companies in the area, including software-giant Microsoft. Floatplanes still call Lake Union home, and if you should venture out on the lake by kayak, sailboard, or boat, be sure to watch out for air traffic.

Two years before the Boeing flight, in 1914, big changes had already begun in Seattle when the Smith Tower was erected. This 42-story building soared above the skyline and was for many years the tallest building west of the Mississippi. That same skyline today is crowded with dozens of skyscrapers that dwarf the Smith Tower. Foremost among these is the new 76-story Columbia Seafirst Center, which is now the tallest building west of Houston.

Despite the significance of these two buildings, the most recognizable structure on the Seattle skyline is the Space Needle. Built in 1962 for Century 21, the Seattle World's Fair, the Space Needle was, and still is, a futuristic-looking structure. Situated just north of downtown—in the Seattle Center complex that was the site of the World's Fair—the Space Needle provides stupendous views of the city and all its surrounding natural beauty.

The 1962 World's Fair was far more than a fanciful vision of the future—it was truly prophetic for Seattle. The emergence of the Emerald City as an important Pacific Rim trading center is a step toward a bright 21st century. The Seattle area has witnessed extraordinary growth in recent years, with the migration of thousands of people in search of jobs, a higher quality of life, and a mild climate. To keep pace with its sudden prominence on the Pacific Rim, Seattle has also been rushing to transform itself from a sleepy Northwest city into a cosmopolitan metropolis. New restaurants, theaters, and museums are cropping up all over the place as new residents demand more cultural attractions. Visitors to Seattle will immediately sense the quickening pulse of this awakening city.

IMPRESSIONS

Seattle is a comparatively new-looking city that covers an old frontier town like frosting on a cake.
—WINTHROP SARGEANT, IN THE NEW YORKER, 1978

ART & ARCHITECTURE

ART   Seattle—and all the Northwest for that matter—has a burgeoning art community. Outside of the fine-art glass produced at the Pilchuck School of Glass, though, Northwestern art has yet to develop a national following as has Southwestern art. Like the American Southwest, the Pacific Northwest has a Native American art heritage, which is evident in Seattle. There are several totem poles around the city, and Northwest Coast Native American designs show up everywhere, from T-shirts to restaurant decor. Several galleries exhibit and sell the works of Native American artists and artisans, and these works command high prices. Carved wooden masks generally start at around $2,000.

ARCHITECTURE   Aside from Seattle's Space Needle, which is one of the city's most immediately identifiable symbols, there is little particularly noteworthy about Seattle architecture. Most of the city burned to the ground in the fire of 1889, so its architectural heritage dates only to the period of rebuilding. Of interest is the fact that the city leaders chose to rebuild *on top of* the rubble. In order to raise the city above the mud flats upon which it was originally built, streets were filled in with any rubble that came to hand. To this day, there are still sections of the old city accessible beneath the streets of the Pioneer Square area. These dark recesses are the focus of the Seattle Underground Tour, a rather off-color look at the city's early years.

After the fire of 1889, Seattle rebuilt in brick and cast iron to prevent another such disaster. Today many of Pioneer Square's 100-year-old buildings, with their unusual cast-iron framed windows, have been restored. Also in this area are the Smith Tower and the much larger Columbia Seafirst Center.

2. RECOMMENDED BOOKS & FILMS

BOOKS

Timothy Egan's *The Good Rain* (1990) provides an enlightening overview of life in the Pacific Northwest, with a chapter devoted to Seattle and the many changes it has gone through in the past century.

If you are interested in learning more about the history of Seattle, there are two books that I'm sure you will find much more entertaining than a standard dry history: *Sons of the Profits* and *Doc Maynard, The Man Who Invented Seattle*. Both are by Bill Speidel, the man who conceived the Seattle Underground Tour. You can pick them up in Seattle or contact the Seattle Underground Tour gift shop, 610 First Ave. (tel. 206/682-1511).

FILMS

The Northwest has never been a major setting for films. Its unpredictable weather makes outdoor photography chancy. However, in recent years a few films have used this area as a backdrop. *An Officer and a Gentleman* (1982) was filmed at Fort Worden State Park in Port Townsend on the Olympic Peninsula. *Twice in a*

Lifetime (1985), a domestic drama starring Gene Hackman and Ann-Margret, was shot in Seattle and its environs. *WarGames* (1983), the story of a teenage computer hacker who inadvertently almost initiates World War III, was also made in the Northwest. *Immediate Family* (1989), starring James Woods and Glenn Close, is another Seattle-based film, about a childless yuppie couple who buy a baby. *The Fabulous Baker Boys* (1989), starring Jeff Bridges, Beau Bridges, and Michelle Pfeiffer, is a story of two Seattle lounge pianists and how their lives are changed by their new singer. *Singles* (1992), with Matt Dillon and Bridget Fonda, focuses on the Seattle singles scene, with a very prominent use of the local "grunge rock" on the soundtrack. *Sleepless in Seattle* (1993), starring Tom Hanks and Meg Ryan, is a romantic comedy that includes some good shots around Seattle.

PLANNING A TRIP TO SEATTLE

Seattle is becoming an increasingly popular destination for travelers, and as its popularity grows, so too does the need for previsit planning. Before leaving home, you should try to make hotel and car reservations. Not only will these reservations save you money, but you won't have to worry about finding accommodations when you arrive. Summer is the peak tourist season in Seattle and reservations are highly advisable, especially if you plan to visit during the Seafair festival in August, when every hotel in town can be booked up.

1. INFORMATION

The sources of information listed here can provide you with plenty of free brochures on Seattle, many with colorful photos to further tempt you into a visit.

If you still have questions about Seattle after reading this book, contact the **Seattle–King County Convention & Visitors Bureau,** 520 Pike St., Suite 1300, Seattle, WA 98101-9927 (tel. 206/461-5840). They'll be happy to send you more information on the city and the surrounding areas. They're open Monday through Friday from 8:30am to 5pm. To find their **Visitor Information Center,** walk up Union Street until it goes into a tunnel under the Washington State Convention and Trade Center. You'll see the information center on your left as you enter the tunnel. The exact address is 800 Convention Place.

These helpful people also operate two **Visitor Information Centers** at Seattle-Tacoma (Sea-Tac) International Airport (tel. 206/433-4679 and 433-5218). You can't miss them—they're right beside the baggage-claim area (by carousels no. 1 and 9). They have brochures on many area attractions and can answer any last-minute questions.

For information on other parts of Washington, contact the **Washington State Tourism Office,** P.O. Box 42500, Olympia, WA 98504-2500 (tel. 206/586-2102 or 586-2088 or toll free 800/544-1800).

WHAT THINGS COST IN SEATTLE	U.S. $
Taxi from the airport to the city center	29.00
Bus ride between any two downtown points	Free
Local telephone call	0.25
Double at Alexis Hotel (very expensive)	180.00
Double at Sixth Avenue Inn (moderate)	80.00
Double at Travelodge Seattle Airport (inexpensive)	50.00
Lunch for one at Cafe Hue (inexpensive)	12.00
Lunch for one at Macheezmo Mouse (inexpensive)	5.00
Dinner for one, without wine, at The Georgian Room (expensive)	35.00
Dinner for one, without wine, at Cafe Sophie (moderate)	20.00
Dinner for one, without wine, at Wild Ginger Asian Restaurant (inexpensive)	13.00
Pint of beer	3.50
Coca-Cola	0.75
Cup of espresso	1.35
Roll of ASA 100 Kodacolor film, 36 exposures	5.75
Movie ticket	6.50
Theater ticket to Seattle Repertory Theater	12.50–29.00

2. WHEN TO GO

CLIMATE

I'm sure you've heard about the climate in Seattle. Let's face it, the city's weather has a bad reputation. As they say out here, "The rain in Spain stays mainly in Seattle." Seattle can make London look like a desert. I wish I could tell you that it just ain't so, but I can't. It rains in Seattle—and rains and rains and rains. However, when December 31 rolls around each year, a funny thing happens: They total up the year's precipitation, and Seattle almost always comes out behind such cities as Washington, DC, Boston, New York, and Atlanta. Most of the rain falls between September and April, so if you visit during the summer, you might not see a drop of rain the entire time. If July in

Seattle is just too sunny for you, take a trip out to the Hoh Valley on the Olympic Peninsula. With more than 150 inches of rain a year, this is the wettest spot in the continental United States.

No matter what time of year you plan to visit Seattle, be sure to bring at least a sweater or light jacket. Summer nights can be quite cool, and daytime temperatures rarely climb above the low 80s. Winters are not as cold as in the East, but snow does fall in Seattle.

To make things perfectly clear, here's an annual weather chart:

Average Temperature & Days of Rain

	Jan	Feb	Mar	Apr	May	June	July	Aug	Sept	Oct	Nov	Dec
Temp. (°F)	46	50	53	58	65	69	75	74	69	60	52	47
Temp. (°C)	8	10	12	14	18	21	24	23	21	16	11	8
Days of Rain	19	16	17	14	10	9	5	7	9	14	18	20

THE FESTIVAL CITY

Seattleites organize a festival at the drop of a rain hat. Summers in the city seem to revolve around the myriad festivals that take place every week. Check the "Tempo Arts & Entertainment" section of the *Seattle Times* on Friday or pick up a copy of *Seattle Weekly* to find out what special events will be taking place during your visit. Remember, festivals here take place rain or shine.

SEATTLE CALENDAR OF EVENTS

FEBRUARY

☐ **Chinese New Year,** International District. Date depends on lunar calendar (may be in January).

☐ **Northwest Flower & Garden Show,** Washington State Convention and Trade Center. Massive show for avid gardeners. Second weekend in February. Tel. 206/789-5333.

☐ **Mardi Gras,** Pioneer Square. Parades and events culminating on Fat Tuesday, the day before Lent and some seven weeks before Easter. Tel. 206/682-4648.

APRIL

☐ **Skagit Valley Tulip Festival,** Mt. Vernon and the Skagit Valley. Tulip fields in bloom an hour north of Seattle, plenty of entertainment on weekends. First through third week of April. Tel. 206/428-8547.

☐ **Cherry Blossom and Japanese Cultural Festival,** Seattle Center. Traditional Japanese spring festival. Last weekend in April. Tel. 206/684-8582.

MAY

- ☐ **Opening Day of Boating Season,** Lake Union and Lake Washington. First Saturday in May.
- ☐ **Seattle International Film Festival,** theaters around town. Tel. 206/324-9996.

✪ **NORTHWEST FOLKLIFE FESTIVAL** *This is the largest folklife festival in the country, with dozens of national and regional folk musicians performing on numerous stages. In addition, craftspeople from all over the Northwest show and sell. Lots of good food and dancing too.*
   ***Where:** Seattle Center.* ***When:** Memorial Day weekend.* ***How:** Free. Tel. 206/684-8582.*

- ☐ **Pike Place Market Festival,** Pike Place Market. A celebration of the market, with lots of free entertainment. Memorial Day weekend. Tel. 206/587-0351.

JUNE

- ☐ **Out to Lunch,** parks throughout Seattle. Free lunchtime jazz and classical music concerts. Phone 206/623-0340 for a schedule. Beginning in late June.
- ☐ **Fremont Street Fair,** Fremont neighborhood. Food, arts and crafts, and entertainment in one of Seattle's favorite neighborhoods. Third weekend in June. Tel. 206/548-8376.

JULY

- ☐ **Fourth of July fireworks,** Elliott Bay and Seattle waterfront. July 4.
- ☐ **Wooden Boat Festival,** Lake Union. Wooden boats, both old and new, from all over the Northwest. Races, demonstrations, food, and entertainment. First weekend in July. Tel. 206/382-BOAT.
- ☐ **Chinatown International District Summer Festival,** International District. Features the music, dancing, arts, and food of Seattle's Asian district. Second Sunday in July.
- ☐ **Bite of Seattle,** Seattle Center. Sample offerings from Seattle's best restaurants. Mid-July. Tel. 206/684-8582.
- ☐ **King County Fair,** King County Fairgrounds, Enumclaw, south of Seattle. Starts the third Wednesday of the month. Tel. 206/825-7777.
- ☐ **Bellevue Jazz Festival,** Bellevue Downtown Park, Bellevue. Showcase for Northwest jazz musicians. Mid-July.

✪ **SEAFAIR** *This is the biggest Seattle event of the year, during which festivities occur every day—parades, hydroplane boat races, performances by the Navy's Blue Angels, a Torchlight Parade, ethnic festivals, sporting events, and open house on naval ships. This one really packs in the out-of-towners and sends Seattleites fleeing on summer vacations.*
   ***Where:** All over Seattle.* ***When:** Third weekend in July*

*to first weekend in August. **How:** Tel. 206/728-0123 for details on events and tickets.*

☐ **Pacific Northwest Arts and Crafts Fair,** Bellevue Square, Bellevue. The largest arts and crafts fair in the Northwest. Last weekend in July. Tel. 206/454-4900.

AUGUST

☐ **Seattle International Chamber Music Festival,** Meany Hall, University of Washington. Tel. 206/233-0993.
☐ **Chief Seattle Days,** Suquamish. Celebration of Northwest Native American culture across Puget Sound from Seattle. Late August. Tel. 206/598-3311.

SEPTEMBER

✪ ***BUMBERSHOOT*** *Seattle's second most popular festival derives its peculiar name from a British term for umbrella— an obvious reference to the rainy weather. Lots and lots of rock 'n' roll music packs Seattle's younger set into Seattle Center. You'll find plenty of arts and crafts on display too.*
    Where: *Seattle Center.* ***When:*** *Labor Day weekend.* ***How:*** *Phone 206/684-7200 for schedule.*

3. WHAT TO PACK

A raincoat, an umbrella, and a sweater or jacket are all absolutely essential any time of year in Seattle. Other than that, you might want to bring skis (snow or water), hiking boots, boat shoes, running shoes, shorts, bicycling shorts, a bathing suit, and just about any other outdoor clothing or equipment you have on hand. The outdoors is a way of life in this part of the country.

4. TIPS FOR THE DISABLED, SENIORS, SINGLES, FAMILIES & STUDENTS

FOR THE DISABLED   Most hotels in Seattle offer handicapped-accessible accommodations, which are noted in the listings in this book.

FOR SENIORS   Be sure to ask about senior discounts when making hotel reservations. Also, museums, theaters, gardens, and tour companies usually offer senior-citizen discounts. These can add up to substantial savings, but you have to remember to ask for the discount.

FOR SINGLES   One of the busiest singles bars in town is the **Pier 70 Bay Café,** at—you guessed it—Pier 70 on the waterfront.

FOR FAMILIES   Many of the less expensive hotels outside the city center allow kids to stay free in their parents' room. At mealtimes, keep in mind that many of the larger restaurants, especially along the waterfront, offer children's menus. If you want to keep the kids entertained all day long, spend the day at **Seattle Center.**

FOR STUDENTS   See "For Students" in Section 3 of Chapter 3.

5. GETTING THERE

BY PLANE

Seattle-Tacoma International Airport (tel. 206/431-4444), known as **Sea-Tac,** is located about 14 miles south of Seattle. It's connected to the city by I-5.

THE MAJOR AIRLINES   Sea-Tac Airport is served by more than 20 airlines. The major carriers include **Alaska Airlines** (tel. 206/433-3100 or toll free 800/426-0333), **American Airlines** (tel. toll free 800/433-7300), **America West** (tel. toll free 800/247-5692), **Continental** (tel. toll free 800/525-0280), **Delta** (tel. 206/433-4711 or toll free 800/221-1212), **Horizon Air** (tel. toll free 800/547-9308), **Northwest** (tel. 206/433-3500 or toll free 800/225-2525), **TWA** (tel. toll free 800/221-2000), **United** (tel. 206/441-3700 or toll free 800/241-6522), and **USAir** (tel. toll free 800/428-4322).

There are also about a dozen foreign airlines offering flights to and from cities all over the world.

In addition to air service at Sea-Tac Airport, there are several small airlines offering seaplane flights between Seattle and the San Juan Islands and British Columbia. **Kenmore Air** (tel. 206/486-1257 or 206/364-6990 or toll free 800/826-1890) is one airline that offers regular flights.

REGULAR AIRFARES AND SUPER APEX   At the time of this writing, round-trip **Super-APEX (Advance Purchase Excursion)** fares from the East Coast were about $400, though these were

---

 FROMMER'S SMART TRAVELER: AIRFARES

1. Shop all the airlines that fly to your destination.
2. Always ask for the lowest-priced fare, not just for a discount.
3. Keep calling the airline—availability of cheap seats changes daily. Airline yield managers would rather sell a seat than have it fly empty. As the departure date nears, additional low-cost seats become available.
4. Watch the newspapers for special offers. You may be able to save several hundred dollars per ticket by changing your vacation plans to fit in with special low-fare offers.

special summer fares. Shortly before the summer rates went into effect, fares had been running about $600 from the East Coast.

The round-trip full **coach** fare was $1,300 with **business class** costing about the same. The round-trip **first-class** fare was between $1,540 and $2,000.

OTHER GOOD-VALUE CHOICES   You may be able to fly for less than the standard APEX fare by contacting a **ticket broker** (also known as a **bucket shop**). These companies advertise in the travel sections of major city newspapers with small boxed ads listing numerous destinations and ticket prices. You won't always be able to get the low price advertised (often it is available to students only), but you are likely to save a bit of money off the regular fare. Call a few and compare prices, making sure you find out about all the taxes and surcharges that may not be included in the initial fare quote.

BY TRAIN

Amtrak trains stop at King Street Station, Third Avenue South and Jackson Street (tel. 206/382-4125), near the Kingdome. Several trains run daily between Seattle and Portland, Oregon. The trip takes about four hours and costs $23 one way. These trains continue south to San Francisco and Los Angeles. There are also daily trains heading east by way of Spokane. For Amtrak reservations, call toll free 800/872-7245.

BY BUS

From the **Greyhound** bus station, Eighth Avenue and Stewart Street (tel. 206/624-3456), buses can connect you to almost any city in the continental United States.

BY CAR

I-5 is the main artery between Seattle and Portland and points south, stretching as far as the Mexican border. I-5 also continues north between Seattle and the Canadian border. **I-90** comes into Seattle from Spokane and from the east—all the way from Boston. **I-405** bypasses downtown Seattle on the east side of Lake Washington, passing through the city of Bellevue instead.

Here are some driving distances from selected cities (in miles):

Los Angeles	1,190
Portland	175
Salt Lake City	835
San Francisco	810
Spokane	285
Vancouver, B.C.	110

BY SHIP

Seattle is a major port. The city is served by the **Washington State Ferries** (tel. 206/464-6400 or toll free 800/84-FERRY in Washington State), the most extensive ferry system in the United States. Ferries travel between Seattle and Vashon Island, Bainbridge Island, and the Olympic Peninsula. In addition, there is service north of Seattle between Anacortes and the San Juan Islands and between Edmonds and Kingston.

IMPRESSIONS

*The serenity of the climate, the innumerable pleasing landscapes,
and the abundant fertility that unassisted nature puts forth,
require only to be enriched by the industry of man with villages,
mansions, cottages, and other buildings, to render it the most
lovely country that can be imagined.*
—CAPTAIN GEORGE VANCOUVER IN 1792 ON ANCHORING OFF WHAT
WOULD ONE DAY BECOME SEATTLE

For high-speed passenger service between Seattle and Victoria, there is the ***Victoria Clipper,*** Pier 69, 2701 Alaskan Way, Seattle, WA 98121 (tel. 206/448-5000 or toll free 800/888-2535). The trip aboard this speedy catamaran takes only 2½ hours. Round-trip fare for adults is $74–$85; for senior citizens, $64–$75; and for children ages 1 to 11, $37–$42.50. Round-trip tickets are substantially cheaper if purchased in advance.

CHAPTER 3

GETTING TO KNOW SEATTLE

- **1. ORIENTATION**
- **• NEIGHBORHOODS IN BRIEF**
- **2. GETTING AROUND**
- **• FAST FACTS: SEATTLE**
- **3. NETWORKS & RESOURCES**

Water, water, everywhere—that's Seattle. This rapidly growing city has water on three sides. Sailboats, seaplanes, kayaks, and sailboards are permanent fixtures of the cityscape and one of the main reasons why many people live here. Any visit to Seattle should include some manner of waterborne activity, and even if you never leave dry land, you'll find your visit affected by water. There are drawbridges all over the Seattle area, and if you're in a hurry, you can bet that the one you have to cross will be delaying traffic. If you happen to be driving across Lake Washington, you might notice that the bridge you are on is rather close to the water; in fact, it's floating on the water. Seattle has some of the only floating bridges in the world.

In between Elliott Bay, Lake Union, and Lake Washington, there are hills—not gentle hills, but the same kind that San Francisco is famous for. There used to be seven hills, just as in Rome, but one of them (now known as the Denny Regrade) was leveled shortly after 1900 to permit commercial construction and to provide fill for the waterfront. This combination of hills and water makes for spectacular views, so be sure to take extra care when driving: Don't let the natural beauty of the city's surroundings distract you. Unfortunately, Seattle has been busy erecting huge skyscrapers in recent years, and many excellent views have been lost to development. The city is trying to put some controls on growth in order to preserve its unique character.

Seattle is a city of neighborhoods. People identify with their neighborhood even more than they identify with the city itself. Although the best way to explore the different neighborhoods is by car, there is an excellent public bus system that will get you in from the airport and all over the city.

1. ORIENTATION

ARRIVING

BY PLANE **Seattle-Tacoma (Sea-Tac) International Airport** (tel. 206/431-4444) is located about 14 miles south of Seattle and is connected to the city by I-5. Generally, allow 30 minutes for the trip between the airport and downtown, and more during rush hour. See "Getting There" in Chapter 2 for information on airlines serving Seattle.

Gray Line Airport Express (tel. 206/626-6088) provides

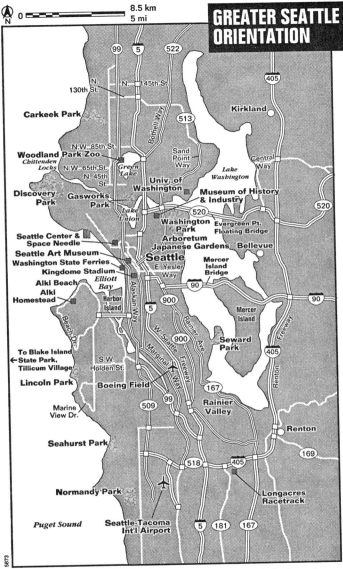

service between the airport and downtown Seattle daily from 5am to midnight. This shuttle van stops at the Stouffer Madison, Holiday Inn–Crowne Plaza, Best Western Executive Inn, Days Inn Town Center, Four Seasons Olympic, Seattle Hilton, Sheraton Seattle, Westin Hotel Seattle, Warwick, and WestCoast Roosevelt. Rates are $7 one way and $12 round-trip.

Shuttle Express (tel. 206/622-1424 or toll free 800/487-RIDE) provides 24-hour service between Sea-Tac and the Seattle area. Their rates vary from $16 to $18. You need to make a reservation to get to the airport, but to leave the airport, just give them a call when you arrive. Push **48** on one of the courtesy phones outside the baggage-claim areas.

Metro Transit (tel. 206/553-3000) operates three buses between the airport and downtown. It's a good idea to call for the current schedule when you arrive in town. At this writing, **no. 174** operates every 15 to 30 minutes from about 5am to midnight; it makes local stops and takes about an hour. On Saturday and Sunday the first buses leave between 6 and 6:30am. For night owls, there's local bus no. 184 that leaves the airport every night at 2:48 and 4:03am. **No. 194,** an express taking only 30 minutes, also departs every 30 minutes and operates between 4:30am and 7:30pm Monday through Saturday. The fare is $1.10 during off-peak hours and $1.60 during peak hours. Nos. 174 and 184 operate to Ninth Avenue and Stewart Street. No. 194 operates to either Third Avenue and Union Street or the Convention Place Station of the Bus Tunnel, depending on the time of day.

A **taxi** into downtown Seattle will cost you about $29. There are usually plenty of taxis around, but if not, call **Yellow Cab** (tel. 206/622-6500) or **Farwest Taxi** (tel. 206/622-1717). The flag-drop charge is $1.80; after that, it's $1.80 per mile.

BY TRAIN   If you arrive in Seattle on an Amtrak train, you will find yourself at the **King Street Station** (tel. 206/382-4125), right across the parking lot from the Kingdome. The heart of downtown Seattle is only a few blocks north.

BY BUS   The **Greyhound bus station,** Eighth Avenue and Stewart Street (tel. 206/624-3456), is slightly northeast of downtown Seattle.

BY CAR   **I-5,** is the main north–south artery through Seattle, running south to Portland and north to the Canadian border. **I-90** comes to Seattle from Spokane, in the eastern part of Washington, and ends just after 23rd Avenue. **Washington Hwy. 99,** the Alaskan Way Viaduct, is another major north–south highway through downtown Seattle; it passes through the waterfront section of the city.

BY SHIP   **Washington State Ferries** (tel. 206/464-6400 or toll free in Washington State 800/84-FERRY) dock at Pier 52. The **Victoria Clipper,** which connects Victoria, British Columbia, with Seattle (tel. 206/448-5000 or toll free 800/888-2535) docks at Pier 69.

TOURIST INFORMATION

Tourist information on Seattle and the surrounding area is available by contacting the **Seattle–King County Convention & Visitors Bureau,** 520 Pike St., Suite 1300, Seattle, WA 98101-9927 (tel. 206/461-5840). The bureau is open Monday through Friday from 8:30am to 5pm. You can stop by their office located at the Washington State Convention & Trade Center, 800 Convention Place, Galleria Level, at the corner of Eighth Avenue and Pike Street (tel. 206/461-5840). To find this information center, walk up Union Street until it goes into a tunnel under the Convention Center. You'll see the information center on your left as you enter the tunnel. This office operates two other **Visitor Information Centers** in the baggage-claim area at Sea-Tac Airport. One is by carousel no. 1 (open daily from 9am to 1:30pm; tel. 206/433-4679) and the other is by carousel no. 9 (open daily from 9:30am to 7:30pm; tel. 206/433-5218).

For information on the rest of Washington State, call the **Washington State Tourism Office,** at 206/586-2102 or 586-2088 or toll free 800/544-1800.

CITY LAYOUT

Although downtown Seattle is fairly compact and can easily be navigated on foot, finding your way through this area by car can be frustrating. The Seattle area has been experiencing phenomenal growth in the past few years, and this has created traffic-congestion problems that must be anticipated. Here are some guidelines to help you find your way around.

MAIN ARTERIES & STREETS   There are three interstate highways serving Seattle. **I-90** comes in from the east and ends downtown. **I-405** bypasses the city completely, traveling up the east shore of Lake Washington through Bellevue. The main artery is **I-5,** which runs through the middle of Seattle. Take the James Street exit west if you're heading for the Pioneer Square area; take the Seneca Street exit for Pike Place Market; or the Olive Way exit for Capitol Hill.

Downtown is roughly defined as extending from **Yesler Way** on the south to **Denny Way** on the north and from Elliott Bay on the west to **Broadway** on the east. Within this area avenues are numbered, whereas streets have names. The exceptions to this rule are the first two roads parallel to the waterfront. They are Alaskan Way and Western Avenue. Spring Street is one way eastbound, and Seneca Street one way westbound. Likewise, Pike Street is one way eastbound, and Pine Street one way westbound. First Avenue and Third Avenue are two-way streets, but Second and Fifth are one way southbound. Fourth Avenue and Sixth Avenue are one way northbound.

FINDING AN ADDRESS   After you become familiar with the streets and neighborhoods of Seattle, there is really only one important thing to remember to find an address: Pay attention to the compass point of the address. Downtown streets have no directional designation attached to them, but when you cross I-5 going east, most streets and avenues are designated "East." South of Yesler Way, which

---

IMPRESSIONS

Its streets are so steep, like those of San Francisco, that you practically need spikes in your shoes, and its politics are almost as spectacular as the scenery.
—JOHN GUNTHER, *INSIDE U.S.A.,* 1947

runs through Pioneer Square, streets are designated "South." West of Queen Anne Avenue, streets are designated "West." The University District is designated "NE" (Northeast); the Ballard, "NW" (Northwest). Therefore, if you are looking for an address on First Avenue South, head south of Yesler Way.

Another helpful hint is that odd-numbered addresses are likely to be on the west and south sides of streets, whereas even-numbered addresses will be on the east and north sides of streets. Also, in the downtown area, address numbers increase by 100 as you move away from Yesler Way going north or south, and as you go east from the waterfront.

STREET MAPS   Even if the streets of Seattle seem totally unfathomable to you, rest assured that even longtime residents sometimes have a hard time finding their way around. Don't be afraid to ask directions. You can obtain a free map of the city from the Seattle–King County Convention & Visitors Bureau or at one of its Visitor Information Centers (see above).

If you happen to be a member of AAA, you can get free maps of Seattle and Washington State from them, either at an office near you or at the Seattle office, 330 Sixth Ave. N. (tel. 206/448-5353). They're open Monday through Friday from 8:30am to 5pm (Wednesday until 6pm).

NEIGHBORHOODS IN BRIEF

Seattle is a city of neighborhoods, partly because it is divided by bodies of water.

International District   The most immediately recognizable of Seattle's neighborhoods, the International District is home to the city's Asian population. It's just south of Yesler Way.

Pioneer Square   Just northwest of the International District is the Pioneer Square Historic District, known for restored old buildings. It's full of shops, galleries, restaurants, and bars.

Capitol Hill   To the northeast, centered along Broadway near Volunteer Park, Capitol Hill is Seattle's cutting-edge shopping district and gay community.

Ballard   In northwest Seattle, bordering Puget Sound, you'll find Ballard, a former Scandinavian community now known for its busy nightlife, but with remnants of its past still visible.

First Hill   Known as Pill Hill by Seattleites, this hilly neighborhood, just east of downtown across I-5, is home to several hospitals as well as the Frye Art Museum.

Queen Anne Hill   This neighborhood is where you'll find some of Seattle's oldest homes, several of which are now bed-and-breakfast inns. Queen Anne is located just northwest of Seattle Center and offers great views of the city. This is one of the most prestigious Seattle neighborhoods.

University District   As the name implies, this neighborhood surrounds the University of Washington in the northeast section of the city. The U District, as it's known to locals, provides all the amenities of a college neighborhood.

Wallingford   This neighborhood is one of Seattle's up-and-comers. Just west of University District and adjacent to Lake Union, it's filling with small, inexpensive-but-good restaurants. There are also interesting little shops.

Downtown   This is Seattle's main business district and can roughly be defined as the area from Pioneer Square in the south to just north of Pike Place Market and from First Avenue to Seventh Avenue. It's characterized by high-rise office buildings and steep streets, and also offers the city's greatest diversity of retail shops.

Fremont   Home to Seattle's best-loved piece of public art—*Waiting for the Interurban*—Fremont is located north of the Lake Washington Ship Canal between Wallington and Ballard. It's a neighborhood of eclectic shops, ethnic restaurants, and artists' studios.

Madison Park   One of Seattle's more affluent neighborhoods, it fronts on the western shore of Lake Washington, northeast of downtown. The centerpiece is the University of Washington Arboretum, including the Japanese Gardens.

2. GETTING AROUND

BY PUBLIC TRANSPORTATION

BUS   Seattle's **Metro bus system** has been voted the best in the country, so be sure to avail yourself of it while you're in town. The best part of riding the bus in Seattle is that as long as you stay within the downtown area, you can ride for free between 4am and 9pm. The **Ride Free Area** is between Alaskan Way in the west, Sixth Avenue in the east, Battery Street in the north, and South Jackson Street in the south. Within this area are Pioneer Square, the waterfront attractions, Pike Place Market, and all major hotels. Two blocks from South Jackson Street is the Kingdome, and six blocks from Battery Street is Seattle Center. Keeping this in mind, you can visit nearly every tourist attraction in Seattle without having to spend a dime on transportation. For more information, phone 206/553-3000.

The Metro's latest innovation is the **Bus Tunnel,** which allows buses to drive underneath downtown Seattle, thus avoiding traffic congestion. The tunnel extends from the International District in the south to the Convention Center in the north, with three stops in between. Commissioned artworks decorate each of the stations, making a trip through the tunnel more than just a way of getting from point A to point B. In fact, the tunnel is becoming a regular tourist attraction. It's open Monday through Friday from 5am to 7pm, on Saturday from 10am to 6pm. When the Bus Tunnel is closed, buses operate on surface streets. Because the tunnel is within the Ride Free Area, there is no charge for riding through it, unless you are traveling to or from outside of the Ride Free Area.

If you travel outside the Ride Free Area, fares range from 85¢ to $1.60, depending on the distance and time of day. Keep in mind that you pay when you get off the bus when traveling out of the Ride Free Area. When traveling into the Ride Free Area, you pay when you get on the bus. Exact change is required.

Discount Passes   On Saturday, Sunday, and holidays, you can purchase an **All Day Pass** for $1.70; it's available on any Metro bus or the Waterfront Streetcar.

FERRY   Washington State Ferries is the most extensive ferry system in the United States and serves numerous cities and towns in the area such as Bremerton, Edmonds, and Bainbridge Island; Vashon Island; Victoria, British Columbia; and the San Juan Islands. At press time, fares from Seattle to Bremerton via car ferry (a 60-minute crossing) were car and driver one way, $6.65 (summer), $5.55 (off season), passengers, $3.30; children and senior citizens, $1.65; children under age 5, free; eastbound from Bremerton to the mainland, there was no charge for passengers. For ferryboat schedule and rate information, you can call via touch-tone phone the Seattle Times Info Line at 206/464-2000 ext. 5500. For information, you can also call the state ferry system at 206/464-6400, or toll free 800/84-FERRY within Washington State.

MONORAIL   If you are planning a visit to Seattle Center, there is no better way to get there from downtown than on the monorail. It leaves from Westlake Center shopping mall (Fifth Avenue and Pine Street). The once-futuristic elevated trains cover the 1.2 miles in 90 seconds and provide a few nice views along the way. The monorail leaves every 15 minutes daily from 9am to midnight during the summer; the rest of the year, Sunday through Thursday from 9am to 9pm, on Friday and Saturday until midnight. The one-way fare is only 60¢ for adults and 25¢ for senior citizens and the handicapped.

WATERFRONT STREETCAR   Old-fashioned streetcars run along the waterfront from Pier 70 to the corner of Fifth Avenue South and South Jackson Street on the edge of the International District, providing another unusual means of getting around in downtown Seattle. The trolley operates Monday through Friday from around 7am to around 6:30pm, departing every 30 minutes; on Saturday, Sunday, and holidays from just after 10am to almost 7pm, departing every 30 minutes. One-way fare is 85¢ in off-peak hours and $1.10 in peak hours. If you plan to transfer to a Metro bus, you can get a transfer good for 90 minutes of bus travel.

BY TAXI

If you decide not to use the public-transit system, call **Yellow Cab** (tel. 622-6500) or **Farwest Taxi** (tel. 622-1717). Taxis can be difficult to hail on the street in Seattle, so it's best to call or wait at the taxi stands at major hotels. The flag-drop charge is $1.80; after that, it's $1.80 per mile.

BY CAR

Before you venture into downtown Seattle in your own car, remember that traffic congestion is severe, parking is limited, and streets are

IMPRESSIONS

. . . on a famous ferry going into famous Seattle, dusk on a November night, the sky, the water, the mountains are all the same color: lead in a closet. Suicide weather. The only thing wrong with this picture is that you feel so happy.
—ESQUIRE MAGAZINE

almost all one way. Be forewarned that you're better off leaving your car outside the downtown area.

CAR RENTALS   For the very best deal on a rental car, make your reservation at least one week in advance. It also pays to shop around and call the same companies a few times over the course of a couple of weeks; the last time I visited Seattle, I was quoted different rates each time I called the major car-rental agencies. If you decide on the spur of the moment that you want to rent a car, check to see whether there are any weekend or special rates available. If you are a member of a frequent-flier program, be sure to mention it: You might get mileage credit for renting a car. Currently, daily rates for a subcompact are around $35, with weekly rates at around $130.

All the major car-rental agencies have offices in Seattle, and there are also plenty of independent companies. I recommend that you try to rent a car from **Budget Rent A Car** (tel. toll free 800/527-0700). They have several offices throughout the Seattle area, including one right in the airport. Budget offices are at Sea-Tac Airport, 17808 Pacific Hwy. S. (tel. 206/682-2277), downtown at Fourth Avenue and Columbia Street (tel. 206/682-4770), and at Westlake Avenue and Virginia Street (tel. 206/682-2277).

Other car-rental companies include **Avis** (tel. toll free 800/331-1212), at Sea-Tac Airport (tel. 206/433-5231) and 1919 Fifth Ave. (tel. 206/448-1700); **Dollar,** at 17600 Pacific Hwy. S. (tel. 206/433-6777) and Seventh Avenue and Stewart Street (tel. 206/682-1316); **Hertz** (tel. toll free 800/654-3131), at Seattle Marriott Hotel (tel. 206/433-5275), Red Lion Hotel/Seattle Airport (tel. 206/246-0159), and 722 Pike St. (tel. 206/682-5050); and **Thrifty,** at 18836 Pacific Hwy. S. (tel. 206/246-7565) and 801 Virginia St. (tel. 206/625-1133).

PARKING   On-street parking is very expensive, extremely limited, and rarely available near your destination. Downtown parking decks (either above or below ground) charge from $7 to $16 per day. You'll save money by parking nearer the Space Needle, where parking lots charge around $6 per day. If you don't mind a bit of a walk, try the south lot at the Kingdome, where all-day parking costs only $2 (best deal in town).

DRIVING RULES   A right turn at a red light is permitted after coming to a full stop. A left turn at a red light is permissible from a one-way street onto another one-way street. If you park your car on a sloping street, be sure to turn your wheels to the curb—you may be ticketed if you don't. When parking on the street, be sure to check the time limit on parking meters; it ranges from 15 minutes to 4 hours. Also be sure to check whether or not you can park in a parking space during rush hour. Don't leave your keys in the ignition and walk away from your car—you might get a ticket.

BY BICYCLE

Downtown Seattle is congested with traffic and is very hilly. Unless you have experience with these sorts of conditions, I wouldn't recommend riding a bicycle downtown. However, there are many bike paths that are excellent for recreational bicycling, and some of these can be accessed from downtown by routes that avoid the steep hills and heavily trafficked streets. See "Participatory Activities" in Section 5 of Chapter 6 for details.

ON FOOT

Seattle is a surprisingly compact city. You can easily walk from Pioneer Square to Pike Place Market. Remember, though, that the city is also very hilly. When you head in from the waterfront, you will be climbing a very steep hill. If you get tired of walking around downtown Seattle, remember that between 4am and 9pm you can always catch a bus for free as long as you plan to stay within the Ride Free Area. Cross streets only at corners and only with the lights in your favor. Jaywalking is a ticketable offense.

FAST FACTS: SEATTLE

Airport **Seattle-Tacoma International Airport (Sea-Tac)** is located about 14 miles south of Seattle; for information call 206/431-4444.

American Express In Seattle, the Amex office is in the Plaza 600 building at 600 Stewart St. (tel. 441-8622). The office is open Monday through Friday from 9am to 5pm.

Area Code The telephone area code in Seattle is **206.**

Babysitters Check at your hotel first if you need a sitter. If they don't have one available, contact **Best Sitters** (tel. 682-2556).

Business Hours **Banks** are generally open weekdays from 9am to 3pm, with later hours on Friday; some have Saturday morning hours. **Offices** are generally open weekdays from 9am to 5pm. **Stores** typically open Monday through Saturday between 9 and 10am and close between 5 and 6pm. Some department stores have later hours on Thursday and Friday evenings until 9pm; many stores are open on Sunday from 11am to 5 or 6pm. **Bars** stay open until 1am; **dance clubs** and **discos** often stay open much later.

Car Rentals See "By Car" in Section 2 of this chapter.

Climate See "Climate" in Section 2 of Chapter 2.

Dentist If you need a dentist while you are in Seattle, contact the **Dentist Referral Service,** the Medical Dental Building, Fifth Avenue and Olive Way (tel. 448-CARE).

Doctor To find a physician in Seattle, check at your hotel for a reference, or call the Medical Dental Building line (tel. 448-CARE).

Driving Rules See "By Car" in Section 2 of this chapter.

Drugstores Conveniently located downtown, **Peterson's Pharmacy,** 1629 Sixth Ave. (tel. 622-5860), has been serving Seattle for more than 50 years. It's open weekdays from 8:30am to 6pm, on Saturday from 9am to 1pm. **Pacific Drugs,** 822 First Ave. (tel. 624-1454), another convenient choice, is open Monday through Friday from 7am to 6pm, on Saturday from 10am to 5pm.

Emergencies For police, fire, or medical emergencies, phone **911.**

Eyeglasses If you have problems with your glasses while in Seattle, try **Davis Optical X-press,** 314 Stewart St. (tel. 623-1758). They are a full-service store and can replace your glasses in an hour.

Hairdressers/Barbers **Gene Juarez Salons** has two

downtown locations: Four Seasons Olympic Hotel, 411 University St. (tel. 628-0011), and at Nordstrom department store, 1501 Fifth Ave. (tel. 628-1405). These full-service beauty salons charge between $22.50 and $45 for a man's or woman's haircut. For an inexpensive haircut, try **Supercuts,** 1550 E. Olive Way (tel. 325-4855), on Capitol Hill.

Holidays   See "Calendar of Events" in Chapter 2, and "Holidays" in "Fast Facts: For the Foreign Traveler" in the Appendix.

Hospitals   One of the hospitals most convenient to downtown Seattle is the **Virginia Mason Hospital & Clinic,** 925 Seneca St. (tel. 583-6433 for emergencies or 624-1144 for information). There is also the **Virginia Mason Fourth Avenue Clinic,** 1221 Fourth Ave. (tel. 223-6490), open Monday through Friday from 7am to 5pm, which provides medical treatment for minor ailments without an appointment.

Hotlines   If you have a touch-tone phone, you'll want to call the **Seattle Times Info Line** at 206/464-2000; this service provides a wealth of information on topics that range from personal health to business news, from entertainment listings to the weather report and marine forecast; you can even obtain complete information on ferry schedules and rates. The local **rape hotline** is 632-7273.

Information   For information on Seattle and the surrounding area, call or write to **Seattle–King County Convention & Visitors Bureau,** Washington State Convention and Trade Center, 520 Pike St., Suite 1300, Galleria Level, Seattle, WA 98101-9927 (tel. 206/461-5840); their office is located at Eighth Avenue and Pike Street. For information on the state of Washington, contact the **Washington State Tourism Office** at 206/586-2102 or 586-2088 or toll free 800/544-1800.

Laundry/Dry Cleaning   The **Waterfront Place Cleaners,** 1017 First Ave. (tel. 206/583-0005), is a dry cleaner, open weekdays from 8am to 6pm. **Dick's,** 115 12th Ave. (tel. 624-0318), offers same-day dry cleaning and hotel/motel valet service; it's open Monday through Friday from 7:30am to 6pm, on Saturday from 7:30am to 1pm. **Downtown St. Regis,** 116 Stewart St. (tel. 448-6366), is a 24-hour coin-operated laundry. If you are staying in the Capitol Hill neighborhood, you can do laundry (or drop it off and have it done for you) at **Cristall Clean,** 1718 Bellevue Ave. (tel. 323-4969), which is open daily 8am to 10pm.

Library   The main branch of the **Seattle Public Library** is at 1000 Fourth Ave. (tel. 386-4636).

Liquor Laws   The legal minimum drinking age in Washington is 21.

Lost Property   If you left something on a Metro bus, call **553-3090,** if you left something at the airport, call **433-5312.**

Luggage Storage/Lockers   There is a luggage-storage facility at Amtrak's King Street Station. It costs $1 per day. The Greyhound bus station, 811 Stewart St., has luggage lockers.

Mail   You can receive mail c/o General Delivery at the main post office (see "Post Office," below).

Maps   You can get a free map of Seattle at the **Visitor Information Centers** in the baggage-claim area at Sea-Tac Airport or at the **Seattle–King County Convention & Visitors Bureau.** See "City Layout" in this chapter.

Newspapers/Magazines   *SeattlePost-Intelligencer*

is Seattle's morning daily, and the *Seattle Times* is the evening daily. The arts and entertainment weekly for Seattle is *Seattle Weekly.*

Photographic Needs **Cameras West,** 1908 Fourth Ave. (tel. 622-0066), is the largest-volume camera and video dealer in the Northwest. Best of all, it's right downtown and also offers 1-hour film processing. It's open Monday through Saturday from 10am to 6pm, and on Sunday from noon to 5pm.

Police For police emergencies, phone **911.**

Post Office Besides the main post office, Third Avenue and Union Street (tel. 442-6340), there are also convenient postal stations in Pioneer Square at 91 Jackson St. S. (tel. 623-1908), and on Broadway at 101 Broadway E. (tel. 324-2588). Hours are 8am to 5:30pm Monday through Friday.

Radio Seattle has dozens of AM and FM radio stations broadcasting every conceivable type of music, in addition to news, traffic updates, sports, and weather. For National Public Radio (NPR) tune to 88.5 FM.

Religious Services The **Church Council of Greater Seattle** (tel. 525-1213) can give you the location of the nearest church of your choice.

Restrooms There are public restrooms in Pike Place Market and the Convention Center.

Safety Although Seattle is rated as one of the safest cities in the United States, it has its share of crime. Take extra precautions with your wallet or purse when you're in the crush of people at Pike Place Market—this is a favorite spot of pickpockets. Whenever possible try to park your car in a garage, not on the street, at night.

Shoe Repairs If you lose a heel or need a new sole, **Busy Shoes/Instant Shoe Repair,** 306 Union St. (around the corner from Third Avenue) (tel. 624-6391), and also at 415 Seneca St. (tel. 467-7386), will get you back on your feet in a hurry.

Taxes The state of Washington makes up for its lack of an income tax with its heavy **sales tax** of 6.5%; King County adds another 1.7% for 8.2% total. **Hotel-room tax** is 15.2% in Seattle.

Taxis To get a cab, call **Yellow Cab** at 622-6500 or **Farwest Taxi** at 622-1717. See also "By Taxi" in section 2 of this chapter.

Television The six local television channels are 4 (ABC), 5 (NBC), 7 (CBS), 9 (PBS), 11 (Independent), and 13 (Fox).

Time Seattle is on **Pacific Time (PT), and Daylight Saving Time,** depending on the time of year, making it three hours behind the East Coast.

Tipping In restaurants if the service has been good, tip 15 to 20% of the bill. Taxi drivers expect about 10% of the fare. Airport porters and bellhops should be tipped about 50¢ per bag. For chambermaids, $1 per night is an appropriate tip.

Transit Information For 24-hour information on Seattle's **Metro bus system,** call 206/553-3000. For information on the **Washington State Ferries,** call 206/464-6400 or toll free 800/84-FERRY. For **Amtrak information,** call toll free 800/872-7245. To contact the **King Street Station** (trains), call 206/382-4125. To contact the **Greyhound bus station,** call 206/624-3456.

Useful Telephone Numbers For police, fire, or medical emergencies, phone **911.** If you have a touch-tone phone, you'll want to call the **Seattle Times Info Line** at 206/464-2000; this service provides a wealth of information on topics that range from personal health to business news, from entertainment listings to the weather report and marine forecast; you can even obtain complete information on ferry schedules and rates.

Weather   If you can't tell what the weather is by looking out the window, or you want to be absolutely sure that it's going to rain the next day, call **526-6087.**

3. NETWORKS & RESOURCES

FOR STUDENTS

The **University of Washington,** located in northeast Seattle, is the largest state university in Washington and also happens to have the second-largest student bookstore in the country. The university's **Visitors Information Center** is located at 4014 University Way NE (tel. 543-9198), and the bookstore is at 4326 University Way NE (tel. 634-3400). **Seattle Pacific University,** 3307 Third Ave. W. (tel. 281-2000), is a Methodist liberal arts university, and **Seattle University,** Broadway and Madison Street (tel. 296-6000) is affiliated with the Roman Catholic church.

If you don't already have one, get an **official student ID** from your school. Such an ID will entitle you to discounts at museums and on performances at different theaters and concert halls around town.

Seattle's **AYH youth hostel** is at 84 Union St. (tel. 206/622-5443). Besides being a place to stay, this hostel has a bulletin board with information on rides, other hostels, camping equipment for sale, and the like.

FOR GAY MEN & LESBIANS

Seattle's large gay community is centered around Capitol Hill. In this chic shopping and residential district, you can find gay restaurants, bars, bookstores, and more. For a guide to Seattle's gay community, get a copy of the **Greater Seattle Business Association (GSBA) Guide Directory.** Their mailing address is 2033 Sixth Ave., Suite 804, Seattle, WA 98121 (tel. 206/443-4722). The **Seattle Gay News** is the community's newspaper. Their offices are at 704 E. Pike St., Seattle, WA 98122 (tel. 206/324-4297).

The **Lesbian Resource Center,** 1208 E. Pine St. (tel. 322-3953), is a community resource center providing housing and job information, therapy, and business referrals. **Thumpers,** 1500 E. Madison St. (tel. 328-3800), is a long-time favorite Seattle gay bar located in the Capitol Hill area. **The Connection** and **Brass Connection,** 722 E. Pike St. (tel. 322-6572 and 324-3436), are a popular restaurant and disco in the heart of Capitol Hill. Although not strictly a lesbian establishment, **Wildrose,** 1021 E. Pike St. (tel. 324-9210), is a tavern primarily for women, with frequent live music. **Beyond the Closet,** 1501 Belmont Ave. (tel. 322-4609), is a gay and lesbian bookstore. **Gaslight Inn** is a bed-and-breakfast in the Capitol Hill area; see Section 3 of Chapter 4 for details.

FOR WOMEN

Seattle is a large city, and all the normal precautions that apply in other cities hold true here. The Pioneer Square area is particularly unsafe for either sex late at night.

Wildrose, 1021 E. Pike St. (tel. 324-9210), is a women's tavern with a friendly atmosphere and frequent live music performances.

The local **rape hotline** is 632-7273.

FOR SENIORS

Be sure to carry some form of photo ID with you when touring Seattle. Most attractions, some theaters and concert halls, and the Washington State Ferries all offer senior-citizen discounts. Also, if you aren't already a member, you should consider joining the **American Association of Retired Persons (AARP),** 601 E. St. NW, Washington, DC 20049 (tel. toll free 800/922-8716). One of the many benefits of belonging to this organization is the 10% discount offered at many motels and hotels.

SEATTLE ACCOMMODATIONS

You generally get a lot for your money in Seattle. Even the most expensive hotel in the city is less expensive than a comparable one in San Francisco or New York. In the following listings, **very expensive** hotels are those generally charging more than $120 per night for a double room; **expensive** hotels, about $90 to $120 per night for a double; **moderate** hotels, about $60 to $90 per night for a double; and **inexpensive** hotels, less than $60 per night for a double. These rates do not include the state and local hotel tax, which comes to 15.2%. A few hotels include breakfast in their rates; others offer complimentary breakfast only on certain deluxe floors. In most cases you will need to tip the bellhops and chambermaids. If tips are included in a hotel's rates, this has been noted. **Parking** rates are per day.

Make reservations as far in advance as possible, especially if you plan a visit during Seafair or another Seattle festival (see "Seattle Calendar of Events" in Chapter 2 for dates of festivals). Also, the San Juan Islands are very busy in summer, so make reservations early.

There are a number of fine bed-and-breakfast establishments in Seattle, and I have listed a few of my favorites. In addition, the **Pacific Bed & Breakfast Agency,** 701 NW 60th St., Seattle, WA 98107 (tel. 206/784-0539; fax 206/782-4036), offers many accommodations, mostly in private homes, in the Seattle area; rates range from $35 to $150 for a double and a small booking fee is charged. They charge $5 for a directory of members.

1. DOWNTOWN

VERY EXPENSIVE

ALEXIS HOTEL & ARLINGTON SUITES, 1007 First Ave. (at Madison St.), Seattle, WA 98104. Tel. 206/624-4844 or toll free 800/426-7033 (outside Washington). Fax 206/621-9009. 54 rms, 55 suites. A/C TV TEL

$ Rates (including continental breakfast and service): $165–$190 single; $180–$200 double; $150–$320 suite. AE, CB, DC, MC, V. **Parking:** $13.

★ Unbelievable as it sounds, this elegant little hotel was once a parking garage. Now listed in the National Register of Historic Places, the 90-year-old building is a sparkling gem. The hotel also has an enviable location halfway between Pike Place Market and Pioneer Square and only two blocks from the waterfront.

In the understated lobby, the peach walls fairly glow in the light of frosted-glass torchères, while bouquets of flowers soften the angular lines and large contemporary paintings add a touch of modern sophistication. Throughout, the hotel is a pleasant mix of old and new, contemporary and antique, giving the Alexis a special atmosphere. The cheerful service—from doormen to chambermaids, none of whom you need to tip—will make you feel as if you are visiting old friends.

Each of the 54 rooms is furnished with antique tables, overstuffed chairs, and brass reading lamps. There are four pillows on every bed, with chocolates on them in the evening. In the black-tiled bath, you'll find a marble counter, luxurious terry-cloth robes, a shaving mirror, a telephone, and a basket of special toiletries. Each room is a little different (there are 18 floor plans), but the nicest by far are the fireplace suites, which have raised king-size beds, whirlpool baths, and wet bars.

If you need that extra bit of space that only a suite can provide, you might want to stay at adjacent Arlington Suites. All the condominium suites are individually decorated and have fully equipped kitchens.

Dining/Entertainment: You'll enjoy highly creative but moderately priced meals at The Painted Table, which is the hotel's main dining room. This informal restaurant takes its name from the colorful, handmade ceramic plates that frame the meals. Each plate is a unique work of art (see Section 5 of Chapter 5 for details). Even more casual, but no less innovative, Volcano Café serves up fiery Latin-influenced dishes that also show hints of Asian flavoring. Just off the lobby, the Bookstore Bar serves light lunches as well as drinks, and is filled with books, magazines, and newspapers for browsing. The Cajun Corner, another casual restaurant run by the hotel, is just down Madison Street.

Services: Room service, concierge, valet/laundry service, morning paper, evening turn down, complimentary evening sherry, shoeshine service.

Facilities: Steamroom, privileges at two sports clubs, wheelchair accommodations.

THE EDGEWATER, Pier 67, 2411 Alaskan Way, Seattle, WA 98121-1398. Tel. 206/728-7000 or toll free 800/624-0670. Fax 206/441-4119. 237 rms. 2 suites. A/C TV TEL
$ **Rates:** $95–$125 single; $95–$180 double; $250 suite. AE, CB, DC, DISC, MC, V. **Parking:** $6.

Built in 1962, Seattle's only waterfront hotel underwent extensive renovation in 1989 and is now once again one of the better hotels in the city. Set back from Alaskan Way on Pier 67, the Edgewater has the feel of a fishing lodge, albeit with all the amenities you'd expect from a deluxe hotel. A vaulted open-beamed ceiling and river-stone fireplace greet you as you enter the lobby, where a wall of windowpaned glass looks out on ships and sailboats on Elliott Bay. Above the lobby's living-room arrangement is a chandelier made from deer antlers. Throughout the building, tartan carpets remind you that this is not your standard stuffy hotel. With such a relaxed atmosphere, it's difficult to believe that the crowded streets of downtown Seattle are only steps away.

The fishing-lodge theme continues in the rooms, which feature rustic lodge-pole pine furniture and plaid comforters on the beds. Half the rooms have minibars and balconies over the water, and all have clock radios and remote-control TVs. In each bright red-and-green bathroom, you'll find a basket of soaps and a shoeshine kit.

Dining/Entertainment: With its dark-green color scheme and duck motif, Ernie's Bar & Grill could have been designed by Eddie Bauer or Ralph Lauren. You'll find Northwest cuisine featured on the menu and a stunning view of the harbor from all the tables. In the pine-walled Lobby Lounge, there is live piano music in the evenings and a fireplace to warm your toes in winter.

Services: Room service, concierge, same-day laundry/valet service, courtesy shuttle to downtown locations.

Facilities: Wheelchair accommodations, gift shop, in-room movies, access to athletic club, no-smoking rooms.

FOUR SEASONS OLYMPIC HOTEL, 411 University St., Seattle, WA 98101. Tel. 206/621-1700 or toll free 800/332-3442 or 800/821-8106 (in Washington State) or 800/268-6282 (in Canada). Fax 206/682-9633. 450 rms, 210 suites. A/C MINIBAR TV TEL

$ Rates: $185–$215 single; $215–$265 double; $170–$1,150 suite. Weekend rates available. AE, CB, DC, MC, V. **Parking:** Valet $15.

Old-fashioned grandeur fit for kings is what you'll find when you step through the doors of this Italian Renaissance palace. Gilt-and-crystal chandeliers hang from the high-arched ceiling; ornate cornices and moldings grace the glowing hand-burnished oak walls and pillars. A huge floral arrangement sits in the middle of the expansive lobby, surrounded by new and antique furnishings and subdued pink-and-gray carpets. At either end, curving stairways lead to the mezzanine level.

In the halls of the 11-floor building are original art and fresh flower arrangements. There were originally 800 rooms here, but during renovation many were combined by taking out walls. Now the 450 rooms are all quite spacious and tastefully appointed with modern furnishings. Remote-control TVs and minibars are standard here, as are hair dryers, plush bathrobes, and large baskets of scented toiletries.

Dining/Entertainment: The Georgian Room is the most elegant restaurant in Seattle. Marble stairs and carpeted terraces lead from the lobby to its doors, and inside, luxurious drapes, a marble floor, antique chairs, and the same ornate moldings that grace the lobby all contribute to the strong feeling of courtly elegance. The menu combines creative Northwest and continental cuisines. (See "Hotel Dining" in Section 5 of Chapter 5 for details.) Downstairs from the lobby is Shuckers, an English pub featuring fresh seafood. In the spacious skylighted Garden Court, more Northwest cuisine is served—but at half the price of meals served in The Georgian Room.

Services: 24-hour room service, concierge, same-day valet/laundry service, 1-hour pressing, complimentary shoeshine, valet parking, massage available.

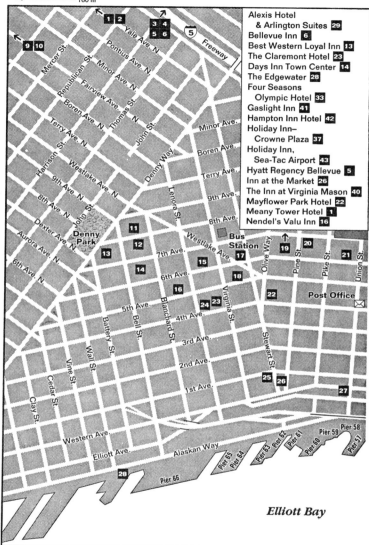

Alexis Hotel
& Arlington Suites 29
Bellevue Inn 6
Best Western Loyal Inn 13
The Claremont Hotel 23
Days Inn Town Center 14
The Edgewater 28
Four Seasons
Olympic Hotel 33
Gaslight Inn 41
Hampton Inn Hotel 42
Holiday Inn–
Crowne Plaza 37
Holiday Inn,
Sea-Tac Airport 43
Hyatt Regency Bellevue 5
Inn at the Market 26
The Inn at Virginia Mason 40
Mayflower Park Hotel 22
Meany Tower Hotel 1
Nendel's Valu Inn 16

Facilities: Indoor swimming pool, whirlpool, sauna, sun deck, health club, wheelchair accommodations, exclusive shopping arcade, no-smoking rooms.

HOLIDAY INN–CROWNE PLAZA, 1113 Sixth Ave., Seattle, WA 98101-3048. Tel. 206/464-1980 or toll free 800/521-2762 or 800/858-0511 (in Washington). Fax 206/340-1617. 415 rms, 28 suites. A/C TV TEL

Pacific Plaza Hotel **32**
Pensione Nichols **25**
Quality Inn City Center **11**
Radisson Hotel **44**
Red Lion Hotel Bellevue **4**
Red Lion Hotel/
   Seattle Airport **45**
Roberta's Bed &
   Breakfast **7**
Salisbury House **8**
Hotel Seattle **31**
Seattle Downtown–
   Lake Union Marriott
   Residence Inn **9**
Seattle Downtown
   Travelodge **12**
Seattle Downtown
   YMCA **30**
Seattle Hilton Hotel **38**
Seattle International
   AYH Hostel **27**

Seattle Marriott Hotel **46**
Seattle YWCA **35**
Sheraton Seattle
   Hotel & Towers **21**
Sixth Avenue Inn **15**
Sorrento Hotel **39**
Stouffer Madison Hotel **36**
Super 8 Motel **47**
Travelodge Seattle Airport **48**
Tugboat Challenger
   Bunk & Breakfast **10**
University Plaza Hotel **2**
Hotel Vintage Park **34**
Warwick Hotel **24**
WestCoast Camlin Hotel **19**
WestCoast Roosevelt Hotel **20**
WestCoast Sea-Tac Hotel **49**
WestCoast Vance Hotel **17**
Westin Hotel Seattle **18**
The Woodmark Hotel
   at Carillon Point **3**

$ Rates: $120–$160 single or double; $225–$500 suite. AE, CB, DC, DISC, JCB, MC, V. **Parking:** Valet $11.

This 34-story tower in the heart of downtown is popular with businesspeople attending conventions at the nearby Washington State Trade and Convention Center. Almost all the rooms offer views of Puget Sound or the Cascade Mountains through large picture windows; ask for one of the higher floors to take advantage of them. The oversized guest rooms all have spacious sitting areas. On the concierge floors, guests receive a complimentary breakfast and afternoon hors d'oeuvres, use of the concierge lounge, and specially furnished rooms.

Dining/Entertainment: The Courtyard Café offers international meals and informal dining in a mezzanine-level atrium. In the evening, Northwest cuisine is served in the Parkside Restaurant, where granite walls and glass blocks combine to create a very contemporary setting. There is also a quiet lounge area on the mezzanine.

Services: Room service, concierge, valet/laundry service, airport shuttle ($7), in-room movies.

Facilities: Whirlpool, sauna, exercise facilities, gift shop, nosmoking rooms.

INN AT THE MARKET, 86 Pine St., Seattle, WA 98101. Tel. 206/443-3600 or toll free 800/446-4484. 65 rms, 9 suites. A/C MINIBAR TV TEL
$ Rates: $95–$170 single; $105–$170 double; $200–$220 suite. AE, CB, DC, DISC, MC, V. **Parking:** $12.

⭐ French country decor is the theme of this inconspicuous little hotel in the middle of Pike Place Market. There is no grand entrance, no large sign—only a plaque on the wall to indicate that this simple brick building in fact houses a very elegant hotel. In the courtyard a fountain bubbles. A small lobby with a fireplace, antique tables, and carved-wood display cabinets will make you think you've stepped into the living room of a French country home. A rooftop deck overlooking the harbor provides a tranquil spot to soak up the sun on summer afternoons.

In the guest rooms, wide bay windows overlook Puget Sound and can be opened to let in refreshing sea breezes. Antiqued furniture (including pine armoires to hide TVs), stocked minibars and refrigerators, coffee makers with complimentary coffee, and well-lit writing desks are amenities that will make you feel right at home here. The huge bathrooms are equipped with telephones and feature baskets of special toiletries from the market. If you check into one of the spacious suites, you'll also have an elegant daybed on which to relax.

Dining/Entertainment: Bacco, the hotel's little bistro, serves simple-but-tasty breakfasts and lunches. Café Dilletante offers light meals, espresso, and handmade chocolates. The hotel's formal dining room is Campagne, an excellent southern French restaurant located across the courtyard from the lobby (see "Hotel Dining" in Section 5 of Chapter 5 for details). In summer, Campagne offers terrace dining.

Services: Limited room service, concierge, valet/laundry service, complimentary limousine service in downtown Seattle.

Facilities: Health spa, wheelchair accommodations, gift shop, hair salon, no-smoking rooms.

MAYFLOWER PARK HOTEL, 405 Olive Way, Seattle, WA 98101. Tel. 206/623-8700 or toll free 800/426-5100 or 800/562-4504 (in Washington). Fax 206/382-6997. 187 rms, 15 suites. A/C TV TEL
$ Rates: $110–$135 single; $120–$155 double; from $155 suite. Children under 18 stay free in parents' room. AE, CB, DC, DISC, MC, V. **Parking:** $8.

If shopping is your favorite sport, you'll really like this hotel. The Mayflower Park is connected by covered walkway to the shops of Westlake Center, and several department stores are within a block. (If you want to spend time at Seattle Center, the monorail starts at Westlake Center and whisks you to the other end faster than you could cross a street.) Built in 1927, the Mayflower Park provides subdued elegance. In the high-ceilinged lobby an antique Chinese screen, Chinese cabinet, grandfather clock, and skylights complement the deep-green carpets and aquamarine overstuffed chairs. Fresh flowers add a colorful touch. Overhead hangs a tubular glass chandelier that once hung in the lobby of the Olympic Hotel.

All rooms have been remodeled in the past few years and are furnished with an eclectic blend of contemporary Italian and traditional European furnishings and Chinese accent pieces. The bathrooms are old-fashioned, small, and lack counter space but have large old tubs that are great for soaking. If you crave space, ask for one of the large corner rooms or a suite. In the larger queen-size rooms and suites, cherry furniture, floral-print bedspreads, and attractive tables all add up to special elegance.

Dining/Entertainment: Clippers restaurant features fresh seafood and French and Italian cuisine. The intimate bi-level restaurant is bright and airy, with marble tables, brass rails, and blond-wood decor. Oliver's lounge provides another cheerful spot for light lunches or drinks and conversation. The room once housed a pharmacy, in which the floor-to-ceiling windows were completely painted over.

Services: Room service, valet/laundry service.

Facilities: Privileges at private athletic club, no-smoking rooms.

SEATTLE DOWNTOWN-LAKE UNION MARRIOTT RESIDENCE INN, 800 Fairview Ave. N., Seattle, WA 98109. Tel. 206/624-6000 or toll free 800/331-3131. 234 suites. A/C TV TEL

$ Rates (including complimentary breakfast): $135 studio suite; $160 one-bedroom suite; $275–$400 two-bedroom suite. AE, CB, DC, DISC, JCB, MC, V. **Parking:** $3–$7.

Located at the north end of downtown Seattle and just across the street from Lake Union, this Marriott Residence Inn is the sort of place that usually is built in the suburbs. A seven-story atrium floods the hotel's plant-filled lobby court with light, while the sound of a waterfall soothes traffic weary nerves. All accommodations here are suites, so you'll buy quite a bit more space for the money. You'll also have use of a full kitchen, complete with dishes, so you can fix your own meals if you like, though the buffet breakfast down in the lobby shouldn't be missed. Guest suites are done in gray and mauve and most have balconies. Most, but not all, of the suites have either a lake or city view. Try for a room as high up as possible for a better view.

Dining/Entertainment: Though the hotel has no restaurant of its own, there are three restaurants across the street that will bill meals to your room.

Services: Complimentary Wednesday night guest reception, nightly dessert, downtown van service; valet/laundry service.

Facilities: Indoor lap pool, children's pool, steam room, sauna, hot tub, exercise room, no-smoking rooms, wheelchair accommodations.

SEATTLE HILTON HOTEL, Sixth Ave. and University St., Seattle, WA 98101. Tel. 206/624-0500 or toll free 800/426-0535 or 800/542-7700 (in Washington). Fax 206/682-9029. 237 rms, 6 suites. A/C TV TEL

$ Rates: $117–$192 single or double; $275–$395 suite. Weekend rates available. AE, CB, DC, DISC, MC, V. **Parking:** $8.50.

When you step into the street-level lobby of the Seattle Hilton, you won't find the check-in desk, no matter how hard you look, because the main lobby is actually up on the 13th floor, though the elevator labels it the lobby floor or second floor. When you finally do reach the lobby, you'll find an attractive pink-marble floor, black-wood pillars, and lots of pink tones and black accents. The overall effect is art deco, with a grand piano and frosted-glass windows further adding to the elegance.

Unfortunately, you won't find a swimming pool or any other athletic facilities here, but you will find very comfortable rooms that are everything you'd expect from a Hilton. Blond woods and pastel walls and carpets give the place a stylish and contemporary feeling. In the bathroom you'll find plenty of fragrant toiletries on hand.

Dining/Entertainment: Macaulay's Restaurant and Lounge is a casual spot serving good old-fashioned American food. Up at the Top of the Hilton, there is international cuisine with a Northwest accent. The views are superb, and there is live music in the evenings. (See "Dining with a View" in Section 5 of Chapter 5 for details.)

Services: 24-hour room service, concierge, valet/laundry service.

Facilities: Gift shop.

SHERATON SEATTLE HOTEL & TOWERS, 1400 Sixth Ave., Seattle, WA 98101. Tel. 206/621-9000 or toll free 800/325-3535. Fax 206/621-8441. 840 rms, 42 suites. A/C MINIBAR TV TEL

$ Rates: $175–$205 single; $195–$230 double; $215–$500 suite. Weekend rates available. AE, CB, DC, MC, V. **Parking:** $13 self-park, $15 valet.

This 35-story tower is the largest hotel in Seattle, and you'll always find the building buzzing with activity. In the spacious lobby, earthy pastels are highlighted by glowing tripod torchère lamps. Above a lounge area with a grand piano hangs a very unusual lighted ceiling sculpture of string baffles that gently sway in the breezes of the air-conditioning system. Potted plants, flower arrangements, and comfortable couches around the lobby offer plenty of places for a quiet moment alone or an opportunity for lively conversation. Also in the lobby, and throughout the rest of the hotel, you'll find numerous works of art, including a large collection of art glass from the Pilchuck School. The top floor of the hotel contains the exercise room and swimming-pool area.

The standard-size rooms are not quite as luxurious as the lobby would suggest, but the king rooms are quite spacious and include a work table with telephone and a couch with a second phone beside it. However, if you book a room in the Towers, the hotel's club floors, you'll get the kind of attention and service you would expect only from a small luxury hotel. Whichever type of room you stay in, make sure it's as high as possible to take advantage of the great views.

Dining/Entertainment: The subdued elegance and outstanding meals at Fuller's continue to win this restaurant awards and recommendations. The very finest and most innovative Northwest cuisine is what has the critics raving (see "Hotel Dining" in Section 5 of Chapter 5 for details). Banners is a less formal restaurant. Gooey's, named for a gigantic local clam, is the hotel's popular lounge and disco. Complimentary happy-hour buffets and live dance music on the weekends keep the crowds content.

Services: 24-hour room service, concierge, valet/laundry service.

Facilities: Indoor swimming pool, whirlpool, sauna, exercise room, wheelchair accommodations, gift shop, no-smoking floors.

STOUFFER MADISON HOTEL, 515 Madison St., Seattle, WA 98104. Tel. 206/583-0300 or toll free 800/468-3571. Fax 206/622-8635. 553 rms, 78 suites. A/C MINIBAR TV TEL

$ Rates: $144–$154 single; $164–$174 double; $164–$184 single suite; $184–$204 double suite. Weekend packages available. AE, CB, DC, DISC, MC, V. **Parking:** $12.

Despite its size, the Stouffer Madison provides friendly service and attention to detail. A spacious lobby graced by attractive Japanese prints is only the beginning of the comforts and amenities here.

All rooms are larger than average and most have views of either Puget Sound or the Cascade Range. Custom-made furniture (including walnut armoires with brass trim), separate seating areas, remote-control TVs, contemporary art, and soft color schemes make every room a winner. In the bath you'll find a nice selection of toiletries. On the Club Floors, you'll find slightly more luxurious accommodations and a lounge in which complimentary continental breakfast and afternoon hors d'oeuvres are served.

Dining/Entertainment: Prego, way up on the 28th floor, serves northern Italian cuisine amid eye-catching views of Seattle. (See "Dining with a View" in Section 5 of Chapter 5 for details.) Down on the second floor, Maxwell's serves American food in a casual café atmosphere; Sunday brunch here is very popular. The lobby court is a convivial lounge, and when the weather permits, tables spill out onto an outdoor terrace complete with waterfall. There's live piano music here in the evenings.

Services: 24-hour room service, concierge, complimentary morning coffee and newspaper, valet/laundry service, complimentary shoeshine, in-room movies, airport shuttle service ($7), turn-down service on club floors, massage available.

Facilities: Indoor swimming pool, whirlpool, fitness room, wheelchair accommodations, no-smoking rooms, beauty salon, florist, gift shop.

HOTEL VINTAGE PARK, 1100 Fifth Ave., Seattle, WA 98101. Tel. 206/624-8000 or toll free 800/624-4433. Fax 206/623-0568. 129 rms, 1 suite. A/C TV TEL

$ Rates: $135–$145 single; $150–$160 double, $370 suite. AE, CB, DC, MC, V. **Parking:** Valet $12.

Small and classically elegant is the best way to describe the Vintage Park. Burnished wood paneling glows in the soft lighting. A black-marble fireplace flanked by shelves full of old books beckons you to sit and relax a while amid Italianate furnishings. To further help you unwind, there are complimentary evening wine tastings featuring Washington wines.

To continue the wine theme, the hotel has named each of its rooms after a Washington winery, and throughout the hotel, you'll likely spot other homages to the grape. Rooms vary quite a bit here, though if you are willing to spend a little more for a deluxe room, you'll experience luxury rarely found in this price range. You'll want to spend your days luxuriating in bed when you see the Arabesque-patterned comforters, pillows, and canopy draperies of deep plum, hunter green, and gold. A minibar is stocked with Washington wines, and there is a large basket of snacks. The bathrooms, though small, feature attractive granite counters, hair dryers, and telephones. Standard rooms, though smaller and less luxuriously appointed, are still very comfortable. Many of these smaller rooms have a wall of mirrors to give the room the feeling of space, and surprisingly the bathrooms in these rooms are larger than in the deluxe rooms. If you're feeling like a splurge, the Chateau St. Michele suite will surround you with a stunningly contemporary decor that includes a four-poster bed, pass-through fireplace, Japanese soaking tub, compact disc stereo piped throughout the suite, and lots of artistic furnishings.

Dining/Entertainment: The adjacent Tulio Restaurant serves Italian meals based on the food of Tuscany, and though the hotel's emphasis is on Washington wines, there are plenty of Italian wines to accompany meals. A small bar adjoins the restaurant.

Services: Room service, concierge, access to health club, complimentary daily newspaper, valet/laundry service.

Facilities: No-smoking rooms.

WARWICK HOTEL, 401 Lenora St., Seattle, WA 98121. Tel. 206/443-4300 or toll free 800/426-9280. 230 rms, 4 suites. A/C TV TEL
$ Rates: $140–$170 single; $155–$185 double; $350 suite. Weekend rates available. AE, CB, DC, DISC, MC, V. **Parking:** $9.50.

Located in the heart of downtown Seattle, only six blocks from Pike Place Market and two blocks from the monorail terminal, the Warwick offers European charm and exceptional service. A sunken lobby with a copper fireplace provides a quiet setting for relaxing conversation. Black mirrored walls, spotlighted bouquets of flowers, and Asian art offer just the right touch of sophistication. A Belgian tapestry depicting woodcutters evokes both the European styling and the Northwest setting of this hotel.

Rooms come with either two double beds or a king-size bed, and many have stocked minibars or minirefrigerators. Modern furnishings in greens and warm beiges, a desk for working, and a couch or an easy chair for relaxing complete the amenities that will help you settle in. On the upper floors, a marble bath with a basket of toiletries and a terry-cloth robe assure you of a fresh start each day, and a telephone in the bath lets you keep in touch.

Dining/Entertainment: Liaison is the hotel's distinctive eatery, serving Northwest-influenced Mediterranean cuisine that uses only the freshest local ingredients. The menu here changes daily, and there is live piano music weekends in the adjacent lounge.

Services: 24-hour room service, concierge, valet/laundry service, complimentary limousine service in downtown Seattle.

Facilities: Indoor swimming pool, whirlpool, sauna, fitness room, wheelchair accommodations.

WESTIN HOTEL SEATTLE, 1900 Fifth Ave., Seattle, WA 98101. Tel. 206/728-1000 or toll free 800/228-3000. Fax 206/728-2259. 822 rms, 43 suites. A/C MINIBAR TV TEL
$ Rates: $140–$165 single; $165–$190 double; from $225 suite.

Children 18 and under stay free in parents' room. AE, CB, DC, DISC, JCB, MC, V. **Parking:** $12, valet $17.

The hallmark cylindrical towers of the Westin chain rise above the downtown Seattle skyline like a pair of honeycombs. Within, you'll find a veritable beehive of activity as tour groups assemble and conventioneers register, and although the hotel has the amenities you'd expect, service can be impersonal and the crowds overwhelming. All rooms have modern furnishings and are done in subdued Mediterranean colors. Some of the nice touches include work desks facing the window and the Seattle views, a bit of art in the bathrooms, and safes for your valuables. The rooms on the upper floors are certainly the best, with fine views of Seattle and Puget Sound. Of Seattle's huge convention hotels, this is my favorite.

Dining/Entertainment: The Palm Court is the Westin's premier, award-winning purveyor of Northwest cuisine. This restaurant sparkles with wide windows, large mirrors, and bright lights, and is considered one of the most romantic restaurants in Seattle. Nikko, which you'll find one floor below the lobby, is one of Seattle's finest Japanese restaurants. Unusual decor here melds traditional Japanese with high-tech contemporary. (See "Hotel Dining" in Section 5 of Chapter 5 for details on both restaurants.) The Market Café is a casual place done up to look as if it belongs in Pike Place Market. In the lobby court you can sip a drink while listening to a pianist tickle the ivories. For music, videos, and dancing, head to Fitzgerald's on Fifth.

Services: Concierge, 24-hour room service, 1-day valet/laundry service, in-room movies.

Facilities: Indoor swimming pool, exercise room, whirlpool, sauna, wheelchair accommodations, no-smoking floors, gift shops, barber, beauty salon.

EXPENSIVE

WESTCOAST CAMLIN HOTEL, 1619 Ninth Ave., Seattle, WA 98101. Tel. 206/682-0100 or toll free 800/426-0670. 136 rms, 4 suites. TV TEL

$ Rates: $80–$101 single; $90–$111 double; $175 suite. AE, CB, DC, DISC, MC, V. **Parking:** $7.

The WestCoast hotel chain has latched onto a brilliant idea and has certainly made the most of it in the Seattle area, where they have seven hotels. Their hotels offer convenient locations as well as European style and service without charging an arm and a leg. Located only a block from the Washington State Convention & Trade Center, the WestCoast Camlin has the feel of a classic European hotel. Sophisticated without being pretentious, small without sacrificing amenities, the Camlin provides personal service at reasonable rates.

The marble floor of the quiet lobby is accented by Oriental carpets, and comfortable chairs and couches are set in living-room arrangements. Large potted plants give the room a homey feeling, while marble walls echo with polish and sophistication. Whenever the weather cooperates, you can visit the outdoor pool with its small sun deck. The accommodations here offer plenty of elbow room, are done in subtle pastel shades, and have attractive floral-print bedspreads and drapes. A few choice toiletries await you in the modern bath.

Dining/Entertainment: The Cloud Room Restaurant & Lounge, on the top floor, serves a varied menu, with an emphasis on fresh seafood. Great views!

Services: Room service, laundry service, in-room movies.

Facilities: Seasonal heated outdoor swimming pool, wheelchair accommodations.

WESTCOAST ROOSEVELT HOTEL, 1531 Seventh Ave., Seattle, WA 98101. Tel. 206/621-1200 or toll free 800/426-0670. Fax 206/233-0335. 118 rms, 32 suites. A/C TV TEL
$ Rates: $95–$110 single; $105–$120 double; $165 suite. AE, DC, DISC, MC, V. **Parking:** $7.

When you walk through the doors of this small hotel, conveniently located a block from the Washington State Convention & Trade Center, you walk into a modern art-deco room in which a long wall of glass blocks illuminates the lobby. Near one entrance stands a shimmering black grand piano beside an Oriental screen. It is all so simple—perfect understated elegance.

The $10 million it cost to renovate this building was well spent. In the guest rooms, which are decorated in eye-pleasing pastels, there are king-size beds, couches, wet bars, recessed lighting, and modern sparklingly white bathrooms. If you choose to stay in one of the limited-edition suites, you can also enjoy your own private whirlpool bath, honor bar, hair dryer, shoeshine machine, and soft terry-cloth robes.

Dining/Entertainment: Just off the lobby is Von's Grand City Café and Martini Manhattan Memorial bar. The restaurant, which can trace its history back 80 years, dedicates itself to preparing juicy steaks, lamb, veal, chicken, and salmon cooked over apple wood. Be sure to have one of the special desserts that are prepared at your table. In the bar you'll be fascinated by the wild array of "objets d'junk" that hangs from the ceiling. Old water skis, a taxi door, and a totem pole are just three of the suspended surprises.

Services: Room service, concierge, valet/laundry service, in-room movies.

Facilities: Exercise room, no-smoking rooms.

WESTCOAST VANCE HOTEL, 620 Stewart St., Seattle, WA 98101. Tel. 206/441-4200 or toll free 800/426-0670. Fax 206/441-8612. 165 rms. A/C TV TEL
$ Rates: $79–$99 single; $89–$109 double. AE, DC, DISC, MC, V. **Parking:** $7.

Built in the 1920s by lumber baron Joseph Vance, the Vance underwent a $7-million restoration in 1990 and reopened as a WestCoast hotel. Typically, the high-ceilinged lobby is very elegant—wood paneling, marble floors, Oriental carpets, tapestry-cloth upholstered chairs and couches, and ornate plasterwork wainscoting and pediments. Accommodations vary in size and some are quite small; the corner rooms compensate with lots of windows. Furniture, in keeping with the style of the lobby, includes an armoire for the TV. Bathrooms have pedestal sinks and windows.

Dining/Entertainment: Salute in Citta Ristorante is a bright and popular Italian restaurant.

Services: Room service, valet/laundry service.

Facilities: No-smoking rooms, wheelchair accommodations.

MODERATE

BEST WESTERN LOYAL INN, 2301 Eighth Ave., Seattle, WA 98121. Tel. 206/682-0200 or toll free 800/528-1234. Fax 206/467-8984. 91 rms, 3 suites. A/C TV TEL

$ Rates: $60–$70 single; $72–$82 double. AE, DC, DISC, MC, V. **Parking:** Free.

A recent remodeling has turned this place into a very attractive and inexpensive city-center accommodation. The deluxe rooms have wet bars, coffee makers, remote-control TVs, king-size beds, and two sinks in the bathrooms. Even the standard rooms come with remote-control TVs. There's no restaurant on the premises, but

 FROMMER'S SMART TRAVELER: HOTELS

VALUE-CONSCIOUS TRAVELERS SHOULD TAKE ADVANTAGE OF THE FOLLOWING:

1. Weekend discounts of 30 to 50%.
2. Lower room rates in the late spring and early fall, when the weather is still good and summer rates are no longer in effect. Rates usually go up in early June.
3. Chain motels, which are very good value and often offer free local calls.
4. The Ys and the AYH youth hostels offer very inexpensive lodgings in downtown Seattle.
5. Lower rates outside of downtown. Downtown hotels are used primarily by business travelers, and their prices reflect this. You can get the same amenities (often more) at lower prices by staying at a hotel away from downtown. The inconvenience is that you must travel into the city each day.
6. Senior citizens and families often get discounts, as do members of AAA. Be sure to ask if there are any such discounts.
7. Advance purchase discounts similar to those offered by airlines. You'll save up to 50% off normal room rates, but you'll pay a penalty if you change your plans.

QUESTIONS TO ASK IF YOU'RE ON A BUDGET:

1. Is there a parking charge? In downtown Seattle, parking charges can add as much as $14 per day to your hotel bill.
2. Does the quoted rate for a given stay include the room tax?
3. Is there a charge for local calls? A surcharge on long-distance calls?
4. Is breakfast included in the rate? Not only bed-and-breakfast inns include breakfast in their service; some moderately priced hotels and even some motels do, too (often only coffee and doughnuts).
5. Does the hotel have a complimentary airport shuttle? This can save you taxi or other airport shuttle fares.

because the Loyal Inn is only five minutes' walk from Seattle Center, it makes a good choice for families.

Services: Complimentary coffee.

Facilities: 24-hour sauna, whirlpool, no-smoking rooms.

THE CLAREMONT HOTEL, 2004 Fourth Ave., Seattle, WA 98121. Tel. 206/448-8600 or toll free 800/448-8601. Fax 206/441-7140. 90 rms, 11 suites. TV TEL

$ Rates: $59–$99 single; $69–$109 double; $99–$159 suite. AE, MC, V. **Parking:** $9.50.

This 1920s downtown hotel was recently remodeled and is now a perfectly adequate and very reasonably priced choice for budget travelers who want to be close to the action. Most rooms include small kitchens, which makes them a great idea for families trying to save on meal expenses. Groups of young travelers may also find these rooms a welcome respite from hostels. The rooms combine old-fashioned touches such as glass doorknobs and modern furnishings. Bathrooms are small and tend to show their age, but otherwise these accommodations are perfectly acceptable. Rooms on the upper floors have good views.

Dining/Entertainment: The Beaver Café is a casual and inexpensive eatery just off the lobby.

Facilities: Coin-operated laundry.

DAYS INN TOWN CENTER, 2205 Seventh Ave., Seattle, WA 98121. Tel. 206/448-3434 or toll free 800/648-6440 or 800/325-2525. Fax 206/441-6976. 90 rms. A/C TV TEL

$ Rates: $74–$81 single; $79–$95 double (discount card good for 10% off regular rates is available). AE, CB, DC, DISC, MC, V. **Parking:** Free.

Conveniently located close to Seattle Center and within walking distance (or a free bus ride) of the rest of downtown Seattle, this three-story hotel offers large, clean accommodations. Modern furniture and pastel color schemes make every room comfortable and attractive.

Dining/Entertainment: The Greenhouse Café & Bar—as its name implies—is a sunny, cheerful place serving breakfast, lunch, and dinner. In the lounge you can sit by the fire or watch the big-screen TV.

Services: Valet/laundry service.

HOTEL SEATTLE, 315 Seneca St., Seattle, WA 98101. Tel. 206/623-5110 or toll free 800/426-2439. 80 rms, 1 suite. A/C TV TEL

$ Rates: $66–$70 single; $72–$76 double; $98–$108 suite. AE, CB, DC, DISC, MC, V. **Parking:** $12.

The 11-story Seattle has seen better days but is still worth considering, since it's one of the least expensive city-center hotels that's still acceptable. Rooms are small but clean. The hotel seems to be very popular with young Japanese travelers, and I'd recommend it primarily for young people who don't expect everything to be perfect. If you want convenience and economical rates, this is the place for you.

Dining/Entertainment: Bernard's on Seneca serves inexpensive German and American food in large portions.

Services: Room service.

Facilities: Gift shop, hair salon.

PACIFIC PLAZA HOTEL, 400 Spring St., Seattle, WA 98104. Tel. 206/623-3900 or toll free 800/426-1165. Fax 206/623-2059. 160 rms. A/C TV TEL

$ Rates (including continental breakfast): $64–$94 single or double. AE, DC, DISC, MC, V. **Parking:** $8.

S Built in 1929, this old hotel was renovated a few years back and offers attractive rooms and excellent value. The building, in the heart of the financial district, is now dwarfed by some of the surrounding skyscrapers. However, you're halfway between Pike Place Market and Pioneer Square, and just about the same distance from the waterfront. Rooms are small and sometimes cramped but they come with such amenities as ceiling fans and alarm clocks. Wingback chairs and cherry-wood finishes on the furnishings give each guest room an elegant touch. Bathrooms are small and dated, but luckily they still have their old-fashioned porcelain shower knobs.

Dining/Entertainment: A Red Robin Restaurant serving gourmet hamburgers is in the basement of the hotel. You can see it through a window in the first-floor lobby.

Services: Valet/laundry service.

Facilities: No-smoking rooms.

SEATTLE DOWNTOWN TRAVELODGE, 2213 Eighth Ave., Seattle, WA 98121. Tel. 206/624-6300 or toll free 800/255-3050. Fax 206/233-0185. 72 rms. A/C TV TEL

$ Rates: $55–$95 single; $60–$90 double. AE, CB, DC, DISC, MC, V. **Parking:** Free.

This conveniently located and moderately priced downtown motel is located about midway between the Washington State Convention and Trade Center and Seattle Center, so it's convenient whether you are here on business or pleasure. The rooms are attractive and some even have balconies. There are clock radios in all rooms, and the baths are large, with baskets of toiletries on the counters.

Dining/Entertainment: There is an adjacent 24-hour restaurant (the Dog House) serving straightforward meals at economical prices.

Services: Complimentary coffee, in-room movies.

Facilities: No-smoking rooms.

SIXTH AVENUE INN, 2000 Sixth Ave., Seattle, WA 98121. Tel. 206/441-8300 or toll free 800/648-6440. 166 rms, 1 suite. A/C TV TEL

$ Rates: $71–$84 single; $80–$93 double; $102–$115 suite (lower rates are for off-season). Children under age 17 stay free in parents' room. AE, CB, MC, V. **Parking:** Free.

You won't have to wonder what time it is here: The huge railway clock behind the front desk takes up an entire wall. Royal-blue carpeting and oversize wicker chairs provide an interesting contrast of casualness and sophistication in the lobby. The deep-blue color scheme is continued throughout the hotel, from the awning over the entrance to the bedspreads and draperies in every guest room. And if you haven't already realized that this is more than your standard moderately priced hotel, one look at your room will convince you: On a small wall shelf is a selection of old hardcover books, and old photos of Seattle provide a glimpse into the city's past. Wicker furniture and a large potted plant give the room the feeling of a tropical greenhouse. There are even brass beds.

Dining/Entertainment: The Sixth Avenue Bar & Grill, located on the second floor, looks out to a Japanese garden that makes dining a very tranquil experience. Prime rib, steak, and seafood are featured on the menu. In the lounge, warm dark-wood paneling and a fireplace are part of the cozy environment.

Services: Room service, valet/laundry service.

Facilities: No-smoking rooms.

INEXPENSIVE

NENDEL'S VALU INN, 2106 Fifth Ave., Seattle, WA 98121. Tel. 206/441-8833 or toll free 800/547-0106. Fax 206/441-0730. 67 rms (all with private bath). A/C TV TEL

$ Rates: $50–$60 single; $55–$65 double. AE, CB, DC, DISC, MC, V. **Parking:** Free.

You'll find this economical motel in the shadow of the monorail (about midway between Westlake Center and the Space Needle). Rooms are a bit small and show their age, but new carpets and wallpaper do a lot to make them feel more comfortable. No-smoking rooms and complimentary coffee are available, and perhaps best of all, there's free parking. You just won't find an acceptable room in downtown for less. I suggest that finicky travelers ask to see a room here before committing.

Y's

SEATTLE DOWNTOWN YMCA, 909 Fourth Ave., Seattle, WA 98104-1194. Tel. 206/382-5000. 185 rms. TEL

$ Rates: $34–$39 single; $39–$43 double ($1 discount to YMCA members). Weekly rates available. MC, V.

This is one of the nicest YMCAs I've ever seen. They welcome men, women, and families, and have rooms with or without private baths. If you want, you can get a room with a TV or just walk down the hall to the TV lounge. All the rooms are fully carpeted and equipped with modern furnishings and comfortable beds. Best of all, you have full use of all the athletic facilities when you stay here. You'd have to stay at the most expensive hotel in the city for facilities like these.

Services: Free local phone calls, baggage storage.

Facilities: Indoor pool, running track, weight room with Nautilus machines, racquetball and squash courts, TV lounges, coin-operated laundry, tailor, barbershop.

SEATTLE YWCA, 1118 Fifth Ave., Seattle, WA 98101. Tel. 206/461-1851. 21 rms (3 with private bathroom, 2 with semiprivate bathroom, 16 with shared bathroom).

$ Rates: $31–$36 single; $42–$48 double. Weekly rates available. MC, V.

This downtown choice for budget-minded women is quite attractive inside. The rooms are small and offer the barest essentials for comfort, but they are economical and clean. Security is also tight, so women traveling alone can sleep peacefully at night. The YWCA offers the same very convenient downtown location as the YMCA, which is only two blocks away. There is a small deli on the premises.

Facilities: Indoor pool ($5).

HOSTEL

SEATTLE INTERNATIONAL AYH HOSTEL, 84 Union St., Seattle, WA 98101-2084. Tel. 206/622-5443. 126 beds.

$ Rates: $15.15 for members. MC, V.

Ⓕ FROMMER'S COOL FOR KIDS: HOTELS

Sheraton Seattle Hotel & Towers *(see p. 36)* The V.I.K. (very important kids) program provides four hours of supervised activities on Saturdays for kids aged 5 to 12: There is a cooking class in Fuller's restaurant, a behind-the-scenes tour of the hotel, a special lunch, and a movie.

Seattle Marriott Hotel *(see p. 47)* With a huge jungly atrium containing a swimming pool and whirlpool spas, kids can play Tarzan and never leave the hotel. There is also a game room that will keep the young ones occupied for hours if need be.

Seattle Downtown YMCA *(see p. 44)* One of the nicest YMCA's I've ever seen. They welcome families and have rooms with or without private baths. You get to use all of the athletic facilities here; for facilities like these, you'd have to stay at the most expensive hotel in Seattle.

This conveniently located hostel is housed in the former Longshoreman's Hall, which was built in 1915. To find it, walk down Post Alley, which runs through and under Pike Place Market, to the corner of Union Street. If you don't provide your own sheets, you can rent them for $2.15 for the duration of your stay. If you plan to stay for three nights or less, you need not be an AYH member, but you'll have to pay a $3 surcharge each night. After your first three nights and any time between June and September, you must buy a membership for $25. There's a kitchen and a self-service laundry.

BED & BREAKFASTS

PENSIONE NICHOLS, 1923 First Ave., Seattle, WA 98101. Tel. 206/441-7125. 10 rms (none with bath), 2 suites (both with bath).

$ Rates (including breakfast): $50 single; $70 double; $150 suite. AE, DISC, MC, V.

If you have ever traveled through Europe on a budget, you have probably stayed at bed-and-breakfast lodgings that started on the second or third floor of a building. This city-center bed-and-breakfast is just such a European-style lodging, and you'll find it up two flights of stairs. Located only a block from Pike Place Market, Pensione Nichols is a touch expensive for what you get, though it is hard to beat the location. Only two of the guest rooms have windows (the two rooms facing the street), but all the rest have skylights. High ceilings and white bedspreads brighten the rooms and make them feel spacious. At the back of the lodging's third floor there is a large lounge area overlooking Eliott Bay.

TUGBOAT CHALLENGER BUNK & BREAKFAST, 1001 Fairview Ave. N., Seattle, WA 98109. Tel. 206/340-1201. 7 rms (4 with private bath). TEL

$ Rates (including full breakfast): $50–$110 single; $65–$135

double. Children by reservation only. AE, DC, MC, V. **Parking:** Free. **Directions:** Yale Street Landing on Chandler's Cove, at the south end of Lake Union.

★ This has to be the most unusual bed-and-breakfast I've ever seen. If you need lots of space, this place is definitely not for you. However, if you love ships and the sea and don't mind cramped quarters, don't pass up this opportunity to spend the night on board a restored and fully operational 45-year-old tugboat. (The only other waterfront hotel in Seattle is the much-pricier Edgewater.) You're welcome to visit the bridge for a great view of Lake Union and the Seattle skyline, or delve into the mechanics of the tug's enormous diesel engine. A conversation pit with granite fireplace fills the cozy main cabin, and in each of the guest cabins you'll find lots of polished wood.

Dining/Entertainment: There is a small bar in the main cabin and several excellent restaurants are nearby.

Facilities: Laundry facilities available, nearby boat-rental center.

---

2. NEAR SEA-TAC AIRPORT

VERY EXPENSIVE

RED LION HOTEL/SEATTLE AIRPORT, 18740 Pacific Hwy. S., Seattle, WA 98188. Tel. 206/246-8600 or toll free 800/547-8010. Fax 206/242-9727. 850 rms, 33 suites. A/C TV TEL

$ Rates: $119–$143 single; $129–$154 double; $175–$395 suite. Weekend packages available. AE, CB, DC, DISC, MC, V. **Parking:** Free.

You'll find Red Lions throughout the Northwest, and they're almost all like this one—big, sprawling, glitzy, with lots of amenities. Built on the banks of a small lake, this Red Lion has seven wings and a 14-story tower. With so many rooms, it isn't surprising that the hotel frequently plays host to conventions. On a sunny day the lobby is filled with light streaming through the greenhouse-type walls. A shake-shingle roof and a Northwest Coast Native American design on the portico are reminders that you're in the Pacific Northwest now.

Take a room in the tower and a glass elevator will whisk you up to your floor, providing a great view of the airport all the way. Red Lion rooms are consistently large—in fact, some of the largest in the hotel business. Whether you book one with two double beds, a queen-size bed, or a king-size bed, you'll have plenty of space to move around. All the rooms have been recently remodeled in relaxing subdued colors.

Dining/Entertainment: Maxi's, up on the 14th floor, is a very elegant large restaurant. The adjacent lounge is on three levels so that you can enjoy the view no matter where you're sitting. In the evenings there's live big-band or rock dance music. Down on the first floor you'll find Seaports, a seafood restaurant open for lunch and dinner. The Coffee Garden is a very casual lobby coffee shop and is open for breakfast, lunch, and dinner.

Services: Room service, concierge, free airport shuttle, valet/laundry service.

Facilities: Heated outdoor swimming pool, exercise room, gift shop, wheelchair accommodations, beauty salon, barbershop.

EXPENSIVE

SEATTLE MARRIOTT HOTEL, 3201 S. 176th St., Seattle, WA 98188. Tel. 206/241-2000 or toll free 800/228-9290. 460 rms, 3 suites. A/C TV TEL

$ Rates: $73–$148 single or double; $250 suite. AE, CB, DC, DISC, MC, V. **Parking:** Free.

With its soaring atrium and tropical greenhouse garden full of flowering plants, a swimming pool, and two whirlpools, this airport-side resort hotel may keep you so enthralled you won't want to leave. There are even waterfalls and totem poles for that Northwest outdoorsy feeling. Best of all, it's always sunny and warm in here, unlike in the real outdoorsy Northwest. In the lobby, there is a huge stone fireplace that will make you think you're at some remote mountain lodge. The waiting area for the Yukon Landing Restaurant has a stuffed moose head and shingle walls that continue the rugged-outdoors theme. You can't pick a better place to stay in the airport area.

Although all rooms are relatively large and attractively decorated in sea-foam green and lavender, the concierge-level rooms are particularly appealing. Attractive Oriental prints decorate the walls. In the bathroom, there are scales, a hair dryer, and a basket of elegantly bottled toiletries. And, of course, there's a concierge on hand to help you and a special lounge with complimentary coffee.

Dining/Entertainment: Yukon Landing Restaurant will have you thinking you're in the middle of the gold rush. Stone pillars; rough-hewn beams and wooden walls; moose, deer, and elk heads on the walls; and deer-antler chandeliers—all make this rustic restaurant very popular. For that gold-rush high life, enjoy the Sunday champagne brunch. The Lobby Lounge is a greenhouse that looks into the larger greenhouse of the atrium. At Gambits, the hotel's disco, you can dance to recorded Top 40 tunes.

Services: Room service, free airport shuttle, valet/laundry service, in-room movies, complimentary coffee.

Facilities: Atrium swimming pool, whirlpool, health club, tanning center, sauna, game room, wheelchair accommodations, no-smoking rooms.

MODERATE

HAMPTON INN HOTEL, Seattle, 19445 International Blvd., Seattle, WA 98188. Tel. 206/878-1700 or toll free 800/426-7866. Fax 206/824-0720. 131 rms, 1 suite. A/C TV TEL

$ Rates (including continental breakfast): $65–$67 single; $75–$77 double; $100 suite (rates lower in winter). AE, CB, DC, DISC, MC, V. **Parking:** Free.

You'll get much more at the Hampton Inn than you'd expect from a small hotel in this price range. All the rooms are attractively furnished with modern appointments and decorated in pleasing pastels. A friendly service-incentive plan assures that each and every member of the staff here will do all that he or she can to make your stay enjoyable. There's even a "satisfaction guaranteed" policy that allows you to stay for free if you aren't entirely satisfied with your stay.

Dining/Entertainment: No restaurant on the premises, but several nearby.

Services: Room service, free restaurant and airport shuttle, valet/laundry service, free local calls, in-room movies.

Facilities: Heated outdoor swimming pool, exercise room, wheelchair accommodations, no-smoking rooms.

HOLIDAY INN, SEA-TAC AIRPORT, 17338 Pacific Hwy. S., Seattle, WA 98188. Tel. 206/248-1000 or toll free 800/465-4329. 260 rms. A/C TV TEL

$ Rates: $71–$101 single or double. AE, CB, DC, DISC, JCB, MC, V. **Parking:** Free.

The lobby here looks as if it could be in some small European hotel. There are slate and marble floors, as well as a fireplace with slate hearth. The swimming pool is enclosed within a contemporary building with a glass-block wall that keeps the room very bright.

Guest rooms feature white-pine or cherry-wood furniture with black trim, including armoires for the TVs. On the executive floors, the overall effect is subtly Asian. Very comfortable easy chairs with hassocks are great for relaxing after a long business day. Rooms on the higher floors also offer good views (ask for a room on the Mount Rainier side of the hotel). Unfortunately, bathrooms in all the rooms tend to lack sufficient counter space. The King Leisure rooms come with sofas, desks, king-size beds, and a bit more room than the standard accommodations.

Dining/Entertainment: In its rotating dining room on the 12th floor, the Top of the Inn features a sweeping vista of the airport and the surrounding area, plus continental and American fare prepared with fresh local ingredients. To entertain you while you dine, there are singing waiters and waitresses, a pianist, and a violinist. The lobby lounge is a dark and lively place serving drinks and complimentary afternoon hors d'oeuvres.

Services: Room service, courtesy airport shuttle, valet/laundry service, in-room movies.

Facilities: Heated indoor pool, exercise room, whirlpool, wheelchair accommodations, coin-operated laundry.

RADISSON HOTEL, 17001 Pacific Hwy. S., Seattle, WA 98188. Tel. 206/244-6000 or toll free 800/333-3333. Fax 206/246-6835. 300 rms, 5 suites. A/C TV TEL

$ Rates: $79–$110 single or double; $150–$350 suite. Weekend and special packages available. AE, CB, DC, DISC, ER, JCB, MC, V. **Parking:** Free.

An abundance of marble and a grand angular entrance give this low-rise hotel more glitz than you might expect. The predominantly green-and-brown decor suggests the Northwest forests, while a garden courtyard planted with spruces and ferns actually brings these famous woods right into the hotel. On sunny days you can dine on a courtyard terrace, although the sound of jets overhead might be a bit too much for you.

Rooms, done in the same brown-and-green color scheme as the rest of the hotel, are furnished with modern appointments. On the Plaza Club level you'll receive a continental breakfast, turn-down service, beverages, hors d'oeuvres, and newspaper.

Dining/Entertainment: Colorful pastels of fresh produce decorate the walls of the Marketplace Café, where standard American fare is offered.

Services: Room service, laundry/valet service, courtesy airport shuttle, massages available.

Facilities: Heated outdoor swimming pool (in garden courtyard), sauna, florist, gift shop, wheelchair accommodations, no-smoking rooms.

WESTCOAST SEA-TAC HOTEL, 18220 Pacific Hwy. S., Seattle, WA 98188. Tel. 206/246-5535 or toll free 800/426-0670. Fax 206/246-5535. 146 rms, 32 suites. A/C TV TEL

$ Rates: $78–$89 single; $88–$99 double. AE, CB, DC, MC, V. **Parking:** Free.

Step into this WestCoast hotel and you enter a world of European styling, comfort, and service. The simple, elegant lines of the lobby—done in subtle pastels and shades of gray—are accentuated by a grand piano, this hotel chain's trademark. Feel free to play whenever the urge strikes.

The spacious, elegantly furnished guest rooms have queen- or king-size beds, writing table, and art deco–style chairs. On the fifth floor, you get special service, including evening turn down, coffee and a newspaper in the morning, plush terry-cloth robes, hair dryers, free local phone calls, and an honor bar. In all the rooms, you'll find bath scales and shoeshine machines.

Dining/Entertainment: Gregory's Bar & Grill is across the parking lot from the main hotel facility. Four nights a week, there is karaoke music in the lounge, which features an aeronautical theme; there is even part of an old airplane hanging from the ceiling. In the restaurant a tropical feeling prevails. Fresh seafood is the specialty here, and there is a daily fresh sheet of specials. Sunday brunch is a good deal at $11.95.

Services: Room service, free airport shuttle, valet/laundry service, in-room movies.

Facilities: Heated outdoor swimming pool, whirlpool, sauna, wheelchair accommodations, no-smoking rooms.

INEXPENSIVE

SUPER 8 MOTEL, 3100 S. 192nd St., Seattle, WA 98168. Tel. 206/433-8188 or toll free 800/843-1991. 119 rms. A/C TV TEL

$ Rates: $50–$60 single; $55–$70 double. AE, CB, DC, MC, V. **Parking:** Free.

There's nothing fancy about Seattle's link of this popular budget-hotel chain—just low prices and clean rooms. The long low-rise simulated-Tudor building is within five minutes of the airport, which makes it very convenient. There's a free airport shuttle and complimentary morning coffee. Facilities include a coin-operated laundry, wheelchair accommodations, and no-smoking rooms.

TRAVELODGE SEATTLE AIRPORT, 2900 S. 192nd St., Seattle, WA 98188. Tel. 206/241-9292 or toll free 800/255-3050. Fax 206/242-0681. 104 rms. A/C TV TEL

$ Rates: $45–$55 single; $50–$60 double. AE, CB, DC, DISC, MC, V. **Parking:** Free.

Another conveniently located and economically priced facility, the Travelodge offers standard motel rooms, although rose carpets and contemporary furnishings lend the rooms a bit more appeal than usual. There's complimentary coffee, a park and fly program, and in-room movies. Facilities include a sauna, a coin-operated laundry, and wheelchair accommodations.

---

3. FIRST HILL & CAPITOL HILL

VERY EXPENSIVE

SORRENTO HOTEL, 900 Madison St., Seattle, WA 98104-9742. Tel. 206/622-6400 or toll free 800/426-1265. Fax 206/343-6155. 76 rms, 35 suites. A/C MINIBAR TV TEL

$ Rates: $130–$160 single or double; $170–$1,000 suite. AE, DC, DISC, MC, V. **Parking:** $10.

Sit by the tiled fireplace in the lobby of the Sorrento and try to imagine all these dark mahogany-paneled walls painted white and the beautiful fireplace hidden, covered over with plywood. That's the state this building was in before it was renovated. Today an old-fashioned European atmosphere reigns at this small hotel. From the wrought-iron gates and palm trees of the courtyard entrance to the plush seating of the octagonal lobby, the Sorrento whispers style and grace, and the service here is as fine as you can expect anywhere in town.

When the Sorrento opened in 1909, there were 150 rooms. Today there are only 76. What this means is that your room will be spacious and unique. No two rooms are alike, but all have remote-control TVs and stereos hidden inside large armoires, minibars and minirefrigerators, plush terry-cloth robes, and dual-line telephones. A couch or easy chair and hassock let you put your feet up and relax after a hard day of touring or working. In the bathroom you'll find a basket of toiletries, including a small sachet to keep your wardrobe smelling fresh. You even have a choice of down or fiber-filled pillows, and in colder months, you'll slip into a bed that has been warmed with an old-fashioned hot-water bottle.

Dining/Entertainment: The Hunt Club, a dark and intimate restaurant with exposed brick walls and louvered doors that can be closed to create private dining areas, serves superb Northwest cuisine (see "Hotel Dining" in Section 5 of Chapter 5 for details). In the adjacent Fireside Room bar, dark-wood paneling continues the clublike, old-world atmosphere. Several nights a week a pianist provides musical atmosphere in this lounge. Afternoon tea is served in the lobby and Fireside Room, and brunch is served on Saturday and Sunday in the Hunt Club.

Services: Room service, concierge, valet/laundry service, complimentary limousine service in downtown Seattle, morning paper, in-room movies.

Facilities: Health-club privileges, wheelchair accommodations.

MODERATE

THE INN AT VIRGINIA MASON, 1006 Spring St., Seattle, WA 98104. Tel. 206/583-6453 or toll free 800/283-6453. Fax 206/223-7545. 79 rms, 3 suites. A/C TV TEL

$ Rates: $79–$119 single or double; $119–$180 suite. Senior-citizen discounts available. Children under 18 stay free in parents' room. AE, CB, DC, DISC, MC, V. **Parking:** Free.

S You may think I've sent you to a hospital rather than a hotel when you first arrive at this small European-style hotel on Pill Hill. It takes its name from the Virginia Mason Hospital, which is next door; in fact, the two buildings are connected. The lobby is small but elegant, with a little brick courtyard just outside. Room sizes vary a lot, since this is an old building, but most have large closets, modern bathrooms (some with windows), and wing-back chairs. The larger deluxe rooms and suites are quite large, and some have whirlpool baths, fireplaces, dressing rooms, hair dryers, and minirefrigerators.

Dining/Entertainment: The Rhododendron Restaurant serves Northwest and traditional cuisine. There is live piano music several nights per week.

Services: Valet/laundry service, concierge, room service, massages, in-room movies.

Facilities: Privileges at nearby fitness center, no-smoking rooms, wheelchair accommodations.

BED & BREAKFASTS

GASLIGHT INN, 1727 15th Ave., Seattle, WA 98122. Tel. 206/325-3654. 9 rms (5 with private bath), 5 suites (all with private bath). TV

$ Rates (including continental breakfast): $58–$89 single or double; $75–$95 suite. AE, MC, V. **Parking:** On street.

This 1906-vintage home was an early spec house—that is, it was considered to be a model home by real-estate investors—and the first house in this neighborhood. Capitol Hill was on the outskirts of the city, but eventually became one of Seattle's poshest neighborhoods. That turn-of-the-century poshness still prevails here, with some modern amenities as well. I'm sure you'll enjoy the backyard swimming pool and sun decks in the summer and the fireplace in the living room in the winter. Each of the rooms is individually decorated and most even have a small refrigerator. Continental breakfast is served in the dining room from 8am on.

An annex next door has six suites with kitchens and dining areas, as well as separate bedrooms and living rooms. These suites also include off-street parking. There's valet/laundry service and an outdoor swimming pool.

ROBERTA'S BED & BREAKFAST, 1147 16th Ave. E., Seattle, WA 98112. Tel. 206/329-3326. 5 rms (4 with private bath).

$ Rates (including full breakfast): $75–$95 single or double. AE, DC, MC, V.

Bibliophile's will be certain to develop an instant rapport with this B&B's namesake innkeeper. Roberta is, to say the least, fond of books and has filled shelves in nearly every room with books both old and new. On a rainy Seattle day, I can think of no better way to spend an afternoon than curled up at Roberta's with a good book. This turn-of-the-century home is on a beautiful tree-lined street just around the corner from Volunteer Park. A big front porch stretches across the front of the house, while inside there are hardwood floors and a mix of antique and modern furnishings. My favorite room is the attic hideaway, which has angled walls, painted wood paneling, lots of skylights, and a claw-foot bathtub. The overall effect of this room is that of a ship's cabin. Breakfast starts with tea or coffee left at your door and continues downstairs in the dining room with a hearty meal that includes home-baked treats.

SALISBURY HOUSE, 750 16th Ave. E., Seattle, WA 98112. Tel. 206/328-8682. 4 rms (all with private bath).
$ Rates (including full breakfast): $69–$83 single; $74–$88 double. AE, DC, MC, V.

This grand old house on tree-lined 16th Avenue East has a wide porch that wraps around two sides. Sit down in one of the white Adirondack chairs and enjoy one of Seattle's prettiest streetscapes. Inside there's plenty to admire as well. Two living rooms (one with a wood-burning fireplace) and a second-floor sun porch provide plenty of spots for relaxing and meeting other guests. On sunny summer days, breakfast may even be served in the small formal garden in the backyard. Guest rooms all have queen-sized beds with down comforters, and one even has a unique canopy bed hung with pink satin. One of the other rooms has an old claw-foot tub in the bathroom. Breakfasts here are deliciously filling and might include fresh fruit, juice, quiche, fresh-baked muffins or bread, or oatmeal pancakes. Cathryn and Mary Wiese, mother and daughter, are the friendly innkeepers.

4. NORTH SEATTLE

EXPENSIVE

MEANY TOWER HOTEL, 4507 Brooklyn Ave. NE, Seattle, WA 98105. Tel. 206/634-2000 or toll free 800/648-6440. 155 rms. A/C TV TEL
$ Rates: $88–$92 single; $100–$104 double. AE, DC, MC, V.
Parking: Free.

If you need to be near the University of Washington and want a view of downtown Seattle and the surrounding hills and water, book a room in this moderately priced high-rise. There is no swimming pool or fitness room here, but the views are superb. Every room is a corner room, and all are pleasingly appointed in peach and deep-green tones. You'll also find an extremely large TV in each room, as well as a clock radio. Though the tiled combination baths are small, they do have baskets of toiletries.

Dining/Entertainment: The Meany Grill features prime rib, steak, and fresh seafood in an elegant atmosphere of deep greens and soft pinks. Brass rails and exposed ceiling beams give it the feeling of an old-fashioned club. The adjacent lounge includes an oyster bar.

Services: Room service, valet/laundry service, complimentary newspaper.

Facilities: Exercise room.

MODERATE

UNIVERSITY PLAZA HOTEL, 400 NE 45th St., Seattle, WA 98105. Tel. 206/634-0100 or toll free 800/343-7040. Fax 206/633-2743. 135 rms, 2 suites. A/C TV TEL
$ Rates: $70–$80 single; $75–$86 double; $125–$165 suite. AE, CB, DC, DISC, MC, V. **Parking:** Free.

You'll think you've been transported to Merrie Olde England when you step through the front door of this hotel. The walls in the lobby and along an adjacent hall are done in scaled-down half-timbered cottage facades. Alas, the guest rooms do not continue the English-village theme. They were, however, remodeled a few years ago in soothing pastels with blond-wood accents. There are comfortable chairs and a remote control for the TV. The hotel takes its name from the nearby University of Washington.

Dining/Entertainment: Excalibur's Restaurant and Lounge is a baronial dining room that completes the English-village theme. Tuesday through Saturday there is live vocal and piano entertainment in the lounge, and on Sundays guests can do their own karaoke singing.

Services: Room service, valet/laundry service, in-room movies.

Facilities: Wheelchair accommodations, heated outdoor swimming pool, fitness room, hair salon.

5. BELLEVUE & KIRKLAND

Across Lake Washington from Seattle, in the area known as Eastside, are two of Washington's fastest-growing cities. Bellevue and Kirkland are at the heart of the region's high-tech industrial growth. These two cities also are bedroom communities with many attractive and wealthy neighborhoods. Should you be out this way on high-tech business or visiting friends, you may find an eastside hotel more convenient than one in downtown Seattle. Keep in mind, however, that Seattleites look on Bellevue as a cultural wasteland and may wonder why you stay there. Don't let them bother you. It's only 15 minutes to downtown Seattle if it isn't rush hour. One bonus of staying here is that rates are a bit lower for the same amenities, and the room tax is also lower (11%).

VERY EXPENSIVE

HYATT REGENCY BELLEVUE, 900 Bellevue Way NE, Bellevue, WA 98004. Tel. 206/462-1234 or toll free 800/233-1234. Fax 206/646-7567. 382 rms, 21 suites. A/C TV TEL
$ Rates: $130–$175 single; $170–$190 double; $175–$1,000 suite. Weekend rates available. **Parking:** $7, valet $11.

Located across the street from the Northwest's largest shopping mall and connected to a smaller and more exclusive shopping center, the Hyatt Regency Bellevue is a sure bet for anyone who likes to shop. This high-rise also offers from its upper floors some good views of Lake Washington and the Seattle skyline. Decor in the public areas is a mixture of traditional European styling and Oriental art and antiques. Guest rooms are done in a pale powder gray with yellow accents and include a marble-top desk and rattan chairs. Tile bathrooms have lots of counter space and an assortment of soaps and lotions. In rooms on the Regency Club floors, you'll also find robes, an iron and ironing board, a hair dryer, extra soaps, a bathroom scale, mineral water, and a jar of candies. These latter rooms also have the best views and include access to a concierge lounge.

Dining/Entertainment: Eques, the hotel's main dining room, is located just off the lobby and serves primarily Mediterranean cuisine. The decor, as the name implies, incorporates various horse images. An adjacent lounge provides a quiet spot for a drink. Chadfield's Sports Pub features green-marble counters, hardwood floors covered with sawdust, and plenty of televisions for monitoring the big game. Light snacks and sandwiches are served in the pub.

Services: 24-hour room service, valet/laundry service, evening turn down.

Facilities: Adjacent health club ($10 per week), with lap pool, steam room, sauna, whirlpool spa, weight room, aerobics room.

THE WOODMARK HOTEL AT CARILLON POINT, 1200 Carillon Point, Kirkland, WA 98033. Tel. 206/822-3700 or toll free 800/822-3700. 100 rms, 25 suites. A/C TV TEL MINIBAR

$ Rates: $140–$175 single; $150–$185 double; $225–$900 suites. Weekend rates. AE, CB, DC, ER, JCB, MC, V. **Parking:** $8.

Water, water everywhere, but hardly a waterfront hotel in sight. Unfortunately, that's the way it is around Seattle, but if you're willing to stay on the east side of Lake Washington in Kirkland, you can stay at the most luxurious waterfront hotel in the metropolitan area. Surrounded by a luxury residential community and shopping center, the Woodmark looks over a wide lawn to the waters of the lake. In the lobby a cosmopolitan sophistication prevails. Classical lines are softened by muted shades of beige and gray, while Oriental antiques and prints of old botanical illustrations provide a touch of international flavor. The overall effect is of being in the living room of a well-traveled friend. Off to one side a wide staircase leading down to the lounge and restaurant curves past a wall of glass that frames the lake beyond.

Guest rooms are no less impressive. When this hotel was planned, they must have asked frequent travelers what they would most like to find in the perfect hotel room. The answers are all here: a VCR, floor-to-ceiling windows that open, terry-cloth robes, oversized towels, a tiny television and a hair dryer in the bathroom, a large work desk, two telephones, computer hookup, complimentary coffee and a coffee maker, a stocked minibar. In addition there are views of the lake from most rooms, so sit back and enjoy.

Dining/Entertainment: The Carillon Room, one floor below the lobby, serves a combination of Northwest and continental cuisines. Decor is an eclectic mix of rustic antiques and classical lines that hint at French country inns. Large windows open onto the lake, though you wouldn't necessarily dine here for the view. Sunday brunch is lavish and delicious. The Carillon Room Lounge is a casual place more evocative of a library than a bar. Wednesday through Sunday there is live piano music in the evenings.

Services: Room service, concierge, courtesy local shopping van, complimentary newspaper, shoeshine service, laundry/valet service, complimentary late-night snacks, video lending library, complimentary use of lap-top computer, cellular phone, pager.

Facilities: Exercise room, business center, no-smoking rooms, wheelchair accommodations.

EXPENSIVE

RED LION HOTEL BELLEVUE, 300-112th Ave. SE, Bellevue, WA 98004. Tel. 206/455-1300 or toll free 800/547-8010. Fax 206/455-0466. 353 rms, 5 suites. A/C TV TEL
$ Rates: $89–$129 single; $104–$144 double; $250–$495 suite. AE, CB, DC, ER, JCB, MC, V. **Parking:** Free.

Located just off I-405 in downtown Bellevue, the Red Lion is as big and glitzy as most other Red Lion properties. An angled atrium towers over the lobby and fills the hotel with light on sunny days (and even on cloudy ones). Though not as sophisticated as the Eastside hotels (see above), the Red Lion offers all the amenities and facilities of a more expensive hotel. Though the guest room decor is rather Spartan, there is plenty of room, including two sinks (one in the bathroom and one in the vanity). Most rooms also have balconies.

Dining/Entertainment: Half the sunlit atrium lobby is given over to the Atrium Café, which serves casual and inexpensive meals. For more elegant dining, there is Misty's, offering gourmet Italian meals. The Quiet Bar provides a peaceful spot for drinks, while Misty's Lounge offers dancing to Top-40 music.

Services: Room service, concierge, valet/laundry service.

Facilities: Outdoor swimming pool, exercise room, gift shop, business center.

MODERATE

BELLEVUE INN, 11211 Main St., Bellevue, WA 98004. Tel. 206/455-5240 or toll free 800/421-8193. Fax 206/455-0654. 180 rms.
$ Rates: $80–$90 single; $85–$95 double. AE, CB, DC, DISC, JCB, MC, V. **Parking:** Free.

The Bellevue is one of the few hotels in the Seattle area that captures the feel of the Northwest in design and landscaping. The sprawling two-story hotel is roofed with cedar-shake shingles and lushly planted with rhododendron, fir, fern, and azalea. Try to book a poolside first-floor room. These rooms, though a bit dark, have sunken, rock-walled patios. Bathrooms include plenty of counter space, and there are built-in hair dryers. There are also clock radios and minirefrigerators in all rooms.

Dining/Entertainment: Jonah's Restaurant and Lounge serves a mix of American and continental dishes, with the occasional touch of Northwest creativity.

Services: Complimentary passes to local athletic club, complimentary local van service, in-room movies.

Facilities: Outdoor swimming pool, exercise room, newsstand, no-smoking rooms.

SEATTLE DINING

Consider yourself very lucky. Seattle is on the cutting edge of culinary creativity these days. For a lot of people, the opportunity to dine at some of Seattle's many excellent restaurants is reason enough to visit the city. Not only is the cuisine highly innovative, but prices are reasonable. For these listings, a restaurant is considered **expensive** if it serves meals, with wine or beer, averaging $25 or more. **Moderate** restaurants offer complete dinners in the $15 to $25 range, and **inexpensive** eateries are those where you can get a complete meal for less than $15.

Northwest cuisine has been generating a lot of publicity in recent years. It is fresh and almost always made with local ingredients. The Northwest has been blessed with a mild climate that's ideal for growing fruit and vegetables; wild mushrooms and greens fill the forests. The grassy hills produce excellent beef and lamb. The rivers and coastal waters abound in seafood. Put these local ingredients together in unexpected combinations, such as fresh salmon with raspberry butter, and you have quintessential Northwest cuisine.

The Northwest is also attracting a great deal of attention among wine lovers. Its climate almost reproduces that of Europe's prime wine-growing regions. Be sure to accompany your dinner with one of these fine local wines.

Seattle is not a late-night city. Many of the finest restaurants open for dinner at 5 or 5:30pm and close by 9:30 or 10pm. There are a few exceptions to this rule, and they are noted. Because the restaurants of Seattle are so popular with both locals and visitors, reservations are advised. If you plan a short stay, especially one over a weekend in summer, I highly recommend making a reservation before you arrive, especially for a restaurant serving Northwest cuisine.

1. DOWNTOWN

EXPENSIVE

IL BISTRO, 93-A Pike St. and First Ave. (inside Pike Place Market). Tel. 682-3049.
   Cuisine: ITALIAN. **Reservations:** Recommended.
$ Prices: Appetizers $9–$12; pastas $11.50–$12.50; main dishes $14–$30. CB, DC, MC, V.

Open: Lunch Tues–Sat noon–3pm; Dinner Sun–Thurs 5:30–10pm, Fri–Sat 5:30–11pm; bar nightly until 2am.

You'll find Il Bistro directly below the famous Pike Place Market sign. The entrance is from the ramp that leads into the bowels of the market, and once inside you'll have the feeling that you're dining in a wine cellar. Il Bistro takes Italian cooking very seriously and puts the Northwest's bountiful ingredients to good use. The region is damp most of the year and brings forth excellent crops of wild and cultivated mushrooms. Watch for them on the menu; they're always a treat.

You won't find the usual antipasti of pickled vegetables here. Instead, the menu lists such mouthwatering starters as mussels sautéed with garlic, basil, tomato, and white wine. Pasta can be a genuine revelation when served with the likes of shiitake mushrooms, hot pepper flakes, vodka, and tomato cream. Long before you arrived, the choice of which main dish to order was decided by the hundreds of loyal fans who insist that the rack of lamb with wine sauce is the best in Seattle. Don't take their word for it—decide for yourself.

CAFE SPORT, 2020 Western Ave. Tel. 443-6000.

Cuisine: NORTHWEST/PACIFIC RIM. **Reservations:** Strongly recommended.

$ Prices: Appetizers $8.25–$11.95; salads $3.75–$8.25; main dishes $10.95–$19.95. AE, DC, MC, V.

Open: Breakfast Mon–Fri 7–10am, Sat–Sun 8:30am–2:30pm; lunch Mon–Fri 11:30am–2:30pm, Sat–Sun 11am–2:30pm; dinner Mon–Sat 5–10pm, Sun 5–9pm.

Seattleites and visitors alike just can't get enough of the excellent food and service here at this *très moderne* restaurant, only steps away from Pike Place Market. The design and decor are geometric, and the lighting tends to accent the many angles. These are softened, however, by niches holding vases of fresh flowers. Small dining rooms with glass walls are perfect for large parties. The animated chatter of contented guests keeps the restaurant lively.

Be sure to start with the creamy and spicy black-bean soup—you'll be glad you did. The seared rare tuna with wasabi butter and an ocean salad is a cross between sushi and Cajun that shows off the imagination of the chef. Creamy desserts are all the rage these days in the Northwest, so be sure to try Café Sport's entry—a smooth-as-velvet crème caramel. In addition to the regular menu items, there are daily specials, including light meals and desserts.

CHEZ SHEA, 94 Pike St., Suite 34, Pike Place Market. Tel. 467-9990.

Cuisine: NORTHWEST. **Reservations:** Required.

$ Prices: Appetizers $5; main dishes $19; fixed-price four-course dinner $35. AE, MC, V.

Open: Dinner only, Tues–Thurs 5:30–9:30pm; Fri–Sun 5:30–10pm.

It's hard to believe that there could be a quiet corner of Pike Place Market, but here it is. Quiet, dark, and intimate, Chez Shea is one of the finest restaurants in Seattle. A dozen candlelit tables, with views across Puget Sound to the Olympic Mountains, are the perfect setting for a romantic dinner. The ingredients used in preparing the

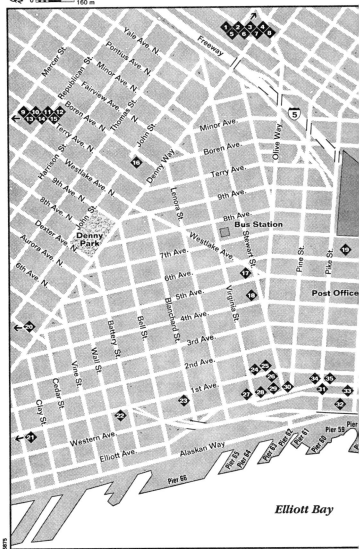

meals here come from the market below, and they are always the freshest and finest. Dinner is strictly fixed price—four courses with a choice of five main dishes, although on weeknights there are also à la carte dinners available.

The menu changes to reflect the season and on a recent winter visit included filet of salmon spiced with tantalizing Chinese sauce made from ginger, cilantro, hoisin, dry sherry, and tangerine zest. To backtrack a bit, the meal started with chicken-filled corn crêpes in *mole rojo,* a spicy, rich sauce that was made without the chocolate

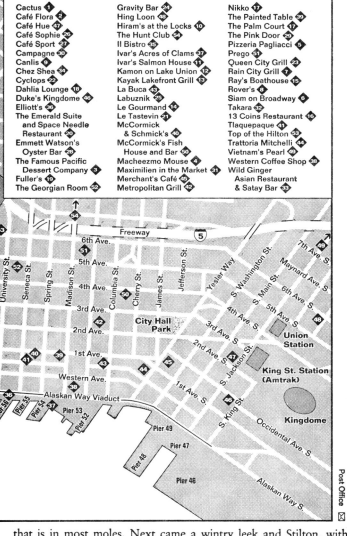

SEATTLE DINING

Cactus ①	Gravity Bar ㉔	Nikko ⑰
Café Flora ②	Hing Loon ㊽	The Painted Table ㊴
Café Hue ㊼	Hiram's at the Locks ⑩	The Palm Court ⑰
Café Sophie ㉖	The Hunt Club ㊴	The Pink Door ㉙
Café Sport ㉗	Il Bistro ㉟	Pizzeria Pagliacci ⑤
Campagne ㉚	Ivar's Acres of Clams ㊲	Prego ㊽
Canlis ⑨	Ivar's Salmon House ⑪	Queen City Grill ㉓
Chez Shea ㉞	Kamon on Lake Union ⑫	Rain City Grill ⑦
Cyclops ㉒	Kayak Lakefront Grill ⑬	Ray's Boathouse ⑮
Dahlia Lounge ⑱	La Buca ㊸	Rover's ⑧
Duke's Kingdome ㊻	Labuznik ㉕	Siam on Broadway ⑥
Elliott's ㊱	Le Gourmand ⑭	Takara ㉜
The Emerald Suite	Le Tastevin ㉑	13 Coins Restaurant ⑯
and Space Needle	McCormick	Tlaquepaque ㊶
Restaurant ⑳	& Schmick's ㊵	Top of the Hilton ㊳
Emmett Watson's	McCormick's Fish	Trattoria Mitchelli ㊹
Oyster Bar ㉘	House and Bar ㊿	Vietnam's Pearl ㊾
The Famous Pacific	Macheezmo Mouse ④	Western Coffee Shop ㊳
Dessert Company ③	Maximilien in the Market ㉛	Wild Ginger
Fuller's ⑲	Merchant's Café ㊺	Asian Restaurant
The Georgian Room ㉜	Metropolitan Grill ㊷	& Satay Bar ㊳

that is in most moles. Next came a wintry leek and Stilton, with garlic, tawny port, roasted walnuts, and chives. Though dessert is à la carte, you'll find it impossible to let it pass you by. I have a weakness for crème brûlée, and here it was flavored with chocolate and accompanied by shortbread stars. Delicious!

DAHLIA LOUNGE, 1904 Fourth Ave. Tel. 682-4142.
  Cuisine: NORTHWEST. **Reservations:** Strongly recommended.

$ Prices: Appetizers $5.25–$8.50; main dishes $12–$20. AE, CB, DC, DISC, MC, V.
Open: Lunch Mon–Fri 11:30am–2:30pm; dinner Mon–Thurs 5:30–10pm, Fri–Sat 5:30–11pm, Sun 5–9pm.

The neon chef holding a flapping fish may suggest that the Dahlia is little more than a roadside diner, but a glimpse inside at the stylish decor will likely have you thinking otherwise. One look at the menu, one bite of any dish, will convince you that this is one of Seattle's finest restaurants. Chef Tom Douglas, who put Seattle's Café Sport on the national map, brings to the Dahlia all his culinary expertise and imagination. Mouth-watering and succulent Dungeness crab cakes, a bow to Douglas's Maryland roots, are the house specialty and should not be missed. Menu influences also extend to the far side of the Pacific Rim, from which the hoisin barbecue with fried rice originates. The house-made gnocchi is always dense and delicious, while the Tuscan bread salad is a meal in itself. The lunch menu features many of the same offerings at slightly lower prices. You can even get half an order of the crab cakes.

ELLIOTT'S, Pier 56 (near Seneca St.). Tel. 623-4340.
Cuisine: SEAFOOD. **Reservations:** Recommended.
$ Prices: Appetizers $5.25–$13; salads $3–$16; main dishes $13–$25. AE, DISC, MC, V.
Open: Sun–Thurs 11am–10pm, Fri–Sat 11am–11pm (later in summer).

Elliott's oyster bar is widely hailed as having the best selection in Seattle. A new menu is printed daily and lists the available oysters and smoked seafood (smoked on the premises). You'll find the long, narrow restaurant enclosed by glass and packed full of junior and senior achievers in business suits. Overhead, the massive timbers of this former pier warehouse have been exposed, while down at floor level etched and frosted glass and pale-aquamarine lighting offer a striking contrast.

Seafood is everything here, and the preparations are primarily Mediterranean, southwestern, and northwestern. Instead of fried fish, you'll encounter such creations as scallops sautéed with tarragon in a Dijon mustard sauce and alder-smoked salmon finished on the mesquite broiler. The selection of wine and microbrewery ale is chosen for its ability to complement the restaurant's various seafood offerings. Meat eaters will find only five menu items to satisfy them; so if you don't eat seafood, it's best not to eat at Elliott's.

MODERATE

CAFE SOPHIE, 1921 First Ave. Tel. 441-6139.
Cuisine: INTERNATIONAL. **Reservations:** Strongly recommended.
$ Prices: Appetizers $4.50–$9; main dishes $10–$14; desserts $3–$6. MC, V.
Open: Lunch Mon–Fri 11am–3pm; dinner Sun–Thurs 5–10pm, Fri–Sat 5–11pm; brunch Sat–Sun 9am–3pm.

A self-consciously stylish restaurant for self-consciously stylish patrons, Café Sophie hearkens back to the grand old days of supper clubs on the Continent. The booths are terribly romantic and there are a couple of tables up front in the lounge area,

**FROMMER'S SMART TRAVELER:
RESTAURANTS**

1. Eat your main meal at lunch, when prices are lower. You can eat at some of the city's best restaurants and try Northwest cuisine for substantially less than what it would cost at dinner.
2. Always ask the price of daily specials; they are almost always several dollars more expensive than the highest-priced main dish on the regular menu.
3. Eat early, between 5 and 7pm. Some restaurants offer sunset dinner specials at greatly reduced prices (and you aren't likely to have to wait as long).
4. Make reservations whenever possible. Even at lunchtime, downtown restaurants fill up. If there is someplace where you particularly want to eat, don't risk being disappointed.
5. Pay attention to how much alcohol you drink; even local wines and beers can be expensive.
6. Eat ethnic—there are lots of good inexpensive Asian restaurants all over the city.
7. Eat at Pike Place Market. There are more than 50 eating establishments here serving all types of food in all price categories.

plus a few more out on the sidewalk, where you can sit and watch the Pike Place Market foot traffic. The menu pulls its gastronomic references from all over the world and changes frequently to keep the loyal patrons returning. On a recent evening, straightforward coq au vin shared the menu with Gorgonzola-and-black-walnut half-moon pasta. Be sure to save plenty of room for one of the luscious desserts; they're the main reason most people come here.

IVAR'S ACRES OF CLAMS, Pier 54. Tel. 624-6852.
Cuisine: SEAFOOD. **Reservations:** Recommended.
$ Prices: Appetizers $2.45–$7; main dishes $10.45–$19. AE, MC, V.
Open: Summer daily 11am–11pm; winter daily 11am–10pm.
Opened in 1938, this is the original Seattle Ivar's. The entrance is directly across Alaskan Way from the Clam Central Station trolley stop, and a few steps from the door is a statue of old Captain Ivar himself, feeding seagulls. The lofty warehouse that houses Ivar's is filled with historic photos of old Seattle and its waterfront. Gleaming brass is everywhere, and there is a spacious lounge area with its own menu of lighter fare. Clams are the main attraction here, as you might have guessed, but every other type of seafood also shows up on the menu. Cajun, Northwest, Italian, French—however you can prepare fish, Ivar's does it and does it well. During happy hour, from 4 to 6:30pm on weekdays, there are half-price appetizers.

LA BUCA, 102 Cherry St. Tel. 343-9517.
Cuisine: ITALIAN. **Reservations:** Strongly recommended.
$ Prices: Appetizers $6–$7; first courses $3.75–$10; main courses $12–$16; lunch main courses $5.50–$9. AE, MC, V.

Open: Lunch Mon–Fri 11:30am–2:30pm; dinner Mon–Thurs 5:30–11pm, Fri–Sat 5:30pm–midnight, Sun 5–10pm.

Turn off of Pioneer Square onto Cherry Street, walk down a flight of steps, and you'll be dining in the Seattle underground. Dark and cavernous with brick arches supporting the ceiling, La Buca is reminiscent of a huge wine cellar. The menu is primarily southern Italian, but goes far beyond spaghetti and meatballs. A half boneless chicken is marinated in olive oil and fresh herbs and served on a bed of polenta and canelline beans, while the saddle of lamb is served with fresh rosemary, figs, port, and Gorgonzola. Appetizers and first courses are equally creative and flavorful. Such dishes as parma ham with marinated dried figs and fresh seasonal fruit; polenta with grilled vegetables, grated Asiago cheese, and a topping of lamb ragoût; and French beans sautéed with pancetta and shallots in a creamy Gorgonzola dressing show off the mouth-watering fare that comes out of La Buca's kitchen.

LABUZNIK, 1924 First Ave. Tel. 441-8899.

Cuisine: EASTERN EUROPEAN. **Reservations:** Recommended.

$ Prices: Appetizers $3.25–$4.25; main dishes $12.50–$23. AE, CB, DC, MC, V.

Open: Dinner only, Tues–Sat 4:30–11pm.

These days when we think of ethnic food we tend to think of Thai, Moroccan, Caribbean, and other exotic cuisines. But before all of these began to appear on the American scene, there was a very different sort of ethnic cuisine—Eastern European. Well, at Labuznik, the meat-and-potatoes meals of Eastern Europe have never been forgotten. Instead, they have been perfected. In Czech, *labuznik* means "lover of good food." Dine here and you'll be a happy labuznik when you leave.

The tasty but tongue-twisting *vepro knedlo zelo* translates into a filling plate of roast pork with cabbage and dumplings. The veal Orloff is deliciously rich with mushrooms, capers, pickles, and cream. A meal here would not be complete without the Sachertorte. A lighter and less expensive menu is served in the bar.

MCCORMICK & SCHMICK'S, 1103 First Ave. Tel. 623-5500.

Cuisine: SEAFOOD. **Reservations:** Recommended.

$ Prices: Appetizers $5–$11.20; main dishes $9–$20; box lunches $8.95. AE, CB, DC, DISC, MC, V.

Open: Mon–Fri 11:30am–11pm, Sat–Sun 5–11pm.

Force your way past the crowds of business suits at the bar and you'll find yourself in a classic fish house. From the café curtains on the windows to the highly polished brass to the sparkling cut glass to the dark-wood paneling, everything about this restaurant shines. Waiters wearing black bow ties will help you find your way through the exhaustingly long sheet of daily specials and equally long wine list.

The well-prepared seafood, lamb, veal, and steak have made McCormick & Schmick's extremely popular with executives from Seattle's surrounding financial community. You, too, can hobnob with the wheelers and dealers for the price of such dishes as mahi mahi with papaya-lime chutney; yellowfin tuna with soy, wasabi, and ginger; or halibut served with hazelnut brown butter. From 3 to 6pm and 10 to 11pm daily, you can get appetizers in the bar for only

$1.95, and if you're in the mood for a downtown picnic, they also prepare box lunches.

MCCORMICK'S FISH HOUSE AND BAR, 722 Fourth Ave. (at Columbia St.). Tel. 682-3900.

Cuisine: SEAFOOD. **Reservations:** Recommended.
$ Prices: Appetizers $2.90–$11.20; main dishes $9.50–$21.20. AE, CB, DC, DISC, MC, V.
Open: Mon–Thurs 11am–11pm, Fri 11am–midnight, Sat 5pm–midnight, Sun 5–10pm.

A recent menu here listed 37 different seafoods from such far-flung locations as Texas, Chile, Hawaii, Idaho, and, of course, Washington—to give you some idea of how committed McCormick's is to bringing you the very best. However, 26 of the listed seafoods were from the Northwest, and this was noted on the menu for those who insist that the freshest is always local. It is immediately apparent that McCormick's is determined to please. The ambience is old-fashioned, with dark-wood booths and a tile floor around the long bar, and the service is fast. The crowds are large; the clientele tends to be very upscale, especially in the bar after the financial offices let out. Both traditional and imaginative Northwest-style cuisine is served, with the menu broken into categories based on how the seafood is cooked.

MAXIMILIEN IN THE MARKET, 81A Pike St. Tel. 682-7270.

Cuisine: FRENCH. **Reservations:** Recommended.
$ Prices: Mon–Thurs fixed-price dinners $13.50–$20; Fri–Sat appetizers $6.25–$8.25; main dishes $8.50–$22. AE, MC, V.
Open: Mon–Sat 7:30am–10pm; brunch Sun 9:30am–4pm.

S Maximilien is not your usual highbrow French restaurant. Dark-green walls and old, well-used tables speak volumes about the ambience here. It is country French, the sort of place you might find in a small village. And the fare is as no-nonsense as the decor, especially on weeknights, when the meals are fixed price and served family-style. On Friday and Saturday evenings, however, dinner is a bit more formal, with such standards as beef tenderloin with béarnaise sauce; escargots bourguignons; and broiled rack of lamb with mint-butter sauce. If you're at the market early, you might stop by for breakfast or lunch, which are less expensive than dinner.

MERCHANTS CAFE, 109 Yesler Way. Tel. 624-1515.

Cuisine: AMERICAN/CONTINENTAL. **Reservations:** Recommended.
$ Prices: Appetizers $2–$7; main dishes $7–$12. CB, DC, MC, V.
Open: Sun–Tues 10am–3pm, Wed–Thurs 10am–7pm, Fri–Sat 10am–9pm.

If you have already been on the highly recommended Seattle Underground Tour, you've had this place pointed out to you. It's Seattle's oldest restaurant and looks every bit of its 100 years. A well-scuffed tile floor surrounds the bar, which came around the Horn in the 1800s. An old safe and gold scales are left over from the days when Seattle was the first, or last, taste of civilization for those bound for, or returning from, the Yukon goldfields. This bar/restaurant has had a long and colorful history. At one time the basement was a card room and the upper floors were a brothel. In fact, this may be the original Skid Row saloon, since Yesler Way was the original Skid Road down which logs were skidded to a sawmill. Straightforward sandwiches and steaks are the mainstays of the menu, though a few more imaginative main dishes also appear.

METROPOLITAN GRILL, 818 Second Ave. Tel. 624-3287.

Cuisine: STEAK. **Reservations:** Recommended.

$ Prices: Appetizers $3.50–$8; main dishes $11–$30. AE, DC, DISC, JCB, MC, V.

Open: Lunch Mon–Fri 11am–3:30pm; dinner Mon–Sat 5–11pm, Sun 5–10pm.

Another reliable restaurant for aspiring financial whiz kids and their mentors, this one is dedicated to meat eaters rather than to seafood lovers. Green-velvet booths, bar stools, and floral-design carpets are the keynote of the sophisticated atmosphere at the Metropolitan. Mirrored walls and a high ceiling trimmed with elegant plasterwork make the dining room feel larger than it actually is, while murals depicting scenes from Seattle history make the local movers and shakers feel secure that one day they, too, will be part of Seattle history.

Perfectly cooked steaks are the primary attraction here, and you'd be foolish not to order one of them. They're considered the best steaks in Seattle by those in the know. A baked potato and a pile of crispy onion rings complete the perfect steak dinner.

THE PINK DOOR, 1919 Post Alley. Tel. 443-3241.

Cuisine: ITALIAN. **Reservations:** Recommended.

$ Prices: Lunch appetizers $4.50–$7; pastas $6–$7; main dishes $7–$9; four-course fixed-price dinner $17.50. MC, V.

Open: Tues–Sat 11:30am–midnight.

If I didn't tell you about this one, you'd never find it. There is no sign out front, only the pink door for which the restaurant is named (watch for a pale-gray wall with flower boxes in the windows between Stewart Street and Virginia Street). Open the door and you step into a cool, dark room with a high ceiling, hanging Chianti bottles, and a fountain in the middle of the floor. Tuesday through Thursday, there's a tarot card reader working the tables so you can find out before your meal whether you're going to enjoy your evening or not. There are also cabaret singers in the evening, and on the weekend there's an accordion player. In summer the action moves outside to the back deck. Be sure to start your meal with the fragrant roasted garlic and ricotta-Gorgonzola spread. I can never get enough seafood when I'm in Seattle, so I highly recommended the cioppino, a flavorful seafood stew. On the other hand, you can opt for the $17.50 four-course fixed-price meal and you won't go wrong.

QUEEN CITY GRILL, 2201 First Ave. Tel. 443-0975.

Cuisine: INTERNATIONAL. **Reservations:** Recommended.

$ Prices: Appetizers $7–$11.50; main dishes $8–$20; lunch main dishes $6–$12. MC, V.

Open: Lunch Mon–Fri 11:30am–2:30pm; dinner Sun–Thurs 4:30–11pm, Fri–Sat 4:30pm–midnight.

Battered wooden floors that look as if they were salvaged from an old hardware store and high-backed wooden booths give the new Queen City Grill the look of instant age. If you didn't know better, you'd think this place had been here since the Great Fire of 1889. Basically a tavern with imaginative and varied meals, the Queen City Grill is a long narrow room with a bar on one side and the booths on the other. Though the restaurant may not sound too inviting, the food will certainly have you contemplating returning again and again. Seafood is the specialty, so you might start with tuna carpaccio accompanied by a lime, ginger, and mustard sauce. The chicken wild rice gumbo is an unusual and tasty salad. There are several daily seafood specials. Dungeness crab cakes and Szechuan prawns are always on the menu.

TAKARA, 1501 Western Ave. Tel. 682-8609.

Cuisine: JAPANESE. **Reservations:** Recommended.

$ Prices: Appetizers $1–$7; sushi $2.50–$8; main dishes $7.50–$16. AE, MC, V.

Open: Mon–Thurs 11:30am–9pm, Fri–Sat 11:30am–9:30pm, Sun (June–Aug) noon–7pm.

If the sight of all the fresh fish in Pike Place Market has you craving some sushi, head down the Pike Market stairs. One flight below Western Avenue, you'll come to Takara, one of the city's best sushi bars. The decor is simple—tile floors, low walls separating booths, and a framed kimono on the wall. You can sit at a table inside or out on the patio (when the weather is good), or pull up a stool at the sushi bar. There is a long menu of Japanese soups, appetizers, and main dishes, but the sushi is the real attraction here. Be sure to order the Seattle roll—made with smoked salmon, of course.

TLAQUEPAQUE BAR, 1122 Post Ave. Tel. 467-8226.

Cuisine: MEXICAN. **Reservations:** Recommended.

$ Prices: Appetizers $4–$7.25; main dishes $8–$16; lunches $5.50–$8.50. AE, DC, DISC, MC, V.

Open: Mon–Thurs 11:30am–11pm, Fri–Sat 11:30am–11:30pm, Sun noon–10pm.

If you enjoy good Mexican food amid noisy revelry, then you are sure to find contentment here. Every Wednesday a strolling mariachi band whoops it up in this cavernous open room, which was once a warehouse. A chandelier made from beer bottles leaves no doubt as to whether or not this restaurant/bar means good times. The menu features regional Mexican fare, primarily broiled over mesquite coals. Cabrito—mesquite-broiled baby goat in ancho chile sauce, a favorite in Monterrey, Mexico—makes a rare North American appearance here. If you have a few friends along, you can order the Tlaquepaque Cadillac Botana Platter, a dinner that includes 10 of the restaurant's specialties.

TRATTORIA MITCHELLI, 84 Yesler Way. Tel. 623-3883.

Cuisine: ITALIAN. **Reservations:** Recommended.

$ Prices: Appetizers $3–$6.50; pastas $5.50–$9.85; main dishes $5.25–$13; lunches $4.50–$7.50. AE, DC, MC, V.

Open: Tues–Fri 7am–4am, Sat 8am–4am, Sun 8am–11pm, Mon 7am–11pm.

Located only a few steps toward the water from Pioneer Square, Trattoria Mitchelli is a cozy place with a friendly old-world atmosphere. The white-tiled waiting area has large windows that let in the warm summer air and salty breezes. An old circular bar in the counter room is a popular after-work and late-night gathering spot; candles flicker in Chianti bottles, and conversation is lively. There is a wide selection of veal dishes, all of which are worth trying. The pizza kitchen and bar features pizza and calzone baked in a wood oven. If you're a night owl, keep Mitchelli's in mind—they serve full meals right through to 4am.

INEXPENSIVE

CAFE HUE, 312 Second Ave. S. Tel. 625-9833.
Cuisine: VIETNAMESE. **Reservations:** Recommended.
$ Prices: Appetizers $1–$4; main dishes $4.50–$19.50. MC, V.
Open: Mon–Fri 11am–10pm, Sat noon–10pm, Sun 5–10pm.

The decor is simple urban chic with exposed brick walls, artful flower arrangements, and a Buddhist altar. Even the flatware and chopsticks are artfully arranged on each table. As you may have already guessed, this is Vietnamese as you have never known it—contemporary and with a French flair. You absolutely must start with the escargots stuffed with pork and ginger. Each little snail comes with its own lemon-grass pull tab. Other unexpected and equally succulent dishes are the stuffed crab and the roast quail. The location is convenient to both Pioneer Square and the International District.

CYCLOPS, 2416 Western Ave. Tel. 441-1677.
Cuisine: AMERICAN. **Reservations:** Not accepted.
$ Prices: Breakfast $4–$6; lunch $3.25–$7.50; dinner $7–$8.50. No credit cards.
Open: Breakfast Sat–Sun 10am–3pm; lunch Mon–Fri 11am–4:30pm, Sat–Sun noon–5pm; dinner daily 5–11pm.

A neighborhood restaurant just a few blocks from Pike Place Market, Cyclops offers a bit of 1950s retro funk. The walls are heavily stuccoed and host art exhibits that change monthly. On display when I last was there were a mechanical umbrella that seemed to breathe and a plastic cowboy with a TV embedded in his head. Along with the interesting art, Cyclops serves variations on standard breakfast fare (weekends only), such as black-bean omelettes, and international favorites, such as Greek chicken stew and pasta Gorgonzola. While you are waiting for your food, you can peruse the magazine rack in the back of the restaurant or use the fortune-telling machine.

DUKE'S KINGDOME, 83 King St. Tel. 622-1092.
Cuisine: AMERICAN. **Reservations:** Recommended.
$ Prices: Appetizers $2.95–$6; main dishes $5–$19.
Open: Lunch Mon–Fri 11–4pm; dinner Sun–Thurs 4–10pm, Fri–Sat 4–11pm.

Duke's attracts sports fans attending games at nearby Kingdome, and may be somewhat rowdy after a game. Fans come to drink in the spacious bar and perhaps have a bowl of Seattle's best clam chowder (the secret is the dill). The airy bar with lots of plants is the focal point of the restaurant and a good place to mix with both locals and tourists. Small dining rooms with wooden beams and checkered tablecloths are cozier and more intimate than the bar. Baked garlic cheese, salads, and sandwiches are among the lighter choices. There are also many seafood dishes, including seafood fettuccine, Dungeness crab cakes, and Alaskan scallops.

EMMETT WATSON'S OYSTER BAR, 1916 Pike Place No. 16. Tel. 448-7721.
Cuisine: SEAFOOD. **Reservations:** Not accepted.
$ Prices: Soups $1.75–$6; main dishes $3–$6. No credit cards.

Open: Sun–Thurs 11:30am–8pm, Fri–Sat 11:30am–9pm.

Tucked away in a rare quiet corner of Pike Place Market (well, actually, it's across the street in the market overflow area), Emmett Watson's looks like a fast-food place, but the service here in fact is infamously slow. The booths are tiny, so it's best to come here on a sunny afternoon when you can sit in the courtyard. The restaurant is named for a famous Seattle newspaper columnist, and there are clippings all over the walls. Oysters on the half shell are the raison d'être for this little place, but the fish dishes are often memorable as well. Check the blackboard for specials.

GRAVITY BAR, 113 Virginia St. Tel. 448-8826.

Cuisine: NATURAL. **Reservations:** Not accepted.

$ Prices: Meals $4–$7; juices $2–$4.75. No credit cards.

Open: Downtown—Mon–Thurs 11am–9pm, Fri 11am–11pm, Sat 10am–11pm, Sun 10am–8pm; Broadway—Mon–Thurs 8am–10pm, Fri–Sat 9am–11pm, Sun 10am–10pm (later in summer).

If you're young and hip and concerned about the food that you put into your body, this is the place you frequent in Seattle. The postmodern neoindustrial decor (lots of sheet metal on the walls, bar, and menus) is the antithesis of the wholesome juices and meals they serve here. The juice list includes all manner of unusual combinations, all with catchy names like Saturn Return or 7 Year Spinach. Be there or be square. Another Gravity Bar is at 415 E. Broadway (tel. 325-7186).

HING LOON, 628 S. Weller St. Tel. 682-2828.

Cuisine: CHINESE. **Reservations:** Not necessary.

$ Prices: Appetizers $1.75–$7.25; main dishes $5.25–$9.

Open: Sun–Thurs 10am–midnight, Fri–Sat 10am–2am.

No atmosphere, bright fluorescent lighting, big Formica-top tables.

🄵 FROMMER'S COOL FOR KIDS: RESTAURANTS

Ivar's Salmon House *(p. 73)* This restaurant is built to resemble a Northwest Coast Native American longhouse and is filled with artifacts that kids will find fascinating. If they get restless, they can go out to the floating patio and watch the boats passing by.

Gravity Bar *(above)* If you're traveling with teenagers, they'll love this place where Seattle's young and hip and health-conscious crowd comes to dine. The decor is postmodern neoindustrial and the food is wholesome, with juices called Saturn Return and 7 Year Spinach.

Merchants Cafe *(p. 63)* Seattle's oldest restaurant may be the original Skid Row saloon. This bar/restaurant looks every bit of its 100 years. The kids will go for the straightforward sandwiches and steaks.

This is the sort of place you would walk by if you were aimlessly searching for a restaurant in the International District. With so many choices in a few square blocks, it is easy to be distracted and attracted by fancy decor. Forget the rest and take a seat in Hing Loon. Seafood is the house specialty and none is done better than the oysters with ginger and green onion on a sizzling platter. For a veggie dish, don't miss the eggplant in Szechuan sauce. If you're feeling really daring, try the cold jellyfish; it's not at all the way you'd imagine it to be. Be careful of the pork dishes, which tend to have Chinese style pork that is mostly fat. The restaurant makes all its own noodles, so you can't go wrong ordering chow mein or chow funn (wide noodles).

WESTERN COFFEE SHOP, 911½ Western Ave. Tel. 682-5001.

Cuisine: AMERICAN. **Reservations:** Not accepted.
$ Prices: Complete meal $4–$6. No credit cards.
Open: Mon–Wed 7am–3pm, Thurs–Fri 7am–3pm and 7pm–1am, Sat 8am–3pm and 7pm–1am, Sun 9am–3pm.

This place is so narrow that you'll probably walk right past it the first time, and once you do find it, you won't be able to get past that big guy on the first counter stool. Persevere and you'll be treated to a real Seattle experience. The Western is a very casual coffee shop sporting a Western theme—toy horses on the counter, cowboy hats here and there, cowboy music on the stereo. The cooking is good old-fashioned home cooking, no Northwest fruit-and-meat combos here. Don't miss the espresso milk shake.

WILD GINGER ASIAN RESTAURANT & SATAY BAR, 1400 Western Ave. Tel. 623-4450.

Cuisine: INDONESIAN/MALAYSIAN. **Reservations:** Recommended.
$ Prices: Appetizers $1.50–$3.75; main dishes $7–$16. AE, DC, DISC, MC, V.
Open: Lunch Mon–Sat 11:30am–3pm; dinner Sun–Thurs 5–11pm, Fri–Sat 5pm–midnight.

With sushi bars old hat these days, the satay bar may be a worthy replacement. Pull up a comfortable stool around the large grill and watch the cooks grill little skewers of anything from fresh produce to fish to pork to prawns to lamb. Each skewer is served with a small cube of sticky rice and a dipping sauce. Order three or four satay sticks and you have a meal. If you prefer to sit at a table and have a more traditional dinner, Wild Ginger can accommodate you. Try the pungent Prawns Assam—tiger prawns in a curry of tamarind, turmeric, candlenuts, chilis, and lemongrass. Accompany your meal with a pot of chrysanthemum tea or a beer from China, Japan, or Singapore for a real Southeast Asian experience. As in Asia, the lunch menu is primarily noodle dishes.

2. SEATTLE CENTER/ LAKE UNION AREA

EXPENSIVE

CANLIS, 2576 Aurora Ave. N. Tel. 283-3313.

Cuisine: AMERICAN. **Reservations:** Strongly recommended. Jacket and tie required for men.

$ Prices: Appetizers $7.50–$12; main dishes $18.50–$35. AE, CB, DC, MC, V.

Open: Dinner only, Mon–Sat 5:30–10:30pm.

Peter Canlis opened his first restaurant at Waikiki in 1947. It proved very popular with Seattleites fleeing Northwest damp, and they wished they had a Peter Canlis restaurant of their own. And in 1950 they got their wish. The restaurant has enjoyed unflagging popularity for more than 40 years now. The reason? It could be the perfectly prepared steaks and seafood, or it could be the excellent service by kimono-clad waitresses, or it could be the view across Lake Union from high on a hillside. Why not find out for yourself?

A huge stone fireplace and stone columns lend a cool, dark air to the main dining room, while outside the tops of fir trees jut into your view of the lake far below. Unusual Asian antiques, including an old door, are displayed throughout the restaurant. A pianist fills the room with his melodies. This is the perfect place to close a big deal or celebrate a very special occasion. The perfect meal? Filet mignon with the restaurant's legendary baked potato, plus a salad tossed at your table, finished off with a Grand Marnier soufflé.

KAMON ON LAKE UNION, 1177 Fairview Ave. N. Tel. 622-4665.

Cuisine: JAPANESE/INTERNATIONAL. **Reservations:** Recommended.

$ Prices: Appetizers $5–$7.50; main dishes $10–$26; lunch $6–$13. AE, DC, JCB, MC, V.

Open: Lunch Mon–Fri 11:30am–2:30pm; dinner Sun–Thurs 5–10pm, Fri–Sat 5–11pm.

If you crave Japanese tonight and your dinner partner can't stand it, try Kamon on Lake Union and its international menu. You'll both be happy. You can also enjoy the sunset over the lake from either the formal dining room or the open-air deck. This is a grand restaurant, with wide steps leading up to the entrance, a spacious lounge with a piano bar, and the longest sushi bar in Seattle.

If you're still not convinced this is the place for you, consider your choices. For an appetizer, you might have smoked Northwest seafood, sushi, oysters on the half shell, or Italian-style calamari. The teppanyaki dinners, cooked tableside by talented chefs, are both entertaining and delicious. Or let the sushi master make a selection of his favorite sushi rolls for you. Five peppercorn New York steak is sure to appeal to anyone who loves steak. There's no question about it—Kamon on Lake Union is the place to go if you have different cravings.

LE TASTEVIN, 19 W. Harrison St. Tel. 283-0991.

Cuisine: FRENCH. **Reservations:** Recommended.

$ Prices: Appetizers $7–$32; main dishes $17–$24. AE, CB, DC, DISC, MC, V.

Open: Lunch Tues–Fri 11:30am–2:30pm; dinner Mon–Sat 5–11:30pm.

Conjure up your image of a classic French restaurant and I bet this is about what it looks like. The use of skylights, picture windows, and trellises (on both walls and ceiling) creates an open, gardenlike atmosphere. Not only is Le Tastevin the largest French restaurant in

Seattle, but it also has the best wine cellar and has won the *Wine Spectator* magazine Grand Award every year since 1984. In fact, wine is nearly an obsession at Le Tastevin. The back of the restaurant's business card has the following old German saying, "Drink and go to heaven, drink wine and you will sleep, sleep and you will avoid sin, avoid sin and you will be saved, ergo, drink wine and be saved." You'll find Le Tastevin between Seattle Center and the waterfront.

If wine isn't your cup of tea, you might start your meal with an exotic frozen, flavored Russian vodka. Don't miss the appetizer of pheasant pâté with Pommery mustard sauce. The salmon baked in a puff-pastry shell and served with pomegranate chardonnay sauce is delicious. For a special meal, try the roast pheasant or chateaubriand, both of which are prepared at your table. The dessert menu includes old favorites and unusual creations. Lunch prices are half those at dinner.

MODERATE

KAYAK LAKEFRONT GRILL, 1200 Westlake Ave. N. Tel. 284-2535.
    Cuisine: SEAFOOD. **Reservations:** Recommended.
$ **Prices:** Appetizers $4–$8; main dishes $9–$15. AE, MC, V.
    Open: Lunch Mon–Fri 11:15am–3pm; dinner Sun–Thurs 5–9:30pm, Fri–Sat 5–10:30pm. Light meals served 3pm–1am.

The marina in front of Kayak brings a very upscale yachting crowd to this large seafood restaurant on Lake Union, but the prices are extremely reasonable. Overhead fans turn languidly, and through the floor-to-ceiling windows you can watch sailboats drift slowly past the looming skyscrapers of downtown. It's all very casually sophisticated.

The Kayak is best known for its grilled fish, but the extensive menu also lists steak, pasta, and chicken, as well as daily specials. Cajun preparations are a staple here, and so are Northwest, Italian, and French dishes. To accompany your meal, there is an excellent selection of wines by the glass or by the bottle. The beer list was chosen by a Michael Jackson, one of the world's leading beer authorities.

3. FIRST HILL, CAPITOL HILL & EAST SEATTLE

EXPENSIVE

RAIN CITY GRILL, 2359 10th Ave. E. Tel. 325-5003.
    Cuisine: NORTHWEST. **Reservations:** Recommended.
$ **Prices:** Appetizers $3.50–$8; main dishes $11–$18; lunches $6–$10. MC, V.
    Open: Lunch Mon–Fri 11:30am–2pm; dinner Mon–Thurs 5:30–9:30pm, Fri–Sat 5:30–10pm, Sun 5:30–9:30pm.

So you came to Seattle expecting to experience one of those legendary crystal-clear days when the mountain is out, but all it's done is rain, rain, rain. Cheer up. Seattleites have learned to laugh about the miserable weather, and one of the best weather jokes in town is the Rain City Grill. The restaurant's ceiling is decorated with dozens of umbrellas hanging upside down. The walls, of course, are painted overcast gray.

All the open umbrellas obviously have not brought bad luck—the meals served here are some of the best in town and display the imaginative flair of Northwest cuisine. On my last visit—drizzly, gray day, of course—the sautéed Dungeness crab cakes with sherry-cayenne mayonnaise were what most appealed to me, but the grilled salmon with pesto butter over roasted pepper coulis was equally mouth watering. Be sure to save room for one of the delectable desserts.

ROVER'S, 2808 E. Madison St. Tel. 325-7442.
   Cuisine: NORTHWEST. **Reservations:** Required.
$ Prices: Appetizers $6–$12.25, main dishes $22.50–$28.50; five-course menu dégustation $39.50–$49.50. AE, DC, MC, V.
   Open: Dinner only, Tues–Sat 5:30–11pm.

Tucked away in a quaint clapboard house behind a chic little shopping center is one of Seattle's most talked about restaurants. Chef Thierry Rautureau received classic French training before falling in love with the Northwest and all the wonderful ingredients it had to offer an imaginative chef.

Voilà! Northwest cuisine with a French accent. Or is it French cuisine with a Northwest accent? Find out for yourself. If the salad of wild greens and edible flowers is on the daily-changing menu, don't pass it by; the flavors are delicately Northwest. Perennial appetizer favorites include warm foie gras salad, usually served with a seasonal fruit-flavored sauce, and a trio of vegetable flans served with an ocean salad and one of Rautureau's imaginative sauces such as black currant or rosemary. Among main dishes, you will almost certainly encounter salmon, perhaps with braised leeks and a dry vermouth sauce; venison, possibly prepared with wild mushrooms, green lentils, and a black pepper sauce; and guinea fowl, which might be served with celery root purée, cranberry chutney, foie gras, and an Armagnac sauce. In summer, don't miss the raspberry desserts—or, for that matter, the desserts at any time of year.

MODERATE

CACTUS, 4220 E. Madison St. Tel. 324-4140.
   Cuisine: NEW MEXICAN. **Reservations:** Recommended.
$ Prices: Appetizers $3–$6; main dishes $8–$13; lunch $6–$8.50. MC, V.
   Open: Lunch Mon–Sat 11:30am–2:30pm; dinner Mon–Sat 5:30–10pm, Sun 5–9pm.

Northwesterners seem constantly to shuttle back and forth between Northwest and Southwest. Perhaps it is the lack of light in winter that sends them winging southward to sunnier states. Now, however, it is not necessary to go any farther than Madison Park to fire up your life with a bit of New Mexican cooking. At Cactus the decor is straight out of Santa Fe, with baskets of Mexican beer by the front door, stucco walls, and Mexican *ranchera* music on the stereo. How about a plate of cactus salad to start—no spines, guaranteed. Yucatán fish, marinated in grapefruit juice, garlic, and achiote seeds and then grilled in lime butter, is always tender, fragrant, and juicy. You can assemble your own fajitas with tender marinated beef, or try a couple of soft tacos. The pork steak adobo, made with smoky chipotle peppers and orange juice is a medley of powerful flavors that shouldn't be missed. For dessert, try the three-milk flan.

INEXPENSIVE

CAFE FLORA, 2901 E. Madison St. Tel. 325-9100.

Cuisine: VEGETARIAN. **Reservations:** Recommended.
$ Prices: Appetizers $2.25–$8.25; main dishes $6–$12. MC, V.
Open: Tues–Fri 11am–10pm, Sat 5–10pm; brunch Sat–Sun 9am–2pm.

Big and bright and airy, this café will dispel any ideas about vegetarian food being boring. This is meatless gourmet cooking and it's delicious. The menu changes weekly and might include a wild mushroom gâteau made with hazelnut pastry and filled with wild mushroom duxelles and served with basil mashed potatoes, yellow cherry tomatoes, asparagus, and a hazelnut vinaigrette. Several unusual pizzas typically are on the menu. A recent Tuscan pizza came with artichokes, calamata olives, goat cheese, red russet potatoes, and pesto. The cheese and fruit plate is a beautiful and light offering that seems to be especially popular at lunch. The dessert tray brought to your table always has plenty of temptations, such as a chocolate mousse pie with whole strawberries inside. In the summer, you can sit on the patio.

PIZZERIA PAGLIACCI, 426 Broadway Ave. E. Tel. 324-0730.

Cuisine: PIZZA. **Reservations:** Not accepted.
$ Prices: Pizza $8–$16.50. AE, MC, V.
Open: Mon–Thurs 11am–11pm, Fri–Sat 11am–1am, Sun noon–11pm.

Pagliacci's pizza was voted the best in Seattle, and they now have three popular locations. Although you can order a traditional cheese pizza, there are much more interesting pies on the menu, like pesto pizza or the sun-dried-tomato primo. It's strictly counter service here, but there are plenty of seats at each of the bright restaurants. For those in a hurry or who just want a snack, there is pizza by the slice. Pagliacci is also at 550 Queen Anne Ave. N. (tel. 285-1232) and at 4529 University Way NE (tel. 632-1058).

SIAM ON BROADWAY, 616 Broadway E. Tel. 324-0892.

Cuisine: THAI. **Reservations:** Recommended.
$ Prices: Appetizers $4–$6; main dishes $5.75–$9; lunches $5–$8. AE, MC, V.
Open: Mon–Thurs 11:30am–10pm, Fri 11:30am–11pm, Sat 5–11pm, Sun 5–10pm.

All the way at the north end of the Broadway shopping district in trendy Capitol Hill is one of Seattle's best inexpensive Thai restaurants. In fact, the food's generally as good as you'll get in Thailand, and that's saying a lot when you can't always come up with all the necessary ingredients. Siam on Broadway is small and very casual. The tom yum soups, made with either shrimp or chicken, are the richest and creamiest I've ever had—also some of the spiciest. If you prefer your food less fiery, let your server know; the cooks will prepare any meal with one to four stars, depending on how much fire you can handle. But remember that they mean it when they say super-hot. The phad thai (spicy fried noodles) is excellent, and the muu phad bai graplau (spicy meat and vegetables, one of my all-time favorites) is properly fragrant with chilis and basil leaves.

VIETNAM'S PEARL, 708 Rainier Ave. S. Tel. 726-1581.
   Cuisine: VIETNAMESE. **Reservations:** Recommended.
$ Prices: Appetizers $2.75–$5.25; main dishes $4.25–$8. AE, MC, V.
   Open: Sun–Thurs 11am–10pm, Fri–Sat 10am–midnight.

Located in an unremarkable neighborhood about a mile or two from Pioneer Square, Vietnam's Pearl is very popular with local Vietnamese. You'll also find plenty of other folks from all over the Seattle area descending on the restaurant's Spartan dining room. What has people driving across town to a neighborhood eatery is great food at budget prices. The menu is long and only shrimp and some fish dishes will run you more than $5.50. If you are willing to order adventurously, you are certain to encounter several new tastes and flavor combinations. The ginger chicken is a particular standout. One of my favorite dishes is minced shrimp wrapped around sugarcane.

4. NORTH SEATTLE

EXPENSIVE

HIRAM'S AT THE LOCKS, 5300 34th Ave. NW. Tel. 784-1733.
   Cuisine: SEAFOOD/STEAK. **Reservations:** Recommended.
$ Prices: Appetizers $2.50–$10; main dishes $13–$35. AE, CB, DC, DISC, MC, V.
   Open: Lunch Mon–Fri 11am–3pm, Sat 11:30am–3pm; dinner Mon–Thurs 4:30–9:30pm, Fri–Sat 4:30–10:30pm, Sun 4:30–9pm; Sun brunch 9am–2:30pm.

Seattle is surrounded by water, both fresh and salt. Here at Hiram's the two come together at the Hiram M. Chittenden Locks, where commercial and private boats of all sizes are raised or lowered during their journey between Puget Sound and Lake Union. The action here makes wonderful entertainment during a meal, and at night the locks are lighted. The restaurant's exterior, constructed of corrugated sheet metal, looks as if it belonged in a warehouse district; however, the interior is as elegant as the prices are high.

   The menu is about equally divided between the regular dishes and the daily specials—and either way, you can't lose. Preparations are frequently in the Northwest style, but more traditional fare can also be found. The steaks are also quite good, and the Sunday buffet is a veritable seafood feast.

MODERATE

IVAR'S SALMON HOUSE, 401 NE Northlake Way. Tel. 632-0767.
   Cuisine: SEAFOOD. **Reservations:** Recommended.

$ Prices: Appetizers $2.45–$7; main dishes $10.45–$19; fish bar $4–$7. AE, MC, V.
Open: Main restaurant—lunch Mon–Fri 11:30am–2pm; dinner Mon–Thurs 5–11pm, Fri 5–11pm, Sat 4–11pm, Sun 4–10pm; Sun brunch 10am–2pm. Fish bar—Sun–Thurs 11am–11pm, Fri–Sat 11am–midnight.

Ivar's commands an excellent view of the Seattle skyline at the far end of Lake Union. Floating docks out back act as magnets for weekend boaters, who abandon their own galley fare in favor of the restaurant's clam chowder and famous alder-smoked salmon. The theme here is Northwest Coast Native American, and the building has even won an award from the Seattle Historical Society for its replica of a tribal longhouse. Inside are many artifacts, including long dugout canoes and historic photographic portraits of Native American chiefs. The dinners even come with Native American cornbread and wild blueberry ice cream. Kids, and adults, love this place.

LE GOURMAND, 425 NW Market St. Tel. 784-3463.
Cuisine: FRENCH. **Reservations:** Required.
$ Prices: Three-course fixed-price dinners $18–$28. AE, CB, DC, MC, V.
Open: Dinner only, Wed–Sat 5:30–9:30pm.

On an otherwise forgettable corner in the Ballard neighborhood of North Seattle stands a tiny building that looks as if it might once have been a laundry or dry cleaner. Chefs Bruce Naftaly and Robin Sanders, former music students who came to Seattle to study voice, have converted this aging storefront into a memorable French restaurant. With only a handful of tables, service is very personal and the atmosphere is homey, with a hint of the country.

On the back of the menu you'll find a list of all the ingredients used at the restaurant, from Sumatran coffee to organically grown herbs and vegetables, and where they come from (neighborhood gardens, in the case of some of the herbs). A nice touch. On my last visit the menu included a pâté of rabbit and chicken livers flavored with cognac, port, and thyme for a starter. There was a choice of six different main dishes, but the roast rack of lamb with a sauce of dark stock, fresh chestnuts, and bosc pears was perfect for a cold winter's night. A choice from the tempting pastry tray is not included in the fixed-price dinner.

RAY'S BOATHOUSE, 6049 Seaview Ave. NW. Tel. 789-3770.
Cuisine: SEAFOOD. **Reservations:** Recommended.
$ Prices: Appetizers $4–$9; main dishes $10–$20; prices slightly lower upstairs. AE, CB, DC, MC, V.
Open: Lunch Mon–Fri 11:30am–2pm; dinner Mon–Thurs 5–10pm, Fri 5–10:30pm, Sat 4:30–10:30pm, Sun 4:30–10pm.

Upstairs at Ray's, where you'll find the lounge, the crowd of suntanned boating types can get pretty rowdy. The restaurant compensates by reducing the price of the food here, but waits of up to an hour for a table are not unusual. Downstairs, everything is quiet, cozy, and sophisticated.

Luckily, everyone gets the same fine meals. As at other Seattle restaurants, fresh herbs are making bold appearances on the menu in dishes such as poached lingcod with mustards, tarragon, and cream.

There are many delicious reasons why this is considered one of the best restaurants in Seattle. Grilled black cod in saké kasu with ginger is a bow to the Japanese influence that has crept into Northwest kitchens.

5. SPECIALTY DINING

LOCAL FAVORITES

I don't know for certain, but suspect that Seattle is the espresso capital of America. Seattleites are positively rabid about coffee. Coffee isn't just a hot drink or a caffeine fix anymore, it's a way of life. Coffeehouses are rapidly overtaking bars as the most popular places to hang out and visit with friends. Espresso and its creamy cousin latte (made with one part espresso to three parts milk) are the stuff that this city runs on, and you will never be more than about a block from your next cup. There are espresso carts parked on the sidewalks, walk-up espresso windows, espresso bars, espresso milk shakes, espresso chocolates, even eggnog lattes at Christmas. The ruling coffee king is **Starbucks,** a chain of dozens of coffee shops where you can buy your java by the cup or by the pound. They sell some 36 types and blends of coffee, and you can find their shops all over the city. (Of course, there is one in Pike Place Market.) **SBC,** formerly Stewart Brothers Coffee and also known as Seattle's Best Coffee, doesn't have as many shops as Starbuck's, but it does have a very devoted clientele.

STREET FOOD

In recent years, Seattle has taken on many of the trappings of urban centers like New York and Chicago. Where once there was no place to grab a quick bite, there are now a variety of street foods available. If you are in a hurry or on a tight budget, street meals may be the way to go in downtown.

Foremost among the city's street offerings is **coffee.** Not your watery American cup o' joe, but rich satisfying espresso, often served with steamed milk as latte. At last count there were more than 150 espresso carts in Seattle, so you need never be more than a few steps away from a latte. Garnish your latte with a sprinkle of cocoa, vanilla, nutmeg, or cinnamon for a true cookie-coffee experience. Espresso carts also sell flavored Italian sodas and the odd cookie or other sweet.

For more substantial meals, you might find a **hot dog** vendor. My favorite is The Good Dog, which can usually be found on Occidental Avenue South near the corner of South Jackson Street. This location is convenient to Pioneer Square and is only a block from the Kingdome. The kosher dogs and Italian sausages can be topped with your choice of half a dozen different gourmet mustards. There are hot pretzels too.

For whopping big **burritos** and **tacos** at very reasonable prices, try Burrito Express just around the corner from the newsstand at Pike Place Market (First Avenue and Pike Street). This is a walk-up window rather than a cart, and folks who work in the area swear the burritos are some of the best in town.

DESSERT

THE FAMOUS PACIFIC DESSERT COMPANY, 420 E. Denny Way. Tel. 328-1950.
Cuisine: DESSERTS. **Reservations:** Not accepted.
$ **Prices:** $3.50–$5.75. MC, V.
Open: Sun–Thurs 11am–11pm, Fri–Sat 11am–midnight.

If you should suddenly be struck by an uncontrollable craving for tiramisu, hazelnut orange torte, zuccotto fiorentino, pear tart with almond cream, raspberry cheesecake, or any other indecently hedonistic dessert, head for the hill—Capitol Hill that is. At any given time you can choose from among more than 30 calorific plates of instant gratification. On the weekends, there is live music in the evenings and a minimum order that can easily be met with one dessert and a coffee.

HOTEL DINING

EXPENSIVE

CAMPAGNE, Inn at the Market, 86 Pine St. Tel. 728-2800.
Cuisine: FRENCH. **Reservations:** Required.
$ **Prices:** Appetizers $4.50–$8; main dishes $13–$25. AE, MC, V.
Open: Lunch (summer only) Mon–Sat 11:30am–2:30pm; dinner daily 5:30–10pm (cafe dining until midnight).

On the far side of the fountain that bubbles in the courtyard of the Inn at the Market, French country decor continues inside the aptly named Campagne. Large windows let in precious sunshine and provide a view of Elliott Bay over the top of Pike Place Market. Cheerful and unpretentious, Campagne is one of the most enjoyable French restaurants in Seattle.

The cuisine of Provence is the specialty of the house, and meals are consistently excellent. The rough-textured pâté de Campagne garnished with niçoise olives and cornichons is delicious, and the sautéed oysters breaded with Provençal herbs and served with aioli will give you a real taste of the south of France. There are daily fresh fish specials that feature whatever happens to be in season—and of high quality—at the nearby market. However, the menu's focus is definitely on locally raised meats, including Vashon Island rabbit on a bed of lemon-thyme fettuccine tossed with a green-peppercorn-and-wild-mushroom sherry sauce; rack of Ellensburg lamb fragrant with a sauce of rosemary, juniper berries, anchovies, and garlic; and beef tenderloin served with a red-wine, shallot, and fresh oregano sauce. Desserts are the equal of any other dish on the menu.

FULLER'S, Seattle Sheraton Hotel & Towers, 1400 Sixth Ave. Tel. 447-5544.
Cuisine: NORTHWEST. **Reservations:** Strongly recommended.
$ **Prices:** Appetizers $5.50–$9; main dishes $17.25–$22.50; prix-fixe dinner $38.50. AE, CB, DC, DISC, JCB, MC, V.
Open: Lunch Mon–Fri 11:30am–2pm; dinner Mon–Sat 5:30–10pm.

Fuller's, named for the founder of the Seattle Art Museum, is dedicated to both the culinary and the visual arts of the Northwest. Each dish is as artfully designed as it is superbly prepared, and surrounding you in this elegant dining room are works of art by the Northwest's best artists. A tiny circle of light illuminates each table as if it were a stage, and it is—a stage for the creative productions of the restaurant's chef. The service is gracious and attentive.

You never know what influences might show up on Fuller's menu, though Mediterranean flavors seem to be predominating of late. A recent menu included on the appetizers list a light and flavorful grilled vegetable strudel with sun-dried tomatoes and goat-cheese tapenade as well as Northwest oysters with pinot noir mignonette. The sweet potato bisque with biryani crème fraîche was smooth and soothing while a salad of warm spinach leaves with smoked duck and honey-sesame dressing was piquant and savory. Entrées are where Fuller's shows its imagination with such dishes as grilled pork loin with apple brandy-blue cheese sauce, sautéed king salmon with a beet buerre blanc, and pan-seared kasu cod with mango chili relish. This latter dish is a Fuller's specialty and is made with a flavorful by-product of saké rice-wine brewing. Local fruit is also put to excellent use in the restaurant's desserts, which should be accompanied by the special coffee tray. Shaved chocolate, cinnamon sticks, whipped cream, and other accompaniments make the coffee alone a dessert unto itself. Lunch, with its lower prices, is especially popular. The wine list reflects the seasonal changes on the menu.

THE GEORGIAN ROOM, Four Seasons Olympic Hotel, 411 University St. Tel. 621-1700.
   Cuisine: CONTINENTAL/NORTHWEST. **Reservations:** Recommended.
$ **Prices:** Appetizers $5.75–$10; main dishes $18–$32; lunch main dishes $11.50–$15.50. AE, CB, DC, MC, V.
   Open: Breakfast Mon–Sat 6:30–11am, Sun 7–11am; lunch Mon–Fri 11:30am–2pm; dinner Mon–Thurs 5:30–10pm, Fri–Sat 5:30–10:30pm; Sun brunch 11:30am–2pm.

Nowhere in Seattle is there a more elegant restaurant—to dine at The Georgian Room is to dine in a palace. The soaring ceiling is decorated with intricate moldings, and the huge windows are framed by luxurious draperies. On a small marble floor in the center of the room stands a baby grand piano on which a pianist plays soothing music at dinner. An antique table nearby holds the evening's dessert selection as well as an immense flower arrangement. The green-and-rose decor beneath the sparkling crystal chandelier is perfectly sophisticated. The excellent service will convince you that your table is the only one being served.

The menu offerings are primarily continental, which is appropriate to the European setting. For less daring diners, the few touches of Northwest flair are a suitable introduction to that cuisine. A recent menu included such tempting presentations as marinated salmon with daikon-cress salad and sweet mustard dressing; Dungeness crab ravioli with pesto cream; sautéed crabmeat with apple blinis, radishes, and an apple-cider sauce; and grilled salmon with battered crayfish tails, acorn squash, and nutmeg butter. For dessert, there's that table in the middle of the room. As you would expect, the wine list is well suited to both the cuisine and the dining room. Sunday brunch is the best in the city.

THE HUNT CLUB, Sorrento Hotel, 900 Madison St. Tel. 343-6156.
   Cuisine: NORTHWEST. **Reservations:** Recommended.

$ Prices: Appetizers $4.75–$11; main dishes $19–$25. AE, DC, MC, V.
Open: Breakfast Mon–Fri 7–11am, Sat–Sun 7–10am; lunch Mon–Fri 11am–2:30pm; brunch Sat–Sun 10am–2:30pm; dinner Sun–Thurs 5:30–10pm, Fri–Sat 5:30–11pm.

The Hunt Club is just the sort of place its name would indicate—dark, intimate, well suited to business lunches and romantic celebrations. Mahogany paneling lines the walls, and stained glass adds splashes of color. If you need a little privacy, folding louvered doors can create private dining areas.

Menus created by executive chef Christine Keff balance French and Asian influences and flavors while stirring in a generous helping of Northwest ingredients. Whether you are having a quick meal in the lounge, a light lunch, or a four-course dinner, you'll find creativity a keystone of the menu. You might start a meal with pork and crab dumplings with lime and chili sauce or an assortment of pâtés and terrines served with homemade pickles. Salads here are particular favorites of mine; try the wild watercress with warm goat cheese and a watercress oil. For a main dish you might try the grilled salmon with Indonesian soy glaze and papaya-ginger salsa or a grilled filet of beef with zinfandel sauce and served with sweet onion jam and ragoût of wild mushrooms. For dessert there are homemade ice creams and sorbets such as honey-rosemary ice cream and strawberry-champagne sorbet, as well as cakes, tortes, and even gingersnap cannolis.

NIKKO, Westin Hotel Seattle, 1900 Fifth Ave. Tel. 322-4641.
Cuisine: JAPANESE. **Reservations:** Strongly recommended.
$ Prices: Appetizers $3–$25; full dinners $18.50–$50; lunch $6.75–$15. AE, CB, DC, DISC, JCB, MC, V.
Open: Lunch Mon–Fri 11:30am–2pm; dinner daily 5:30–10pm.

Traditional Japanese styling meets contemporary Euro-styling at this stunningly trendy Japanese restaurant. Black-slate floors, blond shoji-screen walls, indirect and subtle lighting, and original art on the walls are just some of the details that make Nikko a fascinating place for a meal. Expert sushi chefs, a display teppan-grill bar, and an extensive menu that makes the most of the Northwest's abundance of seafood assure you that Nikko is more than just a pretty place to assuage a hunger. Whether you are grabbing a quick bite of sushi at the bar or sitting cross-legged in a tatami room lingering over a *kaiseki* feast, you'll be pleasantly surprised by the subtle flavors and textures of fine Japanese cooking. If you are here for a full meal, try the clams steamed in saké or the herring roe on kelp for a starter. In fact, with more than 25 appetizers, you just might not stop ordering starters. For entertainment and value, I recommend such one-pot dinners as shabu-shabu or yosenabe. There are even family-style dinners that allow you to sample a wide assortment of dishes.

MODERATE

THE PAINTED TABLE, Alexis Hotel, 92 Madison St. Tel. 624–3646.
Cuisine: NORTHWEST/FRENCH. **Reservations:** Recommended.

$ Prices: Appetizers $6–$9; main dishes $9–$20; lunch main dishes $8–$17. AE, CB, DC, DISC, MC, V.

Open: Breakfast Mon–Fri 6:30–10am, Sat–Sun 8am–noon; lunch Mon–Fri 11:30am–2pm; dinner Sun–Thurs 5:30–10pm, Fri–Sat 5:30–10:30pm.

Artistically presented meals are de rigueur these days at expensive restaurants, but here at The Painted Table it isn't just the main dishes that are works of art, it's the plates as well. Every table is set with colorful hand-painted plates done by West Coast ceramic artists. Should you take a fancy to your plate, you can take it home with you for around $100. If you get the idea that The Painted Table is just a little bit different, wait till you see the assemblage of junk that has been affixed to the dining room wall in an artistic installation of found objects. When the waitperson plops a hunk of delicious bread down right on your table, it isn't because the restaurant has sold off all its bread plates. This is just the restaurant's way of reminding you that despite the location, prices, and clothing of the patrons, this is a casual place.

Rest assured that every dish you order will be as much a work of visual art as culinary art. Salads are beautifully arranged and composed of a half dozen or so distinctive flavors. If you're lucky you might run across smoked duck tamales with mango salsa on the appetizer list. One comes wrapped in a banana leaf and the other in a corn husk. The cambazola and mascarpone cheese ravioli with wild mushrooms and angel hair pasta is my favorite main dish. The ravioli is actually a sheet of thick and chewy green pasta slathered with creamy, fragrant cheeses. The black pepper rum roasted loin of pork with rosemary bread pudding and caramelized onions is another winner. For dessert, try the espresso-flavored crème brûlée.

THE PALM COURT, Westin Hotel Seattle, 1900 Fifth Ave. Tel. 728-1000.

Cuisine: NORTHWEST. **Reservations:** Recommended.

$ Prices: Appetizers $4.75–$6.75; main dishes $13.75–$22.75; lunch main dishes $9. AE, DC, MC, V.

Open: Lunch Tues–Fri 11am–2pm; dinner Tues–Sat 5:30–10pm.

The Palm Court's gardenlike dining rooms are the antithesis of those of other highly acclaimed local hotel restaurants such as Fuller's and the Hunt Club—bright and well lit. Walls of glass and sparkling lights turn it into a giant jewel box. Despite the glimmer and glitz, service is friendly and the atmosphere is always relaxed and casual. The Palm Court's menu these days is primarily Mediterranean with overtones of Northwest here and there. A recent menu included some excellent examples of this melding of flavors from opposite sides of the world. For a cold appetizer, there was smoked king salmon served with mascarpone cheese, roast mushrooms, herbs, and brioche. A salad of poached pear and seasonal greens with a red-wine Gorgonzola vinaigrette showed off some of the region's fine produce, while the Caesar salad with Dungeness crab hinted at the Northwest's bountiful seafood. A long list of main dishes always makes decision making difficult. How can you choose between such dishes as venison medallions with caramelized apples and pickled walnut sauce, basil-wrapped salmon with a pesto of roasted red bell peppers, or pan-roasted duck with grapes, green peppercorns, and braised leeks. For dessert, there is no question—order one of the soufflés, such as that made with Whidbey Island loganberry liqueur. Lunches are much less expensive than dinners, but the menu is not as imaginative.

DINING WITH A VIEW

EXPENSIVE

THE EMERALD SUITE AND SPACE NEEDLE RESTAURANT, Seattle Center, 219 Fourth Ave. Tel. 443-2100.
Cuisine: NORTHWEST. **Reservations:** Required.

$ **Prices:** Breakfast $9.25–$14; lunch $18–$20; dinner appetizers $5–$9; main dishes $23–$38; Sun brunch $15.75–$19.50. AE, CB, DC, MC, V.

Open: Breakfast Mon–Sat 8–11am; lunch Mon–Sat 11am–4pm; dinner Mon–Sat 4–10:45pm, Sun 5–10pm; Sun brunch 9am–3pm.

There may not be a more difficult restaurant in Seattle to get into than the Emerald Suite at the Space Needle. With seating for only 50, the attractively decorated restaurant is cozy, elegant, and almost always booked solid. Both the prices and the views are some of the highest in the city, and this 500-foot-high dining room rotates, assuring you a new vista with each course.

The long appetizers list can be difficult to get past. You'll want to try everything—for example, calamari with basil pesto or a Northwest sampler of prawns, smoked salmon, Dungeness crab, and Northwest lox. Main dishes are savory and mouth-watering, with an emphasis on fragrant sauces. Try the veal medallions sautéed with apple brandy and veal stock. Menus at both the Emerald Suite and the Space Needle Restaurant are quite similar. About the only difference is that the Emerald Suite is smaller and offers slightly more creative cuisine. For the most part, people come expecting a great view and a meal that is almost as good as the scenery.

PREGO, Stouffer Madison Hotel, 515 Madison St. Tel. 583-0300, ext. 3900.
Cuisine: ITALIAN. **Reservations:** Recommended.

$ **Prices:** Appetizers $3.25–$9; pastas $9–$23.25; main dishes $17.50–$25; lunch main dishes $12–$15. AE, CB, DC, MC, V.

Open: Lunch Mon–Fri 11:30am–2pm; dinner Mon–Thurs 5–10pm, Fri–Sat 5–11pm, Sun 5:30–10pm.

You'll be surrounded by the bold colors and shapes of Matisse originals when you dine at this very stylish northern Italian restaurant, where the dining room is split into two levels so all diners get a view. Service is attentive and accommodating.

There is a distinct emphasis on seafood at this outstanding place, and a meal might start with a cioppino with mussels; followed by a pasta course of angel-hair pasta with salmon, prawns, and scallops in smoked-salmon cream sauce; and then a filet of king salmon with pistacchio crust and confit of fennel. Luckily, the pasta courses are available in appetizer proportions for those who were not born with an Italian appetite. In addition to the delicious seafood dishes, there are also plenty of meat dishes, such as rack of lamb with tomato-rosemary jus, Dijon, and parmesan crust and garlic. Lunches are quite a bit less expensive than dinners, but there are far fewer seafood dishes offered.

TOP OF THE HILTON, Seattle Hilton Hotel, Sixth Ave. and University St. Tel. 624-0500.
   Cuisine: CONTINENTAL. **Reservations:** Recommended.
$ Prices: Appetizers $7–$9; main dishes $16–$38; Sun brunch $14–$17. AE, CB, DC, DISC, MC, V.
   Open: Lunch Tues–Fri 11:30am–2pm; dinner Sun 5–10pm, Tues–Thurs 5:30–10pm, Fri–Sat 5:30–11pm; Sun brunch 9:30am–2pm.

There's just no getting around the fact that if you want to dine with a million-dollar view, it's going to cost you a pretty penny. One difference here is the live music in the evenings, which neither the Emerald Suite nor Prego offers. The decor is sparkling sophistication; you'll dine amid shining chrome furniture arranged on two levels. Service is excellent and I'm sure you'll be happy with the food.

The appetizers here are not calculated to astound or surprise—just simple but flavorful stalwarts such as prawn cocktail, steamed clams, peppered brie, and oysters on the half shell. Main dishes, too, are primarily old favorites such as New York steak with sautéed mushrooms, seafood scampi, and surf-and-turf combinations. The tempting display of fresh desserts is placed close to the entrance so that you will be sure to notice it as you arrive; save room. Stop by for lunch and you can get an inexpensive sandwich, or come for the Sunday brunch. Any time of day or night, the view is great.

LIGHT, CASUAL & FAST FOOD

MACHEEZMO MOUSE, 211 Broadway Ave. E. Tel. 325-0072.
   Cuisine: MEXICAN. **Reservations:** Not accepted.
$ Prices: Complete dinner $4–$7.
   Open: Mon–Sat 11am–10pm, Sun noon–10pm. Also at 4129 University Way NE (tel. 206/633-4658).

Portland has such a problem with mice these days that it has started exporting them to Seattle. The Macheezmo Mouse concept of healthy fast food is catching on with the young and active crowd. They come here for delicious low-fat, low-salt, low-cholesterol, low-calorie Mexican food. Everything on the menu tastes even better with plenty of tangy, spicy Boss sauce.

BREAKFAST/BRUNCH

If a restaurant serves brunch, I have noted it in the listings above. The best bets for brunch are the major downtown hotels, and although the prices are high, the spreads are lavish. By far the most lavish is at the Four Seasons Olympic Hotel amid the greenery and glass of the greenhouselike **Garden Court** restaurant (tel. 621-1700). If you're in town on a Sunday, put on your finery and enjoy the feast for $29 to $35; it is served from 10am to 2pm. If you prefer an even tonier brunch, head for the Olympic's **Georgian Room** instead. It's à la carte only and will cost you even more than at the Garden Court. Another notable brunch, for between $14 and $17, is served at the **Top of the Hilton** (tel. 624-0500), where the spectacular views are as impressive as the display of food (see "Dining with a View," above). The Sunday hours here are 9:30am to 2pm.

24-HOUR RESTAURANT
MODERATE

13 COINS RESTAURANT, 125 Boren Ave. N. Tel. 682-2513.

Cuisine: CONTINENTAL. **Reservations:** Recommended for parties of eight or more.

$ Prices: Appetizers $4.50–$9.25; pastas $9.25–$12.95; main dishes $12.95–$30.75. AE, CB, DC, MC, V.

Open: Daily 24 hours.

The name comes from a Peruvian legend about a poor boy who had only 13 coins in his pocket to offer for the hand in marriage of the girl he loved. Embedded in each of the tables at these two restaurants you will find 13 coins. For 25 years the restaurants have been preparing meals with "care and concern." The star attraction is the exhibition cooking, but what keeps fans loyal are the gargantuan proportions. Every meal is enough for two people! The menu offers all the standard continental favorites from steak tartare with capers to veal parmigiana. There's a nice selection of pasta, great steak, egg dishes, and plenty of fresh seafood. At the airport restaurant, there is live jazz seven nights a week. Another 13 Coins is at 18000 Pacific Hwy. S. (tel. 243-9500). For smaller portions at lower prices, stop by for lunch between 11am and 3pm.

CHAPTER 6

WHAT TO SEE & DO IN SEATTLE

- **SUGGESTED ITINERARIES**
- **DID YOU KNOW . . . ?**
1. **THE TOP ATTRACTIONS**
- **FROMMER'S FAVORITE SEATTLE EXPERIENCES**
2. **MORE ATTRACTIONS**
3. **COOL FOR KIDS**
4. **ORGANIZED TOURS**
5. **SPORTS & RECREATION**

Seattle is a relatively new city, and until recently it was considered a cultural backwater rich in natural beauty. Things are changing on the cultural front, but the city's natural surroundings are still one of its primary attractions. You can easily cover all of Seattle's museums and major sights in two or three days. With the help of the itineraries below, you should have a good idea of what not to miss. After that, rent a car and head for the great outdoors. You have your choice of islands, ocean beaches, or mountains, all of which can be enjoyed in any season.

The itineraries outlined here will give you an understanding of the history, natural resources, and cultural diversity that have made Seattle the city it is today.

SUGGESTED ITINERARIES

IF YOU HAVE 1 DAY

Day 1 Start your day in the historic Pioneer Square District and take the earliest Seattle Underground Tour you can. You'll have fun and get a good idea of Seattle's early history. From Pioneer Square, walk down to the waterfront and head north. You'll pass numerous seafood restaurants, all quite good; Ivar's Acres of Clams is the most famous. Stop in at the Seattle Aquarium and learn about the sealife of the region. At Pier 55 you can get a 1-hour harbor tour cruise. Continue along the waterfront until you reach the signs for Pike Place Market, which is on the far side of the elevated highway and up a hill. In the market, you can buy fresh salmon and Dungeness crabs packed to go and much more. From Pike Place Market, walk to the monorail station in Westlake Center, which is at the corner of Pine Street and Fourth Avenue. The monorail will take you to Seattle Center, where you can ride an elevator to the top of the Space Needle, Seattle's best-known landmark. Finish

DID YOU KNOW . . . ?

- The 7,700-foot-long Evergreen Point Bridge is the longest floating bridge in the world.
- There used to be seven hills in Seattle, but now there are only six. Denny Hill was leveled by high-powered water hoses because it was considered too steep for commercial development.
- Seattleites buy more sunglasses per capita than the people of any other U.S. city.
- It rains fewer inches per year in Seattle than it does in New York, Boston, or Washington, D.C.
- The term Skid Row is derived from Skid Road, a road down which logs were skidded to a lumber mill. The very first Skid Road was in Seattle. Today it is called Yesler Way.
- The first Boeing airplane took off from Lake Union in 1916. Boeing is now the largest employer in the Seattle area.
- The geoduck (pronounced "gooeyduck") clam, harvested from Puget Sound, can weigh more than 5 pounds.

the day with dinner at one of the city's many restaurants serving seafood or Northwest cuisine.

IF YOU HAVE 2 DAYS

Day 1 Start your first day in Pioneer Square, as outlined above. After the Seattle Underground Tour, head over to the nearby International District (Chinatown) and have lunch in a Chinese restaurant. Hing Loon is my favorite. After lunch, head over to the waterfront for a harbor cruise, a stop at the aquarium and Ye Olde Curiosity Shop, and dine at one of the seafood restaurants.

Day 2 Start your second day at Pike Place Market, and be sure to arrive early to get the freshest fish (they'll pack it to take on the plane). From here it is only two blocks to the new Seattle Art Museum. After touring the museum, take the lunch tour to Tillicum Village. You'll see Northwest Native American dances while dining on alder-smoked salmon. When you return to Seattle, head for Seattle Center and the Space Needle.

IF YOU HAVE 3 DAYS

Days 1–2 Follow the 2-day strategy outlined above.

Day 3 Take a trip out of the city to the Olympic Peninsula, the San Juan Islands, or the Mount Rainier area. All these trips can be turned into overnighters or longer, but if you plan on a day trip, leave early.

IF YOU HAVE 5 DAYS OR MORE

Days 1–2 Follow the 2-day strategy, as outlined above.

Days 3–4 Stay a night or two somewhere like Port Townsend on the Olympic Peninsula or at a bed-and-breakfast in the beautiful San Juan Islands. Or better yet, take the ferry from the San Juans to the Olympic Peninsula and then back to Seattle. This makes a great loop.

Day 5 Visit Mount St. Helens and stop at the Museum of Flight on your way south.

1. THE TOP ATTRACTIONS

MUSEUM OF FLIGHT, 9404 E. Marginal Way S. Tel. 764-5720.

Located right next door to busy Boeing Field, 10 minutes south of downtown Seattle, is one of the world's best museums dedicated to the history of flight. Aviation buffs will be walking on air when they visit this cavernous repository of some of history's most famous planes. A six-story glass-and-steel building holds most of the collection, and a viewing area lets you watch planes take off and land at the adjacent airport. There is a replica of the Wright brothers' first glider to start things off, and then the exhibits bring you right up to the present state of flight. Suspended in the Great Hall are 20 planes, including a DC-3 and the first air force F-5 supersonic fighter. You'll also see the Blackbird, the world's fastest jet; a rare World War II Corsair fighter rescued from Lake Washington and restored to its original glory; and an exhibit on the U.S. space program featuring an Apollo command module. Other planes have been grounded and can be examined up close. See Section 4, below, for information on a tour of the Boeing plant.

Admission: $5 adults, $3 ages 6–15, under age 6 free.
Open: Daily 10am–5pm (until 9pm Thurs). **Bus:** 124 or 174.
Directions: Take exit 158 on I-5.

MUSEUM OF HISTORY & INDUSTRY, 2700 24th Ave. E. Tel. 324-1126.

You can learn more about the history of Seattle and the Northwest in this museum at the north end of Washington Park Arboretum. There is a Boeing mail plane from the 1920s, plus an exhibit on the 1889 fire that leveled the city. If the Seattle Underground Tour's vivid description of prefire life has you curious about what the city's more respectable citizens were doing back in the 1880s, you can find out here, where re-created storefronts provide glimpses into their lives. This museum also hosts touring exhibitions that address history outside the Northwest.

Admission: $3 adults, $1.50 senior citizens and ages 6–12, under age 6 free. Free to all on Tuesday.
Open: Daily 10am–5pm. **Closed:** Thanksgiving, Christmas, and New Year's Day. **Bus:** 25, 43, or 48.

OMNIDOME FILM EXPERIENCE, Pier 59, Waterfront Park. Tel. 622-1868.

This huge wraparound theater is located adjacent to the Seattle Aquarium, and on my last visit was showing a film about the eruption of Mount St. Helens. The Omnidome, for those who have never experienced it, is a movie theater with a 180° screen that fills your peripheral vision and puts you right in the middle of the action. People with hangovers or who get motion sickness should stay away!

Admission: $5.95 adults, $4.95 senior citizens and ages 13–18, $3.95 ages 6–12, $2.95 ages 3–5.
Open: Sun–Thurs 10am–9pm, Fri–Sat 10am–11pm. **Bus:** 15, 18, or 91; then walk down Pike Place stairs.

PACIFIC SCIENCE CENTER, 200 Second Ave. N., Seattle Center. Tel. 443-2001 or 443-2880.

Although exhibits are aimed primarily at children, the Pacific Science Center is fun for all ages. The main goal of this sprawling complex at Seattle Center is to teach kids about science and to instill a desire to study it. To that end, there are dozens of fun hands-on exhibits addressing the biological sciences, physics, and chemistry. Kids learn how their bodies work, blow giant bubbles, put on shows, build a dam, and play in a rocketship. There is a planetarium for learning about the skies, plus laser shows. Even more interesting are

FROMMER'S FAVORITE SEATTLE EXPERIENCES

Riding the Ferry   There are plenty of harbor tours, but for my money you can't beat the ferries of the Washington State ferry system. For $3.30 you can ride across the sound and back with a great view of the Seattle skyline, and sometimes the Olympic Mountains and Mount Rainier.

Sea Kayaking on Lake Union   Seattle is a city of speedboats, sailboats, sailboards, even floatplanes, but my favorite is the sea kayak. This is the nation's sea-kayak capital, and the waters all around the city are ideal for an afternoon of leisurely paddling. You can even pull up at waterfront restaurants for a meal.

Seattle Underground Tour   The humor is slightly off-color and the history is not what you learn in grade school, but that's what makes this tour so interesting and fun. Go beneath the sidewalks and old buildings of the Pioneer Square area to see what Seattle was like before the Great Seattle Fire of 1889.

A Day at Pike Place Market   There is no better place in Seattle to shop for fresh local and gourmet produce, fish, or meats. The displays are beautiful, even if you don't buy; but the fishmongers will gladly pack a few crabs or a salmon for you to take home on the plane. The market maze also is home to hundreds of craftspeople, vendors, and shops filled with all manner of amazing goods.

A Latte from an Espresso Cart   Seattle is a city of espresso addicts, so you never have to be more than a block or so from your next cup. Colorfully painted espresso carts park on the sidewalks in busy neighborhoods, providing commuters with a quick cup on the way to work. Lattes are the best—they are a three-to-one mixture of milk and espresso. Delicious!

Watching the Salmon Return to Spawn   At The Seattle Aquarium, a fish ladder allows salmon that were hatched here to return from the sea as adults and spawn right on the aquarium grounds. These graceful and powerful fish are an integral part of Northwest culture and it is always reassuring to see them return.

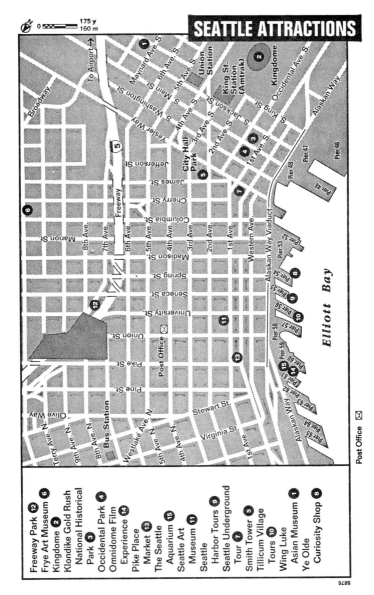

SEATTLE ATTRACTIONS

0 —— 175 y
     160 m

To Airport →

Broadway
Maynard Ave. S.
6th Ave. S.
S. Washington St.
S. Main St.
Union Station
King St. Station (Amtrak)
S. Jackson St.
S. King St.
Occidental Ave. S.
Kingdome
Alaskan Way

Yesler Way
4th Ave. S.
3rd Ave. S.
2nd Ave. S.
1st Ave. S.
City Hall Park
Jefferson St.
James St.
Cherry St.
Columbia St.
Madison St.
Spring St.
Seneca St.
University St.
Union St.
Pike St.
Pine St.

Freeway
7th Ave.
6th Ave.
5th Ave.
4th Ave.
3rd Ave.
2nd Ave.
1st Ave.
Western Ave.
Alaskan Way Viaduct

Marion St.
8th Ave.

Pier 47
Pier 46
Pier 49
Pier 48
Pier 52
Pier 53
Pier 54
Pier 55
Pier 56
Pier 57
Pier 58
Pier 59
Pier 60
Pier 62
Pier 63
Pier 65
Pier 64

Elliott Bay

Post Office ⊠

Bus Station
Olive Way
Terry Ave. N.
9th Ave. N.
8th Ave. N.
Westlake Ave. N.
5th Ave. N.
4th Ave. N.
1st Ave.
Stewart St.
Virginia St.
Alaskan Way

Post Office ⊠

Freeway Park ⑫
Frye Art Museum ⑥
Kingdome ②
Klondike Gold Rush National Historical Park ③
Occidental Park ④
Omnidome Film Experience ⑭
Pike Place Market ⑬
The Seattle Aquarium ⑮
Seattle Art Museum ⑪
Seattle Harbor Tours ⑨
Seattle Underground Tour ⑦
Smith Tower ⑤
Tillicum Village Tours ⑩
Wing Luke Asian Museum ①
Ye Olde Curiosity Shop ⑧

5876

the many special exhibits. There are also special events, such as kayaking classes, reptile shows, a bubble festival, and a science circus. An IMAX® theater has daily showings of short films on its huge 3½-story-high screen. (For map of Seattle Center, see below.)

Admission: $5.50 adults, $4.50 ages 6–13 and senior citizens, $3.50 ages 2–5, under 2 free. IMAX® $4.50 adults, $3.50 ages 6–13 and senior citizens, $2.50 ages 2–5, under 2 free ($1 as add-on to general-admission ticket). Laser show $6 for evening performances,

$1 for matinee performances as add-on to general-admission ticket only.

Open: June–Sept, daily 10am–6pm; Oct–May, Mon–Fri 10am–5pm, Sat–Sun 10am–6pm. **Bus:** 3, 4, 6, 16, 19, 24, or 33. **Monorail:** To Seattle Center station.

PIKE PLACE MARKET, between Pike St. and Pine St. (at First Ave.). Tel. 682-7453.

Pike Place Market, a farmers' market, was founded in 1907 when housewives complained that middlemen were raising the price of produce too high. The market allowed shoppers to buy directly from producers, and thus save on grocery bills. By the 1960s however, the market was no longer the popular spot it had once been. World War II had deprived it of nearly half its farmers when Japanese Americans were moved to internment camps. The postwar flight to the suburbs almost spelled the end for the market, and the site was being eyed for a major redevelopment project. However, a grass-roots movement to save the 7-acre market culminated in its being declared a National Historic District.

Today it is once again bustling, but the 100 or so farmers and fishmongers who set up shop here are only a small part of the attraction. More than 200 local craftspeople and artists can be found selling their creations at different times of the year. There are excellent restaurants, and dozens of shops fill the market area. Street performers—including mimes, sitar players, and hammered-dulcimer players—serenade milling crowds. There is an information booth almost directly below the large Pike Place Market sign where you can pick up a free map and restaurant guide to the market. Watch for the flying fish.

Admission: Free.
Open: Mon–Sat 9am–6pm, Sun 11am–5pm. **Bus:** 15, 18, or 99.

THE SEATTLE AQUARIUM, Pier 59, Waterfront Park. Tel. 386-4320.

The highly acclaimed Seattle Aquarium, in the heart of the waterfront, is a fascinating place to spend a few hours learning about marine and freshwater life in the Northwest. From the underwater viewing dome, you'll get a fish's-eye view of life beneath the waves. A salmon ladder is particularly exciting when the salmon return to the aquarium to spawn (autumn). There is a beautiful large coral-reef tank, as well as many smaller tanks that exhibit fish from local and distant waters. A telling exhibit on the pollution of Puget Sound shows the effect of human population expansion not only on the sound but also on the area's salmon-spawning streams.

The aquarium's newest addition is an interactive tide-pool exhibit and discovery lab that re-creates Washington's wave-swept intertidal zone. As part of the exhibit, a video microscope provides a magnified glimpse of the seldom-seen world of plankton.

Admission: $6.50 adults, $5 senior citizens, $4 ages 6–18, $1.50 ages 3–5.
Open: Labor Day–Memorial Day, daily 10am–5pm; Memorial Day–Labor Day, daily 10am–7pm. **Bus:** 15, 18, or 91; then walk down Pike Place stairs.

SEATTLE ART MUSEUM, First Ave. and University St. Tel. 654-3100.

Seattleites either love the building or hate it, but there is no denying that the Seattle Art Museum has made an impact on downtown Seattle since it's opening at this location in 1992. Some find the museum's facade tastelessly bland, while others claim it is refreshingly minimalist. No matter what you think of the building (designed by noted architect Robert Venturi), it makes a perfect backdrop for the museum's most public work of art. Jonathon Borofsky's *Hammering Man,* a giant black silhouette of a steel sculpture, toils unceasingly in front of the museum's curvilinear facade. Inside, a grand staircase leads from the main entrance to the first of the display floors, which is devoted to special exhibits. One floor higher, you'll find one of the nation's premier collections of Northwest Coast Native American art and artifacts and an equally large collection of African art. These displays juxtapose cultures rich in expressive religious and decorative art. Many pieces in this collection are not kept behind glass, but electronic devices sound alarms if you venture too close. Alarms are constantly sounding, so if the display you are viewing should suddenly begin beeping, just step back. Also on this floor is an extensive collection of Asian art. On the top floor, you'll find the museum's collection of European and American art, covering the ancient Mediterranean to the medieval, Renaissance, and Baroque periods in Europe. A large 18th-century collection and a smaller 19th-century exhibition lead up to a large 20th-century collection that includes a room devoted to Northwest modern art. One room is given over to photography and prints.

Admission: $5 adults, $3 senior citizens and students, ages 6 and under free. Free to all on first Tuesday of each month.

Open: Tues–Sat 10am–5pm (Thurs until 9pm; first Tues of each month until 7pm), Sun noon–5pm. **Bus:** 15, 18, or 91.

SPACE NEEDLE, 203 Sixth Ave. N., Seattle Center. Tel. 443-2100.

From a distance it resembles a flying saucer on top of a tripod, and when it was built it was meant to suggest future architectural trends. Erected for the 1962 World's Fair, the 600-foot-tall tower is the most popular tourist sight in Seattle. At 518 feet above ground level, the views from the observation deck are stunning, and there are displays identifying more than 60 sites and activities in the Seattle area. High-powered telescopes let you zoom in on things. You'll also find a history of the Space Needle, a lounge, and two very expensive restaurants. If you don't mind standing in line and paying quite a bit for an elevator ride, make this your first stop in Seattle so you can orient yourself.

Admission: $6 adults, $5 senior citizens, $4 ages 5–12, ages 4 and under free.

Open: Memorial Day–Labor Day, daily 8am–midnight; day after Labor Day–day before Memorial Day, daily 9am–midnight. **Bus:** 3, 4, 6, 16, 19, 24, or 33. **Monorail:** To Seattle Center station.

2. MORE ATTRACTIONS

MUSEUMS

BURKE MUSEUM, 17th Ave. NE and NE 45th St. Tel. 543-5590.

Located in the northwest corner of the University of Washington campus, the Burke Museum features exhibits on the natural and cultural heritage of the Pacific Rim. It is noteworthy primarily for its Northwest Native American art collection and an active schedule of special exhibits. Down in the basement, there is a large collection of minerals and fossils. In front of the museum stand replicas of totem poles carved in the 1870s and 1880s. There is also an ethnobotanical garden displaying plants used by Northwestern tribes. Campus parking is very expensive on weekdays and Saturday mornings, so try to visit on a Saturday afternoon or a Sunday.

Admission: Donation, $3 adults, $2 students and seniors, $1.50 ages 6–18.

Open: Daily 10am–5pm (Thurs until 8pm). **Bus:** 70, 71, 72, 73, or 74.

FRYE ART MUSEUM, 704 Terry St. (at Cherry St.). Tel. 622-9250.

Most of the paintings in this small museum date from the second half of the 19th century and are primarily by European artists, but there are also paintings by 19th-century Americans and the prolific Wyeth family. A few Russian and Alaskan paintings and monthly contemporary art exhibits complete the picture.

Admission: Free.

Open: Mon–Sat 10am–5pm, Sun noon–5pm. **Bus:** 3, 4, or 12.

KLONDIKE GOLD RUSH NATIONAL HISTORICAL PARK, 117 S. Main St. Tel. 553-7220.

It isn't in the Klondike (which isn't even in the United States) and it isn't really a park (it's a single room in an old store), but it is a fascinating little museum. "At 3 o'clock this morning the steamship *Portland,* from St. Michaels for Seattle, passed up [Puget] Sound with more than a ton of gold on board and 68 passengers." When the *Seattle Post-Intelligencer* published that sentence on July 17, 1897, they started a stampede. Would-be miners heading for the Klondike goldfields in the 1890s made Seattle their outfitting center and helped turn it into a prosperous city. When they struck it rich up north, they headed back to Seattle, the first outpost of civilization, and unloaded their gold, making Seattle doubly rich. It seems only fitting that this museum should be here. Film buffs can catch a free screening of Charles Chaplin's great film *The Gold Rush* the first Sunday of each month at 3pm. Another unit of the park is centered in Skagway, AK.

Admission: Free.

Open: Daily 9am–5pm. **Closed:** Thanksgiving, Christmas, and New Year's Day. **Bus:** 15, 18, 21, 22, 56, 91, or 99.

WING LUKE ASIAN MUSEUM, 407 Seventh Ave. S. Tel. 623-5124.

Asian American culture, art, and history are explored at this museum in the heart of the International District. The emphasis is on the life of Asian immigrants in the Northwest, and special exhibits are meant to help explain customs to non-Asians. Asians, primarily Chinese and Japanese, played an integral role in settling the Northwest, and today the connection of this region with the far side of the Pacific is opening up many new economic and cultural doors.

Admission: $2.50 adults, $1.50 students and senior citizens, 75¢ ages 5–12, under 5 free. Free to all on Thursday.

Open: Tues–Fri 11am–4:30pm, Sat–Sun noon–4pm. **Bus:** 7, 14, 36, or 91.

YE OLDE CURIOSITY SHOP, Pier 54, Alaskan Way. Tel. 682-5844.

It's a museum. It's a store. It's weird! It's tacky! If you have a fascination with the bizarre—and I think we all do—shoulder your way into this crowded shop and erstwhile museum. See Siamese-twin calves, a natural mummy, the Lord's Prayer on a grain of rice, a narwhal tusk, shrunken heads, walrus and whale oosiks (the bone of the male reproductive organ)—in fact, all the stuff that fascinated you as a kid. The collection of oddities was started in 1899 by Joe Standley, who had developed a more-than-passing interest in strange curios.

Admission: Free.

Open: Sun–Thurs 9:30am–6pm, Fri–Sat 9am–9pm. **Bus:** 15, 18, or 91; then walk down Pike Place stairs.

NEIGHBORHOOD

INTERNATIONAL DISTRICT, Fifth Ave. S. to Eighth Ave. S. (between S. Main St. and S. Lane St.).

Seattle's large and prosperous Asian neighborhood is called the International District rather than Chinatown because so many Asian nationalities call this area home. This has been the traditional Asian neighborhood for 100 years or more and you can learn about its history at the Wing Luke Museum (see above). There are of course lots of restaurants and import and food stores, including the huge Uwajimaya (see "Markets" in Section 2 of Chapter 8 for details). Both the Nippon Kan Theatre, 628 S. Washington St. (tel. 467-6807), and the Northwest Asian-American Theater, 409 Seventh Ave. S. (tel. 340-1049), feature performances with an Asian flavor.

TOTEM POLES

OCCIDENTAL PARK, Occidental Ave. S. and S. Washington St.

Totem poles are the quintessential symbol of the Northwest, and although this Native American art form actually comes from farther north, there are quite a few totem poles around Seattle. The four in this shady cobblestoned park were carved by local artist Duane Pasco. The tallest is 35-foot-high *The Sun and Raven,* which tells the story of how Raven brought light into the world. Next to this pole is the *Man Riding a Whale.* This type of totem pole was traditionally carved to help villagers during their whale hunts. The other two figures that face each other are symbols of the Bear Clan and the Welcoming Figure.

PIONEER PLACE, First Ave. and Yesler Way.

The totem pole in this little triangular park at the heart of Pioneer Square has a rather unusual history. The one you see now is actually a copy of the original that stood here, which arrived in Seattle in 1890 after a band of drunken men stole it from a Tlingit village up the coast. In 1938 the pole was set afire by an arsonist. The Seattle city fathers sent a $5,000 check to the Tlingit village requesting a replacement. Supposedly, the response from the village was, "Thanks for paying for the first totem pole. If you want another, it will cost another $5,000." The city of Seattle paid up, and so today Pioneer Square has a totem pole and the city has a clear conscience.

PANORAMAS

SMITH TOWER, 508 Second Ave. Tel. 682-9393.

Despite all the shiny glass skyscrapers crowding the Seattle skyline these days, you can't miss the Smith Tower. It sits off all by itself, a tall white needle on the edge of the Pioneer Square District. At only 42 stories, it was still the tallest building west of the Mississippi for many years after being built in 1914. It isn't nearly as popular as the Space Needle, but there is an observation platform way up near the top. It's worth the trip for not only the view of the city from this end of town, but also for the ride up in the shiny brass-and-copper elevator, which still uses an operator and has glass doors. You should call ahead if you are going out of your way, since the observation floor is sometimes closed due to special functions.

Admission: $2 adults, $1 children.
Open: Mon–Fri 9–11:30am, 1:30–4:30pm, and 5:30–10pm, Sat–Sun 9am–10pm. **Bus:** 15, 17, 18, 21, 22, 56, or 91.

PARKS & GARDENS

FREEWAY PARK, Sixth Ave. and Seneca St.

What do you do when a noisy interstate runs right through the middle of your fair city and you haven't got enough parks for all the suntanners and Frisbee throwers? You could tear up the whole darn thing and turn it into a park, as Portland did with its riverfront freeway, or you could put a roof on the highway and build a park over all the rushing cars and trucks, as Seattle did. Terraced gardens, waterfalls, grassy lawns—they're all here, and they're all smog resistant. They have to be to survive in this environment. You'd never know there's a roaring freeway beneath your feet.

Admission: Free.
Open: Daily dawn to dusk. **Bus:** Any bus that goes to the downtown bus tunnel; Washington State Convention and Trade Center stop.

HIRAM M. CHITTENDEN LOCKS, 3015 NW 54th St. Tel. 783-7059.

These locks connect Lake Washington and Lake Union to Puget Sound and allow boats to travel from the lakes onto open water. The difference between the water levels of the lakes and the sound varies from 6 to 26 feet, depending on the tides and rainfall levels. Mostly used by small boats, the locks are a popular spot for salmon watching. People watch salmon jumping up the cascades of a fish ladder as they return to spawn in the stream where they were born, and windows below the waterline give an idea of what it's like to be a salmon. The best months to see salmon are July and August.

Admission: Free.
Open: Daily 7am–9pm; visitors center 10am–7pm. **Bus:** 17, 43, or 46.

JAPANESE GARDENS, Washington Park Arboretum, Lake Washington Blvd. E. (north of E. Madison St.). Tel. 684-4725.

Situated on 3½ acres of land, the Japanese Gardens are a perfect little world unto themselves. Babbling brooks, a lake rimmed with Japanese irises and filled with colorful koi (Japanese carp), and a cherry orchard for spring color are peaceful any time of year. Unfortunately, noise from a nearby road can be distracting at times. A special Tea Garden encloses a Tea House, where, on the third Sunday of each month at 2 and 3pm, you can attend a traditional tea ceremony.

Admission: $2 adults; $1 senior citizens, the disabled, and ages 6–18.

Open: Mar 1–last Sat in Apr, daily 10am–6pm; last Sun in Apr–May 31, daily 10am–7pm; June 1–Aug 31, daily 10am–8pm; Sept 1–fourth Sat in Oct, daily 10am–6pm; fourth Sun in Oct–Nov 30, daily 10am–4pm. **Closed:** Dec–Feb. **Bus:** 11, 43, or 48.

SNOQUALMIE FALLS PARK, I-90, Exit 27, Snoqualmie, WA.

If you were a fan of the early 1990s television program *Twin Peaks,* you'll immediately recognize this 270-foot waterfall some 35 miles east of Seattle. The park, with its forests and hiking trails, surrounds the falls, while Salish Lodge, a popular weekend retreat for Seattleites, stands on the very brink of the cliff over which the Snoqualmie River cascades. A half-mile trail leads steeply down to the base of the falls, from which you'll get the most famous view of the falls and the lodge. It isn't at all obvious to visitors, but the falls are used to generate hydroelectricity. If you are interested in seeing other familiar scenery from *Twin Peaks,* drive through the nearby town of North Bend, where you can get a piece of "damn good pie." To reach the falls, head east from Seattle on I-90 to exit 27. It takes about 35 to 45 minutes to get there.

VOLUNTEER PARK, E. Prospect St. and 14th Ave. E. Tel. 684-4743.

Volunteer Park is surrounded by the elegant mansions of Capitol Hill and is a popular spot for suntanning and playing Frisbee. A stately conservatory houses a large collection of tropical plants, including palm trees, orchids, and cacti. The Seattle Art Museum (see above) was formerly here.

Admission: Free (park and conservatory).

Open: Daily dawn to dusk; conservatory daily 10am–7pm. **Bus:** 10.

WASHINGTON PARK ARBORETUM, 2300 Arboretum Dr. E. Tel. 543-8800.

Acres of trees and shrubs stretch from the far side of Capitol Hill all the way to the Montlake Cut, a canal connecting Lake Washington to Lake Union. Within the arboretum, there are quiet trails that are most beautiful in spring, when azaleas, cherry trees, rhododendrons, and dogwoods are all in flower. There are more than 5,000 varieties of plants in the 200-acre park. The north end, a marshland that is home to ducks and herons, is popular with kayakers and canoeists (see below for where you can rent a canoe or kayak).

Admission: Free.

Open: Daily dawn to dusk; visitors center Mon–Fri 10am–4pm, Sat–Sun noon–4pm. **Bus:** 11, 43, or 48.

WOODLAND PARK ZOO, 5500 Phinney Ave. N. Tel. 684-4800.

Although the zoo in Portland is better known for elephant, the new elephant habitat here at the noted Woodland Park Zoo is more impressive. It includes a tropical forest, pool, Thai logging camp, and an elephant house designed to resemble a Thai Buddhist temple. A lush tropical rain forest exhibit includes two separate gorilla habitats, and the African savannah habitat is equally impressive. Slated for opening in 1994 are a home for bald eagle, brown bear, and river otter, as well as a temperate forest habitat that includes a petting zoo. The zoo also includes the Family Farm, where kids can marvel at animal babies.

Admission: $6 adults; $4.50 senior citizens and disabled; $3.50 chldren ages 6–17; $1.50 ages 3–5; free under age 3. **Parking:** $1.
Open: Mar 15–Oct 14 daily 9:30am–6pm; Oct 15–Mar 14 9:30am–4pm. **Bus:** 5, 6, or 43.

3. COOL FOR KIDS

Look under "The Top Attractions" and "More Attractions," above, for the following Seattle attractions for kids: **Pacific Science Center, The Seattle Aquarium,** and **Ye Olde Curiosity Shop.**
The places listed in this section are also great for kids. They'll be interested in the arcades and rides at **Seattle Center,** as well as their very own museum, the **Seattle Children's Museum.**
Or you can take them to a sports event. Seattle supports professional football, basketball, and baseball teams (see Section 5 below). And what could be more fun than exploring the **Seattle Underground** (see Section 4 below)!

ENCHANTED VILLAGE & WILD WAVES, 36201 Enchanted Pkwy. S., Federal Way, WA 98003. Tel. 206/661-8000.
The littlest kids can watch the clowns and ride on miniature trains, merry-go-rounds, and the like at Enchanted Village. The older kids, teenagers, and adults will want to spend the hot days of summer riding the wild waves, tubing down artificial streams, and swooshing down water slides.

Admission (to both parks): $18 age 10–adult, $16 ages 3–9, free under age 2.
Open: Enchanted Village only Apr 10–May 23 Sat–Sun 10am–5pm; Enchanted Village and Wild Waves May 24–June 25 daily 10am–6pm; June 26–Sep 6 daily 11am–7pm. Wild Waves closes right after Labor Day for season.
Directions: By car from Seattle, take I-5 south to Exit 142-B, Puyallup.

SEATTLE CENTER, 305 Harrison St. Tel. 684-7200.
This 74-acre amusement park and cultural center was built for the Seattle World's Fair in 1962 and stands on the north edge of downtown at the end of the monorail line. The most visible building at the center is the Space Needle (see above), which provides an outstanding panorama of the city from its observation deck. However, of much more interest to children are the rides (a roller coaster, log flume, merry-go-round, and Ferris wheel) and arcade games. This is Seattle's main festival site, and in the summer months hardly a

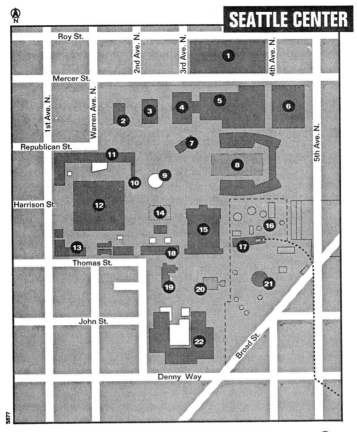

SEATTLE CENTER

weekend goes by without some festival or another filling its grounds. (See map above.)

Admission: Free; pay per ride or game.

Open: Summer, daily 9am–midnight; rest of year, Sun–Thurs 9am–9pm, Fri–Sat 9am–midnight.

Bus: 1, 2, 3, 4, 6, 13, 15, 16, 18, 19, 24, or 33.

THE CHILDREN'S MUSEUM, Center House, Seattle Center. Tel. 441-1767.

Kids have their very own museum in the Center House at Seattle Center. The museum includes plenty of hands-on cultural exhibits, workshops, a child-size neighborhood, an infant and toddler play center, and a soap-bubble center that keeps kids learning and playing for hours.

Admission: $3 adults or children.

Open: Tues–Sun 10am–5pm. **Bus:** 1, 2, 3, 4, 6, 13, 15, 16, 18, 19, 24, or 33.

---

4. ORGANIZED TOURS

BOEING TOUR CENTER, State Rte. 526, Everett, WA. Tel. 342-4801.

Anyone interested in how planes are built will enjoy this free 90-minute tour of the Boeing assembly plant, 30 miles north of Seattle. This is the single largest building, by volume, in the world. Gigantic 747s easily fit inside, and the Seattle Seahawks football team would have no problem playing here. A window opening onto the plant allows you to observe the assembly-line production. There is also a slide and movie presentation in the visitor's center auditorium.

Price: Free.

Tours: Mon–Fri 8:30am–2pm on first-come, first-served basis. Call for current schedule. Children under age 10 not permitted.

CASUAL CABS (tel. 623-2991).

One of the most enjoyable ways to tour the Seattle waterfront and Pioneer Square area is by horse-drawn carriage. You will usually find a few carriages parked along the waterfront near the Seattle Aquarium, and you can hire one on the spur of the moment.

Price: $25 per half hour for up to four adults.

EMERALD CITY CHARTERS, 809 Fairview Place N. Tel. 624-3931.

The islands and bays of Puget Sound are a favorite with the yachting crowd, and if you want to find out why this is such a popular sailing destination, why not step aboard the *Kaholo Makani* for a sunset cruise or tour of the harbor.

Prices: $20–$35.

SEATTLE HARBOR TOURS, Pier 55. Tel. 623-1445.

For your basic see-Seattle-from-the-water cruise, you can't beat this one. You'll learn about the history, geography, and important sights of Seattle on the 1-hour cruise that takes in the Seattle waterfront as well as the harbor facilities.

Prices: $11 adults, $5 children.

Tours: Daily.

SEATTLE UNDERGROUND TOUR, 610 First Ave. Tel. 682-1511 (information), 682-4646 (reservations).

Dirt, corruption, sewers, scandal! With a come-on like that, how can you resist this unusual tour? Never have I enjoyed a guided tour as much as I enjoyed this one, and I'm sure you'll be equally entertained and enlightened (though an appreciation for off-color humor is a prerequisite). Early Seattle had its problems, and when a fire raged through the city in 1889, leveling most of downtown, the city authorities had to start all over again. part of their solution was to build on top of the old city, and today you can still see parts of old Seattle beneath the busy streets of the modern-day metropolis. Best of all, you'll learn a side of local history that official versions avoid. Don't miss this one!

Prices: $5.50 adults, $4.50 senior citizens, $4 students aged 13–17 or with valid ID, $2.50 ages 6–12.

Tours: Daily (hours vary with the month).

TILLICUM VILLAGE TOURS, Pier 56. Tel. 443-1244.

Northwest Native American culture comes alive at Tillicum Village, across Puget Sound from Seattle at Blake Island Marine State Park. Totem poles stand vigil outside a huge cedar longhouse fashioned after the traditional dwellings of Northwest Indians. You'll enjoy a meal of alder-smoked salmon while watching traditional masked dances. All around stand the carved and painted images of fanciful animals, and you can see the park's resident wood-carver create more of these beautiful works of art. After the dinner and dances, you can explore the deep forest that surrounds the clearing in which the lodge stands. There are even beaches on which to relax.

Prices: $39.95 adults, $36.95 senior citizens, $25.95 ages 13–19, $15.95 ages 6–12, $7.95 ages 4–5.

Tours: Daily May–Oct.

5. SPORTS & RECREATION

SPECTATOR SPORTS

BASEBALL The **Seattle Mariners** (AL) are Seattle's major-league baseball team, and they play in the Kingdome from April to October. Monday nights are family nights, with the more expensive seats being sold on a two-for-one basis. Prices range from $5.50 to $11.50. Tickets are available at the Kingdome box office or by calling TicketMaster (tel. 628-0888). Parking is next to impossible, so plan to leave your car behind.

BASKETBALL The **Seattle SuperSonics** (NBA) play professional basketball in the Seattle Center Coliseum from November to about May. Games start at 7pm, and tickets are $7 to $45. Call for schedule and ticket information (tel. 281-5800).

FOOTBALL The **Seattle Seahawks** (NFL) play in the Kingdome from September to December. Games are on Sunday at 1pm, and tickets, at $19 to $35, are very difficult to get. Call for schedule and ticket information (tel. 827-9777). Parking in the Kingdome area is nearly impossible during games, so take the bus.

HORSE RACING Watch the thoroughbreds run and wager a bit on your favorites at **Longacres Race Course,** 1621 SW 16th St., Renton, WA (tel. 206/226-3131), southeast of downtown Seattle. The season runs from April to September. On Saturday, Sunday, and holidays, the first race is at 12:30pm; Thursday and Friday, the first race is at 3pm. Admission is $2.50.

MARATHON The **Seattle Marathon** takes place in November.

There's a runners' hot line in Seattle that you can call for more information on this and other races in the area (tel. 524-RUNS).

PARTICIPATORY ACTIVITIES

BEACHES   **Alki** (rhymes with sky) **Beach,** on Puget Sound, is the nearest beach to downtown Seattle. It stretches for 2½ miles down the west side of the Alki Peninsula, which is the promontory you see across Elliott Bay from Seattle's waterfront. This is a busy beach, and the views across the sound to the Olympic Mountains can be stunning on a clear day. There are also several miles of beaches at **Blake Island State Park,** site of Tillicum Village (see above). You'll need your own boat to get here, though, if you don't plan to come on the Tillicum Village tour.

BICYCLING   **Gregg's Green Lake Cycle,** 7007 Woodlawn St. NE (tel. 523-1822); the **Bicycle Center,** 4529 Sand Point Way NE (tel. 523-8300); and **Sammamish Valley Cycle,** 8451 164th Ave. NE, Redmond (tel. 881-8442)—all rent bikes by the hour and by the day, as well as by the week. Rates range from $4 to $6 per hour and $15 to $20 per day. These three shops are all convenient to the **Burke-Gilman Trail** and the **Sammamish River Trail.** The former is a 12.5-mile trail created from an old railway bed. It starts at **Gasworks Park** and continues to **Kenmore Logboom Park** at the north end of Lake Washington by way of the University of Washington. Serious riders can then connect to the Sammamish River Trail, which leads to Lake Sammamish. There are lots of great picnicking spots along both trails.

FISHING   As you might have guessed from the plethora of seafood restaurants in Seattle, the waters around here are brimming with fish. You can fish the rivers for salmon and steelhead trout, or try the saltwater of Puget Sound for salmon or bottom fish.

GOLF   There are more than a dozen public golf courses in the Seattle area. **Jackson Park Municipal Golf Course,** 1000 NE 135th St. (tel. 363-4747); **Jefferson Park Municipal Golf Course,** 4101 Beacon Ave. S. (tel. 762-4513); and **West Seattle Municipal Golf Course,** 4470 35th Ave. SW (tel. 935-5187)—these are three of the most convenient courses. Greens fees are $20.25 if you're not a King County resident, $13.50 if you are.

HIKING   The areas surrounding Seattle are a hiker's paradise, and hiking, backpacking, and camping are some of the most popular activities in the region. Within an easy drive of the city are three national parks, Mount St. Helens National Volcanic Monument, and numerous national forests, all of which offer hikes of varying lengths and degrees of difficulty.
   Mount Rainier National Park, Tahoma Woods/Star Route, Ashford, WA 98304 (tel. 206/569-2211), is the easiest to reach from Seattle. **Olympic National Park,** 600 E. Park Ave., Port Angeles, WA 98362 (tel. 206/452-0330), is the most varied of the national parks in this region. There are long stretches of isolated beaches, snow-capped mountains, lush rain forests, and hot springs. The **North Cascades National Park,** 2105 Washington Hwy. 20, Sedro Woolley, WA 98284 (tel. 206/856-5700), is adjacent to the Canadian border northeast of Seattle.
   Mount St. Helens National Volcanic Monument, 3029

Spirit Lake Hwy., Castle Rock, WA 98611-9719 (tel. 206/274-4038), has been left as a monument to the power of a volcanic eruption and is an amazing site that should not be missed. A limited number of hikers are allowed to climb the peak each day, but you have to make reservations far in advance.

The **Interagency Committee for Outdoor Recreation,** 4800 Capitol Blvd., KP-11, Tumwater, WA 98504-5611 (tel. 206/753-7140), will send you a trails directory that lists most of Washington's parks with hiking trails.

HORSEBACK RIDING   Down at the south end of Lake Washington near the airport are three outfits that rent horses. **Aqua Barn Ranch,** 15227 SE Renton-Maple Valley Hwy., Renton, WA (tel. 206/255-4618), offers guided rides at the rate of $19.50 per hour; reservations are required. **Kelly's Riding and Boarding Ranch,** 7212 Issaquah-Renton Rd. SE, Issaquah, WA (tel. 206/392-6979), charges $20 for a 70-minute ride. **Tiger Mountain Outfitters,** 24508 SE 133rd St., Issaquah, WA (tel. 206/392-5090), offers a 3-hour ride up Tiger Mountain for $35 in winter and $40 in summer; reservations required.

KAYAKING/CANOEING   Although there is no white water around Seattle, kayaking is still a very popular recreational activity. The boats used are not the tiny white-water boats, but long sea kayaks, often with a rudder for better steering in choppy or windy seas.

Northwest Outdoor Center, 2100 Westlake Ave. N. (tel. 281-9694), is located on Lake Union, and they will rent you a sea kayak for only $7 to $9 per hour. Your third and fourth hours are free on weekdays, and on the weekend your fourth hour is free. You can also opt for guided paddles lasting from a few hours to several days, and there are plenty of classes available for those who are interested. From April to September, the center is open Monday through Friday from 10am to 8pm, on Saturday, Sunday, and holidays from 9am to 6pm; in March and October, daily from 10am to 6pm; and from November to February, Wednesday through Sunday from 10am to 5pm.

The **University of Washington Waterfront Activities Center,** on the university campus behind Husky Stadium (tel. 543-9433), is open to the public and rents canoes for only $3.50 per hour. Rentals are available from February to October, daily from 10am to about an hour before sunset.

SAILBOARDING   Sailboarding is one of Seattle's favorite sports. The local waters are ideal for learning—the winds are light and the water is flat. **Bavarian Surf/Seattle,** 711 NE Northlake Way (tel. 545-WIND), will rent you a board and give you lessons if you need them. Rates are $35 per day for a board. Private lessons are $35 per hour, and a 7-hour group class is $95. The shop is open Monday through Friday from 10am to 6pm and on Saturday from 10am to 5pm.

SAILING   The **Center for Wooden Boats,** 1010 Valley St. (tel. 382-BOAT), has its museum and boat-rental shop at Waterway 4 at the south end of Lake Union. Dedicated to the preservation of historic wooden boats, the center is unique in that many exhibits can be rented and taken out on Lake Union. There are rowboats and large and small sailboats. Rates range from $6 to $15 per hour.

Individual sailing instruction is also available. There is a wooden-boat show held here every year on the Fourth of July. From June 1 to Labor Day, the center is open daily from 11am to 7pm; the rest of the year, Wednesday through Monday from noon to 6pm.

SKIING One of the reasons Seattleites put up with long, wet winters is because they can go skiing within an hour of the city. With many slopes set up for night skiing, it's possible to leave work and be on the slopes before dinner, ski for several hours, and be home in time to get a good night's rest. The ski season in the Seattle area generally runs from mid-November to the end of April.

Equipment can be rented at the ski areas listed below, and at **REI,** 1525 11th Ave. (tel. 323-8333).

Downhill Skiing The largest ski area at Snoqualmie Pass, which is less than 50 miles east of Seattle on I-90, is actually made up of four separate ski areas. **Alpental, Ski Acres, Snoqualmie,** and **Hyak,** 7900 SE 28th St., Suite 200, Mercer Island, WA 98040 (tel. 206/232-8182 or 236-1600 for snow conditions), are all part of a single gigantic complex with more than 65 runs, 24 chair lifts, and **11** rope tows. There are also plenty of cross-country ski trails here. You can rent both cross-country and downhill equipment, and can take lessons at the ski school. Daily lift rates are $10–$17 Monday through Friday, $25 on weekends and holidays. Lift rates for night skiing (5pm to closing) are $10–$15.

Alpental and Snoqualmie are open Tuesday through Friday from 9:30am to 10:30pm, on Saturday from 9am to 10:30pm, and on Sunday from 9am to 6pm (at Alpental) or 9pm (at Snoqualmie). Ski Acres is open Monday and Wednesday through Friday from 9:30am to 10:30pm, on Saturday from 9am to 10:30pm, and on Sunday from 9am to 9pm. Hyak is open December 26 through March 14, Friday from 5 to 10:30pm, Saturday from 9am to 10:30pm, and Sunday from 9am to 6pm.

Crystal Mountain Resort, 1 Crystal Mountain Blvd., Crystal Mountain, WA 98022 (tel. 206/663-2265 or 634-3771 for snow conditions), is a little bit farther away (76 miles southeast of Seattle on Washington Hwy. 410), but the facilities are better than those at Snoqualmie Pass: 10 chair lifts, 43 runs, and night skiing on the weekends. There are rentals, a ski school, a repair shop, and child-care services. The Crystal Mountain Express bus leaves daily at 6:45am from the Seattle Sheraton. Round-trip fares are $19 for adults and $14 for children Monday through Friday, $21 for adults and $16 for children on Saturday and Sunday.

Monday and Tuesday lift tickets are $12; Wednesday through Friday lift tickets are $16; Saturday and Sunday lift tickets are $28 for adults, $19 for children ages 6 to 12, and $20 for senior citizens ages 65 to 69 (free for anyone over 70). Children under age five are $5 anytime. Lower lift ticket prices are available for late afternoon, twilight, night skiing, and beginners lifts. Lift hours are 9am to 4:30pm Monday through Friday, and 8:30am to 10pm on Saturday and Sunday.

Cross-Country Skiing The Seattle area abounds in cross-country skiing opportunities. In the Snoqualmie Pass area, less than 50 miles east of Seattle on I-90, **Ski Acres & Hyak Cross-Country Center,** 7900 SE 28th St., Suite 200, Mercer Island, WA 98040 (tel. 206/434-6646), offers rentals, instruction, and many miles of groomed trails. Ski Acres even has lighted trails for night skiing. The trail fee runs $5 to $9.

If you happen to be in town on a rare clear winter day, head for **Hurricane Ridge** in Olympic National Park, which has its head-quarters at 600 E. Park Ave., Port Angeles, WA 98362 (tel. 206/452-0330). The views of the Olympic Mountains from here are spectacular. Rental equipment is available, but the area is open only on weekends and holidays.

When renting skis, be sure to get a **Sno-Park permit.** These are required in most cleared parking areas near ski trails. They are available at ski shops.

TENNIS   Seattle Parks and Recreation operates dozens of outdoor tennis courts all over the city. The most convenient are at **Volunteer Park,** 15th Ave. East and East Prospect St., and at **Lower Wood-land Park,** West Green Lake Way North. If it happens to be raining and you had your heart set on playing tennis, there are indoor public courts at the **Seattle Tennis Center,** 2000 Martin Luther King Jr. Way S. (tel. 684-4764). Rates here are $11.50 for singles and $15 for doubles for 1¼ hours.

WHITE-WATER RAFTING   Seattle is surrounded by water, but it's flat water. For more thrilling boating experiences you have to head to the Olympic Mountains or Cascade Range. **Olympic Raft and Guide Service,** 464 U.S. 101 W., Port Angeles, WA 98362 (tel. 206/457-7011), offers trips down the Olympic Peninsula's Elwha, Hoh, and Queets rivers. Rates range from $30 to $75 per person. Another outfit that runs trips down rivers all over the state is **Northern Wilderness River Riders,** 23312 77th Ave. SE, Woodinville, WA 98072 (tel. 206/485-RAFT). They charge $50–$75 for a 4-hour trip.

CHAPTER 7

STROLLING AROUND SEATTLE

- **WALKING TOUR—PIONEER SQUARE AREA**

Downtown Seattle is easy to explore on foot. Foremost, of course, are the Pike Place Market and the waterfront, which together form the busiest neighborhood in Seattle. You really don't need a guided tour of this area: Just follow the hoards of people. The historic Pioneer Place neighborhood is a different story. This area has interesting buildings and history that you will probably not want to miss. *Note:* For additional information on some stops, see Chapter 6.

WALKING TOUR — PIONEER SQUARE AREA

Start: Pioneer Place at the corner of Yesler Way and First Avenue.
Finish: Washington Street Public Boat Landing.
Time: Approximately two hours, not including shopping, dining, and museum and other stops.
Best Times: Weekdays, when Pioneer Square and the Seattle Underground Tour are not so crowded.
Worst Times: Weekends, when the area is very crowded.

Seattle is a relatively young city, though founded in 1851, and the buildings surrounding Pioneer Square were erected after the fire of 1889. Today this small section is all that remains of old Seattle. You will probably notice a uniformity of architectural style. This is because many of the buildings were designed by one architect, Elmer Fisher.

Start your tour of this historic neighborhood at the corner of Yesler Way and First Avenue on:

1. **Pioneer Place,** the triangular park in the middle of Pioneer Square. The totem pole here is a replacement of one that burned in 1938. The original pole had been stolen from a Tlingit village up the coast in 1890. Legend has it that after the pole burned the city fathers sent a check for $5,000 requesting a new totem pole. The Tlingit response was, "Thanks for paying for the first one. Send another $5,000 for a replacement." The cast-iron pergola in the park was erected in 1905 as a shelter for a large underground lavatory. Facing the square is the:
2. **Pioneer Building,** one of the architectural standouts of this neighborhood. It houses an antiques mall and several bars, including:
3. **Doc Maynard's** (610 First Avenue), a nightclub featuring live

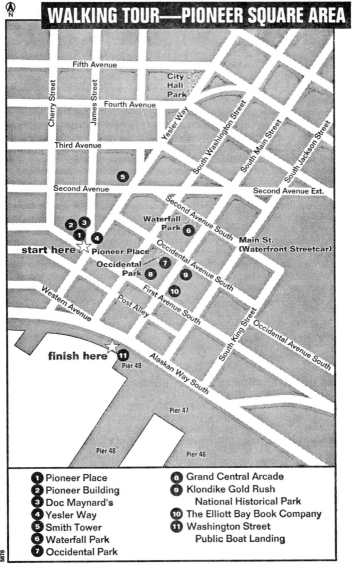

WALKING TOUR—PIONEER SQUARE AREA

Fifth Avenue
City Hall Park
Fourth Avenue
Cherry Street
James Street
Yesler Way
Third Avenue
South Washington Street
South Main Street
South Jackson Street
5
Second Avenue
Second Avenue Ext.
2 **3**
1 **4**
Waterfall Park
Second Avenue South
6
start here Pioneer Place
Main St. (Waterfront Streetcar)
Occidental Avenue South
Occidental Park
7
8 **9**
First Avenue South
10
Western Avenue
Post Alley
South King Street
Occidental Avenue South
finish here **11**
Pier 49
Alaskan Way South
Pier 47
Pier 48
Pier 46

1 Pioneer Place		**8** Grand Central Arcade	
2 Pioneer Building		**9** Klondike Gold Rush	
3 Doc Maynard's		National Historical Park	
4 Yesler Way		**10** The Elliott Bay Book Company	
5 Smith Tower		**11** Washington Street	
6 Waterfall Park		Public Boat Landing	
7 Occidental Park			

rock bands, which is also the starting point of the Seattle Underground Tour, which takes a look at the Pioneer Square area from beneath the sidewalks. Forming the southside of Pioneer Square is:

4. Yesler Way, the original Skid Row. In Seattle's early years, logs were skidded down this road to a lumber mill on the waterfront, and the road came to be known as Skid Road. These days it's trying hard to live down its reputation, but there are still quite a few people down on their luck here.

REFUELING STOP   Across Yesler Way from the pergola is **Merchants Café** (109 Yesler Way), the oldest restaurant in Seattle. If it happens to be time for lunch or dinner, this makes a good place to stop. Meals are moderately priced and well prepared.

Glance up Yesler Way past the triangular parking deck and you'll see:

5. Smith Tower, which was the tallest building west of the Mississippi for a long time. There's a great view of the city from an observatory near the top. This 1914 building is worth a visit just to view the ornate lobby and elevator doors.

Walk down Second Avenue (take the right fork, not Second Avenue Extension) to Main Street and you'll find the shady little:

6. Waterfall Park, with a roaring waterfall that looks as if it had been transported here straight from the Cascade Range. The park was built by United Parcel Service (UPS) and makes a wonderful place for a rest or a picnic lunch. Two more blocks down Main Street toward the water is cobblestoned:

7. Occidental Park, with four totem poles carved by a Northwestern artist. This shady park serves as a gathering spot for homeless people. On the west side of the park is the:

8. Grand Central Arcade, a shopping and dining center created from a restored brick building. Inside, you can watch craftspeople at work in their studios. Across Main Street from Occidental Park is a unit of:

9. Klondike Gold Rush National Historical Park (117 S. Main St.). The small museum is dedicated to the history of the 1897–98 Klondike gold rush, which helped Seattle grow from an obscure town into a booming metropolis. A couple of doors toward the water from this museum is:

10. The Elliott Bay Book Company, on the corner of Main Street and First Avenue. This is one of Seattle's most popular bookstores and has an extensive selection of books on Seattle and the Northwest. Continue down Main Street to the water and turn right. In one block you will come to the:

11. Washington Street Public Boat Landing. This iron openair building was erected in 1920 and today serves as a public dock where people can tie up their boats while they are in Seattle. As recently as 100 years ago, this was a mud flat, but dredging deepened the bay.

SEATTLE SHOPPING

Seattle is a Northwest shopping mecca, and you too are welcome to join the pilgrims as they wander from grand old department stores to tiny specialty shops in search of bargains, great values, one-of-a-kind purchases, and memorable shopping experiences. Whether shopping is your passion or merely an activity in which you occasionally indulge, you should not miss Pike Place Market. Once the city's main produce market, this sprawling building is today filled with hundreds of unusual shops, including quite a few produce vendors' stalls. Just west of Pike Place Market is the Seattle waterfront, where you'll find numerous gift and souvenir shops.

1. THE SHOPPING SCENE

The heart of Seattle's shopping district is the corner of Pine Street and Westlake Avenue. Within one block of this intersection are three major department stores and a shopping mall. These stores include **Nordstrom,** which has gained a name as one of the best department stores in the country; the **Bon Marché,** which is known simply as the **"Bon"** here in Seattle; and **I. Magnin,** which is smaller than the other two but still offers a wide selection.

If you're young at heart and possess a very personal idea of style, head over to Broadway on Capitol Hill to do your shopping. Pioneer Square, Seattle's historic district, is filled with art galleries, antiques shops, and other unusual stores.

Hours Shops in Seattle are generally open Monday through Saturday from 9 or 10am to 5 or 6pm, with shorter hours on Sunday. The major department stores usually stay open later on Friday evenings, and many shopping malls stay open until 9pm Monday through Saturday.

2. SHOPPING A TO Z

ANTIQUES

The three shops listed here are located in Seattle, but for an even larger selection of antiques, head north of Seattle to the town of **Snohomish** (near Everett)—where you'll find one of the largest

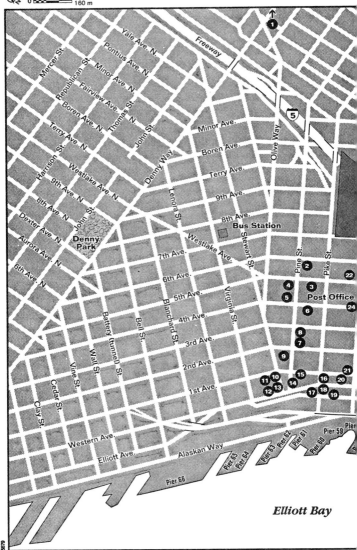

concentrations of antiques dealers in the Northwest and more than 150 shops to keep antiques hunters happy.

HONEYCHURCH ANTIQUES, 1008 James St. Tel. 622-1225.

For high-quality Asian antiques, including Japanese wood-block prints, textiles, furniture, and ivory and wood carvings, few Seattle antiques stores can approach Honeychurch Antiques. Regular special exhibits give this shop the feel of a tiny museum.

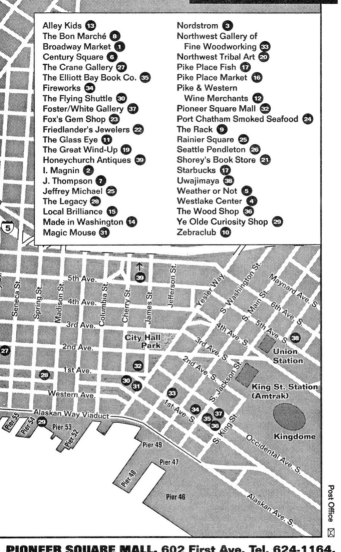

SEATTLE SHOPPING

Alley Kids **13**
The Bon Marché **8**
Broadway Market **1**
Century Square **6**
The Crane Gallery **27**
The Elliott Bay Book Co. **35**
Fireworks **34**
The Flying Shuttle **30**
Foster/White Gallery **37**
Fox's Gem Shop **23**
Friedlander's Jewelers **22**
The Glass Eye **11**
The Great Wind-Up **19**
Honeychurch Antiques **39**
I. Magnin **2**
J. Thompson **7**
Jeffrey Michael **25**
The Legacy **28**
Local Brilliance **15**
Made in Washington **14**
Magic Mouse **31**

Nordstrom **3**
Northwest Gallery of
  Fine Woodworking **33**
Northwest Tribal Art **20**
Pike Place Fish **17**
Pike Place Market **16**
Pike & Western
  Wine Merchants **12**
Pioneer Square Mall **32**
Port Chatham Smoked Seafood **24**
The Rack **9**
Rainier Square **25**
Seattle Pendleton **26**
Shorey's Book Store **21**
Starbucks **17**
Uwajimaya **38**
Weather or Not **5**
Westlake Center **4**
The Wood Shop **36**
Ye Olde Curiosity Shop **29**
Zebraclub **10**

PIONEER SQUARE MALL, 602 First Ave. Tel. 624-1164.
   This underground antiques mall is in the heart of Pioneer Square
and contains 80 shops selling all manner of antiques and collectibles.

THE CRANE GALLERY, 1203-B Second Ave. Tel. 622-7185.
   Chinese, Japanese, and Korean antiquities are the focus of this
shop, which prides itself on selling only the best pieces. Imperial
Chinese porcelains, bronze statues of Buddhist deities, rosewood

furniture, Japanese ceramics, netsukes, snuff bottles, and Chinese archaeological artifacts are just some of the quality antiques you will find here. Some Southeast Asian and Indian objects are also available.

ART GALLERIES

Pioneer Square also has Seattle's greatest concentration of art galleries. Wander around south of Yesler Way and you are likely to stumble upon a gallery showing the very latest contemporary art from the Northwest. There are also many antiques stores and galleries selling Native American art in the Pioneer Square area.

FOSTER/WHITE GALLERY, 311½ Occidental Ave. S. Tel. 622-2833.

Seattle's largest fine-arts dealer represents the foremost contemporary artists of the Northwest, including artists from the Pilchuck School of Glass, renowned for its creative glass sculpture.

There is another Foster/White Gallery in Kirkland at 126 Central Way (tel. 822-2305).

NORTHWEST TRIBAL ART, 1417 First Ave. Tel. 467-9330.

Located next to Pike Place Market, this is another of Seattle's galleries selling Northwest Coast Native American and U.S. Eskimo art. Traditional and contemporary wood carvings, masks, fossilized ivory carvings, soapstone carvings, scrimshaw, jewelry, drums, and even totem poles are available.

THE GLASS EYE, 1902 Post Alley, Pike Place Market. Tel. 441-3221.

The Glass Eye is one of Seattle's oldest art-glass galleries, specializing in glass made from Mount St. Helens ash. These hand-blown pieces all contain ash from the volcano's 1980 eruption.

THE LEGACY, 1003 First Ave. Tel. 624-6350.

Located in the same building as the prestigious Alexis Hotel, The Legacy is Seattle's oldest and finest gallery of contemporary and historic Native American Indian, U.S. Eskimo, and Canadian Inuit art. You'll find a large selection of masks by Northwest Coast Indians, as well as boxes, bowls, baskets, ivory and stone carvings, jewelry, prints, and books. Craftsmanship is of the highest quality. For the serious collector.

BOOKS

ELLIOTT BAY BOOK COMPANY, 101 S. Main St. Tel. 624-6600.

With heavy wooden fixtures, balconies, and a staircase descending to the deli/café in the basement, this could very well be the most aesthetically pleasing bookstore in the Northwest. They have an excellent selection of books on Seattle and the Northwest, so if you want to learn more or are planning further excursions around the region, stop by. It's located in the Pioneer Square neighborhood.

SHOREY'S BOOK STORE, 1411 First Ave. Tel. 624-0221.

In business since 1890, Shorey's will be happy to find you books from the year they opened (or any other year for that matter). Rare, antiquarian, and out-of-print books are their specialty. With more than a million items in stock, Shorey's is sure to have that obscure tome you've been seeking for years. If they don't have it, they'll search the world to find it for you. The store's motto is "The oldest, the biggest, the best!"

CRAFTS

The Northwest is a leading center for craftspeople, and the place to see what they are creating is Pike Place Market. Although there are quite a few permanent shops within the market that sell local crafts, you can meet the artisans themselves on weekends when they set up tables on the main floor.

FIREWORKS, 210 First Ave. S. Tel. 682-8707.

Playful, outrageous, bizarre, beautiful—these are just some of the terms that can be used to describe the eclectic collection of Northwest crafts on sale at this Pioneer Square–area gallery. A table with place setting and food painted onto its top, cosmic clocks, wildly creative jewelry, and children's furniture painted with fun designs are some of the fine and unusual items you'll find here. A second store is at Westlake Center, 400 Pine St. (tel. 682-6462).

NORTHWEST GALLERY OF FINE WOODWORKING, 202 First Ave. Tel. 625-0542.

This store is a showcase for some of the most amazing woodworking you'll ever see. Be sure to stroll through here while in the Pioneer Square area. The warm hues of the exotic woods are soothing and the designs are beautiful. Furniture, boxes, sculptures, vases, bowls, and much more are created by more than 35 Northwest artisans. A second shop is at 317 NW Gilman Blvd., Issaquah, WA (tel. 206/391-4221).

DEPARTMENT STORES

I. MAGNIN, 601 Pine St. Tel. 682-6111.

Though smaller than the other downtown department stores, I. Magnin provides the same excellent service and a surprisingly wide selection of merchandise.

NORDSTROM, 1501 Fifth Ave. Tel. 628-2111.

This is my pick for best department store in Seattle. Known for personal service, Nordstrom stores are rapidly gaining a reputation as one of the premier department stores in the United States. The company originated here in Seattle, and its customers are devotedly loyal. Whether it's your first visit or your 50th, the knowledgeable staff will help you in any way they can. Prices are comparable to those at other department stores, but you also get the best service available. There are very popular sales in June, July, and November (for women) and in January and June (for men).

THE BON MARCHÉ, Third Ave. and Pine St. Tel. 344-2121.

Seattle's only full-line department store, the Bon offers nine floors of merchandise. You'll find nearly anything you could possibly want at this store.

DISCOUNT STORES

J. THOMPSON, 205 Pine St. Tel. 623-5780.

This store sells designer women's clothing at 30 to 70% off retail. Styles are rather conservative.

THE RACK, 1601 Second Ave. Tel. 448-8522.

Discounts similar to those at J. Thompson are available at The Rack, which sells clearance items from Nordstrom.

FASHION

SEATTLE PENDLETON, 1313 Fourth Ave. Tel. 682-4430.

For Northwesterners, and many other people across the nation, Pendleton is and always will be *the* name in classic wool fashions. This store features tartan plaids and Indian-pattern separates, accessories, and blankets. Other Pendleton stores are at Bellevue Square and Tacoma Mall.

WEATHER OR NOT, Westlake Center, 400 Pine St. Tel. 682-3797.

Seattle's inclement weather is legendary, and so it comes as no surprise that there is a store here devoted exclusively to weathering this climate. Weather Or Not sells everything from umbrellas and raincoats to underwater paper, waterproof matches, and floating briefcases.

CHILDREN'S FASHION

ALLEY KIDS, 1904 Post Alley. Tel. 728-0609.

Tucked away on Post Alley, between Pike Place and First Avenue, Alley Kids sells both locally designed and imported children's clothing. If you don't mind spending a bundle on clothes that will be outgrown in a few months, you'll love the selection here.

MEN'S FASHION

JEFFREY MICHAEL, 1318 Fourth Ave. (in Rainier Sq.). Tel. 625-9891.

With five floors of top men's fashions, Jeffrey Michael is Seattle's leading menswear store. Excellent service and reasonable prices.

ZEBRACLUB, 1901 First Ave. Tel. 448-7452.

If you're young and hip and believe that clothes shopping should be an audiovisual experience, make the scene at Zebraclub, where rock videos playing on overhead monitors set the shopping tempo. If you need to get wired beforehand, grab a double espresso from the espresso cart out front. Clothing is casual.

WOMEN'S FASHION

THE FLYING SHUTTLE, 607 First Ave. Tel. 343-9762.

Fashion becomes art and art becomes fashion at this chic boutique-cum-gallery on Pioneer Square. Handwoven fabrics and hand-painted silks are the specialties here, but of course such unique fashions require equally unique body decorations in the form of exquisite jewelry creations. Designers and artists from the Northwest and the rest of the nation find an outlet for their creativity at the Flying Shuttle.

LOCAL BRILLIANCE, 1535 First Ave. Tel. 343-5864.

If you want to return from your trip to Seattle wearing a dress you know no one else at the office will have ever seen before, visit Local

Brilliance. The shop carries a wide selection of fashions by the Northwest's best fashion designers.

FOOD

COFFEE

STARBUCKS, Pike Place Market. Tel. 448-8762.

Seattle has developed a reputation as a city of coffeeholics, and Starbucks is probably the reason why. This company has coffeehouses all over town, but this is probably the most convenient if you are just visiting Seattle. With some 36 types of coffee available by the cup or by the pound, you can do a bit of taste testing before making a decision.

SEAFOOD

After tasting the bounty of seafood available in Seattle, it's almost impossible to do without. Any of the seafood vendors in Pike Place Market will pack your fresh salmon or Dungeness crab in an airline-approved container that will keep it fresh for up to 48 hours.

PIKE PLACE FISH, 86 Pike Place, Pike Place Market. Tel. 682-7181.

Located just behind Rachel, the life-sized bronze pig, this fishmonger is famous for flying fish. Pick out a big silvery salmon, ask them to filet it, and watch the show. The floor salesman, who usually keeps up a loud sales patter, calls out to the folks behind the counter that a fish is on the way, and the next thing you know, your salmon is flying over the counter and in moments is fileted and wrapped. They'll also deliver your packaged order to your hotel, ready to carry onto your plane. Another Pike Place Fish is at Crossroads Mall in Bellevue (tel. 644-7402).

PORT CHATHAM SMOKED SEAFOOD, 1306 Fourth Ave., Rainier Sq. Tel. 623-4645.

Northwest Coast Native Americans relied heavily on salmon for sustenance; to preserve the fish for times of the year when the fish weren't running, they used alder-wood smoke. This tradition is still carried on today to produce one of the Northwest's most delicious food products. This store sells smoked sockeye, king salmon, rainbow trout, black cod, and oysters—all of which will keep without refrigeration until the package is opened.

GIFTS/SOUVENIRS

Pike Place Market is the Grand Central Terminal of Seattle souvenirs, with stiff competition from Seattle Center and Pioneer Square.

MADE IN WASHINGTON, Pike Place Market (Post Alley at Pine St.). Tel. 467-0788.

Washington takes pride in what it produces, whether it's salmon, wine, or Northwest Native American masks. You'll find a selection of Washington State products in this shop, which is an excellent place to pick up gifts for all those who didn't get to come with you on your visit to Seattle. Other Made in Washington locations include Westlake

Center (tel. 623-9753); Bellevue Square, Bellevue, WA (tel. 454-6907); Gilman Village (tel. 392-4819); and Northgate (tel. 361-8252).

JEWELRY

FOX'S GEM SHOP, 1341 Fifth Ave. Tel. 623-2528.
This is Seattle's premier jeweler. Among other elegant lines, they feature the Tiffany Collection.

FRIEDLANDER'S JEWELERS, 1400 Fifth Ave. Tel. 223-7474.
This company has been doing business in Seattle since before the great fire of 1889 and stocks a wide selection of jewelry, watches, and fine crystal.

MALLS/SHOPPING CENTERS

BROADWAY MARKET, 401 Broadway E. Tel. 322-1610.
A trendy mall located in the stylish Capitol Hill neighborhood, the Broadway Market houses numerous small shops and restaurants with reasonable prices.

CENTURY SQUARE, Fourth Ave. and Pike St.
More fine stores are in this upscale mall a block from Westlake Center.

RAINIER SQUARE, 1326 Fifth Ave.
Only two blocks away from Westlake Center, Rainier Square is filled with about 60 upscale shops and restaurants. Built on the bottom floors of several skyscrapers, Rainier Square mall is a veritable maze.

WESTLAKE CENTER, 400 Pine St. Tel. 467-1600.
This covered shopping mall is in the heart of the downtown shopping district and includes some 80 specialty shops. The monorail terminal is on the second floor of the mall.

MARKETS

PIKE PLACE MARKET, Pike St. and First Ave. Tel. 682-7453.
Pike Place Market is one of Seattle's most famous landmarks and tourist attractions. Not only are there produce vendors, fishmongers, and butchers, but also artists, craftspeople, and performers. A trip here can easily be an all-day affair. Hundreds of shops are tucked away in hidden nooks and crannies on the seemingly endless levels. Many of Seattle's best restaurants are located in or near this megamarket.

UWAJIMAYA, 519 Sixth Ave. S. Tel. 624-6248.
Typically, your local neighborhood supermarket has a section of Chinese cooking ingredients; it's probably about 10 feet long, with half that space taken up by various brands of soy sauce. Now imagine your local supermarket with nothing *but* Asian foods, housewares, produce, and toys. That's Uwajimaya, Seattle's Asian supermarket in the heart of the International District.

TOYS

MAGIC MOUSE, 603 First Ave. Tel. 682-3229.

Adults and children alike have a hard time pulling themselves away from this, the most fun toy store in Seattle. It is conveniently located on Pioneer Square and specializes in European toys.

THE GREAT WIND-UP, Pike Place Market. Tel. 621-9370.

You guessed it—they sell windup toys (and battery-operated toys too). 1950s and 60s nostalgia toys and candies also fill the store.

THE WOOD SHOP, 320 First Ave. S. Tel. 624-1763.

Just two blocks away is another Seattle favorite that sells wooden toys and puppets. This place is worth a look even if you're not in the market for toys.

WINE

The Northwest is rapidly becoming known as a producer of fine wine. The relatively dry summer with warm days and cool nights provides a perfect climate for growing grapes. After you have sampled Washington or Oregon vintages, you might want to take a few bottles home.

PIKE & WESTERN WINE MERCHANTS, Pike Place Market. Tel. 441-1307.

Visit this shop for an excellent selection of Northwest and French wine. The extremely knowledgeable staff will be happy to send you home with the very best wine available in Seattle.

SEATTLE NIGHTS

Though Seattleites spend much of their free time enjoying the natural surroundings, they have not overlooked the more cultured evening pursuits. Theater, opera, and ballet flourish here, and music lovers will find a plethora of classical, jazz, and rock offerings. If you are a fan of chamber music, you're in good company in Seattle. Much of the evening entertainment is clustered in the Seattle Center or Pioneer Square area, which makes a night out on the town surprisingly easy. To make things even easier, you can buy half-price tickets at **Ticket/Ticket,** which has two sales booths. The Pike Place Market location, First Avenue and Pike Street (tel. 324-2744), is the more convenient location if you are staying downtown. This booth is open Tuesday through Sunday from noon to 6pm. The other booth is on the second floor of the Broadway Market, 401 Broadway E. (same telephone number). It's open Tuesday through Sunday from 10am to 7pm. The booths offer half-price day-of-show tickets only and levy a service charge of 50¢ to $3 depending on the ticket price, but you still save lots of money. If you want to pay full price with your credit card, call **Ticketmaster Northwest** (tel. 628-0888), open Monday through Saturday from 8am to 10pm and on Sunday from 10am to 6pm.

To find out what's going on when you are in town, pick up a copy of **Seattle Weekly** (75¢), which is Seattle's weekly arts-and-entertainment newspaper. You'll find it in bookstores, convenience stores, grocery stores, and newsstands. The Friday **Seattle Times** also has a guide, "Tempo," to the week's arts and entertainment offerings. A free weekly listing is **Seattle Guide,** which you can pick up at the Seattle–King County Convention & Visitors Bureau information center, Washington State Convention & Trade Center, 800 Convention Place, Level 1 Galleria, at Eighth Avenue and Pike Street (tel. 461-5840).

1. THE PERFORMING ARTS

The main venues for the performing arts in Seattle are clustered in the Seattle Center. Here, in the shadow of the Space Needle, you'll find the Opera House, Bagley Wright Theater, Intiman Playhouse, Center House Theatre, Pacific Arts Center, Seattle Center Coliseum, and Memorial Stadium.

MAJOR CONCERT & PERFORMANCE HALLS

A Contemporary Theater. Tel. 285-5110.
Bagley Wright Theater. Tel. 443-2222.
Broadway Performance Hall. Tel. 323-2623.
Empty Space Theatre. Tel. 547-7500 or 587-3737.
Intiman Playhouse. Tel. 626-0782.
Meany Theater. Tel. 543-4880.
New City Theatre and Art Center. Tel. 323-6800.
Paramount Theatre. Tel. 682-1414.
Seattle Opera House. Tel. 389-7676.
The 5th Avenue Theatre. Tel. 625-1900.

MAJOR PERFORMING ARTS COMPANIES

OPERA & CLASSICAL MUSIC

NORTHWEST CHAMBER ORCHESTRA, 411 University St. Tel. 343-0445.

Chamber music is very popular in Seattle, and the Northwest Chamber Orchestra presents some of the very finest. Active for more than 20 seasons now, it is a showcase for Northwest performers. The annual "Bach by Popular Demand" baroque music festival is the highlight of the season, which runs from September to April.

Prices: $15–$18; student and senior-citizen discounts.

SEATTLE INTERNATIONAL CHAMBER MUSIC FESTIVAL, Meany Theater, University of Washington. Tel. 233-0993.

For a week and half in late August, Seattle classical music lovers are treated to some of the world's finest chamber music at this festival. Until a few years ago Seattle hosted the Santa Fe Chamber Music Festival, but then it was decided the Emerald City deserved its own festival.

Prices: $20.

SEATTLE OPERA ASSOCIATION, Seattle Opera House, Fourth Ave. and Mercer St. Tel. 389-7676.

The Seattle Opera is an internationally recognized company best known for its productions of Wagner's four-opera *The Ring of the Nibelungen.* The company offers six productions during its season, which runs from July to May.

Prices: $28–$95.

SEATTLE SYMPHONY ORCHESTRA, Seattle Opera House, Fourth Ave. and Mercer St. Tel. 443-4747.

The Seattle Symphony Orchestra is conducted by Gerard Schwarz, who also conducts the New York Chamber Symphony and is music director of New Jersey's Waterloo Music Festival and New York City's Mostly Mozart Festival. The season here runs from September

to May, and performances are on Monday and Tuesday evenings. There are also family, pops concerts, and children's programs.
Prices: $9–$45.

THEATER

A CONTEMPORARY THEATER (ACT), 100 W. Roy St. Tel. 285-5110.

This theater offers slightly more adventurous productions than the other major theater companies in Seattle, although it is still not as avant-garde as some of the smaller companies. The season runs from May to December, when they close the year with a well-loved version of *A Christmas Carol.*
Prices: $12–$23.

EMPTY SPACE THEATRE, 3509 Fremont Ave. N. Tel. 547-7500 or 587-3737.

In the Pioneer Square area, this theater offers a six-play season that runs from October to June. If you enjoy the new and the unusual, the Empty Space will more than likely have something for you.
Prices: $10–$19.

INTIMAN THEATRE COMPANY, Intiman Playhouse, Seattle Center, 201 Mercer St. Tel. 626-0782.

This company has a very dedicated following in the Seattle area. The theater season runs from May through December. The theater is small, seating only 424 people, so you are always assured a good seat. Past seasons have included the world premiere of the Pulitzer Prize–winner *The Kentucky Cycle.* The original version of J. M. Barrie's *Peter Pan* is an annual holiday-season production.
Prices: $12–$24 for most tickets.

NEW CITY THEATRE AND ART CENTER, 1634 11th Ave. Tel. 323-6800.

Located in Capitol Hill, Seattle's hippest neighborhood, this is the city's most daring theater venue. As you would expect, the productions here are calculated to keep the local art crowd talking. You'll find everything from performance artists to plays by local playwrights, even a bit of cabaret now and then.
Prices: $3–$12.

SEATTLE REPERTORY THEATER, Bagley Wright Theater, Seattle Center. Tel. 443-2222.

The Rep season picks up where the Intiman leaves off, giving Seattle excellent year-round theater. The season is October to May, with six plays performed in the main 856-seat theater and three more in the intimate PONCHO theater, which seats only 142. The Rep has been around for more than a quarter century and is consistently outstanding. Productions range from classics to contemporary to Broadway musicals.
Prices: $12.50–$29.

THE 5TH AVENUE THEATRE, 1308 Fifth Ave. Tel. 625-1900.

First opened in 1926 as a vaudeville house, The 5th Avenue Theatre is a loose re-creation of the imperial throne room in Beijing's Forbidden City. When vaudeville lost popularity, this opulent setting was used as a movie theater. In 1980 a $2.6-million renovation was undertaken and the theater once again opened as a venue for live stage performances. Since then, major touring companies—with such stars as Katharine Hepburn, Richard Harris, and Lauren Bacall—have played The 5th Avenue. In addition to national touring shows, the theater now has its own resident musical-theater company. Don't pass up an opportunity to attend a show at Seattle's most beautiful theater.

Prices: $20–$40.

DANCE

ON THE BOARDS, Washington Hall Performance Gallery, 153 14th Ave. Tel. 325-7901.

This is Seattle's premier modern-dance company, satisfying the city's year-round craving for innovative dance. The Northwest New Works Festival, which is held every spring, is one of the season's highlights. In addition to performances by the company, there are special appearances by internationally known artists.

Prices: $5–$16.

PACIFIC NORTHWEST BALLET, Seattle Opera House, Fourth Ave. and Mercer St. Tel. 628-0888.

If you happen to be in Seattle in December, try to get a ticket to this company's performance of *The Nutcracker*. In addition to outstanding dancing, you'll enjoy sets and costumes by children's book author Maurice Sendak. During the rest of the season, which runs from October to May, the company presents a wide range of classics and world premieres, with an emphasis on the choreography of George Balanchine.

Prices: $10–$52.

2. THE CLUB & MUSIC SCENE

If you have the urge to do a bit of nightclubbing and barhopping while in Seattle, there's no better place to start than in Pioneer Square. Good times are guaranteed whether you want to laugh it up at a comedy club, hang out in a good old-fashioned bar, or do a little dancing.

CABARET

CABARET DE PARIS, Crepe de Paris Restaurant, Rainier Sq., 1305 Fourth Ave., Suite 1015. Tel. 623-4111.

Crepe de Paris is one of Seattle's oldest French restaurants, and though it fries up a mean crêpe, it is better known these days as the city's favorite cabaret. Thursday through Saturday nights, talented performers entertain with humor, music, and dance. The cabaret's annual performance of *Waiter, There's a Slug in My Latte* has become a perennial favorite and usually returns with the slug-breeding, heavy rains of April.

Admission: $12 plus dinner off the menu.

COMEDY CLUBS

COMEDY UNDERGROUND, 222 S. Main St. Tel. 622-4540.

What is it about the Seattle Underground that induces people to tell jokes? Remember all those horrendous ones you heard during the Seattle Underground Tour? Maybe it's all those sewer gases that affect people down here. Whatever the reason, this underground (literally) nightspot in the Pioneer Square area is dedicated to laughter. Local and nationally known comedians whiff their fair share of the laughing gases when they perform here.

Admission: $3–$7.50.

SEATTLE IMPROV, 1426 First Ave. Tel. 628-5000.

What's the difference between December and June in Seattle? Answer: June has only 30 days. If you're a fan of the Showtime Comedy Club Network, you'll probably see someone here who you've seen on TV. Not all the jokes are about the local weather, but you can bet there will be a few on any given night. The Seattle Improv also has a very good restaurant serving Northwest cuisine. Reservations are required for dinner.

Admission: Sun, Tues–Thurs $6; Fri–Sat $10. Two-drink minimum.

FOLK, COUNTRY & ROCK

For the past few years, Seattle bands have been making rock 'n' roll headlines with their distinctive "grunge" rock sound. By the time you reach town, the hype may have faded and the A&R men may have moved on to Portland or Pocatello. If the Seattle sound is still riding the crest of the wave, however, grab a copy of *Seattle Weekly* and check the club listings for where the hot new bands are appearing.

BACKSTAGE, 2208 Northwest Market St. Tel. 781-2805.

This is Seattle's top venue for contemporary music of all kinds and packs in the crowds most nights. The audience ranges from drinking age up to graying rock 'n' rollers. The music runs the gamut from Afro pop to zydeco. If you want to find out who's hot in the Northwest, check this place out.

Admission: $7–$14.

BALLARD FIREHOUSE, 5429 Russell St. Tel. 784-3516.

A similarly eclectic assortment of musical styles finds its way onto the bandstand of this converted firehouse in the old Scandinavian section of northwest Seattle. Now it's just the music that's hot, and that's the way they want to keep it. You might catch one of your jazz favorites here, or maybe someone who used to be famous but decided to make good music instead of selling out for big bucks. People having dinner here get the best tables.

Admission: $5–$12.

CENTRAL CAFE, 207 First Ave. Tel. 622-0209.

Seattle's only "second class tavern"—that's what the sign out front claims, and more than a few people wind up inside just to find out what a second-class tavern is really all about. The crowd is young and the music is rock and rhythm-and-blues. You can catch both local and out-of-town bands here. On weekends this is one of the clubs participating in the "joint cover" program: For $7 you can get into nine different clubs in the Pioneer Square area.

Admission: $4–$7.

DOC MAYNARD'S, 610 First Ave. Tel. 682-4649.

By day it's the starting point of the family-oriented Seattle Underground Tour, but by night it's one of Seattle's most popular clubs for live rock 'n' roll. This place attracts all types of rock-music lovers, and you'll be welcome as long as you like your music loud.

Admission: $6–$12.

KELLS, 1916 Post Alley, Pike Place Market. Tel. 728-1916.

 This friendly Irish pub has the look and feel of a casual Dublin pub. They pull a good Guinness stout and feature live traditional Irish music Wednesday through Saturday. This is also a restaurant serving traditional Irish meals, and there's even a patio dining area (something you aren't likely to find in a pub in Ireland, where it rains even more than in Seattle).

Admission: Fri–Sat only, $3.

JAZZ & BLUES

DIMITRIOU'S JAZZ ALLEY, 2033 Sixth Ave. Tel. 441-9729.

 This is *the* place for great jazz music in Seattle. Cool and sophisticated, Dimitriou's books only the very best performers and is reminiscent of New York jazz clubs.

Admission: $6.50–$12.50.

NEW ORLEANS CREOLE RESTAURANT, 114 First Ave. S. Tel. 622-2563.

If you like your food and your jazz hot, check out the New Orleans. There's live music seven nights a week. Tuesday is Cajun night, but the rest of the week you can hear Dixieland, R&B, jazz, and blues. This is one of the "joint cover" clubs (nine clubs for $7).

Admission: Weeknights free, weekends $7.

DANCE CLUBS/DISCOS

GOOEY'S, Seattle Sheraton, Sixth Ave. and Pike St. Tel. 621-9000.

Artsy high-tech styling and a multilevel dance floor make Gooey's a hit with the young and restless crowd. During happy hour there's a free appetizer buffet that features some surprisingly tasty and unusual dishes. The dance music goes on late into the night. The peculiar name is a reference to the amazing giant clam of the Northwest, which is spelled geoduck but pronounced "goo-ee-duck."

Admission: $3.

PIER 70 BAY CAFE, 2815 Alaskan Way. Tel. 728-7071.

Over on the waterfront is a cavernous place popular with Seattle's singles set. There's live Top 40 dance music nightly, and the restaurant has great views of Elliott Bay. However, the folks here are usually too busy checking each other out to notice the romantic parade of lights as the ferry leaves the harbor. Oh well. Let's dance.

Admission: $5.

GAY CLUBS

NEIGHBOURS, 1509 Broadway. Tel. 324-5358.

This has been the favorite disco of Capitol Hill's gay community for years, and recently word has gotten out to straights that it's a fun

dance club. Still, the clientele is primarily gay. Weekend buffets are extremely popular.
Admission: Free.

3. THE BAR SCENE

BREW PUBS

BIG TIME BREWERY AND ALEHOUSE, 4133 University Way NE. Tel. 545-4509.

Located in the University District and decorated to look like a turn-of-the-century tavern complete with 100-year-old back bar and wooden refrigerator, the Big Time serves up three to five of its own brews, which you can see being made on the premises.

TROLLEYMAN, 3400 Phinney Ave. N. Tel. 548-8000.

This is the taproom of the Redhook Ale Brewery, one of the Northwest's most celebrated microbreweries. It's located in a restored trolley barn on the Lake Washington Ship Canal. You can sample the ales brewed here, have a bite to eat, and even tour the brewery if you are interested.

SPECIALTY BARS

SPORTS BARS

FX MCRORY'S STEAK, CHOP, AND OYSTER HOUSE, 419 Occidental Ave. S. Tel. 623-4800.

Also very popular, FX McRory's is a glittery drinking-and-dining establishment with an old-fashioned saloon feel to it. However, the clientele is upscale, and you're likely to see members of the Seahawks or the SuperSonics at the bar. The original Leroy Neiman paintings on the walls lend class to this sports bar. You'll also find Seattle's largest selection of bourbon and microbrew beers and ales.

SNEAKERS, 567 Occidental Ave. S. Tel. 625-1340.

Located almost directly across the street from the Kingdome, Sneakers is a favorite of Seattle sports fans, especially before and after Seahawks games. The walls are covered with celebrity signatures and old sports photos; the day's sports pages are plastered on the restroom walls so you can keep current; and a TV broadcasting sports events is never out of view.

BANKER'S BARS

MCCORMICK & SCHMICK'S, 1103 First Ave. Tel. 623-5500.

If the mahogany paneling, sparkling cut glass, and waiters in bow ties don't convince you that you're drinking with money, a glance at the clientele will. Happy hour is very busy as brokers wind down with a few stiff drinks. If you long to rub shoulders with the movers and shakers of Seattle, this is the place for you.

MCCORMICK'S FISH HOUSE & BAR, 722 Fourth Ave. Tel. 682-3900.

This dining-and-drinking establishment provides the same atmosphere as McCormick's & Schmick's. Elbow your way up to the bar during after-work hours and you just might overhear a hot tip on the market. Be sure to look your best when you stop in here for a drink or two.

ATMOSPHERIC BARS

TLAQUEPAQUE, 1122 Post Alley. Tel. 467-8226.

★ There are rowdier bars in Seattle, but few have the atmosphere of this cavernous Mexican cantina. Strolling mariachi musicians, strumming for their lives and wailing at the tops of their lungs, keep the crowds of diners and drinkers happy. Overhead is a massive chandelier made from Mexican beer bottles. The bar used to be a warehouse, and still they need more space!

BILLIARD PARLOR

JILLIAN'S BILLIARD CLUB AND CAFE, 731 Westlake Ave. N. Tel. 223-0300.

There was a time when people who wore a suit and tie to work wouldn't dream of going into a pool hall after a hard day at the office, but not anymore. Jillian's has changed all that. The bar here is from the famous Algonquin Bar and fits in nicely with the view of the lake.

GAY BAR

THUMPERS, 1500 E. Madison St. Tel. 328-3800.

Perched high on Capitol Hill with an excellent view of downtown Seattle, Thumpers is a classy bar done up with lots of oak. The seats by the fireplace are perfect on a cold and rainy night. Great snacks to go with the drinks.

4. MORE ENTERTAINMENT

MOVIES

The **Seattle International Film Festival** has become quite an affair in recent years. It's held every May, with 150 films being screened during the festival. They are shown at **The Egyptian,** 801 E. Pine St. (tel. 323-4978), and the **Market Theater,** 1428 Post Alley (tel. 382-1171).

The **Market Theater,** mentioned above, shows foreign and independent films year-round. **Harvard Exit,** 807 E. Roy St. (tel. 323-8986), often shows films that can't find a screen elsewhere in the city. However, the most eclectic programming is to be found in the University District at **Grand Illusion,** 1403 NE 50th Ave. (tel. 523-3935), and **Neptune,** NE 45th Ave. and Brooklyn St. NE (tel. 633-5545), which is Seattle's repertory theater.

CHAPTER 10

EASY EXCURSIONS FROM SEATTLE

1. MOUNT RAINIER
2. MOUNT ST. HELENS
3. OLYMPIC PENINSULA
4. SAN JUAN ISLANDS

I strongly recommend that you make one or more of these trips so that you get a sense of what life is like in the Northwest. Seattleites are nearly inseparable from their natural surroundings—the forests, the mountains, and the waters— and spend as much time in them as they can. At least some part of each of the areas described below can be visited on long day trips. However, to circle the Olympic Peninsula, visit all the major San Juan Islands, or to fully explore the Cascade Range requires an overnight trip or longer. Regardless of how much time is available, be sure to at least sample the Northwest's natural beauty by visiting one of these areas.

1. MOUNT RAINIER

Weather forecasting for Seattle laymen is a simple matter: Either "the Mountain" is out and the weather is good, or it isn't (out or good). "The Mountain" is of course Mount Rainier, the 14,410-foot-tall dormant volcano that looms over Seattle on clear days. Mount Rainier may look as if it were on the edge of town, but it's actually 90 miles southeast of the city.

The mountain and some 235,400 acres surrounding it are part of Mount Rainier National Park, which was established in 1899 as the fifth U.S. national park. From downtown Seattle, the easiest route to the mountain is via I-5 south to exit 127. Then take Washington Hwy. 7 south, which in some 30 miles becomes Washington Hwy. 706. The route is well signposted.

WHAT TO SEE & DO

You'd be well advised to leave as early as possible, especially if you are heading to the mountain on a summer weekend. Traffic along the route and crowds at the park can be daunting. Before leaving, you might contact the park for information. Write or call Mount Rainier National Park, Tahoma Woods, Star Route, Ashford, WA 98304 (tel. 206/569-2211). Keep in mind that during the winter the four visitor centers in the park are only open on weekends.

On the way to the park on Washington Hwy. 7, you might want to stop in the town of **Elbe** to ride on the **Mount Rainier Scenic Railroad** (tel. 206/569-2588). The old steam trains pull vintage cars through lush forests and over old bridges, then wind up at Mineral

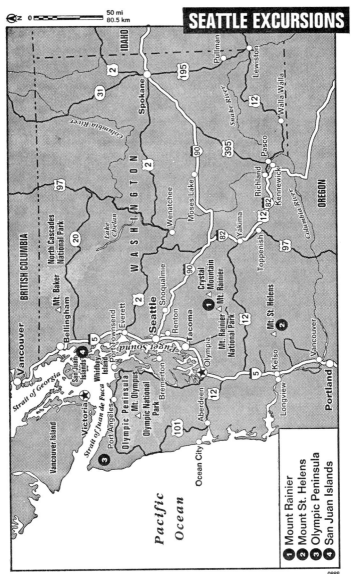

SEATTLE EXCURSIONS

① Mount Rainier
② Mount St. Helens
③ Olympic Peninsula
④ San Juan Islands

Lake. The trip covers 14 miles and takes an hour and a half. Fares are $6.95 for adults, $5.95 for senior citizens, $4.95 for ages 12 to 17, and $3.95 for children under age 12. The train operates daily from June 15 to Labor Day, with departures at 11am, 1:15pm, and 3:30pm. From Memorial Day to June 15 and from Labor Day to the end of September, the train operates on weekends only.

If you plan ahead, you can also ride the **Cascadian Dinner Train** from Morton (farther south on Hwy. 7) to Elbe. This 4-hour, 40-mile trip includes a prime rib dinner and costs $55 per person.

IMPRESSIONS

*There is a great deal in the remark of the discontented traveller:
'When you have seen a pine forest, a bluff, a river, and a lake,
you have seen all the scenery of western America. Sometimes
the pine is three hundred feet high, and sometimes the rock is,
and sometimes the lake is a hundred miles long. But it's all the
same don't you know. I'm getting sick of it.'*
—RUDYARD KIPLING

The dinner train operates on summer Sundays only and prepaid reservations are required.

Mount Rainier National Park admission is $5 per motor vehicle or $2 per person for pedestrians and bicyclists. Just past the main southwest entrance (Nisqually), you'll come to Longmire, site of the National Park Inn, Longmire Museum (exhibits on the park's natural and human history), a hiker information center that issues backcountry permits, and a ski-touring center where you can rent cross-country skis in winter. The road then continues climbing to Paradise (elevation 5,400 feet), the aptly named mountainside aerie that affords a breathtaking close-up view of the mountain. Paradise is the park's most popular destination, so expect crowds. During July and August the meadows here are ablaze with wildflowers. The circular Henry M. Jackson Memorial Visitor Center provides 360° panoramic views, and a short walk away is a spot from which you can look down on Nisqually Glacier. It's not unusual to find plenty of snow at Paradise as late as July. In 1972 the area set a world's record for snowfall in one year—93.5 feet!

In summer you can continue beyond Paradise to the Ohanapecosh Visitor Center, where you can walk through a forest of old-growth trees, some more than 1,000 years old. Continuing around the mountain, you'll reach the turnoff for Sunrise. At 6,400 feet, Sunrise is the highest spot accessible by car. A beautiful old log lodge serves as visitor center. From here you can see not only Mount Rainier, seemingly at arm's length, but also Mounts Baker and Adams.

If you want to avoid crowds and see a bit of dense forest or hike without crowds, head for the park's Carbon River entrance in the northwest corner. This is the least visited region of the park, because it only offers views to those willing to hike several miles uphill. Carbon River is formed by the lowest-elevation glacier in the contiguous 48 states.

WHERE TO STAY

Besides the three accommodations listed below, there are several **campgrounds** in Mount Rainier National Park.

MODERATE

**ALTA CRYSTAL RESORT, 68317 S.R. 410 E., Greenwater,
WA 98022. Tel. 206/663-2500.** 24 rms.
$ Rates: $69–$149 single to quad. AE, MC, V. **Parking:** Free.
Though this condominium resort, located north of the national park,

is most popular in winter when skiers flock to Crystal Mountain's slopes, there is also plenty to do in summer. Accommodations are in one-bedroom and loft chalets. The former sleep up to four people and the latter provide bed space for up to eight people. No matter what size condo you choose, you'll find a full kitchen and fireplace. The loft chalets include two bathrooms and skylights. The grounds are wooded and ski slopes are just minutes away. This is the closest lodging to the northeast park entrance and the Sunrise area.

Dining/Entertainment: The nearest restaurant is eight miles away at the Crystal Mountain ski area.

Facilities: Outdoor swimming pool, tennis courts, hiking trails, riding stables.

NATIONAL PARK INN, P.O. Box 108, Ashford, WA 98304. Tel. 206/569-2275. 25 rms (18 with private bath).
$ Rates: $60 single or double without bath; $84 single or double with bath; $110 single, double, or triple in two-room unit with bath. MC, V. **Parking:** Free.

Located in Longmire in the southwest corner of the park, this rustic lodge was opened in 1920 and fully renovated in 1990. With only 25 rooms and open all year, the National Park Inn makes a great little getaway or base for exploring Mount Rainier. The inn's front veranda has a view of the mountain, and in summer you can dine here. Inside, there's a guest lounge with a river-rock fireplace that's perfect for winter-night relaxing. Guest rooms vary in size, but come with rustic furniture, new carpeting, clock radios, and coffee makers. Because of the vintage of the hotel, several rooms have shared bathrooms. If you don't mind the inconvenience, these rooms are a great deal. Because this lodge is open in the winter, it is particularly popular with cross-country skiers.

Dining/Entertainment: The inn's restaurant has a limited menu that nevertheless manages to offer something for everyone. There's also a small bar.

Facilities: Gift shop, cross-country ski rentals adjacent, wheelchair accommodations, no-smoking rooms.

PARADISE INN, P.O. Box 108, Ashford, WA 98304. Tel. 206/569-2275. 129 rms (116 with private bath), 1 suite.
$ Rates: $64 single or double with shared bath; $90 single or double with bath; $116 single, double, or triple for a two-room unit with bath; $123 single, double, or triple suite. MC, V. **Parking:** Free. **Closed:** Early Oct–mid May.

Built in 1917 high on the flanks of Mount Rainier in an area aptly known as Paradise, this rustic lodge offers breathtaking views of the mountain and nearby Nisqually Glacier. Cedar-shake siding, huge exposed beams, cathedral ceilings, and a gigantic stone fireplace all add up to a quintessential mountain retreat. A warm, cozy atmosphere prevails. As at the National Park Inn, guest rooms vary in size and some have shared baths. Be sure to specify the type of room you'd like. Miles of trails and meadows spread out from the lodge making this the perfect spot for some relatively easy alpine exploring.

Dining/Entertainment: The inn's large dining room serves three meals a day. The legendary Sunday brunch, served from 11am to 2:30pm, costs $16.80.

Facilities: Gift shop, no-smoking rooms.

2. MOUNT ST. HELENS

For many visitors to the Northwest, a trip to see Mount St. Helens is far more important than a trip to Mount Rainier. Mount St. Helens, an active volcano southwest of Rainier, erupted on May 18, 1980, and attracted worldwide attention for many months. The devastation wrought by this eruption is as awesome a sight as the Grand Canyon and should not be missed. Before heading out to the mountain, you may want to stop by the Omnidome Film Experience (p. 85) on the waterfront to see the film about the eruption.

WHAT TO SEE & DO

Today the area surrounding the volcano is designated the **Mount St. Helens National Volcanic Monument.** There are numerous information centers and viewing sites, and it is even possible to climb to the top now, although only a few permits are handed out each day and reservations for weekends must be made far in advance. The main **visitors information center** is located at Silver Lake (tel. 206/274-6644), five miles east of I-5 (Exit 49) on Washington Hwy. 504. Included in the center's extensive exhibits are photos of the eruption and its effects on the region. The center is open daily from 9am to 6pm in summer and from 9am to 5pm daily in winter. Farther east on Hwy. 504 (at milepost 47), you'll come to the new Coldwater Ridge Visitor Center. This center offers programs and exhibits on the events leading up to and following the eruption. It's located only eight miles from the crater and offers truly spectacular views. Opening hours here are the same as at the main visitor information center.

For the best views of the blown-down forest or Spirit Lake, take U.S. 12 (Exit 68 of I-5). Head east to the town of Randle and then south on local Route 25. You can stop at **Woods Creek information center** for further information. This is my favorite approach to the volcano. The two-way road is only one lane wide (with turnouts), and you travel through mile after mile of tree trunks that were toppled by the force of the explosion. It's an amazing sight that will forever remind you of the power of nature.

For more information, contact **Mount St. Helens National Volcanic Monument,** 42218 NE Yale Bridge Rd., Amboy, WA 98601 (tel. 206/247-5473). For climbing permits, phone 206/247-5800.

3. OLYMPIC PENINSULA

On a clear day, the view west from the Seattle waterfront is almost as spectacular as the view of Mount Rainier to the east. The snow-capped Olympic Mountains shimmer in the sun on the far side of Puget Sound. All around them are lush green hills and mountains. This is the Olympic Peninsula, site of **Olympic National Park,** 600 E. Park Ave., Port Angeles, WA 98362 (tel. 206/452-4501). Of all the possible excursions from Seattle, in my opinion this is the most worthwhile. There are other mountains and islands, but nowhere else in the continental United States will you find such extensive rain forest. The 150 inches of rain that fall annually on the peninsula's **Hoh Valley** make Seattle's climate look dry. Between Bainbridge Island on the east side of the peninsula and the Hoh Valley on the west, there are spectacular mountain views, lakes, ocean beaches, museums, even a restored Victorian town full of restaurants and bed-and-breakfast inns.

If you have time only for a taste of the Olympic Peninsula, I suggest a visit to **Hurricane Ridge** to view the Olympic Mountains and a stop in **Port Townsend.** It will take you at least two days to make the trip to the Hoh Valley rain forest and back, but it's well worth it. I would happily give up a day in Seattle to make this trip.

Start by taking a **Washington State Ferry** to **Bainbridge Island.** For ferry information, phone 206/464-6400 or toll free 800/84-FERRY.

SUQUAMISH MUSEUM

Your first stop, heading north on Washington Hwy. 305, should be at the **Suquamish Museum,** located on Sandy Hook Road (tel. 206/598-3311), which is just after you cross Agate Pass Bridge between Bainbridge Island and the mainland on Washington Hwy. 305. The museum is dedicated to the Suquamish and Chief Sealth, from whom Seattle derived its name. In addition to exhibits covering Suquamish early history, there are canoe-carving and Native American art demonstrations. Nearby is the grave of Chief Sealth, the site of a Suquamish village and longhouse, and the Suquamish Fish Hatchery. The museum is open from Memorial Day to September, daily from 10am to 5pm; and October to May, Friday through Sunday from 11am to 4pm. Admission is $2.50 for adults, $2 for senior citizens, and $1 for children.

PORT TOWNSEND

North of Suquamish Museum, watch for the turnoff to Port Townsend. Around 1900 this town was an important port, but when the transcontinental railroad stopped in Seattle instead of here, the community lost much of its regional importance. Port Townsend's ornate Victorian homes, built by wealthy merchants, were ignored for years. In the past decade or so, however, the elaborate homes have been restored and the town is once again alive with activity, this time as a popular tourist destination. The downtown area is lined with turn-of-the-century brick buildings filled with interesting shops and restaurants. On a bluff above town are the Victorian homes for which

IMPRESSIONS

What can we do with the western coast, a coast of 3,000 miles, rockbound cheerless, uninviting, and not a harbour on it? What use have we for such a country? I will never vote one cent from the public treasury to place the Pacific Ocean one inch nearer Boston than it is now.
—DANIEL WEBSTER, QUOTED IN NANCY WILSON ROSS, *FARTHEST REACH,* 1944.

the town is now so famous. There are dozens of the ornately decorated and brightly painted houses looking out across the sound. Many are bed-and-breakfasts, and the best part of a visit to Port Townsend is the chance to stay in one of these old homes.

WHAT TO SEE & DO

Built in 1868, the **Rothschild House,** at the corner of Taylor and Jefferson streets, is open to the public. Although the house is filled with Victorian antiques, the exterior is quite plain looking compared with some of its neighbors. It's open April 1 to October 1, daily from 11am to 4pm; September to April, only on Saturday and Sunday from 11am to 4pm. Admission is $2 for adults, $1 for children. You can also tour the **Commanding Officer's Quarters** at nearby **Fort Worden State Park.** The house is open April to October, daily from 10am to 5pm.

For further information on Port Townsend, contact the **Port Townsend Chamber of Commerce,** 2437 E. Sims Way, Port Townsend, WA 98368 (tel. 206/385-2722).

WHERE TO STAY
Moderate

MANRESA CASTLE, Seventh and Sheridan Streets (P.O. Box 564), Port Townsend, WA 98368. Tel. 206/385-5750 or toll free (in Washington) 800/732-1281. Fax 206/385-5883. 41 rms, 8 suites (all with private bath).
$ Rates (including continental breakfast): $64–$70 double; $85–$175 tower suite. MC, V.

If you are searching for even greater splendor than a mere Victorian home can furnish, consider staying at Port Townsend's very own castle. Built in 1892 by a wealthy baker, this reproduction of a medieval castle later became a Jesuit retreat and school. Today Manresa Castle is the town's most elegant accommodation by far and also its best deal. A traditional elegance pervades the hotel's lounge and dining room, so you should be sure to have at least one meal and a drink here. Guest rooms have a genuine, vintage feeling. The best deal in the hotel is the tower suite during off season. For $100 a night, you'll get a huge room with sweeping views from its circular seating area.

Bed-and-Breakfasts

ANN STARRETT MANSION, 744 Clay St., Port Townsend, WA 98368. Tel. 206/385-3205 or toll free 800/321-0644. 11 rms (8 with private bath).
$ Rates (including full breakfast): $70–$165 single or double. AE, DISC, MC, V.

Built in 1889 for $6,000 as a wedding present for Ann Starrett, this Victorian jewel box is by far the most elegant and ornate bed-and-breakfast in Port Townsend. A three-story turret towers over the front door of this cream, teal blue, and green mansion. Inside, you enter a museum of the Victorian era. Every room is exquisitely furnished in period antiques. In fact, if you aren't staying here, you can still have a look during one of the afternoon house tours ($2). Breakfast is an extravaganza that can last all morning and will certainly have you considering skipping lunch.

F.W. HASTINGS HOUSE/OLD CONSULATE INN, 313 Walker St., Port Townsend, WA 98368. Tel. 206/385-6753. 8 rms (all with private bath).
$ Rates (including full breakfast): $59–$155 double. AE, MC, V.
Though not quite as elaborate as Starrett Mansion, the Old Consulate Inn is another example of the sort of Victorian excess that is so wonderfully appealing today. The attention to detail and quality craftsmanship both in the original construction and the restoration of this elegant mansion are evident throughout. Despite its heritage, however, the Old Consulate avoids being a museum and instead is just a comfortable-yet-elegant place to stay. For entertainment, you'll find a grand piano, a billiard table, and a VCR, as well as stunning views out most of the windows. A multicourse breakfast is meant to be lingered over.

WHERE TO DINE
Inexpensive

KHU LARB THAI, 225 Adams St. Tel. 206/385-5023.
Cuisine: THAI. **Reservations:** Suggested.
$ Prices: Appetizers $4.50–$7; main dishes $6–$8.50. AE, MC, V.
Open: Sun–Thurs 11am–9pm, Fri–Sat 11am–10pm.
Located just half a block off busy Water Street, Khu Larb seems a world removed from Port Townsend's sometimes overdone Victorian decor. Thai easy-listening music plays on the stereo and you are surrounded by cheap souvenirs from Thailand. Don't let this lack of atmosphere put you off. One taste of any dish on the menu and you'll be convinced that this is great Thai food. Particularly memorable is *tom kha gai,* a sour and spicy soup with a coconut milk base. The steamed clams with ginger are another excellent dish. If you are feeling adventurous, try black rice pudding for dessert.

AROUND THE PENINSULA
WEST OF PORT TOWNSEND

Continuing around the Olympic Peninsula on U.S. 101, you next reach the town of **Sequim.** This area is an Olympic Peninsula anomaly. Because Sequim is in the rain shadow of the Olympic Mountains, the town receives only about 13 inches of rain per year. For contrast, keep in mind that the Hoh Valley, on the other side of the mountains, gets upward of 150 inches per year. Because of its sunny climate, Sequim has become a very popular retirement community.

A few miles from Sequim is the small town of **Dungeness,** which is regionally famous for its crabs. If you'd like to try some Dungeness crabs, follow the signs to the Three Crabs restaurant, 101 Three Crabs Rd. (tel. 206/683-4264).

A little farther west is **Port Angeles,** the largest city on the Olympic Peninsula. **Olympic National Park** maintains a visitors center at 3002 Mount Angeles Rd. (tel. 206/452-0330). You can watch an orientation slide program, buy books and maps, find out about trail and road conditions throughout the park, and ask about the availability of campsites and rooms in the park's lodges. The visitors center is open daily from 9am to 4pm (longer hours in summer). Park admission is $3 per motor vehicle and $2 per person for pedestrians and bicyclists and is charged at various entrance stations around the park. After you've paid once, you don't have to pay again if you visit another region of the park that same day.

From here, you should continue up to **Hurricane Ridge** if it's a clear day. Hurricane Ridge is in Olympic National Park, 17 miles from U.S. 101, and is at an elevation of 5,230 feet. There are sweeping panoramas of the Olympic Mountains and the forests of the park. Drive slowly and be alert; deer like to graze beside the road. There is another **visitors information center** here that's open daily.

Six miles west of Port Angeles, you'll see the turnoff for **Elwha Valley.** Five miles up this road are two campgrounds and trailheads for backcountry trails. There is also a short nature trail opposite the entrance station.

LAKE CRESCENT

Back on U.S. 101, you next come to Lake Crescent, which offers camping, hiking, boating, and fishing on a beautiful lake that is a landlocked fjord. The road runs alongside the lake for 11 miles, providing many excellent views.

Lake Crescent Lodge, HC 62, Box 11, Port Angeles, WA 98362-9798 (tel. 206/928-3211), is a historic hotel on the edge of the lake. Accommodations are available in the lodge, cottages, and modern motel rooms. Rates range from $65 to $124 single or double.

About 1½ miles past the western end of Lake Crescent is the turnoff for **Sol Duc Hot Springs Resort,** P.O. Box 2169, Port Angeles, WA 98362 (tel. 206/327-3583). The popular mineral hot springs are open from mid-May through September. An all-day pass to the hot pools costs $5.10 for adults and $4.10 for senior citizens. There are also modern cabins available if you want to stay overnight. Rates are $73 to $81 single or double. There is also a campground here with full-hookup RV sites going for $14 per night. Other amenities include a gourmet restaurant, a poolside deli, an espresso counter, a grocery and gift shop, and a massage therapist.

NEAH BAY

Turn off U.S. 101 at the crossroads of Sappho and you'll be on your way (via Hwy. 112) to the northwesternmost point in the continental United States, **Neah Bay,** in the middle of the **Makah Indian Reservation.** The **Makah Cultural and Research Center,** Washington Hwy. 112 (tel. 206/645-2711), will fill you in on the fascinating Indian history of this area. Most artifacts on display are from a Native American village that was completely covered by mud slides 2,000 years ago. Admission is $4 for adults, $3 for children, students, and senior citizens. In summer the museum is open daily from 10am to 5pm; the rest of the year it is only open Wednesday through Sunday. At Neah Bay you get your first glimpse of the **Pacific Ocean.** As you walk along the beach, watch for whale, seal, and sea lion.

LA PUSH BEACHES

My favorite Olympic Peninsula **beaches** are those near the tiny town of La Push. To reach La Push from Neah Bay, it is necessary to backtrack to Sappho and then continue west on U.S. 101 until you see the signs for the La Push turnoff. **Second Beach** and **Third Beach** are both more than a mile from the road on well-maintained trails. The reward for those who make the walk is a secluded beach piled high with driftwood logs and surrounded by cliffs and deep forest. Offshore, there are rocky islands that are home to birds, seals, and sea lions.

HOH RIVER VALLEY & KALALOCH

South of Forks, which is the turnoff for La Push, you finally reach the Hoh River Valley and its **rain forest.** It is 12 miles from the highway to the visitors information center, campgrounds, and rain forest nature trails. There are several trails of differing lengths and difficulty originating at the visitors center, but no matter which one you choose, you will be surrounded by a verdure the likes of which you have probably never seen. Mosses three feet long hang from the branches of the trees. Groves of new trees sprout from decaying tree stumps. Ferns cover the forest floor.

Kalaloch, 34 miles south of Forks, is known for its beaches and tide pools. The **Kalaloch Lodge,** H.C. 80 (P.O. Box 1100), Forks, WA 98331 (tel. 206/962-2271), is the place to stay in this area. Its main lodge and cottages are perched on a bluff above the water. Rates are $48 to $135 for a double.

QUINAULT VALLEY

Quinault Valley, located 35 miles south of Kalaloch, is the Olympic Peninsula's other major rain forest. Lake Quinault fills the valley east of the highway. Along the North Shore Drive, there are two trails into the rain forest: One is a half mile long and the other four miles long.

Also on the shores of the lake is **Lake Quinault Lodge,** South Shore Rd. (P.O. Box 7), Quinnault, WA 98575 (tel. 206/288-2571 or toll free in Washington, 800/562-6672, fax 206/288-2415). The lodge was built in the mid-1920s and still has many of its original furnishings. Although not all the rooms in the original building have private baths, they are much more appealing than those in the newer wing of the lodge. For those who prefer warmer water than the lake offers, there is a heated indoor pool, whirlpool baths, and a sauna. Rates are $78 to $99 for a double.

You can once again return to the ocean beaches by turning west in the town of **Humptulips. Moclips** and **Pacific Beach,** on the coast, are popular beach resort towns with all the amenities you'd expect to find.

HOQUIAM & RETURN

Continuing on to Ocean City and heading east on Washington Hwy. 109, you come to the town of **Hoquiam.** If you didn't stay at the Manresa Castle in Port Townsend, you can still visit the Olympic Peninsula's other castle—**Hoquiam Castle,** 515 Chenault Ave. (tel. 206/533-2005). The 20-room mansion was built in 1897 for a local timber baron. The castle is open for tours mid-June to Labor Day, daily from 10am to 5pm; the rest of the year, on Saturday and Sunday from 11am to 5pm (closed in December). Tickets for the tour are $3 for adults, $2 for senior citizens, and $1 for children under 16.

In Hoquiam you leave U.S. 101 and drive east on U.S. 12 to

Olympia, Washington's state capital. From Olympia, I-5 will return you to Seattle in about an hour.

---

4. SAN JUAN ISLANDS

Seattleites love the water, and when they want to enjoy some serious sailing, sea kayaking, or simply the unequaled water-and-island views, they head for the San Juan Islands. Dotting the blue waters of Puget Sound, the 172 San Juans were named by early Spanish explorers who came as far north as Puget Sound, claimed the land for Spain, and then never returned. Only three islands—**Orcas, San Juan,** and **Lopez**—have much in the way of development, and only these three and Shaw Island are reachable by public ferry. It is this limited access and relative remoteness that has made the San Juans an idyllic getaway. Harried city dwellers escape to the islands to enjoy rural tranquillity and the many recreational activities. Bicycling along winding roads tops the list of popular island pastimes, which include sailing, hiking, kayaking, swimming, scuba diving, whale watching, and salmon fishing. Of course, the islands wouldn't be nearly so popular if it weren't for the dozens of bed-and-breakfast inns, small resorts, and excellent little restaurants that cater to vacationers in search of rejuvenation.

I must, however, warn you of the summer crowds on the islands. Though the San Juans have fewer than 15,000 permanent residents, more than 200,000 people visit each summer. Visitors wait in line for hours to board ferries, accommodations and campgrounds are booked months in advance, and reserving at a restaurant can be nearly impossible. I suggest that, if at all possible, you visit the San Juans in the off-season. The weather won't be quite as pleasant as in summer, but because these islands get only half the rainfall of Seattle, you will likely find refuge from the rain. If you must visit in summer, try to come during the week and don't leave the mainland without a room or campground reservation. For those seeking real solitude, nothing is more relaxing than a sail or paddle (by kayak) through the islands. Deserted islands, tiny coves, and wave-swept rocky shores offer days of exploration.

For more information on the islands, contact **San Juan Islands Visitor Information Services,** P.O. Box 65, Lopez Island, WA 98261 (tel. 206/468-3663). If you are interested in kayaking in the San Juans, contact **Shearwater Adventures,** P.O. Box 787, Eastsound, WA 98245 (tel. 206/376-4699), or **San Juan Kayak Expeditions,** P.O. Box 2041, Friday Harbor, WA 98250 (tel. 206/378-4436). If you are interested in bicycling around the islands, contact **Island Bicycles,** 380 Argyle St., Friday Harbor, WA 98250 (tel. 206/378-4941), or **Dolphin Bay Bicycles** on Orcas Island (tel. 206/376-4157).

GETTING THERE   Although the islands are only about 85 miles north of Seattle, it takes several hours to reach them. There are no bridges to the islands, so you'll have to take one of those huge **Washington State Ferries** (tel. 206/464-6400 or toll free 800/ 84-FERRY). If you have the time and are planning to spend a few days in the islands, I'd recommend taking **Washington Hwy. 20** north from Seattle. This narrow road winds across scenic Whidbey

Island before reaching Anacortes, where the ferries dock. If you're in a hurry, you can take **I-5** to the northern end of Washington Hwy. 20 and reach Anacortes that way. Another alternative is to fly from Seattle. **Kenmore Air, 950** Westlake Ave. N. (tel. 206/486-1257 or toll free 800/826-1890), provides regular floatplane service to five towns in the San Juans. Flights leave from the west side of Lake Union, north of downtown Seattle.

If you have come north on Washington Hwy. 20, be sure to stop at **Deception Pass State Park,** which is just over the bridge from Whidbey Island and before the turnoff for Anacortes. The park isn't far from Anacortes, so you should make a point of visiting even if you took I-5. Turbulent currents surge over the rocks as tidal waters are squeezed into a narrow channel by the point and an island. The sight is as awe-inspiring as a waterfall.

BED-AND-BREAKFASTS On San Juan, Orcas, and Lopez islands, there are a number of bed-and-breakfast inns that are very popular in the summer. You can find out about these inns by contacting **San Juan Islands Visitor Information Services,** P.O. Box 65, Lopez Island, WA 98261 (tel. 206/468-3663).

SEEING THE ISLANDS

SAN JUAN ISLAND

Though San Juan Island is the last stop for the ferry from Anacortes (except for the one ferry a day that continues on to Victoria, British Columbia), it is the most developed and most popular of the islands. The ferry dock is in downtown Friday Harbor, the largest and busiest town in the islands. Here you'll find most of the trappings of a tourist town—gift shops, frozen yogurt vendors, restaurants, motels, and bed-and-breakfasts. Despite the tourist orientation of Friday Harbor, the historic little community preserves the genuine feeling of an island town. Wooden Victorian buildings line the streets near the marina and ferry landing, and spreading out from downtown are quiet neighborhoods full of restored homes dating back to the turn of the century.

There isn't a whole lot to do in Friday Harbor other than stroll around, but the town does have one unique claim. It is home to the **Whale Museum,** 62 First St. (tel. 206/378-4710), which is the only museum in the United States dedicated entirely to whales. The museum is open daily from 11am to 4pm. Admission is $3 for adults, $2.50 for senior citizens, $1.50 for children ages 5 to 11, and free for children under age 5.

Whale watching is popular throughout the San Juans, and the whale most often sighted here is the much-maligned killer whale, correctly known as the orca. While riding the ferries through the islands, keep your eyes peeled for their characteristic knife-edged dorsal fins. If you're lucky, you might even see one breach (jump completely out of the water). **Lime Kiln State Park,** 10 miles west of Friday Harbor, is a good spot for whale watching, especially during the summer.

San Juan Island was nearly the site of a battle between the British and the Americans in 1859. The two countries had only recently agreed upon the border between the United States and Canada, and it seems someone forgot to tell a British pig on San Juan Island. The pig unknowingly crossed the border, illegally, to have dinner in an

American garden. The owner of the garden didn't take too kindly to this and shot the pig. The Brits, rather than welcoming this succulent addition to their evening's repast, threatened redress. In less time than it takes to smoke a ham, both sides were calling in reinforcements. Luckily, this pigheadedness was defused and armed conflict was avoided. **San Juan Island National Historical Park,** P.O. Box 429, Friday Harbor, WA 98250 (tel. 206/378-2240), commemorates the "Pig War" with two parks on different sides of the island—one called **American Camp** and the other **British Camp.** You can visit buildings that are much as they might have looked in 1859.

Roche Harbor Resort, P.O. Box 4001, Roche Harbor, WA 98250 (tel. 206/378-2155), is the largest resort on the island and includes a historic Victorian hotel, marina, restaurant, and lounge. The rooms in the old Hotel de Haro building have the most character, but they don't have private bathrooms. Request one of the old cottages or a modern condominium for more comfortable accommodations. Rates range from $45 to $120 per night for one or two people.

The best restaurants on the island are **Café Bissett,** 1709 West St. (tel. 206/378-3109), serving Northwest and Mediterranean cuisine; **Springtree Café,** 310 Spring St. (tel. 206/378-4848), serving Northwest cuisine; **Duck Soup Inn,** 3090 Roche Harbor Rd. (tel. 206/378-4878), serving continental cuisine; and **Roberto's** (tel. 206/378-6333), on the corner of First and A streets, serving Italian food. Rates are $60 to $120 single or double.

ORCAS ISLAND

Orcas Island is a favorite of nature lovers. **Moran State Park,** which covers 5,175 acres of the island, is the largest park in the San Juans. If the weather is clear, you'll find great views from the summit of **Mount Constitution,** which rises 2,409 feet above Puget Sound. There are also five lakes, 32 miles of hiking trails, fishing, hiking, boating, biking, camping in the park, and an environmental learning center. For campground reservations or more information, contact **Moran State Park,** Star Route, Box 22, Eastsound, WA 98245 (tel. 206/376-2326).

Rosario Resort and Spa, 1 Rosario Way, Eastsound, WA 98245-2222 (tel. 206/376-2222 or toll free 800/562-8820), is the island's premier hotel. The hotel's central building is the Moran Mansion, which was built in 1905 and is a National Historic Building. The spa features three heated pools, whirlpools, a health club, a beach, boat rentals, tennis courts, and nature trails. Rates range from $63 to $140 single or double (more expensive suites are also available).

The best restaurants on the island are **Christina's,** on the waterfront in Eastsound (tel. 206/376-4904), serving Northwest seafood; **La Famiglia,** Prune Alley, Eastsound (tel. 206/376-2335); **Ship Bay Oyster House,** on the road to Rosario Resort (tel. 206/376-5886), serving steak and seafood; and **Café Olga,** in Olga (tel. 206/376-5098), serving creative deli fare.

LOPEZ ISLAND

Of the three islands that offer accommodations other than camp-grounds, Lopez is the least developed and most laid-back. This is not to say, however, that there is nothing to do here. Lopez is the most popular island with bicyclists, who find its gentle hills to be the easiest on the islands. **Spencer Spit State Park** (tel. 206/468-2251), located on the northeast side of the island, offers a mile of beach at the base of forested hills. The views across a narrow channel to Frost Island and Flower Island are excellent. Down on the southwest end of the island, you'll find Shark Reef Sanctuary, a small park with a short hiking trail that leads through forest to a rocky shoreline. The currents of the San Juan Channel swirl past the rocks here, and seals, otters, porpoises, and whales can sometimes be seen here. This is a great bicycling destination or picnicking spot.

Islander Lopez Marina Resort, P.O. Box 197, Lopez Island, WA 98261 (tel. 206/468-2233 or toll free 800/736-3434), in tiny Lopez Village, offers several types of accommodation, from simple small rooms to much larger rooms with balconies and great views. Rates range from $50 to $115 for a single or double room.

The island's best restaurant is the **Bay Café,** across from the old post office in Lopez Village (tel. 206/468-3700), serving Northwest cuisine.

INTRODUCING PORTLAND

Portland likes to think of itself as a big little city. It long ago gave up trying to compete with Seattle for the title of the Northwest's Pacific Rim trade capital. By giving up this goal, it has been able to concentrate on being a very livable city. Compared to the rapid growth in the Seattle area, Portland's progress is moving slowly. However, this hasn't prevented the city from opening new cultural venues, a new convention center, and some very appealing hotels and restaurants that are as good as any you'll find elsewhere.

1. CULTURE, HISTORY & BACKGROUND

GEOGRAPHY/PEOPLE

Located at the junction of the Columbia and Willamette rivers in northwestern Oregon, Portland is a compact city of about 453,000 people. Some 1.5 million people live in the metropolitan area. The West Hills act as backdrop for the handful of skyscrapers in the downtown area, making the cityscape as you enter from the east one of the most impressive in the country. The view from the West Hills, looking out over the city to Mount Hood, is even more inspiring.

The individualist spirit that prompted pioneers to follow the Oregon Trail is still very much alive. Oregonians are proud of their heritage and value their active life-style, and the people of Portland are at the forefront of environmental policy. City planning here generally focuses on the quality of life rather than on economic progress at any cost, as is the case in some other cities. Of course, it

IMPRESSIONS

Oregon is seldom heard of. Its people believe in the Bible, and hold that all radicals should be lynched. It has no poets and no statesmen.
—H. L. MENCKEN, *AMERICANA,* 1925

WHAT'S SPECIAL ABOUT PORTLAND

Beaches
☐ Cannon Beach has Haystack Rock, just offshore.
☐ Oswald West State Park—the beach is a mile walk through dense forests.

Buildings
☐ The Portland Building (1980), by Michael Graves, is considered the first postmodern building in the United States.
☐ The Oregon Convention Center (1990), with its twin glass spires, has become Portland's most readily identifiable landmark.

Museum
☐ The American Advertising Museum is the only museum of its kind in the country.

Gardens
☐ The gardens of the Japanese Garden Society of Oregon, in Washington Park, are considered the equivalent of any in Japan.

Festival
☐ The Portland Rose Festival, which had its start more than 100 years ago, is a 3-week-long June extravaganza celebrating the start of the rose-blossoming season.

Natural Spectacles
☐ Columbia Gorge boasts dozens of waterfalls, high cliffs, and scenic highways.
☐ Mount Hood, an extinct volcano, has year-round skiing and hiking.

Shopping
☐ At the Portland Saturday Market, which is held on Sundays also, local artisans sell their creations.

Zoo
☐ Metro Washington Park Zoo, known for an elephant-breeding program, recently opened an African rain-forest exhibit.

Great Neighborhoods
☐ Old Town (also known as Skidmore District) boasts outstanding examples of cast-iron-fronted buildings from 100 years ago. There are also dozens of boutiques and galleries, as well as the Portland Saturday Market.
☐ Nob Hill is Portland's trendiest neighborhood. Old Victorian homes have been converted into boutiques and restaurants.

Offbeat
☐ The Church of Elvis offers 24-hour psychic readings.

Regional Food & Drink
☐ Innovative chefs are cooking up a quiet storm at Portland's restaurants—and at very reasonable prices.
☐ Portland is the microbrewery capital of America. These small breweries produce delicious and unusual ales.
☐ The Oregon wine industry is winning awards in international competitions.

does rain quite a bit, but residents will tell you that's what keeps the land green. Portlanders are happy to put up with the drizzly months in exchange for the glorious summers. The same aspects that make Portland one of the most livable cities in the world also make it one of the most visitable.

HISTORY

EARLY DAYS   Portland was once a very inexpensive piece of property. In 1844 it sold for $50, double the original price of Manhattan Island. Before that, it had been purchased for just 25¢, although the original purchaser had to borrow the quarter. Remember that there was nothing here at the time. This was a wilderness, and anyone who thought it would ever be anything more was either foolish or extremely farsighted.

Asa Lovejoy and William Overton, the two men who staked the original claim to Portland, were the latter: farsighted. From this spot on the Willamette River they could see snow-capped Mount Hood 50 miles away; they liked the view and figured other people might also. These two were as disparate as a pair of founding fathers could be. Overton was a penniless drifter. No one is sure where he came from, or where he went when he left less than a year later. Lovejoy had attended Harvard College and graduated from Amherst. He was one of the earliest settlers to venture by wagon train to the Oregon country.

These two men were traveling by canoe from Fort Vancouver, the Hudson's Bay Company fur-trading center on the Columbia River, to the town of Oregon City on the Willamette River. Midway through their journey they stopped to rest at a clearing on the west bank of the Willamette. Overton suggested they stake a claim to the spot. It was commonly believed that Oregon would soon become a U.S. territory and that the federal government would pass out free 640-acre land claims. Overton wanted to be sure that he got his due. Unfortunately, he didn't have the 25¢ required to file a claim. In exchange for half the claim, Lovejoy loaned him the money. Not a bad return on a 25¢ investment!

Wanderlust struck Overton before he could do anything with his claim, and he bartered his half to one Francis Pettygrove for $50 worth of supplies and headed off for parts unknown. Overton must have thought he had turned a pretty deal—from a borrowed quarter to $50 in under a year is a respectable return. Pettygrove, a steadfast Yankee like Lovejoy, was a merchant with ideas on how to make a fortune. Alas, all poor Overton got in the end was a single street named after him.

Pettygrove lost no time in setting up a store on the waterfront, and now with a single building on the site, it was time to name the town. Pettygrove was from Maine and wanted to name the new town for his beloved Portland; Lovejoy was from Boston and wanted that name for the new settlement. A coin was flipped, Pettygrove called it correctly, and a new Portland was born.

Portland was a relative latecomer to the region. Oregon City, Fort Vancouver, Milwaukie, and St. Helens were all doing business in the area when Portland was still just a glimmer in the eyes of Lovejoy and Overton. But in 1846 things changed quickly. Another New Englander, Capt. John Couch, sailed up the Willamette, dropped anchor in Portland, and decided to make this the headquarters for his shipping company.

Another enterprising gentleman, this one a Southerner named Daniel Lownsdale, opened a tannery outside town and helped build a road through the West Hills to the wheat farms of the Tualatin Valley. With a road from the farm country and a small port to ship the wheat to market, Portland rapidly became the most important town in the region.

With the 1848 discovery of gold in California (by a former Oregonian), and the subsequent demand for such Oregon products as grain and timber, Portland became a booming little town of 800.

By the late 1880s Portland was connected to the rest of the country by several railroad lines, and by 1900 the population had grown to 90,000. In 1905 the city hosted the Lewis and Clark Exposition, that year's World's Fair, which celebrated the centennial of the explorers' journey to the Northwest. The fairgrounds, landscaped by John Olmsted, successor to Central Park (New York City) designer Frederick Law Olmsted, were a great hit. The city of Portland also proved popular with visitors; by 1910 its population had exploded to 250,000.

By this time, however, there were even more roses than there were people. Since 1888 Portland had been holding an annual rose show, but in 1907 it had blossomed into a full-fledged Rose Festival. Today the annual festival, held each June, is still Portland's favorite celebration. More than 400 varieties bloom in the International Rose Test Gardens in Washington Park, lending Portland the sobriquet City of Roses.

20TH CENTURY The 1900s have been a roller-coaster ride of boom and bust for Portland. The phenomenal growth of the city's first 50 years has slowed. Timber and agriculture have been the mainstays of the Oregon economy, but the lumber-industry recession of recent years has nearly crippled the Oregon economy. Luckily, the Portland area has developed a high-tech industrial base that has allowed it to weather the storm and continue to prosper.

Portlanders tend to have a different idea of prosperity than residents of most other cities. Since its beginnings, nature and the city's relationship to it have been an integral part of life here. As far back as 100 years ago the Willamette River was a favored recreation site, with canoe clubs racing on its clean waters. But the industries of the 20th century brought the pollution that killed the river. Downtown Portland lost its preeminence as a shipping port, and eventually the wharves were torn down and replaced by a freeway. This was akin to cutting out Portland's very heart and soul. But the freeway did not last long.

With the heightened environmental awareness of the 1960s and 70s, Portland's basic character and love of nature began to resurface. A massive cleanup of the Willamette was undertaken—and was eventually so successful that today salmon once again can be seen from downtown Portland. The freeway was torn up and replaced with Tom McCall Waterfront Park (or just Waterfront Park), a large expanse of lawns, trees, fountains, and promenades. But this is only one in a grand network of parks. The city is ringed with them, including Forest Park, the largest wooded city park in the United States, and Washington Park, which is home to the International Rose Test Garden, Japanese Gardens, Metro Washington Park Zoo, and Hoyt Arboretum. Mount Hood, only 90 minutes from downtown, and the hundreds of thousands of acres of national forest surrounding it are well utilized by the outdoors-conscious citizens of this green city.

Being a "big little city," Portland isn't interested in growth quite so much as Seattle, its main competitor in the Northwest. Economic progress is less important to the city than quality of life. Portland is a clean city, a polite city. Littering is almost unheard of, and in case a bit of trash does make it to the streets and sidewalks, there's a special cleaning crew that works overtime to keep the downtown area sparkling. The city's Percent for Art program also ensures a beautiful downtown. Every new public building must spend slightly more than 1% of building costs on public art.

Portland could be considered a bit eccentric. Many Portlanders claim that the hippies of the 1960s are alive and well and selling their crafts at the Portland Saturday Market. You won't find any Styrofoam containers at fast-food restaurants in Portland; they've been banned because of the difficulty of disposing of them after use. Likewise, damaging aerosols have also been banned. And although I haven't been able to verify this statistic, a reliable local source tells me that Portland has the country's highest per capita consumption of Grape Nuts.

IMPRESSIONS

Oregon . . . a pleasant, homogeneous, self-contained state, filled with pleasant, homogeneous, self-contained people, overwhelmingly white, Protestant, and middle class. Even the working class was middle class.
—ARTHUR M. SCHLESINGER JR., *ROBERT KENNEDY AND HIS TIMES,*
1978

2. RECOMMENDED BOOKS & FILMS

BOOKS

The Journals of Lewis and Clark (various editions) will give you an idea of what this area was like almost two centuries ago. Although this fascinating journal does not focus directly on the Portland area, it was this report of Meriwether Lewis and William Clark's famous 1803–06 expedition that first introduced the rest of the world to the Pacific Northwest. *The Oregon Trail* (1849), by Francis Parkman, Jr., chronicles the grueling travels of the first pioneers to settle in the Oregon country. It was the rich soils of the Willamette and Tualatin river valleys just outside Portland that lured families to undertake such an arduous trip. *Caesars of the Wilderness,* by Peter C. Newman, focuses on the role of the Hudson's Bay Company in opening up this part of the West.

FILMS

Come See the Paradise (1990) has a few shots of a vintage Portland in its story of a Caucasian man's love for his Japanese wife during World War II. *Drugstore Cowboy* (1989), by Portland director Gus van Sant, relates the exploits of a band of drug-crazed criminals who work around Portland. The film stars Matt Dillon and received much acclaim when it was released. *My Own Private Idaho,* another film by Gus van Sant, stars Keanu Reeves and River Phoenix and focuses on the street life of runaway teenagers.

CHAPTER 12

PLANNING A TRIP TO PORTLAND

Planning before you leave can make all the difference between enjoying your trip and wishing you had stayed home. For many people, in fact, planning a trip is half the fun of going. You can write to the addresses below for interesting packets of information that are created to get you excited about your upcoming trip. One of your first considerations should be when you want to visit. Summer is the peak season in the Northwest. That's when the sun shines and outdoor festivals and events take place. During the summer, hotel and car reservations are almost essential; the rest of the year, they are highly advisable. You usually get better rates by reserving at least one or two weeks in advance.

1. INFORMATION

For information on Portland and the rest of Oregon, contact the **Portland/Oregon Visitors Association,** Three World Trade Center, 26 SW Salmon St., Portland, OR 97204-3299 (tel. 503/222-2223 or toll free 800/962-3700). They also have an information booth by the baggage-claim area at Portland Airport. Another organization with brochures helpful in planning a Portland visit is the **Association for Portland Progress,** 520 SW Yamhill St., Suite 100, Portland, OR 97204 (tel. 503/224-8684). This is the same group that provides the Portland Guide service, those invaluable people who walk the streets of Portland answering any and all questions about the city. Also helpful is the **Portland Metropolitan Chamber of Commerce,** 221 NW Second Ave., Portland, OR 97209 (tel. 503/228-9411).

WHAT THINGS COST IN PORTLAND — U.S. $

Taxi from the airport to the city center	21.00
Bus or tram ride between downtown points	Free
Local telephone call	.25
Double at The Heathman Hotel (very expensive)	155.00
Double at Riverside Inn (moderate)	85.00
Double at Cypress Inn-Portland Downtown (inexpensive)	57.00
Lunch for one at B. Moloch (moderate)	10.00
Lunch for one at Macheezmo Mouse (inexpensive)	5.00
Dinner for one, without wine, at L'Auberge (expensive)	35.00
Dinner for one, without wine, at Alexis Restaurant (moderate)	20.00
Dinner for one, without wine, at Mayas Tacquerie (inexpensive)	6.00
Pint of beer	2.75
Coca-Cola	1.00
Cup of espresso	1.25
Roll of ASA 100 Kodacolor film, 36 exposures	5.50
Admission to the Portland Art Museum	4.50
Movie ticket	1.00–6.00
Oregon Symphony ticket at Arlene Schnitzer Concert Hall	9.50–45.00

2. WHEN TO GO

CLIMATE

This is the section you've all been looking for. You've all heard about the horrible weather in the Northwest. It rains all year, right? Wrong! The Portland area has some of the most beautiful summer weather in the country—warm, sunny days with clear blue skies and cool nights perfect for sleeping. During the months of July, August, and September, it almost never rains. And the rest of the year? Well, yes, it rains in those months and it rains regularly. However, the rain is generally a fine mist and not the torrential downpour most people associate with the word rain. In fact, it often rains less in Portland than it does in New York, Boston, Washington, DC, and Atlanta.

IMPRESSIONS

The green damp England of Oregon.
—ALISTAIR COOKE, *ALISTAIR COOKE'S AMERICA,* 1973

There, now I've let the secret out. Let the stampede begin! Winters here aren't too bad, either. They're warmer than in the Northeast, but there is snow in nearby mountains. In fact, there's so much snow on Mount Hood, only 90 minutes from downtown Portland, that you can ski right through the summer.

Of course you're skeptical about the amazing information I just presented, so here are the statistics.

Average Temperature & Days of Rain

	Jan	Feb	Mar	Apr	May	June	July	Aug	Sept	Oct	Nov	Dec
Temp. (°F)	40	43	46	50	57	63	68	67	63	54	46	41
Temp. (°C)	4	6	8	10	14	17	20	19	17	12	8	5
Days of Rain	18	16	17	14	12	10	4	5	8	13	18	19

A CITY OF FESTIVALS

There is nothing Portland enjoys more than a big get-together. Because of the winter weather conditions, these festivals, free concerts, and fairs tend to take place in summer. Not a week goes by then without some sort of event. For a complete list of special events in and around Portland, send a self-addressed 9-by-12 envelope and 75¢ for a monthly listing or $1.50 for an annual listing to **Portland/ Oregon Visitors Association,** Three World Trade Center, 26 SW Salmon St., Portland, OR 97204-3299. To find out what's going on during your visit, pick up a copy of **Willamette Week, Portland Guide** (available in hotels), or the Sunday **Oregonian.** Some of the larger and more popular special and free events are listed there.

While you're in town, keep your ears peeled and you might find out about other free concerts, such as the Music on the Roof Friday-lunchtime concerts at Yamhill Market or the Jazz on the Water Friday-evening concerts on the patio at the Harborside Restaurant in RiverPlace.

Portland Parks and Recreation also sponsors concerts in more than half a dozen parks throughout the city every summer. Write to them at 1120 SW Fifth Ave., Portland, OR 97204, for a free schedule of concerts.

Portland is especially proud of its Waterfront Park, and rightfully so. Not too many years ago this 2-mile-long park with its fountains and sweeping lawns was a busy freeway. You'll find that a lot of festivals take place here throughout the year. If you happen to be in town and see tents and crowds in the park, you can be sure it's one of Portland's favorite festivals in swing.

PORTLAND CALENDAR OF EVENTS

FEBRUARY

☐ **Portland International Film Festival,** various theaters around the city. Tel. 503/221-1156.

MARCH

☐ **Winter Games of Oregon,** Timberline Ski Area, Mount Hood Meadows, Mt. Hood SkiBowl. Alpine and Nordic ski competitions. Tel. 503/272-3311.

APRIL

☐ **Hood River Blossom Festival,** Hood River. Celebration of the blossoming of the orchards outside the town of Hood River. Tel. toll free 800/366-3530.

MAY

☐ **Cinco de Mayo Festival,** Hispanic celebration with food and entertainment. Tel. 503/823-4572.
☐ **Mother's Day Rhododendron Show,** Crystal Springs Rhododendron Gardens. Mother's Day. Tel. 503/771-8386.

JUNE

☐ **Rhythm and Zoo,** Metro Washington Park Zoo. Rhythm and blues concerts are held on Thursday nights from June to August. Tel. 503/226-1561.
☐ **Your Zoo and All That Jazz,** Metro Washington Park Zoo. Jazz concerts are held on Wednesday nights from June to August. Tel. 503/226-1561.

۞ PORTLAND ROSE FESTIVAL   *From its beginnings back in 1888, when the first rose show was held, the Rose Festival has blossomed into Portland's biggest celebration. The festivities now span 3½ weeks and include a rose show, parade, rose queen contest, music festival, car races, footrace, boat races, even a snow-skiing competition up on Mount Hood. Most of the events take place in the first 2 weeks of June, and hotel rooms can be hard to come by. Plan ahead.*
   Where: *All over the city.* ***When:*** *First 3 weeks of June.* ***How:*** *Contact the Portland Rose Festival Association, 220 NW Second Ave., Portland, OR 97209 (tel. 503/227-2681), for information on tickets to specific events.*

☐ **Peanut Butter & Jam Sessions,** Pioneer Courthouse Square, free lunchtime jazz concerts. They're held every Tuesday and Thursday, mid-June to mid-August. Tel. 503/223-1613.

JULY

☐ **Multnomah County Fair,** Portland Exposition Center. Tel. 503/281-2437.
☐ **Oregon Brewers Festival,** Waterfront Park. America's largest festival of independent brewers features lots of local microbrews and music.
☐ **Fourth of July Fireworks,** Vancouver, WA. "What about the Fourth of July?" you ask. Doesn't anything special happen in Portland then? Well, not exactly. Portland just can't compete with

the fireworks spectacle that Vancouver puts on. It's the biggest display west of the Mississippi. Vancouver is just across the river, and you can see the fireworks from plenty of spots in Portland. For a closeup view, head up to Jantzen Beach. For an elevated perspective, climb up in the West Hills.

☐ **Waterfront Blues Festival,** Waterfront Park. Early July. Tel. 503/282-0555.

☐ **Portland Highland Games,** Mount Hood Community College, Gresham. Late July. Tel. 503/293-8501.

☐ **Cathedral Park Jazz Festival,** under St. John's Bridge in Cathedral Park. Free performances by nationally known jazz artists. End of July.

AUGUST

☐ **The Bite,** Waterfront Park. Portland's finest restaurants serve up sample portions of their specialties at this food and music festival. A true gustatory extravaganza. Tel. 503/248-0600.

☐ **Mount Hood Festival of Jazz,** Mount Hood Community College, Gresham (less than 30 minutes from Portland). For the serious jazz fan, this is the festival of the summer. It features the greatest names in jazz. Tel. 503/666-3810.

☐ **Artquake,** radiating out from Pioneer Courthouse Square along Broadway, Portland's grandest festival of the arts. Visual arts, all types of music, theater, dance, festival foods, and a crafts market are all part of this celebration. Late August and early September. Tel. 503/227-2787.

OCTOBER

☐ **Hood River Harvest Festival,** Hood River. Celebration of the harvest season with crafts and food booths, pie-eating contests, and lots of entertainment. Tel. toll free 800/366-3530.

DECEMBER

☐ **Festival of Trees,** Oregon Convention Center. Extravagantly decorated Christmas trees are displayed among gingerbread houses and trains. Tel. 503/235-7575.

☐ **Winter Solstice Festival,** Oregon Museum of Science and Industry. In a 4,000-year-old tradition, the lengthening of the days is celebrated with entertainment, arts and crafts, and special events. Dec. 20 or 21. Tel. 503/797-4000.

3. WHAT TO PACK

A raincoat, an umbrella, and a sweater or jacket are all absolutely essential in Portland at any time of year. Other than that, you might want to bring skis (snow or water), hiking boots, boat shoes, running shoes, shorts, bicycling shorts, a bathing suit, and just about any other outdoor clothing or equipment you have on hand. The outdoors is a way of life in this part of the country.

4. TIPS FOR THE DISABLED, SENIORS, SINGLES, FAMILIES & STUDENTS

FOR THE DISABLED   Many hotels listed in this book feature special rooms for the disabled. I have tried to note this in all cases, but if you don't see mention in a listing, be sure to ask when making a reservation.

All MAX light-rail (trolley) system stations have wheelchair lifts, and there are two wheelchair spaces available on each train. Be sure to wait on the platform lift. Many of the Tri-Met buses also are equipped with wheelchair lifts and wheelchair spaces. Look for the wheelchair symbol on buses, schedules, and bus stops. There is also a special door-to-door service provided for people who are not able to use the regular Tri-Met service. Phone 503/238-4952 for information.

Broadway Cab (tel. 227-1234) and **Radio Cab** (tel. 227-1212) both have vehicles for transporting the disabled.

FOR SENIORS   Many hotels, museums, theaters, gardens, and tour companies offer special discounts for senior citizens. I have noted this in listings. Also, while you are in Portland try to pick up a copy of **Spectrum,** a monthly newspaper for senior citizens. Call 244-2227 to find out where you can obtain a copy.

FOR SINGLE TRAVELERS   Portland has a lively singles nightlife, and some of the liveliest spots are the popular discos at the **Red Lion hotels.** If you're looking for someone to talk sports with, head over to **Champions,** the sports bar at the Portland Marriott, 1401 SW Front Ave. (tel. 226-7600).

FOR FAMILIES   At many hotels in Portland, kids stay free in their parents' room. Be sure to check the listings or ask when you contact a hotel. As many as three children under age six can ride free with an adult on Tri-Met buses and MAX.

FOR STUDENTS   Student discounts are available at many museums, theaters, and concert halls. Be sure to carry a current student ID and ask about discounts.

5. GETTING THERE

BY PLANE

Portland International Airport (PDX) (tel. 503/335-1234), Oregon's main airport, is located nine miles northeast of downtown Portland, adjacent to the Columbia River. The airport is relatively small but offers some amenities you wouldn't expect at a facility this size. Tops on this list is the PDX Conference Center, which offers businesspeople a secluded and quiet working space.

THE MAJOR AIRLINES   About 15 carriers service Portland Airport to and from some 100 cities worldwide. The major airlines include **Alaska Airlines** (tel. 503/224-2547 or toll free 800/426-0333), **America West** (tel. 503/228-0737 or toll free 800/247-5692), **American Airlines** (tel. toll free 800/433-7300), **Continental** (tel. 503/249-4626 or toll free 800/525-0280), **Delta** (tel. toll free 800/221-1212), **Horizon** (tel. toll free 800/547-9308), **Morris Air** (tel. toll free 800/466-7747), **Northwest** (tel. toll free 800/225-2525), **TWA** (tel. 503/282-1111 or toll free 800/221-2000), **United Airlines** (tel. toll free 800/241-6522), and **USAir** (tel. toll free 800/428-4322).

REGULAR AIRFARES AND SUPER APEX   At the time of this writing, round-trip **Super-APEX (Advance Purchase Excursion)** fares from the East Coast were about $400, though these were special summer fares. Shortly before summer rates went into effect, fares had been running about $600 from the East Coast.

The round-trip **coach** fare was around $1,300, with **business class** about the same. The round-trip **first-class** fare was between $1,540 and $2,000.

OTHER GOOD-VALUE CHOICES   Check the Sunday travel section of a major newspaper for ads from **ticket brokers** (also called **bucket shops**). These ads are typically small boxes with a list of destinations and prices. You'll usually find that the brokers sell airline tickets at a discount. When an airline runs a special deal, however, you won't always do better at the bucket shops.

BY TRAIN

Amtrak passenger trains connect Portland with Seattle, San Francisco, Salt Lake City, and the rest of the country and stop at Union Station, 800 NW Sixth Ave. (tel. 503/273-4865), about 10 blocks from the heart of downtown Portland. For Amtrak schedule information and reservations, call toll free 800/872-7245.

BY BUS

Greyhound Bus Lines connects Portland with the rest of the country. The bus station is at 550 NW Sixth Ave. (tel. 503/243-2323).

 FROMMER'S SMART TRAVELER:
AIRFARES

1. Shop all the airlines that fly to your destination and shop ahead. The lowest fares are usually on 14- or 30-day advance-purchase tickets.
2. Always ask for the lowest-priced fare, not just for a discount.
3. Keep calling the airline—availability of cheap seats changes daily. Airline yield managers would rather sell a seat than have it fly empty. As the departure date nears, additional low-cost seats become available.
4. Watch the newspapers for special offers. You may be able to save several hundred dollars per ticket by changing your vacation plans to fit in with special low-fare offers.

BY CAR

Portland is linked to the rest of the U.S. by a number of Interstate highways and smaller roads. I-5 runs north to Seattle and south as far as San Diego. I-84 runs east as far as Salt Lake City. I-405 arcs around the west and south of downtown Portland. I-205 bypasses the city to the east. U.S. 26 runs west to the coast.

Here are some driving distances from selected cities (in miles):

Los Angeles	1,015
San Francisco	640
Seattle	175
Spokane	350
Vancouver, B.C.	285

CHAPTER 13

GETTING TO KNOW PORTLAND

- **1. ORIENTATION**
- **• NEIGHBORHOODS IN BRIEF**
- **2. GETTING AROUND**
- **• FAST FACTS: PORTLAND**
- **3. NETWORKS & RESOURCES**

Portland's compactness makes it a wonderfully easy city to explore. Although the airport is in the northeastern part of the city, most important sights and hotels are in the southwestern part. The Willamette River forms a natural dividing line between the eastern and western portions of the city, while the Columbia River forms a boundary with the state of Washington to the north. The West Hills, Portland's prime residential district, are a beautiful backdrop for this attractive city. Covered in evergreens, the hills rise to a height of 1,000 feet at the edge of downtown. Within these hills are Metro Washington Park Zoo, the International Rose Test Garden, the Japanese Gardens, and several other attractions. When you're ready to leave Portland and explore the beautiful Oregon countryside, it's easy to drive away on an Interstate and be far from the city in 30 minutes.

1. ORIENTATION

ARRIVING

BY PLANE   Portland International Airport (PDX) (tel. 503/ 335-1234) is located nine miles northeast of downtown Portland. The trip into town is entirely on interstates and takes about 20 minutes. The airport is small enough to be convenient but large enough to offer amenities you wouldn't expect. Tops on this list is the **PDX Conference Center,** which offers businesspeople a secluded and quiet working space. There are meeting rooms, fax machines, computer workstations, secretarial help, and more. This was the first such airport conference center in the United States. Also at the airport is the **Oregon Market,** a shopping mall featuring Oregon-based retail stores and food and beverage vendors. You can pick up a pair of Nike's as you run to make your flight or hook into a fresh salmon packed to go.

There's an information booth by the baggage-claim area where you can pick up maps and brochures and find out about transportation into the city.

Many downtown hotels provide courtesy shuttle service to and from the airport. Be sure to check at your hotel when you make a reservation. This is by far the best way to get in from the airport.

The next best way, if you haven't rented a car at the airport, is to take the **Raz Transportation Downtown Shuttle** (tel. 503/246-3301). They'll take you directly to your hotel for $7. They operate every 30 minutes from 5am to midnight daily.

Tri-Met public bus no. 12 leaves the airport approximately every 15 minutes from 5:30am to 11:50pm for the trip to downtown Portland. The trip takes about 40 minutes and costs $1. The bus between downtown and the airport operates between 5am and 12:30am and leaves from SW Sixth Avenue and Main Street.

A **taxi** into town costs around $21.

BY TRAIN Amtrak trains use historic **Union Station,** 800 NW Sixth Ave. (tel. 503/273-4865). For Amtrak schedule and fare information and reservations, call toll free 800/872-7245.

BY BUS The **Greyhound bus station** is located at 550 NW Sixth Ave. (tel. 503/243-2323).

BY CAR Portland's major interstates and smaller highways are **I-5** (north and south), **I-84** (east), **I-405** (circles around the west and south of downtown Portland), **I-205** (bypasses the city to the east), and **U.S. 26** (west).

If you have rented a car at the airport and want to reach central Portland, follow signs for downtown. These signs will take you first to I-205, then I-84, which brings you to the Willamette River. Take the Morrison Bridge exit to cross the river.

TOURIST INFORMATION

The **Portland/Oregon Visitors Association Information Center** is at Three World Trade Center, 26 SW Salmon St., Portland, OR 97204-3299 (tel. 503/222-2223 or toll free 800/962-3700). The association also maintains an information booth by the baggage-claim area at Portland Airport. If you happen to see two people walking down a Portland street wearing matching kelly-green hats and jackets, they are probably members of the **Portland Guide** service run by the Association for Portland Progress (tel. 503/224-8684). They'll be happy to answer any question you have about the city.

CITY LAYOUT

Portland is located in northwestern Oregon at the confluence of the Columbia and Willamette rivers. To the west are the West Hills, which rise to more than 1,000 feet. Some 90 miles west of the West Hills are the spectacular Oregon coast and the Pacific Ocean. To the east are rolling hills that extend to the Cascade Range, about 50 miles away. The most prominent peak in this section of the Cascades is Mount Hood (11,235 feet), a dormant volcanic peak that looms over the city on clear days. From many parts of Portland it's also possible to see Mount St. Helens, another volcano, which erupted spectacularly in 1980.

With about 1.5 million people in the entire metropolitan area, Portland is a relatively small city. This is especially evident when one begins to explore the compact downtown area. Nearly everything is

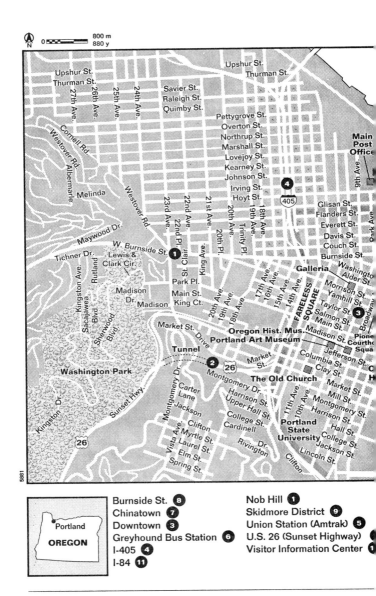

Burnside St. **8**	Nob Hill **1**	
Chinatown **7**	Skidmore District **9**	
Downtown **3**	Union Station (Amtrak) **5**	
Greyhound Bus Station **6**	U.S. 26 (Sunset Highway)	
I-405 **4**	Visitor Information Center **1**	
I-84 **11**		

Portland
OREGON

accessible on foot, and the city authorities do everything they can to encourage this.

MAIN ARTERIES & STREETS   I-84 (Banfield Freeway or **Expressway)** enters Portland from the east. East of the city is **I-205,** which bypasses downtown Portland and runs past the airport. **I-5 (East Bank Freeway)** runs through on a north–south axis, passing along the east bank of the Willamette River directly across from downtown. **I-405 (Stadium Freeway** and **Foothills**

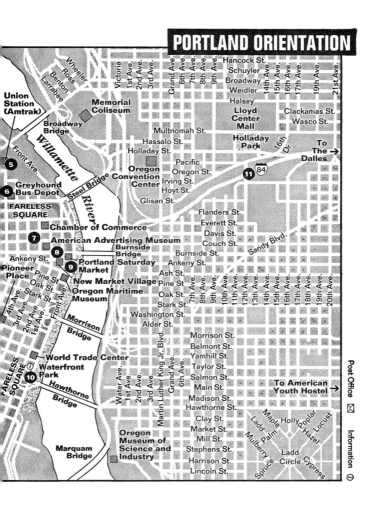

Freeway) circles around the west and south sides of downtown. **U.S. 26 (Sunset Highway)** leaves downtown heading west toward Beaverton and the coast. **Oregon Hwy. 217 (Beaverton–Tigard Highway)** runs south from U.S. 26 in Beaverton.

The most important artery within Portland is **Burnside Street.** This is the dividing line between north and south Portland. Dividing the city from east to west is the **Willamette River,** which is crossed by eight bridges in the downtown area. All these bridges are named: from north to south they are Fremont, Broadway, Steel, Burnside,

Morrison, Hawthorne, Marquam, and Ross Island. There are additional bridges beyond the downtown area.

For convenience sake I'll define downtown Portland as the 300-block area within **Fareless Square.** This is the area in which you can ride for free on the city's public buses and the MAX light-rail system. Fareless Square is bounded by I-405 on the west and south, by Hoyt Street on the north, and by the Willamette River on the east.

FINDING AN ADDRESS   Finding an address in Portland can be easy if you keep a number of things in mind. Almost all addresses in Portland, and even extending for miles beyond the city, include a map quadrant—NE (Northeast), SW (Southwest), and so forth. The dividing line between east and west is the Willamette River; between north and south it's Burnside Street. Any downtown address will be labeled either SW (Southwest) or NW (northwest). An exception to this rule is the area known as North Portland. Streets here have a plain "North" designation. This is the area across the Willamette River from downtown going toward Jantzen Beach.

Avenues run north–south and streets run east–west. Street names are the same on both sides of the Willamette River. Consequently, there is a Southwest Yamhill Street and a Southeast Yamhill Street. In northwest Portland street names are alphabetical going north from Burnside to Wilson. Front Avenue is the road nearest the Willamette River on the west side, and Water Avenue is the nearest on the east side. Beyond these are numbered avenues. On the west side you'll also find Broadway and Park Avenue between Sixth Avenue and Ninth Avenue. With each block, the addresses increase by 100, beginning at the Willamette River for avenues and at Burnside Street for streets. Odd numbers are generally on the west and north sides of the street, and even numbers on the east and south sides.

Here's an example. You want to go to 1327 SW Ninth Avenue. Because it's in the 1300 block, you'll find it 13 blocks south of Burnside and, because it's an odd number, on the west side of the street.

Getting to the address is a different story, since streets in downtown Portland are mostly one way. Front Avenue is two way, but then First, Third, Fifth, Broadway, and Eleventh are one way southbound. Alternating streets are one way northbound.

STREET MAPS   Contact the **Portland/Oregon Visitors Association,** Three World Trade Center, 26 SW Salmon St., Portland, OR 97204-3299 (tel. 503/222-2223 or toll free 800/962-3700), for a free map of the city. **Powell's "City of Books,"** 1005 W. Burnside St. (tel. 503/228-4651), has an excellent free map of downtown that also includes a walking-tour route and information on many of the sights you'll pass along the way. Members of the **American Automobile Association** can obtain a free map of the city at the AAA offices at 600 SW Market St. (tel. 503/222-6734) and 8555 SW Apple Way in Beaverton (tel. 503/243-6444).

NEIGHBORHOODS IN BRIEF

Downtown   This term usually refers to the business and shopping district south of Burnside and north of Jackson Street between the Willamette River and 13th Avenue. You'll find the major department stores, dozens of restaurants, most of the city's performing arts venues, and almost all of the best hotels in this area.

Chinatown   Portland has had a Chinatown almost since the earliest days. It is entered through the colorful Chinatown Gate at West Burnside Street and Fourth Avenue.

Skidmore District   Also known as Old Town, this is Portland's original commercial core and overlaps with Chinatown for a few streets. The center of this district is the Skidmore Fountain at SW Ankeny Street and SW Front Avenue. Many of the restored buildings in this neighborhood have become retail stores, which, along with the presence of the Portland Saturday Market here, has made this one of Portland's popular shopping districts. There are also half a dozen or so nightclubs.

Nob Hill   Centered along NW 23rd Avenue at the foot of the West Hills, Nob Hill is an old residential neighborhood that now includes interesting shops and restaurants. This is by far the most stylish neighborhood in town. It's named for Nob Hill in San Francisco.

Irvington   Though not as attractive as Nob Hill, Irvington, centered around Broadway in northeast Portland, is equally trendy. For several blocks along Broadway you'll find unusual boutiques, stores selling imports, and lots of excellent-but-inexpensive restaurants.

Hollywood District   One of the latest neighborhoods to attract attention in Portland is the Hollywood District of northeast Portland. This area, which centers around the busy commercial activities of Sandy Boulevard near 42nd Avenue, came into being in the early years of this century. The name is taken from the Hollywood Theater, an art deco–style area landmark. Throughout this neighborhood are craftsman-style houses and vernacular architecture of the period.

Sellwood   Situated in the southeast, this is Portland's antiques-store district and contains many restored Victorian houses. There are also excellent restaurants.

Hawthorne District   This enclave of southeast Portland is full of eclectic boutiques, moderately priced restaurants, and hip college students from nearby Reed College.

2. GETTING AROUND

BY PUBLIC TRANSPORTATION

FREE RIDES   Portland is committed to keeping its downtown uncongested, and to this end it has invested heavily in its public-transportation system. The single greatest innovation and best reason to ride the Tri-Met public buses and the MAX light-rail system is that they're free within an area known as the **Fareless Square.** That's right, free! There are 300 blocks of downtown included in the Fareless Square, and as long as you stay within the boundaries, you don't pay a cent. The Fareless Square covers the area between I-405 on the south and west, Hoyt Street on the north, and the Willamette River on the east.

BUS   Tri-Met buses operate daily over an extensive network. You can pick up the *Tri-Met Guide,* which lists all the bus routes with times, or individual route maps and time schedules at the **Tri-Met**

Customer Assistance Office, behind and beneath the waterfall fountain at Pioneer Courthouse Square (tel. 238-7433). The office is open Monday through Friday from 9am to 5pm.

Outside Fareless Square, fares on both Tri-Met buses and MAX are $1 or $1.30, depending on how far you travel. You can also make free transfers between the bus and the MAX light-rail system. A **day ticket** costing $3.50 is good for travel to all zones and is valid on both buses and MAX. Day tickets can be purchased from any bus driver.

Portland's other great public transportation innovation is the **Portland Transit Mall.** Nearly all Tri-Met buses pass through the Transit Mall on SW Fifth Avenue and SW Sixth Avenue. These two streets have very limited automobile access, being almost entirely devoted to pedestrians and public transit. There are brick sidewalks and streets, flower-filled planters, fountains, and sculpture to enhance the beauty of these streets, as well as umbrella-shaped glass shelters for waiting on rainy days. Each shelter indicates which bus stops there. Just walk along the street until you find the stop you need. Once you're at the right shelter, you'll see a lighted display with the next departure time.

MAX   The **Metropolitan Area Express (MAX)** is Portland's aboveground light-rail system that now connects downtown Portland with the eastern suburb of Gresham. MAX is basically a modern trolley; reproductions of vintage trolley cars operate during certain times on weekends. You can ride MAX for free if you stay within Fareless Square, which includes all the downtown area. However, be sure to buy your ticket before you board MAX if you're traveling out of Fareless Square. Fares are the same as on buses. There are ticket-vending machines at all MAX stops that tell you how much to pay for your destination; these machines also give change. The MAX driver cannot sell tickets. There are ticket inspectors who randomly check tickets. If you don't have one, you can be fined $250.

The MAX light-rail system crosses the Transit Mall on SW Morrison Street and SW Yamhill Street. Transfers to the bus are free.

BY TAXI

Because most everything in Portland is fairly close together, getting around by taxi can be economical. Although there are almost always taxis waiting in line at major hotels, you won't find them cruising the streets—you'll have to phone for one. **Broadway Cab** (tel. 227-1234) and **Radio Cab** (tel. 227-1212) both offer 24-hour radio-dispatched service and accept American Express, Discover, MasterCard, and VISA credit cards. Fares are $2 for the first mile and $1.50 for each additional mile.

BY CAR

CAR RENTALS   For the best deal on a rental car, I highly recommend making a reservation at least one week before you arrive in Portland. It also pays to call several times over a period of a few weeks just to ask prices; the last time I rented a car, the same company quoted me different prices every time I called to ask about rates. Remember the old Wall Street adage: Buy low! If you didn't have time to plan ahead, ask about special weekend rates or discounts you might be eligible for. And don't forget to mention that you are a frequent flyer: You might be able to get miles for your car rental. Also, be sure to find out whether your credit card pays the collision-damage waiver, which can add a bundle to the cost of a rental. Currently, daily rates for a subcompact are around $35 and weekly rates are around $140.

You'll find the major car-rental companies represented in Portland, and there are also many independent and smaller car-rental agencies listed in the Portland Yellow Pages. Inside the main arrivals terminal at Portland International Airport, right behind the baggage-claim area, you'll find the following companies:

Avis (tel. 503/249-4950 or toll free 800/831-2847).

Budget (tel. 503/249-6500 or toll free 800/527-0700), which also has offices downtown at 2033 SW Fourth Ave., on the east side at 2323 NE Columbia Blvd., and in Beaverton at 10835 SW Canyon Rd.

Dollar (tel. 503/249-4792 or toll free 800/800-4000), which also has an office downtown at NW Broadway and NW Davis St. (tel. 503/228-3540).

Hertz (tel. 503/249-8216 or toll free 800/654-3131), which also has an office downtown at 1009 SW Sixth Ave. (tel. 503/249-5727).

National (tel. 503/249-4900 or toll free 800/227-7368).

Outside the airport is **Thrifty,** at 10800 NE Holman St. (tel. 503/254-6563 or toll free 800/367-2277), which also has an office downtown at 632 SW Pine St. (tel. 503/227-6587).

PARKING   Portland is lucky in having far more downtown parking facilities than most cities its size. However, as you probably know, this is never enough. Parking downtown can be a problem, especially if you show up weekdays after workers have gotten to their offices. There are a couple of very important things to remember when parking downtown.

When parking on the street, be sure to notice the meter's time limit. These vary from as little as 15 minutes (these are always right in front of the restaurant or museum where you plan to spend 2 hours) to long-term (read long walk). Most common are 30- and 60-minute meters. You don't have to feed the meters after 6pm or on Sunday.

If you're going shopping, look for a red-and-green sign that says "2 hr free park downtown" at pay parking lots. Spend $15 or more at any participating merchant and you get two hours of free parking. Rates in public lots range from 75¢ up to about $2 per hour.

DRIVING RULES   You may turn right on a red light after a full stop, and if you are in the far left lane of a one-way street, you may turn left into the adjacent left lane at a red light after a full stop.

BY BICYCLE

Bicycles are a very popular way of getting around Portland. The downtown stoplights are timed at 13 miles per hour, so a bicycle can easily keep up with automobile traffic. For leisurely cycling, try the promenade in Waterfront Park. There's another esplanade path on the east side of the river between the Hawthorne and Burnside bridges. The Terwilliger Path runs for 10 miles from Portland State University to Tryon Creek State Park in the West Hills. You can pick up a copy of a bike map of the city of Portland at any bike shop. At **Agape Cycle & Sport,** 2314 SE Division St. (tel. 230-0317), you can rent a road or mountain bike for $15 to $25 a day. They're open Monday to Saturday from 10am to 6pm.

ON FOOT

City blocks in Portland are about half the size of most city blocks elsewhere, and the entire downtown area covers only about 13 blocks by 26 blocks. These two facts make Portland a very easy place to explore on foot. The city has been very active in encouraging people to get out of their cars and onto the sidewalks downtown. The sidewalks are wide, and there are many small parks with benches for resting, fountains for cooling off, and works of art for soothing the soul.

If you happen to spot a couple of people wearing kelly-green baseball caps and jackets and navy-blue pants, they're probably a pair of Portland Guides. These informative souls are there to answer any questions you might have about Portland—"Where am I?" for instance. Their job is simply to walk the streets and answer questions.

FAST *PORTLAND*

Airport   **Portland International Airport (PDX)** is located nine miles northeast of downtown Portland; for information call 503/335-1234.

American Express   The **American Express Travel Service Office** (tel. 226-2961) is located at 1100 SW Sixth Ave.—corner of Sixth and Main. The office is open Monday through Friday from 9am to 5pm. You can cash American Express traveler's checks and exchange foreign currency here.

Area Code   The area code for Portland and the entire state of Oregon is **503.**

Babysitters   Call **Rent-A-Mom** (tel. 222-5779) if your hotel doesn't offer babysitting services.

Business Hours   In Portland **banks** are generally open Monday through Thursday from 9am to 3pm, with later hours (to 6pm) on Friday. **Offices** are generally open Monday through Friday from 8:30 or 9am to 5 or 5:30pm. In general, **stores** in the downtown area are open Monday through Friday from 10am to 6pm. Many stores have later hours one or two times a week—usually on Monday and Friday evenings. **Bars** stay open until 1 or 2:30am.

Car Rentals   See Section 2 of this chapter.

Climate   See "Climate" in Section 2 of Chapter 12.

Dentist   If you need a dentist while you are in Portland, contact the **Multnomah Dental Society** for a referral (tel. 223-4731).

Doctor   If you need a physician while in Portland, contact the **Multnomah County Medical Society** for a referral (tel. 222-0156).

Driving Rules   See Section 2 of this chapter.

Drugstore   Convenient to most downtown hotels, **Central Drug,** 538 SW Fourth Ave. (tel. 226-2222), is open Monday to Friday from 9am to 6pm, on Saturday from 9am to 5pm.

Emergencies   For police, fire, or medical emergencies, phone **911.**

Eyeglasses   Stocking a wide range of designer eyeglass frames, **Zell Optical,** 816 SW Morrison St. (tel. 228-0104), has been in business for more than 40 years. They perform optical examinations and will be happy to replace your lost glasses.

Hairdressers/Barbers   **Dionne's Coiffures,** 1975 SW First Ave. (tel. 227-5565), is a full-service salon for men, women, and children. They even offer computer video-graphic hair styling. Open daily.

Holidays   See "Calendar of Events" in Chapter 12 and "Holidays" in "Fast Facts: For the Foreign Traveler" in the Appendix.

Hospitals   Three area hospitals are **Good Samaritan,** 1015 NW 22nd Ave. (tel. 229-7711); **St. Vincent Hospital,** 9205 SW Barnes Rd. (tel. 291-2115), off U.S. 26 (Sunset Highway) before Oregon Hwy. 217; and the **Oregon Health Sciences University Hospital,** 3181 SW Sam Jackson Park Rd. (tel. 494-8311), just south of the city center.

Hotlines   **AIDS,** 223-2437; **battered women,** 235-5333; **child abuse,** 731-3100; **alcohol and drug helpline,** 232-8083; **rape,** 235-5333; **suicide prevention,** 223-6161.

Information   For tourist information, contact **Portland/ Oregon Visitors Information Association** at Three World Trade Center, 26 SW Salmon St., Portland, OR 97204-3299 (tel. 503/275-9750 or toll free 800/962-3700). While you're in Portland, if you spot members of the **Portland Guide service**—dressed in kelly-green hats and jackets—they'll be happy to answer any question you have about the city.

Laundry/Dry Cleaning   **Downtown Cleaners** offers dry cleaning at two locations, 609 SW Third Ave. (tel. 227-7881), and 621 SW Washington St. (tel. 226-1255); open Monday through Friday from 7am to 6pm, on Saturday from 10am to 2pm. **Starting Point Laundromat,** 302 NW Sixth Ave. (tel. 222-3316), is open daily from 7am to 8pm.

Library   The **Multnomah County Library,** 801 SW 10th Ave. (tel. 248-5123), is Portland's largest library. It's open Monday through Thursday from 10am to 8pm, on Friday and Saturday from 10am to 5:30pm, and on Sunday from 1 to 5pm.

Liquor Laws   The legal minimum drinking age in Oregon is 21.

Lost Property   If you lose something on a bus or the MAX, call **238-4855** Monday through Friday from 10am to 5pm. If you lose something at the airport, call **335-1277.**

Luggage Storage/Lockers   You'll find coin-operated luggage-storage lockers at the **Greyhound bus station,** 550 NW Sixth Ave.

Mail   You can receive mail c/o General Delivery at the main post office (see "Post Offices," below).

Maps   See Section 1 of this chapter.

Newspapers/Magazines   Portland's morning daily newspaper is the *Oregonian.* For arts and entertainment information and listings, pick up a free copy of *Willamette Week.* Another free weekly that has information about Portland is the *Portland Downtowner.* The *Portland Guide* is a weekly tourism guide to Portland and is available at hotels.

Photographic Needs   Flashback Foto, 900 SW Fourth Ave. (tel. 224-6776), offers 1-hour film processing. It's open Monday through Friday from 7am to 7pm, on Saturday from 9am to 6pm, and on Sunday from noon to 5pm. **Camera World,** 500 SW Fifth Ave. (tel. 222-0008), is the largest camera and video store in the city; open Monday through Friday from 9am to 6pm, on Saturday from 10am to 6pm, and on Sunday from 11am to 5pm.

Police   To reach the police, call **911.**

Post Offices   The **main post office,** 715 NW Hoyt St. (tel. 294-2410), is open Monday through Friday from 7:30am to 6:30pm, Saturday from 8:30am to 5pm. There are also convenient post offices at 204 SW Fifth Ave. (tel. 221-0202), open Monday through Friday from 8:30am to 5pm, and 1505 SW Sixth Ave. (tel. 221-0199), open Monday through Friday from 8:30am to 5pm.

Radio   There are more than 30 AM and FM radio stations in the Portland area. Together they offer every imaginable type of music, news, and sports. KOPB-FM (91.5) is the local National Public Radio station.

Religious Services   In the downtown area you can find the following churches and synagogues: **First Baptist,** 909 SW 11th Ave. (tel. 228-7465); **St. James Lutheran,** 1315 SW Park Ave. (tel. 227-2439); **First Presbyterian,** 1200 SW Alder St. (tel. 228-7331); **First Unitarian,** 1034 SW 13th Ave. (tel. 228-6389); **First Christian,** 1314 SW Park Ave. (tel. 228-9211); **St. Stephen's Episcopal,** 1432 SW 13th Ave. (tel. 223-6424); **St. Michael's Roman Catholic,** 424 SW Mill St. (tel. 228-8629); **Sixth Church (Christian Science),** 1331 SW Park Ave. (tel. 227-6024); **Congregation Beth Israel (Reform),** 1931 NW Flanders St. (tel. 222-1069); **Congregation Neveh Sholom (Conservative),** 2900 SW Peaceful Lane (tel. 246-8831); **Congregation Kesser Israel (Orthodox),** 136 SW Meade St. (tel. 222-1239); and **First United Methodist,** 1838 SW Jefferson St. (tel. 228-3195).

Restrooms   There are public restrooms underneath Starbuck's coffee shop in Pioneer Courthouse Square and in downtown shopping malls.

Safety   Because of its small size and emphasis on keeping the downtown alive and growing, Portland is still a relatively safe city; in fact, strolling the downtown streets at night is a popular pastime. Take extra precautions, however, if you venture into the entertainment district along West Burnside Street or Chinatown at night. Parts of northeast Portland are controlled by street gangs, so before visiting any place in this area, be sure to get very detailed directions so that you don't get lost. If you plan to go hiking in Forest Park, don't leave anything valuable in your car. This holds true in the Old Town district as well.

Shoe Repair   Busy Shoes, 533 SW Alder St. (tel. 223-0046), is the spiffiest-looking shoe-repair shop I've ever seen. They're set up to resemble a tiny diner, with bar stools and a little counter. They'll fix your shoes while you wait, any time Monday through Friday from 9am to 6pm.

Taxes   Portland is a shopper's paradise—there's no sales tax. However, there is a 9% tax on hotel rooms within the city of Portland. Outside the city, the room tax varies.

Taxis   To get a cab, call **Broadway Cab** at 227-1234 or **Radio Cab** at 227-1212. See also Section 2 of this chapter.

Television   Channels in Portland are 2 (ABC), 6 (CBS), 8 (NBC), 10 (PBS), 12, 24 (religious), and 49. All major cable networks are also available.

Time   Portland is on **Pacific Time,** making it three hours behind the East Coast.

Tipping   In restaurants, if the service has been good, tip 15 to 20% of the bill. Taxi drivers expect about 10% of the fare. Airport porters and bellhops should be tipped about 50¢ per bag. For chambermaids, $1 per night is an appropriate tip.

Transit Information   For bus information, call the **Tri-Met Customer Assistance Office** at 503/238-RIDE. They're open Monday through Friday from 7:30am to 5:30pm. You can pick up a *Tri-Met Guide* from their office located beneath the waterfall fountain at Pioneer Courthouse Square. For **Amtrak** schedule and fare information, call toll free 800/872-7245. To reach **Union Station** (for train arrival times only), call 503/273-4865. For the **Greyhound bus station**, call 503/243-2323.

Useful Telephone Numbers   You may find the following telephone numbers useful during your stay in Portland: **Alcoholics Anonymous** (tel. 223-8569), **Portland Center for the Performing Arts Information Hotline** (tel. 796-9293), and the **Nike Runner's Hotline** (tel. 223-7867).

Weather   If it's summer, it's sunny; otherwise, there's a chance of rain. This is almost always a sufficient weather forecast in Portland, but for specifics, call weather information (tel. 236-7575).

3. NETWORKS & RESOURCES

FOR STUDENTS   There are no huge universities in Portland, but there are a number of smaller ones. **Portland State University,** 724 SW Harrison St. (tel. 725-3000), in downtown Portland, is a state-run commuter college. The **University of Portland,** 5000 N. Willamette Blvd. (tel. 283-7911), in North Portland, is operated by the Holy Cross Fathers of Notre Dame. The parklike campus is situated on a scenic bluff high over the Willamette River. **Reed College,** 3203 SE Woodstock St. (tel. 771-1112), a small private college of the liberal arts in southeastern Portland, was an anachronism when it opened in 1911. It shunned fraternities, sororities, athletics, and other aspects of college life in favor of academic excellence. Today it ranks highest in the number of Rhodes Scholars produced for a college of its size.

FOR GAY MEN & LESBIANS   Gay men and women visiting Portland should be sure to pick up a free copy of *Just Out,* a monthly newspaper for the gay community. You can usually find copies at **Powell's Books,** 1005 W. Burnside St., or phone 236-1252 to find out where you can obtain a copy. The newspaper covers local news of interest to gays. They also publish a resource guide for lesbians and gays called *The Just Out Pocket Book*. Call the above number to find out where you can get a copy. The guide is a free directory of Portland businesses that welcome gay customers.

FOR WOMEN   **Old Wives' Tales,** 1300 E. Burnside St. (tel. 238-0470), is a restaurant that, although not strictly for women, has for years been popular with feminists and single mothers. It's open Monday through Thursday from 8am to 10pm, on Friday from 8am to 11pm, on Saturday from 9am to 11pm, and on Sunday from 9am to 10pm. They have a small browsing library and a children's playroom.

The women's **crisis hotline** number is 235-5333.

FOR SENIORS   In addition to the discounts senior citizens can get at events, museums, hotels, and on tours, there is a local monthly newspaper specifically for older citizens: *Spectrum*. Call 244-2227 for information on where you can pick up a copy.

IMPRESSIONS

We want you to visit our State of Excitement often. Come again and again. But for heaven's sake, don't move here to live. Or if you do have to move in to live, don't tell any of your neighbors where you are going.
—GOV. TOM MCCALL, 1971

CHAPTER 14

PORTLAND ACCOMMODATIONS

1. DOWNTOWN
- **FROMMER'S SMART TRAVELER: HOTELS**
- **FROMMER'S COOL FOR KIDS: HOTELS**

2. NORTH PORTLAND

3. NORTHEAST PORTLAND

4. SOUTHEAST & SOUTHWEST PORTLAND

5. NEAR THE AIRPORT

6. BEAVERTON/TIGARD AREA

Although room rates are slowly creeping up to what they are in other major U.S. cities, Portland's hotels are still relatively inexpensive. In the following listings, **very expensive** hotels are those charging more than $120 per night for a double room; **expensive** hotels, $90 to $120 per night for a double; **moderate** hotels, $60 to $90 per night for a double; and **inexpensive** hotels, less than $60 per night for a double. These rates do not include the hotel-room tax of 9%. A few hotels include breakfast in their rates, and this has been noted in the listings; others offer complimentary breakfast only on certain deluxe floors. In most cases you will need to tip the bellhops and chambermaids. If tips are included in a hotel's rates, I have noted this also. **Parking** rates are per day.

If you are planning to visit during the busy summer months, make reservations as far in advance as possible and be sure to ask if special rates are available. Almost all large hotels offer weekend discounts of as much as 50%. For other days, you might be able to obtain a discount simply by asking for one. Who knows—if the hotel isn't busy, you just might be able to negotiate.

If you enjoy staying in bed-and-breakfast homes and inns, you may wish to contact **Northwest Bed & Breakfast Travel Unlimited,** 610 SW Broadway, Portland, OR 97205 (tel. 503/243-7616). This service represents more than 75 B&Bs in the Portland and Seattle areas. It also lists homes throughout Oregon, Washington, and British Columbia and in parts of California. Included are some unhosted city apartments, mountain cabins, and beach houses. You might order the *Directory of West Coast Homes* for $7.95, and reservations can then be made by contacting the service. All homes have been inspected and are clean and comfortable. Many offer airport pick up. Rates average between $30 and $55 for singles and between $40 and $70 for doubles.

For information on other B&Bs in Portland and the rest of Oregon, contact **Portland Innkeepers,** P.O. Box 69292, Portland, OR 97201; **Oregon Bed & Breakfast Directory,** 230 Red Spur Dr., Grants Pass, OR 97527; or **Oregon Bed & Breakfast Guild,** P.O. Box 3187, Ashland, OR 97520.

1. DOWNTOWN

VERY EXPENSIVE

THE BENSON HOTEL, 309 SW Broadway, Portland, OR 97205. Tel. 503/228-2000 or toll free 800/426-0670. Fax 503/226-4603. 289 rms, 47 suites. A/C TV TEL
$ Rates: $130–$165 single; $130–$190 double; $155–$600 suite. AE, CB, DC, DISC, ER, JCB, MC, V. **Parking:** Valet $10.

With its mansard roof and French baroque lobby, the Benson, built in 1913, exudes old-world sophistication and elegance. Circassian walnut from Russia covers the lobby walls, framing a marble fireplace. A marble staircase with wrought-iron railing leads from the grand lobby to the mezzanine, and Austrian crystal chandeliers hang from the ornate plasterwork ceiling. It's easy to imagine movie stars or royalty rushing in surrounded by popping flashbulbs. The Benson underwent a $16-million face-lift a few years ago and is looking as fresh as the day it opened, but unfortunately, room rates took a corresponding leap upward.

The guest rooms, housed in two towers above the lobby, have all been redone in shades of pale gray, with elegant classic French Second Empire furnishings that include large desks and armoires that hide the TVs. The deluxe queens are particularly roomy and come with seven pillows per bed. Baths have also been upgraded and include pedestal sinks, but very little shelf space for spreading out your toiletries.

Dining/Entertainment: In the vaults below the lobby is The London Grill (see next chapter), one of Portland's best dining establishments. Open for breakfast, lunch, and dinner, it features fresh seafood specialties. Trader Vic's, on the ground floor, has become an international institution over the years, and this branch of the famous Polynesian-motif restaurant and bar serves up all the expected meals and colossal cocktails. The Lobby Court serves a buffet lunch from 11:30am to 2pm Monday through Friday, and cocktails until midnight on weekdays and 1am on weekends. Both the London Grill and Trader Vic's also have their own bars.

Services: 24-hour room service, concierge, valet parking, in-room movies, airport shuttle service ($7 each way), valet/laundry service.

Facilities: Privileges at nearby athletic club, gift shop, no-smoking floor.

GOVERNOR HOTEL, SW 10th Ave. and Alder St., Portland, OR 97205. Tel. 503/224-3400 or toll free 800/554-3456. Fax 503/224-9426. 100 rms, 32 suites. A/C TV TEL MINIBAR
$ Rates: $135–$165 single; $155–$185 double; $185–$600 suite. Weekend and special packages available. AE, CB, DC, MC, V. **Parking:** Valet $10.

Governor Hotel, which opened in 1909, not long after the 1905 Lewis and Clark Exposition, is one of Portland's several historic hotels and is listed on the National Register of Historic Places. In 1992 this hotel reopened after a massive renovation that turned the landmark building into an homage to the Lewis and Clark Expedition. Throughout the hotel, you'll spot references to the famous explorers, but it is the wall mural in the lobby that most captures the attention. Scenes from Lewis and Clark's journals are depicted in sepia tones that help give the lobby its Western appeal. A fireplace and heavy overstuffed leather chairs add to the ranch atmosphere of the lobby.

Guest rooms, on the other hand, are anything but rustic, and instead feature an Asian influence, such as painted porcelain lamps and black-and-gold lacquered tables. Because this is an old building and most rooms did not originally have bathrooms, rooms vary considerably in size. The least expensive are rather small but are nevertheless very comfortable. Unfortunately bathrooms are in general quite small and lack counter space. Suites on the other hand are quite spacious, and some even have huge patios overlooking the city. Many of the suites also have their own fireplaces.

Dining/Entertainment: Celilo (pronounced suh-LIE-low), the hotel's restaurant, is a grand, old-fashioned hall with burnished wood columns, slowly turning overhead fans, and raised booths along the outside walls (see next chapter). The menu features a mix of Northwest cuisine with a distinct pan-Pacific influence. Between the lobby and the restaurant, you'll find the Celilo Lounge and the Dome Room. The latter is notable for its stunning stained-glass dome skylight. Both these rooms sport Asian motifs. There is live jazz in the lounge Thursday through Saturday nights.

Services: 24-hour room service; concierge; personal computers, fax machines available; complimentary morning newspaper and coffee, afternoon tea, and evening wine; overnight shoeshine; valet/laundry service.

Facilities: Business center; wheelchair and hearing-impaired accommodations; Princeton Athletic Club, in basement, with lap pool, running track, whirlpool spa, steam rooms, sauna, exercise room.

THE HEATHMAN HOTEL, SW Broadway at Salmon St., Portland, OR 97205. Tel. 503/241-4100 or toll free 800/551-0011. Fax 503/790-7110. 152 rms, 16 suites. A/C TV TEL

$ Rates: $135–$175 single; $155–$195 double; $185–$375 suite. Weekend and other packages available. AE, CB, DC, MC, V. **Parking:** $9.

Understated luxury, style, and sophistication have made the Heathman the finest hotel in Portland. Opened in 1927, it is listed on the National Register of Historic Places. Original art, from 18th-century oil paintings to Andy Warhol prints, give the place a museum atmosphere. A marble-and-teak lobby opens onto the Tea Court, where a fireplace, sweeping staircase, grand piano, and the original eucalyptus paneling create a warm atmosphere.

Every guest room is decorated with original works of art and photographs, matching bedspreads, and unusual Roman shades in English chintzes, torchère lamps, rattan bedsteads, and glass-topped tables. An elegant wood armoire hides the remote-control TV. Live plants impart a homey feel. In the bath you'll find European soaps and shampoos, plush terry-cloth robes, and large towels.

Dining/Entertainment: The Heathman Restaurant and Bar is one of the finest restaurants in Portland, and has been receiving rave reviews since it opened. The menu, which changes seasonally,

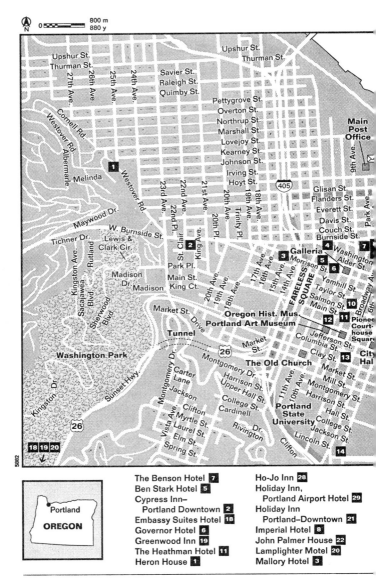

The Benson Hotel **7**	Ho-Jo Inn **28**
Ben Stark Hotel **5**	Holiday Inn,
Cypress Inn–	Portland Airport Hotel **29**
Portland Downtown **2**	Holiday Inn
Embassy Suites Hotel **18**	Portland–Downtown **21**
Governor Hotel **6**	Imperial Hotel **8**
Greenwood Inn **19**	John Palmer House **22**
The Heathman Hotel **11**	Lamplighter Motel **20**
Heron House **1**	Mallory Hotel **3**

emphasizes fresh local produce, seafood, and game, all combined in imaginative and delectable creations. B. Moloch/Heathman Bakery & Pub, the hotel's informal, but equally popular, second restaurant is located two blocks away at 901 SW Salmon St. The emphasis is similar, but prices are much lower. The two restaurants have cozy bars. (See next chapter for details on both.) At the hotel's Mezzanine Bar, there is live jazz music several nights a week for most of the year. Afternoon tea is served daily in the Lobby Lounge.

Services: 24-hour room service, concierge, valet parking, 350

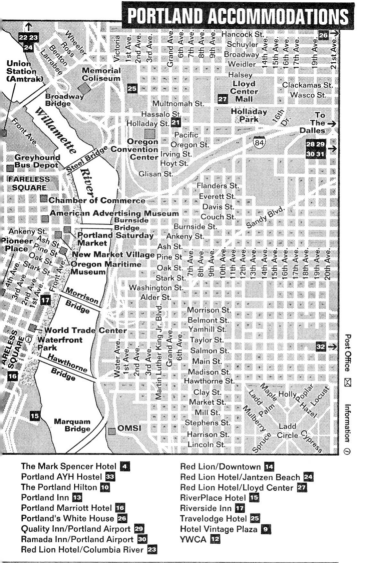

PORTLAND ACCOMMODATIONS

The Mark Spencer Hotel **4**
Portland AYH Hostel **33**
The Portland Hilton **10**
Portland Inn **13**
Portland Marriott Hotel **16**
Portland's White House **26**
Quality Inn/Portland Airport **29**
Ramada Inn/Portland Airport **30**
Red Lion Hotel/Columbia River **23**

Red Lion/Downtown **14**
Red Lion Hotel/Jantzen Beach **24**
Red Lion Hotel/Lloyd Center **27**
RiverPlace Hotel **15**
Riverside Inn **17**
Travelodge Hotel **25**
Hotel Vintage Plaza **9**
YWCA **12**

film videotape library, valet/laundry service, complimentary newspaper, airport shuttle, waterproof running map.
   Facilities: Privileges at nearby athletic club, wheelchair accommodations, no-smoking rooms, in-room exercise equipment, gift shop.

THE PORTLAND HILTON HOTEL, 921 SW Sixth Ave., Portland, OR 97204-1296. Tel. 503/226-1611 or toll free 800/HILTONS. Fax 503/220-2565. 455 rms, 16 suites. A/C TV TEL

$ Rates: $95–$145 single; $115–$165 double; $280–$900 suite. Weekend and other packages available. AE, CB, DC, MC, V. **Parking:** Valet $16.

Centrally located near businesses, the performing arts center, and several museums, this modern high-rise attracts many tour groups and conventions and is always bustling with activity. The marble-walled lobby is intimate and quiet, and there are three restaurants within steps.

All rooms, renovated in the past few years, are decorated in relaxing pastels and floral prints. Comfortable wingback chairs, tables, and desks make both businesspeople and those with time to relax feel right at home. Be sure to request a floor as high as possible to take advantage of the views. The corner rooms with king-size beds are particularly nice.

Dining/Entertainment: From its 23rd-floor aerie, Alexander's offers a striking panorama of Portland, the Willamette River, and snow-covered Mount Hood (see next chapter). Back down at lobby level is the informal Twigs restaurant, with its popular lunchtime salad buffet. Up a flight of stairs from the lobby is the International Club and Lounge. Pettygrove's is a casual lounge just off the lobby.

Services: Room service, concierge, in-room movies, laundry/ valet service, overnight shoeshine service.

Facilities: Fitness center, heated outdoor swimming pool, gift shop, beauty salon/barber, business center, wheelchair accommodations, no-smoking floors.

PORTLAND MARRIOTT HOTEL, 1401 SW Front Ave., Portland, OR 97201. Tel. 503/226-7600 or toll free 800/228-9290. Fax 503/221-1789. 503 rms, 28 suites. A/C TV TEL

$ Rates: $109–$150 single; $109–$160 double; $300–$350 suite. Weekend and other packages available. AE, CB, DC, DISC, ER, JCB, MC, V. **Parking:** Valet $14.

Just across Front Avenue from the Willamette River, the Portland Marriott is the flashiest of the city's hotels. A massive portico complete with lava-rock waterfall and bamboo deer scarer ushers you into a high-ceilinged lobby filled with bright lights. Red floral carpets, small groupings of comfortable lavender chairs, and gentle piped-in classical music tone down the glitz.

Almost all the accommodations have small balconies. Ask for a room overlooking the river, throw back the glass door to the balcony, and consider that the view used to be of a noisy freeway. On a clear day Mount Hood looms in the distance. The decor in the rooms is simple but attractive.

Dining/Entertainment: The King's Wharf restaurant features fresh seafood, Northwest specialties, and a view of the river below. Fazzio's is a family restaurant serving breakfast, lunch, and dinner. Champions is a very popular sports bar with all the requisite sports memorabilia on the walls; after night games there's dancing to recorded music. The lobby bar attracts a much more sedate and sophisticated clientele, as is obvious from the small library of books available to guests.

Services: Room service, concierge floor, in-room movies, valet/ laundry service, shoeshine stand, babysitting service, valet parking, video checkout and message viewing, massage.

Facilities: Exercise room, indoor pool, whirlpool, saunas, games room, weight room, sun deck, beauty salon, gift shop, newsstand, no-smoking floors.

RIVERPLACE HOTEL, 1510 SW Harbor Way, Portland, OR 97201. Tel. 503/228-3233 or toll free outside Oregon 800/227-1333. Fax 503/295-6161. 84 rms, 45 suites. A/C TV TEL

$ Rates (including continental breakfast): $155 single; $175–$190 double; $190–$210 junior suite, $210–$500 suite. AE, CB, DC, MC, V. **Parking:** Valet $10.

With the sloping lawns of Waterfront Park to one side and the Willamette River at its back doorstep, the RiverPlace occupies an enviable location in downtown Portland. If you prefer the quiet atmosphere of a European-style small resort over the crowds of a convention hotel, try the RiverPlace. As part of the renovation of the city's waterfront, this complex incorporates not only this fine hotel but shops, restaurants, and condominiums. The promenade along the waterfront, with a marina full of private boats floating below, is Portland's best spot for a sunset stroll.

Spacious rooms are decorated with wingback chairs, teak tables, writing desks, and lacquered armoires. Nearly half the rooms here are suites, and these come with wood-burning fireplaces, wet bars, and whirlpool baths. In all rooms you can open the large windows to let in cool breezes that waft down the Willamette. In the bath you'll find a delightful assortment of luxurious soaps, shampoos, lotions, and gels. In the closet are terry-cloth robes and sweatsuits (this is a fitness-oriented city)! Forget your running shoes? Don't worry. Ring down to the desk and they'll send up a pair (and a running map so you can find your way back to the hotel). Planning a long stay in town? The hotel can arrange for you to stay in one of their adjacent condominiums. Keep in mind that there is a no-tipping policy in effect except for food and beverage service.

Dining/Entertainment: The Esplanade Restaurant overlooks the river. Northwest and continental cuisines are the specialty here (see next chapter). For al fresco dining there's the Patio, featuring sandwiches, burgers, and steaks. Just off the lobby is a very comfortable bar where light meals are served to the accompaniment of live piano music and a crackling fire in cool weather.

Services: 24-hour room service, concierge, turn-down service, in-room movies, complimentary shoeshine, valet/laundry service, complimentary morning paper.

Facilities: Whirlpool, sauna, privileges at nearby athletic club, wheelchair accommodations, in-room computer and fax connections, voice mail.

HOTEL VINTAGE PLAZA, 422 SW Broadway, Portland, OR 97205. Tel. 503/228-1212 or toll free 800/243-0555. Fax 503/228-3598. 107 rms, 21 suites. A/C MINIBAR TV TEL

$ Rates (including continental breakfast): $145 single; $165 double; $165–$205 suite. AE, CB, DC, DISC, MC, V. **Parking:** Valet $10.

This recently renovated deluxe hotel sports Italianate decor and a wine theme that plays up the budding Oregon wine industry. The intimate lobby is divided into two seating areas with low lighting and comfortable easy chairs. In the main seating area, there is a fireplace flanked by bookshelves that hold old volumes. Soaring up from the lobby is a 10-story atrium that gives this old building a very modern feel.

All accommodations are different, and though the starlight rooms and two-level suites are real scene-stealers, the standard rooms also have much to recommend them. Roman window shades and old Italian architectural prints are elements of the Italianate decor. Long pink granite counters, gold-tone designer faucets, and green-taffeta shower curtains and walls make the bathrooms here the classiest in town. However, it is the starlight rooms that are truly extraordinary. Though small, they have greenhouse-style wall-into-ceiling windows that provide very romantic views at night and let in lots of light during the day. These rooms have wicker furniture and pale-pastel color schemes, creating a tropical feel. The two-level suites, some with Japanese soaking tubs and one with a spiral staircase, are equally stunning. On the concierge club floors, you get special treatment.

Dining/Entertainment: Ristorante Pazzo is a dark and intimate trattoria just off the lobby (see next chapter). You can gaze into the restaurant through a wall of glass, and prominently displayed wine racks remind you of the hotel's theme once again. Hotel guests get preferential seating in the restaurant.

Services: Complimentary evening wine, shoeshine service, morning newspaper, valet/laundry service, concierge floors, turndown service.

Facilities: Executive gym, business center, no-smoking rooms, wheelchair accommodations.

EXPENSIVE

RED LION HOTEL/DOWNTOWN, 310 SW Lincoln St., Portland, OR 97201. Tel. 503/221-0450 or toll free 800/547-8010. Fax 503/226-6260. 235 rms, 3 suites. A/C TV TEL

$ Rates: $93–$103 single; $108–$125 double; $225–$325 suite. Weekend and other packages available. AE, CB, DC, MC, V.
Parking: Free.

Situated on a shady tree-lined street on the southern edge of downtown Portland, this low-rise hotel offers convenience and comfort. The design and landscaping reflect the Northwest. A glass-enclosed walkway leads to the lobby from the parking lot, and in the courtyard surrounding the swimming pool are lush plantings of evergreens and other shrubs.

Red Lion Inns are noted for the spaciousness of their guest rooms, and this one is no exception. Large windows let in lots of precious Northwest light when the sun shines. All rooms come with king- or queen-size beds.

Dining/Entertainment: The Cityside Restaurant offers a wide variety of well-prepared meals, with the focus on fresh local seafood. In the adjacent Cityside Lounge, there is karaoke nightly. Club Max is the hotel's disco, with recorded Top 40 music Monday through Saturday.

Services: Room service, complimentary airport shuttle, valet/laundry service.

Facilities: Outdoor pool, gift shop, wheelchair accommodations, coin laundry.

MODERATE

IMPERIAL HOTEL, 400 SW Broadway, Portland, OR 97205. Tel. 503/228-7221 or toll free 800/452-2323. 136 rms. A/C TV TEL

$ Rates: $55–$65 single; $65–$75 double. AE, CB, DC, DISC, MC, V. **Parking:** Free.

Although it doesn't quite live up to its regal name, this older hotel—catercorner to the Benson Hotel—is a fine choice if you're on a budget. It recently underwent a complete renovation that, surprisingly, didn't raise the rates more than $20. Rooms here are clean and comfortable, with new furniture (psuedo–Louis XIV) and lavender color schemes. Bathrooms are older (they even have porcelain shower knobs) but in good shape. The corner king rooms, with large windows, are the best choices here. All rooms come with clock radios, and local phone calls are free.

Dining/Entertainment: The hotel's restaurant/lounge is a popular meeting place with downtown businesspeople.

Services: In-room movies, valet/laundry service, room service.

Facilities: Wheelchair accommodations.

F FROMMER'S SMART TRAVELER: HOTELS

VALUE-CONSCIOUS TRAVELERS SHOULD TAKE ADVANTAGE OF THE FOLLOWING:

1. Weekend discounts of 30 to 50%.
2. Lower room rates in the late spring and early fall, when the weather is still good and summer rates are no longer in effect. Rates usually go up in early June.
3. Apartment hotels, which are very good value, help save on dining bills, and often offer free local calls.
4. The Y and the AYH Hostel offer very inexpensive lodgings in downtown Portland.
5. Lower rates outside of downtown. Downtown hotels are used primarily by business travelers, and their prices reflect this. You can get the same amenities (often more) at lower prices by staying at a hotel away from downtown. The inconvenience is that you must travel into the city each day.
6. Senior citizens and families often get discounts, as do members of AAA. Be sure to ask if there are any such discounts.

QUESTIONS TO ASK IF YOU'RE ON A BUDGET:

1. Is there a parking charge? In downtown Portland, parking charges can add as much as $16 per day to your hotel bill.
2. Does the quoted rate for a given stay include the room tax?
3. Is there a charge for local calls? A surcharge on long-distance calls?
4. Is breakfast included in the rate? Not only bed-and-breakfast inns include breakfast in their service; some moderately priced hotels and even some motels do too (often only coffee and doughnuts).
5. Does the hotel have a complimentary airport shuttle? This can save you taxi or other airport shuttle fares.

MALLORY HOTEL, 729 SW 15th Ave., at Yamhill St., Portland, OR 97205-1994. Tel. 503/223-6311 or toll free 800/228-8657. Fax 503/223-0522. 143 rms, 13 suites. A/C TV TEL

$ Rates: $55–$75 single; $60–$100 double; $90–$100 suite. AE, CB, DC, MC, V. **Parking:** Free (a real plus this close to downtown).

⑤ The older and old-fashioned Mallory on the edge of Portland's business district is a sort of poor man's Benson Hotel. Although the neighborhood and the hotel's exterior are unassuming, the lobby exhibits an unexpected grandeur. It is done in deep forest greens and ornate gilt-plasterwork wainscoting. A crystal chandelier hangs from the ceiling, and soft light filters through a frosted lead-glass skylight.

The rooms are not as luxurious as the lobby might suggest, but they are comfortable and clean. With rates this low, you might want to go for one of the king-size suites. These rooms are about as big as they come, with walk-in closets, minirefrigerators, and sofa beds. All rooms have new carpets, drapes, and furniture.

Dining/Entertainment: The dining room at the Mallory continues the grand design of the lobby. Heavy drapes hang from the windows, and faux-marble pillars lend just the right air of imperial grandeur.

Services: Free local calls, 2pm checkout, in-room movies, valet/laundry service.

THE MARK SPENCER HOTEL, 409 SW 11th Ave., Portland, OR 97205. Tel. 503/224-3293 or toll free 800/548-3934. Fax 503/223-7848. 103 rms. A/C TV TEL

$ Rates: $65 studio, single or double; $84 one-bedroom. Lower weekly and monthly rates are also available. Children 12 and under stay free in parents' room. AE, CB, DC, MC, V.

If you're planning an extended stay in Portland and need to be within walking distance of downtown, this is the place for you. Although the hotel is not in the best neighborhood in the city, it's just around the corner from Jake's Famous Crawfish, one of Portland's oldest and most popular restaurants. The building itself has been attractively restored, with flower baskets hanging from old-fashioned street lamps out front.

Both studios and one-bedrooms feature kitchenettes and attractive modern furnishings, including plush-velvet wingback chairs and couches in some rooms. Walk-in closets are a definite plus for those planning a long stay in town.

Services: Free housekeeping, coin-operated laundry and valet service, private mailboxes, personal phone lines.

Facilities: Privileges at nearby athletic club, no-smoking rooms.

PORTLAND INN, 1414 SW Sixth Ave., Portland, OR 97201. Tel. 503/221-1611 or toll free 800/648-6440. 180 rms. A/C TV TEL

$ Rates: $67 single; $72–$77 double. AE, CB, DC, MC, V. **Parking:** Free.

Located in the heart of downtown, Portland Inn is an excellent choice for budget-minded business travelers and family vacationers. From the moment you walk into the royal-blue-and-beige lobby and see the humongous railway clock behind the tiny check-in desk, you'll know you've stumbled on something unusual. You'll be even more surprised to discover a small library of old hardbound books in every room. In addition, there are brass beds and framed old photos of Portland and movie stars. Each room has a wall of glass—to let in lots of sunlight—and may even have live plants.

Dining/Entertainment: With its art-deco lamps, brass rails, and wood trim, the Portland Bar & Grill is popular for its oyster bar and free happy-hour hors d'oeuvres.

Services: Valet/laundry service, complimentary newspaper.

Facilities: Outdoor swimming pool, athletic facilities.

RIVERSIDE INN, 50 SW Morrison Ave., Portland, OR 97204. Tel. 503/221-0711 or toll free 800/648-6440. Fax 503/274-0312. 137 rms. A/C TV TEL

$ Rates: $75 single; $85–$90 double. AE, CB, DC, DISC, MC, V. **Parking:** Free.

Overlooking Waterfront Park and located on the MAX light-rail transit system line, Riverside has many unexpected features. As the name implies, you are only steps from the Willamette River, but you are also close to businesses, fine restaurants, and shopping. Colorful fine-art posters enliven the walls of the small lobby, giving the seating area a very homey feel. Rooms, many with excellent views of the river and Morrison Bridge, feature a small library of hardbound books, brass beds, modern furnishings, and attractive framed posters.

Dining/Entertainment: The Riverside Café & Bar is a bright and airy restaurant with large windows looking out over the Waterfront Park and the river. Fresh seafood is the specialty here.

Services: Room service, valet/laundry service, complimentary newspaper, complimentary fitness club membership.

INEXPENSIVE

CYPRESS INN-PORTLAND DOWNTOWN, 809 SW King St., Portland, OR 97205. Tel. 503/226-6288 or toll free (in Oregon) 800/445-4205 or (outside Oregon) 800/225-4205. 82 rms (all with private bath). A/C TV TEL

 FROMMER'S COOL FOR KIDS: HOTELS

Holiday Inn, Portland Airport Hotel *(see p. 180)* The indoor swimming pool and video game room will keep kids entertained no matter what the weather.

Red Lion Hotel/Lloyd Center *(see p. 176)* Let the kids loose in the huge Lloyd Center Shopping Mall across the street and they'll stay entertained for hours. There is even an ice-skating rink in the mall.

Portland Marriott Hotel *(see p. 168)* The game room and indoor pool are popular with kids, and just across the street is 2-mile-long Tom McCall Waterfront Park, which runs along the Willamette River.

$ Rates (including continental breakfast): $50–$62 single; $57–$69 double. AE, DC, DISC, MC, V. **Parking:** Free.

Though the standard rooms here are rather cramped, for just a few dollars more you can get a much larger room, which may even have a kitchenette. Because the motel sits a little bit up into the hills west of downtown, it has some nice views over the city. You'd expect to spend quite a bit more for such views, which makes these rooms a good value. Another plus here is that you are within walking distance of both the Nob Hill shopping and restaurant district and Washington Park, which is home to the Japanese Gardens and the International Rose Test Garden. Be sure to avail yourself of the courtesy airport shuttle.

BED & BREAKFAST

HERON HAUS, 2545 NW Westover Rd., Portland, OR 97210. Tel. 503/274-1846. Fax 503/274-1846. 5 rms. TV TEL

$ Rates (including continental breakfast): $85–$250 single or double. AE, MC, V. **Parking:** Free.

A short walk from the bustling Nob Hill shopping and dining district of northwest Portland, Heron Haus offers outstanding accommodations and spectacular views. There is even a small swimming pool with sun deck.

Surprisingly, the house still features some of the original plumbing. In most places this would be a liability but not here, since the plumbing was done by the same man who plumbed Portland's famous Pittock Mansion. Many of that building's unusual bath features are to be found at the Heron Haus as well. One shower has seven shower heads; another has two. In another room there's a modern whirlpool spa that affords excellent views of the city.

HOSTEL

BEN STARK HOTEL, 1022 SW Stark St., Portland, OR 97205. Tel. 503/274-1223. Fax 503/274-1033. 96 rms (48 with private bath). TV TEL

$ Rates (including continental breakfast): Hostel $12–$15; single or double without bath $25–$40; single or double with bath $30–$45. AE, DISC, MC, V.

If you're a hardened hosteler or budget traveler used to Spartan accommodations that provide a place to crash and little more in the way of comforts, the Ben Stark should meet with your approval. Rooms are quite basic, but as you would expect, you'll meet some interesting folks hanging around the common areas. Actually the building, erected in 1912, is one of Portland's few remaining historic hotels, and the owners are working hard to restore some of its lost grandeur. Mahogany doors and claw-foot tubs are just two of the classic touches here. Facilities include a laundry, bike storage area, luggage storage room, safe deposit boxes, and no-smoking rooms.

Y

YWCA, 1111 SW 10th Ave., Portland, OR 97205. Tel. 503/223-6281. 13 rms.

$ Rates: $6–$10 in dorm; $15 in shared room with shared bath; $20 single with shared bath down the hall, $23 single with semiprivate bath; $27 double in a private room with shared bath, $30 double with semiprivate bath. MC, V.

If you are a woman traveling on a budget, you might want to check out this very conveniently located Y. Accommodations are simple, as you would expect, but the atmosphere is friendly. There's a TV lounge for guests, as well as a microwave and refrigerator where you can store a few foodstuffs. For an additional charge you can use the athletic facilities.

2. NORTH PORTLAND

Located in North Portland, on Hayden Island in the Columbia River, is the shopping and resort area of Jantzen Beach, named for the famous swimwear manufacturer that originated in Portland. Although you'll find Red Lion Inns throughout the West, including three others in Portland, the pair listed here are two of the nicest and most impressive. One warning: Both hotels are in the flight path for the airport, and although the rooms themselves are adequately insulated against noise, the swimming pools and sun decks are not.

VERY EXPENSIVE

RED LION HOTEL/COLUMBIA RIVER, 1401 N. Hayden Island Dr., Portland, OR 97217. Tel. 503/283-2111 or toll free 800/547-8010. Fax 503/283-4718. 351 rms, 8 suites. A/C TV TEL

$ Rates: $99–$125 single; $114–$140 double; $195–$400 suite. Weekend and other packages available. Children under 18 stay free in parents' room. AE, CB, DC, MC, V. **Parking:** Free.

An attractive low-rise design that's slightly reminiscent of a Northwest Native American longhouse has kept this hotel popular for many years. The lobby, on the other hand, features lots of cherry wood and faux green-marble accents for that Ivy League look.

As with all Red Lions, the rooms are spacious and comfortable, and are done in shades of sea-foam green and mauve. Floral-print bedspreads with a beige background, as well as framed watercolors, give the rooms a country-cottage appeal.

Dining/Entertainment: The Coffee Garden, just off the lobby, offers coffee-shop meals from early morning to late at night. Great views of the Columbia River are to be had at Brickstones Restaurant, which features an international menu emphasizing fresh local seafoods. For late-night entertainment, there's the Brickstones Bar, where live rock bands perform on weekends. For a quieter atmosphere, try the aptly named Quiet Bar, a small glass-walled octagonal building just off the lobby and overlooking the pool.

Services: Room service, complimentary airport shuttle, valet/laundry service.

Facilities: Heated outdoor swimming pool, whirlpool spa, putting green, gift shop, barbershop, beauty salon.

RED LION HOTEL/JANTZEN BEACH, 909 N. Hayden Island Dr., Portland, OR 97217. Tel. 503/283-4466 or toll free 800/547-8010. Fax 503/283-4743. 320 rms, 8 suites. A/C TV TEL

$ Rates: $100–$125 single; $115–$160 double; $350–$450 suite. AE, CB, DC, DISC, ER, JCB, MC, V. **Parking:** Free.

Everything about this resort hotel is spacious. An imposing portico that reflects Northwest tribal designs leads to the massive lobby, which is fronted by a long wall of glass. Thick carpets muffle every sound. Intricately carved dark woods impart a warmth and Northwest feel.

Arranged in wings around a central garden courtyard and swimming pool, the rooms are as large as you're likely to find in any hotel. Most have balconies and excellent views of the river and sometimes Mount St. Helens. The baths, each with a nice assortment of soaps, shampoos, and lotions, are equally spacious.

Dining/Entertainment: Elegant dining in plush surroundings can be found in Maxi's Restaurant, which specializes in traditional continental cuisine prepared with flair. For much more casual dining there's the Coffee Garden in the lobby. Thursday through Saturday nights come alive to the sound of live rock 'n' roll bands at Maxi's Lounge, an art nouveau extravaganza.

Services: Room service, complimentary airport shuttle, valet/laundry service.

Facilities: Heated outdoor pool, tennis courts, wheelchair accommodations, gift shop, helicopter port, privileges at nearby athletic club ($5).

3. NORTHEAST PORTLAND

VERY EXPENSIVE

RED LION HOTEL/LLOYD CENTER, 1000 NE Multnomah St., Portland, OR 97232. Tel. 503/281-6111 or toll free 800/547-8010. Fax 503/284-8553. 476 rooms, 18 suites. A/C TV TEL

$ Rates: $77–$139 single; $77–$154 double; $145–$535 suite. AE, CB, DC, DISC, ER, JCB, MC, V. **Parking:** Free.

In the busy lobby of this modern high-rise, glass elevators shuttle up and down through the skylighted ceiling. Massive overstuffed chairs and couches with built-in tables are surrounded by plants, which create a warm greenhouse atmosphere. Spreading out in different directions are hallways leading to the restaurants, gift shops, a swimming pool, and an elegant lounge. Large leaf patterns in bas-relief decorate the walls, and tubular-glass chandeliers sparkle overhead.

As you've come to expect, the Red Lion's rooms are spacious beyond compare, and the views from the higher floors are stunning. On a clear day you can see Mount Hood, Mount St. Helens, and even Mount Rainier.

Dining/Entertainment: Maxi's Restaurant, with its stained-glass chandeliers and baffled ceiling, is just off the lobby but surrounded by a low wall of plants. Local seafood, steaks, and wild game are the well-prepared specialties here. If you're more in the mood for Mexican, cross the lobby to Eduardo's Cantina, where stucco walls, tile floors, rough-hewn wood beams, and rattan chairs will transport you down Mexico way. Family dining is possible in the Coffee Garden, which opens directly onto the lobby. For those seeking a quiet place for conversation and a drink, there's the Quiet Bar. In Maxi's Lounge you'll find two dance floors and live music on the weekends.

Services: Room service, concierge, complimentary airport shuttle, in-room movies, valet/laundry service.

Facilities: Heated outdoor swimming pool, wheelchair accommodations, exercise room, gift shop.

EXPENSIVE

HOLIDAY INN PORTLAND-DOWNTOWN, 1021 NE Grand Ave., Portland, OR 97232. Tel. 503/235-2100 or toll free 800/HOLIDAY. Fax 503/238-0132. 174 rms, 2 suites. A/C MINIBAR TV TEL

$ Rates: $80 single; $90 double; $250 suite. Special packages for senior citizens. AE, CB, DC, MC, V. **Parking:** Free.

This reasonably priced hotel, located across the street from the architecturally striking Oregon Convention Center, is a popular choice with conventioneers who don't want to spend an arm and a leg. Because Portland's MAX light-rail system stops one block from the hotel, this is also a convenient location if you want to go downtown.

You'll find all the rooms attractively furnished in pastel colors and modern decor with an Asian touch. Large tables, writing desks, two phones, and comfortable armchairs allow guests to spread out. Upper floors have good views either west to the city skyline or east to the Cascades and Mount Hood, and the twin peaks of the Convention Center loom just across the street.

Dining/Entertainment: Windows, the hotel's aptly named top-floor restaurant, provides the hotel's best views and is a popular dining spot. You can dine on fresh Northwest cuisine or just have a drink in the lounge.

Services: Room service, valet/laundry service.

Facilities: Sauna, fitness center.

TRAVELODGE HOTEL, 1441 NE Second Ave., Portland, OR 97232. Tel. 503/233-2401 or toll free 800/255-3050. Fax 503/238-7016. 236 rms, 1 suite. A/C TV TEL

$ Rates: $78–$93 single; $88–$103 double; $264–$279 suite. AE, CB, DC, MC, V. **Parking:** Free.

Convenient to both the city center and the Convention Center, the Travelodge offers excellent views from its modern 10-story building. Soothing pastels are used in the small lobby and in the guest rooms, all of which have large windows to let in as much of that rare Northwest sunshine as possible. In the baths you'll find marble countertops and tile floors, and a coffee maker in every room. There is also an executive club floor offering additional security, bathrobes and hair dryers, free local phone calls, and complimentary continental breakfast, morning newspaper, and nightcap.

Dining/Entertainment: Traders, just off the lobby, is the hotel's restaurant, and fresh seafood is the specialty. For cocktails and conversation, there's the adjacent Encore Lounge.

Services: Room service, in-room movies, complimentary airport shuttle, valet/laundry service, free jogging maps.

Facilities: Heated outdoor swimming pool, wheelchair accommodations, no-smoking rooms, women's floor, privileges at nearby athletic facility.

INEXPENSIVE

HO-JO INN, 3939 NE Hancock St., Portland, OR 97212. Tel. 503/288-6891. Fax 503/288-1995. 48 rms. A/C TV TEL

$ Rates: $38 single; $42–$53 double. AE, CB, DC, DISC, MC, V. **Parking:** Free.

Located in the Hollywood District of northeast Portland about halfway between the airport and downtown, Ho-Jo Inn is an excellent choice in the budget range. All rooms are exceptionally large and were renovated a few years ago. Attractive modern furniture and comfortable beds will make your stay here enjoyable. Take a stroll around the neighborhood and you'll see why they call this the Hollywood District—the same style of southern California Hollywood architecture prevails. There are valet service, free coffee, and a coin laundry. The Inn offers wheelchair-accessible rooms.

BED & BREAKFASTS

JOHN PALMER HOUSE, 4314 N. Mississippi Ave., Portland, OR 97217. Tel. 503/284-5893. 7 rms (2 with private bath), 2 suites.

$ Rates (including continental breakfast): $50–$85 single or double; $95–$135 single or double suite. AE, DISC, MC, V.

Even before you set foot inside the door of this restored Queen Anne Victorian home in an unassuming neighborhood in North Portland, you know that you've stumbled onto something special. Cross the Italianate veranda, step through the double stained-glass doors, and you are enveloped in the Victorian era. The interior has been done with all the flair for which that period was known. Dozens of different wallpapers turn the walls into a coordinated riot of colors and patterns.

Guest accommodations are actually in two houses: the main Palmer House and Grandma's Cottage. Each room in the main house is decorated with massive Victorian furnishings, and stained-glass windows throughout the house filter the sunlight into magical hues. In one bedroom there's a stuffed moose head that seems to take up almost the entire room. Decor in Grandma's Cottage is much simpler. In the morning you will be served a delicious gourmet breakfast. There is also a whirlpool in a gazebo, plus a croquet court.

For an additional fee, you can indulge whatever Victorian fantasy you might have. Have a horse-drawn carriage carry you to the inn. Perhaps you'd like your own private butler or maid. Lacy Victorian sleepwear might be what you need to help you sleep better at night. A massage? You name it, and the Sauters will try to accommodate you.

Dining/Entertainment: Saturday and Sunday, high tea is served from 1 to 3pm; after tea, a tour is given. The price of tea and tour is $12.50. The Palmer House also offers fine dining by reservation (48 hours ahead) at 6 and 8:15pm.

PORTLAND'S WHITE HOUSE, 1914 NE 22nd Ave., Port-land, OR 97212. Tel. 503/287-7131. 6 rms (all with private bath).

$ Rates (including full breakfast): $88–$104 single; $96–$112 double; some rates lower in winter. MC, V.

This imposing Greek-revival mansion bears a more than passing resemblance to its namesake in Washington, DC. Massive columns frame the entrance and a patio area where, on sunny days, you can sit at a table and enjoy a picnic lunch. A long semicircular driveway sweeps up to the entrance, and a fountain bubbles in the garden. This is a no-smoking inn, and hosts Larry and Mary Hough prefer guests who are more than 12 years old. There is free airport pick up and afternoon tea.

Behind the mahogany doors is a huge entrance hall with original hand-painted wall murals. To your right is the parlor, with its French windows and piano. To your left is the formal dining room, where the large breakfast is served amid sparkling crystal chandeliers. A double staircase leads past a large stained-glass window to the second-floor accommodations.

Canopy and brass queen beds, antique furnishings, and bathrooms with claw-foot tubs await you at the end of a weary day. Request the balcony room and you can gaze out past the Greek columns and imagine you're the president.

4. SOUTHEAST & SOUTHWEST PORTLAND

YOUTH HOSTELS

By the time you visit Portland, the new **Portland International Gateway Hostel** may have opened its doors. It will be located at the corner of SW 11th Avenue and SW Washington Street and should have at least 100 beds. In addition to small dorms, there will be some single and double rooms. There are also plans to include a rooftop café, a ground-floor café, and a travel shop.

PORTLAND AYH HOSTEL, 3031 SE Hawthorne Blvd., Portland, OR 97214. Tel. 503/236-3380. 50 beds. **Bus:** 5 from downtown or 12 then 5 from airport.

$ Rates: $14 member, $17 nonmember. JCB, MC, V.

The Hawthorne District is a shopping and dining area popular with students, artists, and musicians, so it makes an ideal location for a youth hostel. Housed in an old house on a busy street, this hostel is small and has primarily dormitory beds. The common room is also small, but a large wraparound porch makes up for the lack of space inside. There is a large kitchen where guests can prepare their own meals, with a grocery store a short walk away. However, an all-you-can-eat pancake breakfast for 50¢ shouldn't be missed. Located just down the street is an AYH Travel Center, where hostel members can get student IDs, and buy books, travel packs, and Eurailpasses. Membership is $10 per year for youths under 17, $25 for adults, and $15 for senior citizens over 55. Between May and September, the hostel offers van tours to Mount St. Helens, the Columbia River Gorge, and the Oregon coast.

5. NEAR THE AIRPORT

EXPENSIVE

HOLIDAY INN, PORTLAND AIRPORT HOTEL, 8439 NE Columbia Blvd., Portland, OR 97220-1382. Tel. 503/ 256-5000 or toll free 800/HOLIDAY. Fax 503/256-5000, ext. 149. 286 rms, 17 suites. A/C TV TEL

$ Rates: $92–$125 single; $98–$131 double; $130–$325 suite. AE, CB, DC, DISC, MC, V. **Parking:** Free.

A Southwest motif reigns at this Holiday Inn in the Northwest. From the outside the building looks unremarkable, but once you're inside you enter a mezzanine-level lobby overlooking a large covered courtyard. Spanish-tile awnings, a bubbling fountain, and a swimming pool beneath a ramada all help create the Southwest flavor. The courtyard dining area has an al fresco feel. In your room you'll find pleasant subdued colors and a large bath—everything you'd expect of a Holiday Inn.

Dining/Entertainment: John Q's offers traditional gourmet dining. The Coffee Shop is open early and late. Music and dancing are offered every night at the Flirts Dance Club.

Services: Room service, in-room movies, complimentary airport shuttle, valet/laundry service.

Facilities: Indoor pool, exercise room, whirlpool, sauna, video games room, wheelchair accommodations, gift shop.

MODERATE

QUALITY INN/PORTLAND AIRPORT, 8247 NE Sandy Blvd., Portland, OR 97220. Tel. 503/256-4111 or toll free 800/228-5151. Fax 503/254-1507. 120 rms, 4 suites. A/C TV TEL

$ Rates: $67–$100 single; $77–$100 double; $100 suite. AE, CB, DC, DISC, ER, MC, V. **Parking:** Free.

Although the rooms here are a bit small and dark, they are very comfortable and clean, and the attractively landscaped surroundings more than make up for any inadequacies in the accommodations. If you are willing to spend a bit more, there are suites and rooms with whirlpool baths.

Dining/Entertainment: Steamers Restaurant specializes in fresh seafood. If you're a fan of the steam era, you'll love this place. There are plenty of old photos on the walls, and bits and pieces rescued from paddle wheelers and steam locomotives. Zanzibar is the hotel's tropical-theme lounge.

Services: Complimentary airport shuttle, complimentary hors d'oeuvres from 5 to 7pm, same-day valet service, complimentary morning newspaper, free local phone calls.

Facilities: Heated outdoor pool, laundry facilities.

RAMADA INN/PORTLAND AIRPORT, 6221 NE 82nd

Ave., Portland, OR 97220. Tel. 503/255-6511 or toll free
800/272-6232. Fax 503/255-8417. 202 rms, 108 minisuites, 4
suites. A/C TV TEL

$ Rates: $74–$110 single or double; $74–$120 minisuite; $295–
$595 suite. AE, CB, DC, DISC, MC, V. **Parking:** Free.

Located three miles from the airport, this Ramada Inn is convenient
to the interstate for quick access to downtown Portland. Rooms are
done in attractive lavenders and grays and come with queen-size or
double beds. If you stay in one of the minisuites, you'll find a
microwave, wet bar, refrigerator, and remote-control TV, in addition
to the sofa bed and the art deco and Asian styling. These minisuites
are definitely worth the few dollars extra they cost.

Dining/Entertainment: O'Callahan's, the spacious two-level
dining room and lounge, specializes in Cajun food, extra-large
sandwiches, and seafood.

Services: Room service, complimentary airport shuttle, valet/
laundry service.

Facilities: Heated outdoor swimming pool, whirlpool spa,
sauna, fitness room, business center.

6. BEAVERTON/TIGARD AREA

VERY EXPENSIVE

**EMBASSY SUITES HOTEL, 9000 SW Washington Square
Rd., Tigard, OR 97223. Tel. 503/644-4000** or toll free
800/EMBASSY. Fax 503/641-4654. 250 suites. A/C TV TEL

$ Rates (including full breakfast): $109–$132 single; $142 double.
AE, DC, DISC, MC, V. **Parking:** Free.

Beaverton and Tigard are at the heart of Oregon's rapidly
growing high-tech industries, and whether you are traveling on
business or for pleasure, this outstanding nine-story hotel
should be your first choice in the area. It is built around a soaring
atrium, with colorful kites suspended high above the gardenlike
lobby and courtyard dining area. Tropical plants are everywhere, and
waterfalls add their pleasant music. In the evening and during brunch
there's live piano music in the lobby garden dining area. A glass
elevator whisks guests to their rooms.

As the name implies, every room is a suite—each beautifully
decorated in pale greens and pastels, with plush carpets. In the sitting
room you'll find a huge stereo console TV, potted plants, a relaxing
couch, a telephone, and a large table. There are also a microwave,
minirefrigerator, and wet bar in each suite. In the bedroom you'll find
another TV, a clock radio, and a second phone. The bath is equally
appealing with its generous basket of fragrant soaps, shampoos, and
lotions on the large counter.

Dining/Entertainment: At the elegant Crossroads Restaurant,
Northwest cuisine is the order of the day. For more casual dining and
for the delicious Sunday brunch, seat yourself amid the lush foliage of
the Atrium. For relaxing, socializing, and dancing, there's the
Crossroads Lounge, with live entertainment and a cozy fireplace.

Services: Room service, valet/laundry service, nightly manag-
er's reception with complimentary drinks, courtesy transportation to
Washington Square Mall, complimentary newspapers.

Facilities: 24-hour indoor pool, whirlpool, sauna, fitness room and privileges at nearby health club, wheelchair accommodations.

MODERATE

GREENWOOD INN, 10700 SW Allen Blvd., Beaverton, OR 97005. Tel. 503/643-7444 or toll free 800/289-1300. Fax 503/626-4553. 260 rms. A/C TV TEL

$ Rates: $72–$87 single; $82–$97 double. AE, CB, DC, DISC, MC, V. **Parking:** Free.

Two-story buildings set amid attractively landscaped grounds give the Greenwood the feel of a small resort, though it is only 10 minutes from downtown Portland. Beaverton, a western suburb of Portland, is at the heart of a rapidly growing area for high-tech industries. If you are in the area to do business in the "Silicon Forest," the Greenwood is well located. Guest rooms are large and comfortable and done in neutral tones with exposed brick accents. There's plenty of counter space for toiletries. Executive rooms, which cost only $10 extra, are exceptional, with original artwork on the walls, a desk/work area, natural-wood furnishings, and a warm coppery color scheme.

Dining/Entertainment: The Pavilion Bar and Grill serves moderately priced meals in a plant-filled atrium dining room. Six nights a week there is live Top 40 dance music in the hotel's Wanigan Lounge, while the Pavilion Bar provides a quiet spot for a drink.

Services: Access to nearby athletic club; complimentary beverages, morning newspaper, shopping shuttle.

Facilities: Exercise room, sauna, outdoor swimming pool, hot tub, no-smoking rooms, wheelchair accommodations.

INEXPENSIVE

LAMPLIGHTER MOTEL, 10207 SW Parkway, Portland, OR 97225. Tel. 503/297-2211. 56 rms (all with private bath). A/C TV TEL

$ Rates: $35 single; $38–$45 double. AE, DC, DISC, MC, V.

If you are looking for a clean, inexpensive place only 10 minutes from downtown, try Lamplighter, located just off U.S. 26 at the Cedar Hills/Barnes Road exit. Some rooms feature kitchenettes, and complimentary coffee is available in the lobby. Rooms away from the highway are quietest.

PORTLAND DINING

Portland may not be garnering as much praise for its Northwest cuisine as Seattle, but there certainly are restaurants here that are every bit the equal of Seattle's. Young and innovative chefs are cooking up a quiet storm in Portland these days, and prices are very reasonable. For these listings, I considered a restaurant **expensive** if a meal with wine or beer would average $25 or more. **Moderate** restaurants offer complete dinners in the $15 to $25 range, and **inexpensive** eateries are those where you can enjoy a complete meal for less than $15.

To learn more about Northwest cuisine, see the introduction to Chapter 5, "Seattle Dining."

Be sure to accompany your dinner with one of Oregon's fine wines. Quite a few have won taste-test competitions with California and French wines in recent years.

Many of Portland's finest restaurants are open for dinner between only 5 or 5:30pm and 9:30 or 10pm. There are a few exceptions to this rule and I have noted these. Making reservations is always a good idea, especially if there are five or more in your group.

1. DOWNTOWN & OLD TOWN

EXPENSIVE

COUCH STREET FISH HOUSE, 105 NW Third Ave., at Couch St. Tel. 223-6173.
   Cuisine: SEAFOOD. **Reservations:** Strongly recommended.
$ Prices: Appetizers $6.95–$8.95; main dishes $11.50–$20; four-course sunset dinners $10.95. AE, CB, DC, DISC, MC, V.
   Open: Dinner only, Mon–Thurs 5–10pm, Fri–Sat 5–11pm, Sun 5–9:30pm.

S Located in the heart of Old Town, this award-winning restaurant specializes in the Northwest's freshest seafood. The restaurant occupies two historic structures, one of which is merely the facade of an Italianate Victorian hotel built in 1883; this, in fact, must be the only historic parking lot in the country. The other historic building has been completely remodeled into a dark and intimate restaurant. Antiques and exposed brick abound.

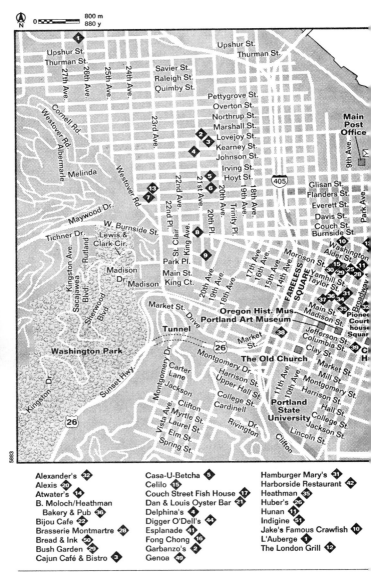

Alexander's ③②	Casa-U-Betcha ⑤	Hamburger Mary's ③①
Alexis ②⓪	Celilo ⑮	Harborside Restaurant ④②
Atwater's ⑭	Couch Street Fish House ⑰	Heathman ③⑤
B. Moloch/Heathman	Dan & Louis Oyster Bar ②①	Huber's ②⑥
Bakery & Pub ③⑥	Delphina's ④	Hunan ⑬
Bijou Cafe ②②	Digger O'Dell's ④④	Indigine ⑤①
Brasserie Montmartre ②⑧	Esplanade ④①	Jake's Famous Crawfish ⑩
Bread & Ink ⑤⓪	Fong Chong ⑯	L'Auberge ①
Bush Garden ②③	Garbanzo's ②	The London Grill ⑫
Cajun Café & Bistro ③	Genoa ④⑨	

The succulent seafood main dishes run the gamut from panfried oysters coated with a crust of Oregon hazelnuts to mesquite-grilled salmon to such classics as lobster thermidor and shrimp scampi. Red meat eaters are also served with the likes of rack of lamb and filet mignon in Madeira glace.

HARBORSIDE RESTAURANT, 0309 SW Montgomery St. Tel. 220-1865.

Cuisine: SEAFOOD. **Reservations:** Recommended.

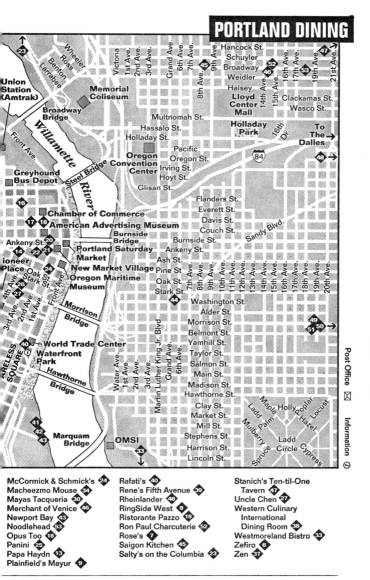

PORTLAND DINING

Union Station (Amtrak)

Wheeler
Ross
Benton
Larrabee

Victoria
1st Ave.
2nd Ave.
3rd Ave.

Grand Ave.

6th Ave.
7th Ave.

9th Ave.

Hancock St.
Schuyler
Broadway
Weidler
Halsey

Memorial Coliseum

8th Ave.

14th
15th

16th Ave.
17th Ave.
19th Ave.

21st Ave.

Clackamas St.
Wasco St.

Lloyd Center Mall

Broadway Bridge

Multnomah St.
Hassalo St.
Holladay St.

Willamette

Oregon Convention Center

Pacific
Oregon St.
Irving St.
Hoyt St.
Glisan St.

16th Dr.

Holladay Park

To The Dalles →

84

Greyhound Bus Depot

Steel Bridge

River

Front Ave.

Flanders St.
Everett St.
Davis St.
Couch St.

Sandy Blvd.

Chamber of Commerce
American Advertising Museum

Burnside Bridge
Burnside St.

Ankeny St.
Ash St.
Pine St

Portland Saturday Market
New Market Village
Oregon Maritime Museum

Oak St
Stark St.

7th Ave.
8th Ave.
10th Ave.
11th Ave.
12th Ave.
13th Ave.
14th Ave.
15th Ave.
16th Ave.
17th Ave.
18th Ave.
19th Ave.
20th Ave.

ioneer Place

4th Ave.
Oak St.
Stark St.

3rd Ave.
2nd Ave.
1st Ave.
Front Ave.

Morrison Bridge

Washington St.
Alder St.
Morrison St.
Belmont St.
Yamhill St.
Taylor St.
Salmon St.
Main St.
Madison St.
Hawthorne St.
Clay St.
Market St.
Mill St.
Stephens St.
Harrison St.
Lincoln St.

Water Ave.
1st Ave.
2nd Ave.
3rd Ave.

Martin Luther King Jr. Blvd.

Grand Ave.
6th Ave.

RELESS SQUARE

World Trade Center
Waterfront Park

Hawthorne Bridge

Marquam Bridge

OMSI

Maple
Holly
Poplar
Hazel
Locust

Ladd
Palm
Mulberry
Spruce

Ladd Circle

Cypress

Post Office ☒   Information ①

McCormick & Schmick's ❖24
Macheezmo Mouse ❖34
Mayas Tacqueria ❖30
Merchant of Venice ❖46
Newport Bay ❖43
Noodlehead ❖53
Opus Too ❖18
Panini ❖25
Papa Haydn ❖13
Plainfield's Mayur ❖9

Rafati's ❖40
Rene's Fifth Avenue ❖39
Rheinlander ❖48
RingSide West ❖8
Ristorante Pazzo ❖19
Ron Paul Charcuterie ❖52
Rose's ❖7
Saigon Kitchen ❖45
Salty's on the Columbia ❖23

Stanich's Ten-til-One Tavern ❖47
Uncle Chen ❖27
Western Culinary International Dining Room ❖38
Westmoreland Bistro ❖33
Zefiro ❖6
Zen ❖37

$ Prices: Appetizers $4.50–$9.90; main dishes $5.50–$18; lunches $4.75–$10. AE, CB, DC, DISC, MC, V.
Open: Lunch daily 11:30am–2pm; dinner Sun–Thurs 5–10pm, Fri–Sat 5–11pm.

Anchoring the opposite end of RiverPlace from the RiverPlace Hotel is this large and very popular restaurant. The clientele is mostly upscale, especially at lunch and in the après-work hours. The sparkling cut-glass windows and doors at the restaurant's entrance are an unexpected bit of tradition in an otherwise modern-looking establishment. Tall walls of glass are fronted by four dining levels, so everyone gets a view of the river and marina below. Because it's so popular, the place tends to be noisy and the help seems a bit harried; however, don't let this detract from the fine food. Nearly any time of year, if the weather is good, you'll find folks dining al fresco along the promenade in front of the restaurant.

Although seafood (such as crab-stuffed salmon, razor clams with rémoulade sauce, and grilled sea scallop fettuccine) is the main attraction here, the menu is quite extensive. The long list of hot and cold salads is very tempting. There are a dozen pasta dishes and even pizzas made with such unusual ingredients as blue cheese and apples.

JAKE'S FAMOUS CRAWFISH, 401 SW 12th Ave. Tel. 226-1419.

Cuisine: SEAFOOD. **Reservations:** Recommended for dinner.

$ Prices: Appetizers $2–$13; main dishes $10–$29. AE, CB, DC, DISC, MC, V.

Open: Lunch Mon–Fri 11:30am–2pm; dinner Mon–Thurs 5–11pm, Fri–Sat 5pm–midnight, Sun 5–10pm.

⭐ Jake's has been serving up crawfish (crayfish)—like miniature lobsters—since 1909 at an address that has housed a restaurant or bar since 1892. The back bar came all the way around Cape Horn in 1880, and much of the rest of the restaurant's decor looks just as old and well-worn. The noise level after work, when local businesspeople pack the bar, can be deafening, and the wait for a table can be long if you don't make a reservation. However, don't let these obstacles dissuade you from visiting this Portland institution.

A large selection of seafood and an extensive wine list make this one of the city's most popular restaurants. There's a daily menu sheet listing 15 to 20 specials, all of which are fresh from the market. However, there is really no question about what to eat at Jake's—crawfish are always on the menu and may be prepared any of five different ways. If you really want something else, their other seafoods and steaks are equally delectable.

MCCORMICK & SCHMICK'S, 235 SW First Ave. Tel. 224-7522.

Cuisine: SEAFOOD. **Reservations:** Strongly recommended.

$ Prices: Appetizers $5–$22; main dishes $10–$22; bar meals $2.25; lunches $5–$11. AE, DC, MC, V.

Open: Lunch Mon–Fri 11:30am–2pm; dinner Sun–Thurs 5–10pm, Fri–Sat 5–11pm; bar meals Mon–Sat 2–5pm and 9:30pm–midnight.

Although it opened in 1979, McCormick & Schmick's feels as if it has been around as long as Jake's. The owners wanted to open a restaurant/bar that was based on traditional seafood establishments. What they succeeded in creating was a very popular place noted for the freshness of its ingredients. Both the up-and-coming and the already-there keep this place bustling.

Whether it's king salmon or Dungeness crab, seafood is king here. The oysters in the oyster bar go by name, including Olympia, Royal Miyagi, and Quilcene. The daily fresh menu sheet begins with a listing of what's available that day and might list 25 different types of seafood; it even lists the home port of each offering. If you aren't interested in live oysters as an appetizer, there are plenty of cooked seafoods to start you out. Some outstanding main dishes on a recent visit included grilled rainbow trout with Dungeness crab and lemon hazelnut cream, bluefin tuna with tandoori lime glaze and pickled ginger, and alder-smoked sturgeon with cilantro pesto. The extensive wine list features excellent Oregon wines, and while you're waiting for a table, you might want to try one of the more than 30 single malt scotches available.

OPUS TOO RESTAURANT & JAZZ DE OPUS BAR, 33 NW Second Ave. Tel. 222-6077.

Cuisine: SEAFOOD/STEAK. **Reservations:** Recommended.
$ Prices: Appetizers $4.25–$8; main dishes $10–$21. AE, CB, DC, MC, V.
Open: Lunch Mon–Sat 11:30am–3pm; dinner Tues–Sat 5pm–midnight, Sun–Mon 5–11pm. Bar open until 2am.

Anyone who has outgrown sushi but still enjoys the camaraderie and floor show of a sushi bar should stop by this popular restaurant in the heart of Portland's Old Town. Solo diners can sit at the grill bar and watch the cooks mesquite-broil thick seafood steak, beefsteak, and chops. The flames leap and dance; the steaks sizzle. What a show! You'll know you've found the right place when you see the window full of artfully arranged fresh seafood steak. In the bar, you can listen to excellent jazz recordings and share an intimate moment with someone special. Though the menu is short compared with those of other nearby seafood restaurants, Opus Too makes up for this by grilling your order to perfection and then offering you a choice of eight different sauces.

RINGSIDE WEST, 2165 W. Burnside St. Tel. 223-1513.

Cuisine: STEAK. **Reservations:** Recommended.
$ Prices: Appetizers $3–$8; steaks $11–$20; seafood main dishes $15–$34. AE, MC, V.
Open: Dinner only, Mon–Sat 5pm–12:30am, Sun 4–11:30pm.

Stop a Portlander on the street and ask where to get the best steak in town and you will invariably be pointed in the direction of RingSide. Though boxing is the main theme of the restaurant, the name delivers a two-fisted pun as well, referring to the incomparable onion rings that should be an integral part of any meal here. Have your rings with a side order of one of their perfectly cooked steaks for a real knockout meal.

There is also a **RingSide East** at 14021 Northeast Glisan Street (tel. 255-0750), on Portland's east side, with the same menu. It's open for lunch Monday through Friday from 11:30am to 2:30pm; and for dinner Monday through Saturday from 5pm to midnight and on Sunday from 4pm.

ZEN RESTAURANT, 910 SW Salmon St. Tel. 222-3056.

Cuisine: JAPANESE. **Reservations:** Required for a tatami room.
$ Prices: Appetizers $2.50–$15; main dishes $9–$40. AE, CB, DC, MC, V.
Open: Lunch Mon–Fri 11:30am–2pm; dinner Mon–Sat 5–10pm.

Step through the door here and you'll know you are about to have a dining experience. A rock garden just inside helps guests forget the busy streets outside. For further meditation and contemplation on the Japanese aesthetic, there are ikebana flower arrangements. Step into a tatami room, pull the shoji behind you, and the transformation is complete—you're in Japan.

When in this part of Japan, there's only one meal to order and that's the kaiseki dinner, a Japanese gourmet feast that requires 24-hour advance notice to prepare. Among the numerous courses offered, you might delight in shrimp wrapped in plum leaves, a delicately flavored clear broth with a few choice vegetables, a bit of sushi, perhaps some succulent noodles, and of course fresh fish, thinly sliced beef, and tempura. Each serving is a work of art, and an evening spent here will soothe your body and soul.

MODERATE

ALEXIS RESTAURANT, 215 W. Burnside St. Tel. 224-8577.

Cuisine: GREEK. **Reservations:** Recommended.

$ Prices: Appetizers $3.50–$14; main dishes $9–$14. AE, CB, DC, DISC, MC, V.

Open: Lunch Mon–Fri 11:30am–2pm; dinner Mon–Thurs 5–10pm, Fri and Sat 5–11pm, Sun 4:30–9pm.

Alexis is a classic Greek taverna, and the crowds keep it packed as much for the great food as for the fun atmosphere. On weekends there's belly dancing and live music, and if you happen to be in town on March 25, you can help Alexis celebrate Greek Independence Day with a rousing big party.

The menu has all your Greek favorites. The main dishes are good, but the appetizers are out of this world. The not-to-be-missed list includes saganaki (panfried cheese flamed with ouzo), kalamarakia (perfectly fried squid), octopus, and the tart and creamy avgolemono soup. Accompany these with Alexis's own fresh bread (so good it's sold in grocery stores), and wash it all down with a bottle of Demestica wine for a meal beyond compare.

B. MOLOCH/HEATHMAN BAKERY & PUB, 901 SW Salmon St. Tel. 227-5700.

Cuisine: NORTHWEST. **Reservations:** Not accepted.

$ Prices: Salads $4–$8.25; main dishes $5.50–$9. AE, DC, DISC, MC, V.

Open: Mon–Thurs 7am–11pm, Fri 7am–midnight, Sat 8am–midnight, Sun 8am–11pm.

At B. Moloch, corporate climbers and bicycle messengers rub shoulders, quaff microbrews, and chow down on creative pizzas baked in a wood-burning oven. Get here before the downtown offices let out or you won't get a seat. The atmosphere is bright and noisy amid an industrial decor softened by colorful images of salmon.

Ostensibly, this is the bakery for the Heathman Hotel dining room a block away, and to that end a cavernous wood-burning brick oven was installed. Luckily, someone had the idea to bake a few pizzas in that amazing oven, and today those very nouvelle pizzas are the mainstay of the menu here. If you're in the mood for pizza like you'll never get from Mario's back home, try the pie with smoked lamb, feta cheese, spinach, and smoke-dried tomatoes. In addition to pizza, there are sandwiches, pasta dishes, great salads, and daily specials. My personal favorites are the small plates such as grilled goat

---

 **FROMMER'S SMART TRAVELER:
RESTAURANTS**

1. Eat your main meal at lunch, when prices are lower. You can eat at some of the city's best restaurants and try Northwest cuisine for substantially less than what it would cost at dinner.
2. Always ask the price of daily specials; they are almost always several dollars more expensive than the highest-priced main dish on the regular menu.
3. Eat early, between 5 and 7pm. Some restaurants offer sunset dinner specials at greatly reduced prices (and you aren't likely to have to wait as long).
4. Make reservations whenever possible. Even at lunchtime, downtown restaurants fill up. If there is someplace where you particularly want to eat, don't risk being disappointed.
5. Pay attention to how much alcohol you drink; even local wines and beers can be expensive.
6. Eat ethnic—there are lots of good inexpensive Asian restaurants all over the city.

---

cheese and smoked tomatoes or Northwest game pâté. You have to place your order at the counter here, but a waitress will bring the food to your table.

Though the name B. Moloch is rarely used by people in the know, who refer to this place as Heathman Bakery, you might be interested to learn that the restaurant takes its name from the 19th-century French artist who painted the caricatures that hang behind the counter. Next door to the restaurant, on the other side of a wall of glass, is a microbrewery. You can sit in the bar here and watch the brewers at work while sipping one of their beers.

BRASSERIE MONTMARTRE, 626 SW Park Ave. Tel. 224-5552.

Cuisine: CONTINENTAL/FRENCH. **Reservations:** Recommended.

$ Prices: Appetizers $4–$7; main dishes $8.50–$18. AE, CB, DC, MC, V.

Open: Lunch Mon–Fri 11:30am–2:30pm; dinner daily 5:30–10pm; brunch Sat–Sun 10am–2:30pm; bistro menu available daily from 2pm–closing.

Though the menu lacks the creativity of other continental and French restaurants in Portland, The Bra (as it's known) is hardly the stodgy and expensive place its full name implies. There is nightly jazz music from 8:30pm on Monday to Thursday and Sunday and from 9pm on Friday and Saturday, and on every table you'll find a paper tablecloth and a container of crayons. Let your artistic ambitions run wild while you wait for dinner or linger over drinks. Tuesday through Saturday, a magician performs amazing feats of digital dexterity.

This playfulness is balanced out by spacious and dark formal dining rooms. Massive white pillars, black-and-white tile floors, velvet banquettes, and silk lamp shades lend an air of fin de siècle Paris. With all this elegance and entertainment, prices are surprisingly reasonable. When I last visited, the most expensive item on the menu was a mixed grill for $16.95. You might start your meal with a ménage à trois of pâtés, then have a cup of onion soup with three cheeses, move on to salmon with lingonberry-and-ginger butter, and finish off with one of the divinely decadent pastries. The wine list is neither extensive nor expensive. And if you've grown attached to your tabletop art, they'll be happy to let you take it with you.

BUSH GARDEN, 900 SW Morrison St. Tel. 226-7181.

Cuisine: JAPANESE. **Reservations:** Strongly recommended.
$ Prices: Appetizers $2.50–$9.50; main dishes $10.50–$25; lunches $5.50–$11. AE, CB, DC, DISC, JCB, MC, V.
Open: Lunch Mon–Fri 11:30am–1:45pm; dinner Mon–Sat 5–9:45pm, Sun 5–8:45pm.

Japanese businessmen are delighted when their companies send them on assignment to Portland. Why? Because here they can get Japanese food that's as good as back home, and it costs far less. Groups, and anyone seeking privacy and a special experience, should have their meal in one of the traditional tatami rooms with the shoji rice-paper-screen walls. If you can't sit cross-legged through dinner, don't worry, beneath the low tables are wells that allow you to sit as you are accustomed.

The moment you step through the door here, enticing aromas greet you—the outstanding salmon teriyaki, perhaps, or the delicate tempura. If there are two or more of you, you should definitely opt for one of the special dinners. Shabu-shabu is my favorite; you get to do the cooking yourself. For the ultimate Japanese banquet, order the kaiseki dinner, which includes two appetizers, sushi or sashimi, tempura, fish, beef, and dessert.

DAN & LOUIS OYSTER BAR, 208 SW Ankeny St. Tel. 227-5906.

Cuisine: SEAFOOD. **Reservations:** Recommended.
$ Prices: Appetizers $2.50–$8.95; main dishes $6–$12. AE, CB, DC, MC, V.
Open: Sun–Thurs 11am–10pm, Fri–Sat 11am–11pm.

Dan & Louis has been serving up succulent oysters since 1907. The oysters come from Dan and Louis's own oyster farm on Yaquina Bay, OR—they don't come much fresher than this. Half the fun of eating here is enjoying the old-fashioned surroundings. The front counter is stacked high with candies and cigars much as it would have been in the 1920s. The walls are covered with founder Louis Wachsmuth's own collection of old and unusual plates. Beer steins line the shelves, and nautical odds and ends are everywhere.

Louis began his restaurant business serving only two items—oyster stew and oyster cocktails. These two are still on the menu, and as good today as they were 85 years ago. Main courses are simple, no-nonsense seafood dishes, mostly fried, but the prices are great.

HUBER'S, 411 SW Third Ave. Tel. 228-5686.

Cuisine: CONTINENTAL. **Reservations:** Recommended.
$ Prices: Appetizers $2–$5.50; main dishes $4.50–$16. AE, DC, DISC, MC, V.
Open: Lunch Mon–Fri 11am–4pm; dinner Mon–Thurs 5–10pm, Fri–Sat 5–11pm.

Portland's oldest restaurant first opened its doors to the public in

1879, though it didn't move to its present location until 1911. You'll find this very traditional establishment tucked inside the Oregon Pioneer Building. It's easy to miss, since the only sign for Huber's is the name in gold lettering on the building's front door. Down a quiet hallway you'll come to a surprising little room with vaulted stained-glass ceiling, Philippine mahogany paneling, and the original brass cash register. The house specialty has been turkey since the day the first Huber's opened, so there really isn't any question of what to order, even though the menu now features a wide selection of continental and American classics. You can gobble turkey sandwiches, turkey Delmonico, turkey nouvelle, or turkey mushroom pie. The menu even has wine recommendations to accompany your different turkey dishes. Lunch prices are lower, with the turkey sandwich the star of the hour.

HUNAN, 515 SW Broadway, at Morgan's Alley. Tel. 224-8063.

Cuisine: CHINESE. **Reservations:** Required for five or more.

$ Prices: Appetizers $2.50–$5.75; main dishes $6.50–$24; lunch main dishes $4.25–$6. MC, V.

Open: Mon–Thurs 11am–9pm, Fri 11am–10pm, Sat noon–10pm, Sun 5–9pm. **Parking:** SW 10th Ave. and Washington St., with refund after 6pm.

Located at the end of Morgan's Alley, which is lined with interesting little shops and boutiques, is one of Portland's most reliable Chinese restaurants. Hunan exudes a quiet sophistication. Saltwater and freshwater aquariums bubble and glow in the cool darkness, and ivory statues are displayed in wall niches.

Although the menu lists such appetizing main dishes as champagne chicken and Peking duck, there are two items that should absolutely not be missed. General Tso's chicken is both crispy and chewy at the same time, and the succulent sauce has just the right touch of fire. Lover's eggplant is "dedicated to those of our guests with romantic inclinations as well as to all genuine lovers of eggplant," states the menu. With an introduction like that, how can you pass it by? Beautifully presented and prepared chunks of creamy eggplant are truly an eggplant lover's dream come true.

NEWPORT BAY RESTAURANT, 0425 SW Montgomery St. 227-3474.

Cuisine: SEAFOOD. **Reservations:** Recommended.

$ Prices: Appetizers $1–$9; main dishes $9–$18; lunches and light main dishes $5–$9. AE, CB, DC, DISC, MC, V.

Open: Mon–Thurs 11am–11pm, Fri–Sat 11am–midnight, Sun 9am–11pm (brunch 9am–3pm).

Though there are Newport Bay restaurants all over Portland, this one has the best location. It's in the middle of the Willamette River. Well, not actually in the middle, kind of to one side. If you feel this building rocking while you dine, it's no surprise—it's floating. And if you happen to have your own boat, you can just tie up at the dock. Located in the marina at Portland's beautiful RiverPlace shopping-and-dining complex, Newport Bay provides excellent views of the river and the city skyline, especially from the deck. Inside, the atmosphere is cheery and the service is efficient.

Nearly everything on the menu has some sort of seafood in it—even the quiche, salads, and pastas. Main dishes are mostly straightforward and well prepared, nothing too fancy. The short wine list focuses on West Coast wines at reasonable prices. Be sure to save room for the sour-cream-and-raisin pie!

PLAINFIELD'S MAYUR RESTAURANT & ART GALLERY, 852 SW 21st Ave. Tel. 223-2995.

Cuisine: INDIAN. **Reservations:** Recommended.
$ **Prices:** Appetizers $2–$5; main dishes $10–$16. AE, DISC, MC, V.
Open: Dinner only, daily 5:30–10pm.

★ In the words of a friend, "With an Indian restaurant like Mayur's, who needs anything else?" Located in an elegant old Portland home, this is in fact the city's premier Indian restaurant (and includes an art gallery). You can watch the cooks bake bread and succulent tandoori chicken in the only tandoor show kitchen in Oregon. The atmosphere is refined, with bone china and European crystal, and the service is informative and gracious. In addition to the three floors of dining rooms inside, there is a patio out back.

Every dish on the menu is perfectly spiced so that the complex flavors and aromas of Indian cuisine shine through. Be sure to ask them to go easy on the chili peppers if you can't handle spicy food. A tray of condiments accompanies each meal, and consider yourself very lucky if it happens to include the tiny stuffed chili peppers that fire-eaters adore. The dessert list is also an unexpected and pleasant surprise. The hot masala milk, made with their own cardamom liqueur, is ambrosial, and the flan recipe is coveted by a famous food magazine. Save room!

RAFATI'S ON THE WATERFRONT, 25 SW Salmon St. Tel. 248-9305.

Cuisine: SEAFOOD/STEAK. **Reservations:** Strongly recommended.
$ **Prices:** Appetizers $2.75–$6.75; main dishes $13.75–$18.75. AE, JCB, MC, V.
Open: Lunch Mon–Fri 11:30am–2pm; dinner Mon–Thurs 5:30–9pm, Fri–Sat 5:30–10pm.

Popular with executives and other business types, this small restaurant overlooking Tom McCall Waterfront Park prides itself on the award-winning wine list, excellent service, and well-prepared steak and seafood. The steak is only the finest corn-fed, dry-aged beef, and the seafood, lamb, and veal are of equal quality and freshness.

The specialty of the house is flame broiling over mesquite charcoal. With this in mind, you might try sturgeon sautéed with raspberries, mint, and cream; filet mignon glazed with cream, cognac, whisky, and green peppercorns; raspberry teriyaki chicken; or any of the other mouth-watering offerings. And Rafati's seafood paella, though not mesquite broiled, is an outstanding mélange of fresh flavors from the sea. For dessert, there are outstanding seasonal fruit tarts. Be sure to peruse the extensive wine list, which features local, California, and imported wine.

WESTERN CULINARY INTERNATIONAL DINING ROOM, 1316 SW 13th Ave. Tel. 223-2245 or toll free 800/666-0312.

Cuisine: CONTINENTAL. **Reservations:** Required.
$ **Prices:** Four-course lunch $7.95; six-course dinner $15–$20. MC, V.

Open: Lunch Tues–Fri 11:30am–1pm; dinner Tues–Fri 6–8pm.

If you happen to be a frugal gourmet whose palate is more sophisticated than your wallet can afford, you'll want to schedule a meal here. The dining room serves four- to six-course gourmet meals prepared by advanced students at prices even a budget traveler can afford.

Meals are served in a quiet dining room done in pleasing pastels. The decor is modern and unassuming, and the students who wait on you are eager to please. For each course you have a choice among two to five offerings. A sample dinner menu might begin with consommé of Brunoise, followed by pâté of rabbit, a pear sorbet, grilled mahi mahi with citrus lime vin blanc, Chinese salad with smoked salmon, and divine chocolate-mousse cake. Remember, that's all for less than $20! Reservations are strongly recommended, so you don't miss out on this treat. The four-course lunch for only $7.95 is an even better deal.

INEXPENSIVE

FONG CHONG, 301 NW Fourth Ave. Tel. 220-0235.

Cuisine: CHINESE. **Reservations:** Not accepted.

$ Prices: Appetizers $3–$5.50; main dishes $4.50–$10; dim sum meals, under $10. No credit cards.

Open: Mon–Thurs 11am–9pm, Fri–Sun 11am–10pm; dim sum 11am–3pm.

Some of the most popular Chinese restaurants in Portland are in grocery stores, including this one. Don't worry, you won't be eating between the aisles; the restaurant occupies its own room. Although most of the food here is above average, the dim sum is the best in the city. Flag down a passing cart and point to the most appetizing-looking little dishes. Be careful or you might end up with a plate of chicken feet. At the end of the meal, your bill is calculated by the number of plates on your table.

HAMBURGER MARY'S, 840 SW Park Ave. Tel. 223-0900.

ⓕ FROMMER'S COOL FOR KIDS: RESTAURANTS

Brasserie Montmartre *(see p. 189)* Though this is more of an adult restaurant, there are paper tablecloths and crayons to keep kids entertained and even a strolling magician most evenings.

Dan & Louis Oyster Bar *(see p. 190)* You'll think you're eating in the hold of an old sailing ship, and all the fascinating stuff on the walls will keep kids entertained.

Hamburger Mary's *(see above)* Your kids can play with the Etch-a-Sketch while they wait for the omelet they've created from the 22 possible ingredients. This place serves one of the best hamburgers in Portland—always a perennial favorite with little ones—at a price that won't bust your budget.

Cuisine: BURGERS. **Reservations:** Not accepted.
$ Prices: $4.70–$10. AE, CB, DC, MC, V.
Open: Daily 7am–2am.

As the name implies, this is a place to eat a hamburger—one of the best hamburgers in Portland. It's thick and juicy, piled high with crisp lettuce and ripe tomatoes, and served on a whole-wheat bun. You can't miss this little place—a tiny building surrounded by skyscrapers. Step inside and you enter a crowded room where the walls and ceiling are covered with everything from a rusting sousaphone to an upside-down floor lamp. Grab a table, snag the Etch-a-Sketch, and sink back into childhood fantasies. Stop by in the morning (or whenever you're ready for breakfast) and create your own omelet from the list of 22 possible ingredients.

PANINI, 620 SW Ninth Ave. Tel. 224-6001.
Cuisine: ITALIAN. **Reservations:** Not accepted.
$ Prices: Antipasti $4–$7; sandwiches $4.95; pasta $7.50; pizza $3.25–$5.50. No credit cards.
Open: Mon–Fri 7am–7pm, Sat 8am–5pm.

"Panini" is Italian for a little roll, a reference to small sandwiches. Panini bars can be found all over Italy, and also in Portland. This hole-in-the-wall sandwich shop looks as if it were lifted from a Florentine back street and tucked into a Portland back street. Blue-and-white tile floors, big glass cases full of beautiful sandwiches, and painted mugs hanging on the wall beside the espresso machine give Panini a thoroughly Italian atmosphere. Even the waiters look Italian. The only drawbacks are the limited seating and the short hours. Panini gets my vote for best place in Portland for a quick lunch.

2. NORTHWEST PORTLAND

EXPENSIVE

L'AUBERGE, 2601 NW Vaughn St. Tel. 223-3302.
Cuisine: NORTHWEST/FRENCH. **Reservations:** Required.
$ Prices: Appetizers $4–$7.75; main dishes $18–$25.50; six-course, fixed-price dinner $45. AE, CB, DC, DISC, MC, V.
Open: Dinner only, Mon–Thurs 5pm–midnight, Fri–Sat 5pm–1am, Sun 5pm–midnight.

Located at the edge of the industrial district, this little country cottage offers some of the best French and Northwest cuisine in Portland and has done so for many years. The restaurant is divided into the main dining room and the lounge and deck area, where an à la carte international-bistro menu is available. On Sunday nights the French flavor is forsaken in favor of succulent ribs, and a movie is shown in the bar. A more formal atmosphere reigns in the main dining room, even on Sunday nights. A fireplace and a few antiques create a homey feel, and etched glass between booths lends an air of sophistication. A few works of contemporary art add drama to the setting.

The fixed-price dinners feature meals with a French origin but translated with a Northwest accent. If you happen to be dining downstairs, be sure to stop by the bar first to have a look at the delectable morsels on the dessert tray. Dinners start with bread and pâté, followed by a soup or fish course, sorbet, and salad. There are always four choices of main dishes, such as filet mignon with port reduction, hazelnuts, and cambazola; or grilled salmon with a coulis of sweet peppers and Kalamata olives. This is all topped off with a choice from that dessert tray.

MODERATE

CAJUN CAFÉ & BISTRO, 2074 NW Lovejoy St. Tel. 227-0227.

Cuisine: CAJUN. **Reservations:** Suggested for lunch, strongly recommended for dinner.

$ Prices: Appetizers $2.75–$8; main dishes $9–$20; main dishes at lunch $5–$10. AE, CB, DC, MC, V.

Open: Lunch Mon–Fri 11:30am–2:30pm; dinner Sun–Thurs 5:30–9:30pm, Fri–Sat 5:30–10:30pm; limited menu available all day.

The Cajun Café sits on a busy corner in the fashionable Nob Hill district. Out front, there are a few tables for taking advantage of summer sunshine; inside, the decor is bright even on a dreary winter day. The menu here changes almost daily, but you can be sure that you'll find quite a few offerings that not only fire up your Cajun tastebuds but that also confound your Creole sensibilities with ingredients and combinations never before seen on any bayou. How about blackened salmon on a bed of radicchio and watercress? Perhaps blackened ahi tuna with mango-jalapeño salsa or chanterelle and shiitake mushroom pasta made with tomato linguine appeal to you. Prices at lunch are about half the dinner prices and the lunch menu includes many of the same dishes.

CASA-U-BETCHA, 612 NW 21st Ave. Tel. 222-4833.

Cuisine: MEXICAN. **Reservations:** Recommended.

$ Prices: Appetizers $2.75–$7.75; main dishes $8.75–$13.25.

Open: Lunch Mon–Fri 11:30am–2:30pm; dinner Sun–Thurs 5–10pm, Fri–Sat 5–11pm.

If you like your restaurant to be a work of art, slide into one of the wacky industrial-chic booths at this trendy nouvelle Mexican restaurant. Garishly painted walls, a huge snake sculpture, flashing chile pepper lights, and metal-pipe cacti create a real "scene" at Casa-U-Betcha. Located on an up-and-coming street with fringe art galleries, a repertory movie theater, and a 1950s furniture store, this is Portland's hippest Mexican restaurant. Big baskets of regular and blue corn chips with bowls of red and green salsa wait on every metal-topped table. I find the appetizers menu so fascinating that I usually just make a meal of a couple of these and skip the combo dinners and other Mexican main dishes. My favorite appetizer is the Mexican sushi made with tortillas, smoked salmon, black beans, jicama, guacamole, and wasabi. The soy-ginger-jalapeño dipping sauce that comes with it is a real knockout. Another Casa-U-Betcha is located at 1700 NE Broadway (tel. 282-4554).

DELPHINA'S, 2112 NW Kearney St. Tel. 221-1195.

Cuisine: ITALIAN. **Reservations:** Strongly recommended; required for Back Kitchen Dinner.

$ Prices: Appetizers and soups $3–$10; pastas $11–$15; main dishes $15–$18. AE, DC, MC, V.

Open: Lunch Mon–Fri 11:30am–2:30pm; dinner daily 5–11pm.
Long a Nob Hill mainstay, Delphina's offers excellent Italian food in
a casual neighborhood-bistro atmosphere. The tile floors, exposed
brick walls, and café curtains on the windows all contribute to the
comfortable feeling, while smiling, friendly service makes you feel
right at home. Be sure to notice the colander lamps hung from the
ceiling.

Northern Italian fare predominates here, but southern Italian and
even Pacific Northwest manage to sneak onto the menu. You might
want to try the Oregon rabbit, which is prepared a different way each
week, or a tenderloin of pork sautéed in a sauce of juniper berries,
garlic, white wine, and butter. Delphina's most unusual meal is the
Back Kitchen Dinner for parties of seven or eight people. You get to
dine in the bustling kitchen, where the chef surprises you with a
multicourse menu that your Italian mother-in-law would envy.

**ZEFIRO RESTAURANT & BAR, 500 NW 21st Ave. Tel.
226-3394.**
   Cuisine: MEDITERRANEAN. **Reservations:** Required.
$ **Prices:** Appetizers $4–$8; main dishes $12.50–$17.50. AE,
   MC, V.
   Open: Lunch Mon–Fri 11:30am–2:30pm; dinner Mon–Thurs
   6–10pm, Fri 6–11pm, Sat 5:30–11pm.

⭐ The Northwest restaurant graveyard is crowded with ghosts of
daring restaurants that served imaginative cuisine, garnered
rave reviews, and disappeared as quickly as a luscious crème
brûlée. Luckily for the adventurous palates of Portland, Zefiro has
not suffered this ignoble fate. Unpainted fiberboard walls and tiny
black-matte halogen lamps hanging from the ceiling lend this
restaurant a minimalist urban chic that allows the outstanding
creativity of the kitchen to take to the fore.

The menu can only be categorized as Mediterranean, with
old-style French and Italian predominating. However, Moroccan,
Greek, Spanish, and even Asian influences creep in. Don't be
surprised if you find yourself asking your waiter to define unfamiliar
menu terms. For a starter, be sure to try the fragrant bowl of warm
polenta with marjoram and mascarpone if it happens to be on the
menu. Salads, with diverese ingredients like fennel, blood orange,
and radishes with mint-citrus vinaigrette, are always menu highlights.
Roasted mahi mahi with an herb salsa verde made from tarragon,
parsley, thyme, oregano, capers, garlic, lemon, and olive oil was a
recent entrée that captured all the fragrance of a Mediterranean herb
garden in one dish. For dessert fresh-fruit sorbet served with
fresh-baked cookies is smooth, flavorful, and refreshing.

INEXPENSIVE

**ROSE'S RESTAURANT AND DELICATESSEN, 315 NW
23rd Ave. Tel. 227-5181.**
   Cuisine: DELI. **Reservations:** Suggested for dinner.
$ **Prices:** Main dishes $5–$9; desserts $3–$4. CB, DC, MC, V.
   Open: Sun–Thurs 7am–11pm, Fri–Sat 8am–midnight.
Dieters should not step through the door of this famous Portland
deli. Immediately inside is a large counter displaying the cakes, sweet
rolls, and pastries that have made Rose's famous. It's not that the
desserts here are any better than anywhere else (although they are
delicious), it's just that the portions are monstrous. A cinnamon roll is

roughly 6 inches by 4 inches by 4 inches! Never mind saving room for dessert, save room for the meal. Rose's is also a New York–style kosher deli with a huge selection of main dishes and giant sandwiches. Other Rose's are located at 12329 NE Glisan St. (tel. 254-6545) and in Beaverton Town Square in Beaverton (tel. 643-4287).

3. SOUTHEAST PORTLAND

EXPENSIVE

DIGGER O'DELL'S RESTAURANT AND OYSTER BAR, 532 SE Grand Ave. Tel. 238-6996.

Cuisine: CAJUN. **Reservations:** Recommended.

$ Prices: Appetizers $4–$12; main dishes $10–$20. AE, DISC, MC, V.

Open: Lunch Mon–Fri 11am–2pm; dinner Mon–Sat 5–11pm, Sun 3–10pm.

People have been dying to get into this place for years. In fact, when these historic buildings known as the Barber Block were erected in 1890, they housed Barber & Hill, Undertakers & Embalmers. Some 50 years later the buildings housed the Nickelodeon Theatre, a popular vaudeville venue. Today the restaurant's name recalls the building's varied past in its reference to the Irish gravedigger from the 1940s radio show "The Life of Riley."

Beautifully restored, the Barber Block is now home to Portland's first, and still most popular, Cajun restaurant. The interior decor is elegantly Victorian, as befits a building of this age. A sweeping staircase leads up to a mezzanine dining area. Gumbo, jambalaya, blackened fish and steak—all your favorites are here, prepared with fresh Northwest ingredients. Digger's is also an oyster bar, and you'd be remiss if you didn't start your meal with fresh Northwest oysters. Thursday through Saturday nights, there is live music in the lounge.

GENOA, 2832 SE Belmont St. Tel. 238-1464.

Cuisine: ITALIAN. **Reservations:** Required.

$ Prices: Fixed-price four-course dinner $36; seven-course dinner $45. AE, CB, DC, MC, V.

Open: Dinner only, Mon–Sat 5:30–9:30pm (four-course from 5:30–6pm only).

Without a doubt, this is the best Italian restaurant in Portland, and with only 10 tables, it's also one of the smallest dining spots in town. Everything is made fresh in the kitchen, from the breads to the luscious desserts that are temptingly displayed on a maple burl table just inside the front door. This is an ideal setting for a romantic dinner, and service is personal, as only a restaurant of this size can provide.

The fixed-price menu changes every couple of weeks, so you can keep coming back again and again and never tire of the menu. On a recent evening, dinner started with *bagna cauda,* a super-rich fondue made with cream, garlic, anchovies, and butter into which are dipped fresh vegetables and breadsticks. The soup was a spicy shrimp bisque and the pasta course was a Tuscan specialty—wide noodles with a sauce of wild boar marinated with juniper berries, bay leaves, rosemary, and Chianti and then stewed in pancetta, marjoram, tomato, and balsamic vinegar. A simple salad of mixed seasonal greens followed. For a main dish there was a choice between grilled salmon garnished with caramelized red onions, golden raisins, pine nuts, orange and lemon zest, clove, cinnamon, and sherry wine vinegar; a confit of duck leg and thinly sliced duck breast with a reduction of black currants, duck demiglaze, shallots, and Dijon mustard; or a veal rib chop stuffed with sautéed dried porcini mushrooms, fresh wild chanterelles, and imported prosciutto and sautéed in a sauce of marsala, white wine, and veal demiglaze. The dessert selection was calculated to throw the indecisive into convulsions: caramelized tarts of apples and pears, chocolate nut tortes, creamy custards, *gelati,* and *granite.* To top it off, there was fresh seasonal fruit to cleanse the palate.

MODERATE

BREAD & INK CAFE, 3610 SE Hawthorne St. Tel. 239-4756.
  Cuisine: NORTHWEST. **Reservations:** Recommended.
$ **Prices:** Appetizers $2–$6.75; main dishes $5.25–$14.50; Sun brunch $11.50. MC, V.
  Open: Breakfast Mon–Fri 7–11:30am, Sat 8am–noon; lunch Mon–Fri 11:30am–3pm; dinner Mon–Thurs 5:30–9pm, Fri–Sat 5:30–10pm; Sun brunch 9am–2pm.

Bread & Ink has been voted one of the best restaurants in Oregon, but don't expect a stuffy atmosphere here. This is a casual neighborhood café, bright and airy, with pen-and-ink artwork on the walls and fresh flowers on every table.

Every meal here is carefully and imaginatively prepared using fresh Northwest ingredients. The last time I visited, I had an unusual preparation of salmon marinated with juniper berries, salt, pepper, and sugar. This dish was influenced by traditional Northwest Native American cooking. Desserts are a mainstay of Bread & Ink's loyal patrons, so don't pass them by. The Yiddish Sunday brunch is one of the most filling in the city.

INDIGINE, 3725 SE Division St. Tel. 238-1470.
  Cuisine: INDIAN/INTERNATIONAL. **Reservations:** Required.
$ **Prices:** Appetizers $3.50; main dishes $15–$19; Sat-night Indian feast $25. MC, V.
  Open: Dinner only, Tues–Sat 5:30–10pm.

At Indigine you can take your tastebuds dancing through tantalizing flavors the likes of which you may never have encountered before. Step through the door of this brown house with a red roof, red trim, and a riotous little flower and herb garden and you are halfway into the kitchen, which gives you the distinct feel of dining at a friend's house. If only all my friends could cook this well.

The menu at Indigine is eclectic, with Indian, Mexican, French, and American offerings during the week and an extravagant Indian feast on Saturday evenings. In what must be the greatest understatement on any Portland menu, the regular meals are called "Simple Suppers." These begin with freshly baked rolls and a salad basket of definitively fresh vegetables, usually accompanied by a vegetable dip such as herbed guacamole. When the irresistibly tempting appetizer tray comes around, keep in mind that dinner portions here are large enough for two people. During the week you can sample some of Indigine's flavorful Indian cuisine by ordering either the tandoori dinner or the vegetarian sampler. On the other hand, the creamy seafood enchilada perfectly mixes cheeses with shrimp and scallops so fresh you can almost smell the salt air. Before it's too late, stop and save room for one of the luscious desserts, such as ginger cheesecake. If you have never had Indian chai (tea), don't miss this opportunity— it's flavored with cardamom.

WESTMORELAND BISTRO AND WINES, 7015 SE Milwaukie Ave. Tel. 236-6457.
   Cuisine: NORTHWEST. **Reservations:** Required.
$ **Prices:** Appetizers $3.25–$4.50; main dishes $13.25–$18. MC, V.
   Open: Lunch Tues–Sat 11am–4pm; dinner Tues–Sat 5–8:30pm.
Westmoreland Bistro and Wines is easy to miss. It's small, it's nondescript, and it's located in a neighborhood that, though attractive, is not one of the city's busiest. Yet, there are people who wouldn't miss a chance to eat here on a visit to Portland. In fact, I've heard that some folks come all the way from Seattle just to have dinner here. Why? Because the Westmoreland's chef is Caprial Pence, who helped put the Northwest on the national restaurant map with the innovative cuisine she served at Fuller's restaurant in the Seattle Sheraton. Here at her own restaurant she continues her innovative kitchen wizardry for a new following of Portlanders. The menu changes every two weeks and is limited to four or five main dishes and as many appetizers, all listed on a blackboard. About half the restaurant is given over to a superb selection of wine, and if you simply crave a glass of great local wine, you can sit at the wine bar. Even though this is a strong contender for best restaurant in Portland, it is a very casual place. There's no need to dress up, but you do need to make reservations well in advance (at least a week ahead for Friday or Saturday night). I'm a sucker for roast garlic and goat cheese, and here you can slather them on crunchy, chewy crostini bread. Salads are simple and delicious and made with only the finest greens and vegetables. Main dishes combine perfectly cooked meat and fish, such as crispy tea-smoked duck or lightly breaded oysters, with vibrant sauces like cranberry-shallot compote or sweet red pepper pesto. Desserts, such as chocolate-almond-ricotta cake, are rich without being overly sweet. You'll get a large piece of whatever you order, so save room.

4. NORTHEAST PORTLAND

INEXPENSIVE

MERCHANT OF VENICE, 1432 NE Broadway. Tel. 284-4558.
   Cuisine: ITALIAN. **Reservations:** Not accepted.
$ **Prices:** Sandwiches $2.75–$4.25; main dishes $5.25–$9.50. AE, MC, V.
   Open: Mon–Thurs 11am–9pm; Fri–Sat 11am–10pm.
If you're over on the east side and want a quick, inexpensive lunch or dinner, duck in at Merchant of Venice, a tiny café and deli

specializing in pizza, pasta, and sandwiches. The prices are great and the food is hard to beat. The pizza here is what has locals raving. Try the Merchant of Venice, which is topped with homemade chicken sausage, mushrooms, and artichokes. If you'd rather go for a sandwich, try the Shylock, which is stuffed with chicken salad made with celery, olives, sun-dried tomatoes, capers, and herb mayonnaise. There aren't too many tables here, so you might want to consider this a take-out place.

NOODLEHEAD, 1708 NE Broadway. Tel. 282-8424.

Cuisine: CHINESE. **Reservations:** Recommended.

$ Prices: Appetizers $3.50–$6.25; main dishes $5.25–$8.50. AE, DC, MC, V.

Open: Mon–Fri 11am–11pm; Sat–Sun 5–11pm.

Maybe you already guessed from the name that this is not your ordinary Chinese restaurant, and when you see Noodlehead, you'll know for sure that this isn't your local Lucky Dragon. Though the dishes on the menu are, for the most part, familiar, the decor is Memphis contemporary (and I don't mean Memphis, Tennessee). A purple velvet bench winds sinuously through the narrow dining room. The back wall is covered with gold leaf, and a side wall is a high-gloss black. Throw in a few green-velvet upholstered walls, red-dyed wood, and funnel-shaped overhead lamps that sprout fiber-optic noodles and you have the setting for an ultrahip postcontemporary eatery. Noodlehead does for Chinese what the adjacent Casa-U-Betcha does for Mexican, so its not surprising to learn that they are under the same ownership. Looks aside, the food is great and if you keep your eyes open you'll find some unusual combinations of flavorings.

RHEINLANDER, 5035 NE Sandy Blvd. Tel. 288-5503.

Cuisine: GERMAN. **Reservations:** Strongly recommended.

$ Prices: Complete meals $10–$15; early dinners $7–$10. AE, MC, V.

Open: Mon–Fri 4:30–9:30pm, Sat 4–10pm, Sun 3:30–9pm; Sun brunch 10am–2pm.

⑤ There's no mistaking this restaurant. It's the only building around with a Black Forest cottage facade and polka music blaring from a loudspeaker out front. For more than 25 years, Rheinlander has been known as Portland's most fun restaurant. Let the singing waiters and strolling musicians in lederhosen entertain you while you feast on good old-fashioned German cooking served in belt-loosening portions.

If you can put together a group of six or more people, order the Family Feast. It's served family style, so everyone can have as much as he or she wants. If you don't have a family, try the sampler platter; it has most of the same items. Early-evening dinners cost several dollars less than those served later, and the crowds are waiting at the door at opening time. For more casual dining, try the adjacent **Gustav's Bier Stube,** a grand, baronial hall that serves sandwiches and quick meals to accompany their many beers and ales. Gustav's is open longer hours than the Rheinlander.

RON PAUL CHARCUTERIE, 1441 NE Broadway. Tel. 284-5347.

Cuisine: PACIFIC NORTHWEST. **Reservations:** Not accepted.

$ Prices: Appetizers and lighter fare $2.75–$8; sandwiches $5.25–$7; main dishes $6–$13. MC, V.
Open: Mon–Thurs 8am–10:30pm, Fri 8am–midnight, Sat 9am–midnight.

Chef Ron Paul has become a Portland institution over the years. He started out with a catering business that became so popular that clients demanded he open a restaurant. This is a casual deli-style place in an upwardly mobile neighborhood in northeast Portland. Light streams in the walls of glass illuminating long cases full of tempting pasta and vegetable salads, cheeses, quiches, pizzas, sandwich fixings, and, most tempting of all, shelves covered with decadent desserts. After 5pm, there are specials such as lamb in filo with goat cheese and mint or spring vegetable ravioli with asparagus, snow peas, and a red pepper coulis. The menu changes daily so you might want to stop by several times during a visit to Portland.

SAIGON KITCHEN, 835 NE Broadway. Tel. 281-3669.
Cuisine: VIETNAMESE/THAI. **Reservations:** Suggested.
$ Prices: Appetizers $1.25–$7; main dishes $5.25–$16. MC, V.
Open: Daily 11am–10:30pm.

Vietnamese restaurants have been opening around Portland's east side. They are generally quite inexpensive, offer amazing variety, and provide some of the most interesting flavor combinations this side of Thailand. Saigon Kitchen is among the best of these restaurants. Don't expect a fancy atmosphere inside this pink stucco building, just good home cooking, Vietnamese style. If the menu proves too bewildering, try a combination dinner and let the kitchen make the decisions. The spring rolls shouldn't be missed, however, nor should the curried chicken. The salads, such as shrimp and barbecued pork, are tangy and spicy. There is even a menu of Thai dishes for those who prefer this similar cuisine. Another Saigon Kitchen is at 3954 SE Division St. (tel. 236-2312).

5. SPECIALTY DINING

Juice bars have been proliferating in Portland and their growing popularity is giving coffeehouses a run for the money. A tall glass of fresh pear, carrot, pineapple, and ginger juice will give you a charge that's almost as invigorating as a cup of espresso. If you want to try kicking the coffee habit and getting into the juice habit, stop by the **Energy Bar,** 834 SW 10th Avenue (tel. 274-1964); **Limbo,** Yamhill Market, 110 SW Yamhill St. (tel. 224-3450); or **Mo' Juice,** 720 NW 21st St. (tel. 223-2182). Prices generally range from $2 to $4.

LOCAL FAVORITE

STANICH'S TEN-TIL-ONE TAVERN, 4915 NE Freemont St. Tel. 281-2322.
Cuisine: BURGERS. **Reservations:** Necessary for lunch.
$ Prices: $2.25–$4.10. No credit cards.
Open: Mon–Sat 11am–11:30pm. (Kelly St., Mon–Thurs 11am–10:30pm, Fri–Sat 11am–11:30pm).

According to Portlanders and the local press, the best burger in town is to be had at Stanich's, a neighborhood tavern that has been serving state governors and a regular lunchtime crowd since 1949. The menu features mostly hamburgers, and Stanich's self-proclaimed "world's greatest hamburger"—a cheeseburger with fried egg, ham, bacon, cheese, and all the trimmings—is definitely not for the faint of heart. Another Stanich's is at 5627 SW Kelly St. (tel. 246-5040).

DESSERT

PAPA HAYDN, 701 NW 23rd Ave. Tel. 228-7317.
 Cuisine: ITALIAN. **Reservations:** Not accepted.
$ **Prices:** Appetizers $6; main dishes $8–$15; desserts $3.50–$5. AE, MC, V.
 Open: Tues–Thurs 11:30am–11pm, Fri–Sat 11:30am–midnight, Sun 10am–3pm.

Say the words Papa Haydn to a Portlander and you'll see eyes glaze over. A wispy, blissful smile will light up that Portlander's face, and then praises will spill forth. What is it about this little bistro that sends locals into accolades of superlatives? Just desserts. That's right, though Papa Haydn is a respectable Italian restaurant, it is legendary for dessert. At last count the menu included 25 decadent delicacies. Specials add to this list. Oregon filbert torte, raspberry gâteau, black velvet, Georgian peanut butter mousse torte, los gatos, boccone dolce. These are just some of the names that stimulate a Pavlovian response in locals. But don't take my word for it, go see for yourself, go *taste* for yourself. Expect a line at the door (that's the real price you pay for a Papa Haydn symphony). Another Papa Haydn is at 5829 SE Milwaukie Ave. (tel. 232-9440).

HOTEL DINING

EXPENSIVE

THE LONDON GRILL, The Benson Hotel, 309 SW Broadway. Tel. 228-2000.
 Cuisine: CONTINENTAL. **Reservations:** Required.
$ **Prices:** Appetizers $5.75–$8.25; main dishes $18.25–$22.50; Sun brunch $19.50. AE, CB, DC, DISC, ER, JCB, MC, V.
 Open: Sunday champagne brunch 9:30am–1pm. Breakfast Mon–Fri 6:30–11am, Sat–Sun 6:30–9am; lunch Mon–Sat 11:30am–2pm; dinner Sun–Thurs 5–10pm, Fri–Sat 5–11pm.

Down in the basement of the luxurious Benson Hotel is one of Portland's top restaurants. Modeled after the original London Grill, which was a favorite with Queen Elizabeth I, it has a dark decor and a vaulted ceiling that further enhances the wine-cellar feel of the room. Mahogany paneling reflects the glowing chandeliers, and on cold nights a fire roars in the fireplace. Service by tuxedoed waiters is impeccable. Both breakfast and lunch are popular with business executives.

 The chef emphasizes uncompromising gourmet meals. The ingredients are always fresh and of the highest quality, including many of the finest local fruits and vegetables. If you have a craving for some imaginative Northwest cuisine, this restaurant should set your tastebuds singing. Grilled Cornish game hen with tangy blood-orange sauce and grilled butterflied filet of beef with mango chutney are two such main dishes. The Sunday champagne brunch is the most elegant in the city.

MODERATE

CELILO, Governor Hotel, SW 10th Ave. and Alder St. Tel. 224-3400.
   Cuisine: NORTHWEST. **Reservations:** Strongly recommended.
$ Prices: Appetizers $6.50–$9.75; main dishes $12.50–$18.75; lunch main dishes $8.75–$14.75. AE, CB, DC, MC, V.
   Open: Breakfast Mon–Fri 6:30–10:30am, Sat 7:30–10:30am; lunch Mon–Sat 11:30am–2pm; dinner Sun–Thurs 5–10pm, Fri–Sat 5–11pm; Sun brunch 10am–2pm.

Celilo (pronounced Suh-LIE-low) is named for the region of the Columbia River where Native Americans once congregated to fish for salmon, which they would then smoke over alder-wood fires. Not surprisingly you'll find plenty of salmon on the menu. You'll also find a casual western elegance in the restaurant's decor. Ceiling fans revolve slowly high above your head, and curtained booths line the two walls of windows. Pull the curtains shut on your table and you'll feel as though you are dining in an old Pullman railroad car. You'd be remiss if you didn't start your meal with a little salmon of one sort or another such as alder-smoked lox served with dilled cucumbers, asparagus vinaigrette, and onion bread. On the other hand, you might have your smoked salmon in a Northwest Caesar salad. For a main dish you might want to try something that includes three more salmon preparations (grilled with lemon-soy sauce, steamed in rice paper, and baked over alder wood). This is not to say that Celilo *only* serves salmon. You'll also find well-prepared steak, veal, chicken, and other seafoods on the menu.

ESPLANADE RESTAURANT, RiverPlace Hotel, 1510 SW Harbor Way. Tel. 295-6166.
   Cuisine: NORTHWEST. **Reservations:** Recommended.
$ Prices: Appetizers $2.95–$6.50; main dishes $12–$19. AE, CB, DC, MC, V.
   Open: Breakfast Mon–Fri 6:30–10:30am, Sat 6:30–11am, Sun 6:30–10am; lunch Mon–Fri 11:30am–2:30pm; dinner daily 5:30–10pm; brunch Sun 11am–2:30pm.

The Esplanade, surrounded by the quietly sophisticated European-resort atmosphere of the RiverPlace Hotel, is one of the city's few waterfront restaurants. Understated elegance and expansive views of the marina and the city's bridges combine for a stunning setting, and even on the grayest day of Portland's long winter, the pale-yellow walls, colorful contemporary art, and huge flower arrangements will cheer you up.

However, it's the superb cuisine that is truly calculated to brighten your day. Imaginative combinations of fresh seasonal ingredients capture the spirit of the Northwest. Among the appetizers on a recent menu were irresistibly spicy crab cakes with chili mint aïoli and cheese raviolis with papaya and lime. The main dishes included such tempting fare as roast duck with raspberry sauce, prawns and andouille sausage with black pepper linguine, and grilled beef tenderloin with polenta.

THE HEATHMAN RESTAURANT AND BAR, The Heathman Hotel, SW Broadway at Salmon St. Tel. 241-4100.
   Cuisine: NORTHWEST/CONTINENTAL. **Reservations:** Required.

$ Prices: Appetizers $5.50–$8.50; main dishes $15–$25. AE, CB, DC, MC, V.
Open: Breakfast Mon–Fri 6:30–11am, Sat 6:30am–noon, Sun 6:30am–3pm; lunch Mon–Fri 11am–2pm, Sat noon–3pm; dinner Sun–Thurs 5–10pm, Fri–Sat 5–11pm.

The menu in this elegant hotel dining room changes seasonally, but one thing remains constant: The ingredients are the very freshest of Oregon and Northwest seafoods, meat, wild game, and produce. Small and bright, the restaurant exudes a bistro atmosphere. On the walls are Andy Warhol's Endangered Species—a rhino, zebra, lion, panda, and others—part of the Heathman's extensive collection of classic and contemporary art.

Both the adventurous diner and the traditionalist will find on the menu appealing dishes that reflect the season and the bounty of the Northwest. A recent winter menu offered roast Muscovy duck with toasted pine nuts, medjool dates, and sauce romaine as well as dry-aged beef tenderloin with Oregon truffle butter and marchand de vin sauce. Local fruit appears in many of the rich desserts. In the bar, there are Northwest microbrewery beers on tap, while an extensive wine list spotlights Oregon.

RISTORANTE PAZZO, Hotel Vintage Plaza, 422 SW Broadway. Tel. 228-1515.
Cuisine: ITALIAN. **Reservations:** Strongly recommended.
$ Prices: Appetizers $5–$8; main dishes $8–$17; lunch main dishes $7–$11. AE, CB, DC, DISC, MC, V.
Open: Breakfast Mon–Fri 7–10:30am, Sat–Sun 8–10:30am; lunch Mon–Sun 11:30am–2:30pm; dinner Sun–Thurs 5–10pm, Fri–Sat 5–11pm.

The Italianate elegance of Hotel Vintage Plaza demands an Italian restaurant, and as luck would have it, Italian food has of late been enjoying a renaissance under the title of Mediterranean cuisine. Whatever you want to call the style of meals served at Pazzo, I call it great. The atmosphere is not nearly as rarefied as in the adjacent hotel lobby, and, in fact, if you take a seat at Pazzo's bar, you'll be ducking hanging hams, sausages, and garlic braids. Rustic decor and the sterotypical red-and-white-checked tablecloths speak of an Italian country ristorante, though the city passes by just outside. As you step through the restaurant's front door, you'll find yourself staring into a glass case full of roasted garlic bulbs. If you aren't a fan of garlic, you might want to turn around and walk right out again. Garlic is all-pervasive at Pazzo (except on the dessert menu). You can start with a rosemary-crust pizzetta topped with roasted garlic and cambazola cheese and then move on to a Caesar salad with plenty of anchovies, garlic, parmesan, and croutons. You don't have to have a ton of garlic in every dish. The smoked-salmon filled ravioli with asparagus and lemon-cream sauce lets other flavors shine through. Consider yourself fortunate if the mixed grill of shrimp, scallops, salmon, clams, seafood sausage, and pancetta wrapped oysters happens to be on the list. Delicious!

DINING WITH A VIEW
EXPENSIVE

ALEXANDER'S, Portland Hilton Hotel, 921 SW Sixth Ave. Tel. 226-1611.

Cuisine: CONTINENTAL. **Reservations:** Recommended.
$ Prices: Appetizers $4–$8.50; main dishes $18–$38; table d'hôte menu $29. AE, CB, DC, MC, V.
Open: Dinner only, Mon–Sat 5:30–10pm.

Way up on the 23rd floor of the Hilton is this excellent continental restaurant. Be sure to have a drink in the lounge, which looks out over the densely wooded West Hills. Move on to the dining room and you are treated to a view encompassing Mount Hood, the Willamette River, and downtown Portland. The entrance to the restaurant is past a wall of rough stones, which creates a rustic mountain resort atmosphere. However, lavender tones and flowers on the tables leave no doubt as to the sophisticated ambience at Alexander's.

Fresh seafood is the star on the menu, and you can choose from six fresh fish dishes, prepared either charbroiled, poached, or sautéed with lemon butter. There are also specialties such as salmon in orange sauce or poached with pear sauce. Breast of duck and breast of pheasant both make artful appearances as well. You'll be stopped in your tracks by the dessert tray by the front door. The combinations of chocolate and fresh fruit are gorgeous and delicious.

ATWATER'S RESTAURANT AND LOUNGE, U.S. Bancorp Tower, 111 SW Fifth Ave. Tel. 275-3600.

Cuisine: NORTHWEST. **Reservations:** Required.
$ Prices: Appetizers $6–$8; main dishes $16–$28; fixed-price meals—$26 three courses, $35 five courses ($53 with wine); Sun brunch $17–$21.50. AE, CB, DC, MC, V.
Open: Dinner daily 5:30–10:30pm; Sun brunch 10am–3pm.

Atwater's whispers elegance from the moment you step off the elevator on the 30th floor. A rosy light suffuses the hall at sunset, and blond-wood trim fairly glows in the warm light. Oriental carpets on a blond-hardwood floor and large, dramatic flower arrangements on dark-wood tables add splashes of color throughout the restaurant. In the middle of the dining room is a glass-enclosed wine room that would put many wineshops to shame. Far below you are the Willamette River and Portland, and off in the distance stands Mount Hood.

Pacific Northwest cuisine is the specialty here, and it's done to perfection. The combinations of ingredients are unexpected and delectable. Roast breast and sausage of duckling with raspberry port sauce is one such combination. For an appetizer, you should indulge in the cured salmon with sturgeon caviar, asparagus, and a lemon-herb dressing.

SALTY'S ON THE COLUMBIA, 3839 NE Marine Dr. Tel. 288-4444.

Cuisine: SEAFOOD. **Reservations:** Strongly recommended.
$ Prices: Appetizers $3.75–$16; main dishes $14–$28. AE, DC, DISC, MC, V.
Open: Lunch Mon–Fri 10am–2pm, Sat–Sun 11am–2pm; dinner Mon–Thurs 5–9pm, Fri–Sat 5–10pm, Sun 4:30–9pm; Sun brunch 10am–2pm.

Despite Portland's two rivers, there aren't many waterfront restaurants, and Salty's is by far the best. Located out on the Columbia River near the airport, this sprawling restaurant offers views that take in river, mountains, and forests. A huge anchor out front and a miniature lighthouse on the roof let you know you've found the place, while inside you'll walk past tanks full of lobster and cases of fresh fish on ice. Preparations here, especially on the daily specials menu, are creative and portions are large. Salmon is particularly popular, and much of the year, you'll see salmon fishermen in the river just off shore. Try it smoked over alder wood, which is a traditional Northwest preparation. A few choice offerings of steak and chicken dishes offer options to those who don't care for seafood. A warning: Though the decks look appealing, the noise from the airport can be distracting.

LUNCH

RENE'S FIFTH AVENUE, 1300 SW Fifth Ave. Tel. 241-0712.
  Cuisine: CONTINENTAL. **Reservations:** Recommended.
$ **Prices:** $7–$9. MC, V.
  Open: Mon–Fri 11:30am–2:30pm.

Comfortable and elegant, this 21st-floor lunch spot is always crowded. Local businesspeople flock here as much for the great view as for the food. The menu, though short, is varied and includes daily specials and plenty of seafood. You won't find a view this good at better prices anywhere else in the city.

LIGHT, CASUAL, FAST FOOD

MACHEEZMO MOUSE, 723 SW Salmon St. Tel. 228-3491.
  Cuisine: MEXICAN/HEALTHY. **Reservations:** Not accepted.
$ **Prices:** $3–$5.50. Cash only.
  Open: Mon–Sat 11am–9pm, Sun noon–8pm.
Portland has a problem with mice; they seem to be popping up everywhere. Known for both its low-fat, low-salt cooking and its unusual contemporary art, Macheezmo Mouse is a fast-food restaurant for those who care about their health. The menu is primarily Mexican and lists the calorie count for each meal. Most dishes have also been approved by the American Heart Association. This is what fast food should be like. Other locations are 811 NW 23rd Ave. (tel. 274-0500), 3553 SE Hawthorne Blvd. (tel. 232-6588), 1200 NE Broadway (tel. 249-0002), and in Pioneer Place (tel. 248-0917).

MAYAS TACQUERIA, 1000 SW Morrison St. Tel. 226-1946.
  Cuisine: MEXICAN. **Reservations:** Not accepted.
$ **Prices:** $2.25–$7.95. AE, MC, V.
  Open: Mon–Sat 11am–10pm, Sun noon–8pm.
Nothing fancy here, just good home-cooked Mexican food—fast—and you can watch the cooks prepare your meal just as in any tacqueria in Mexico. The menu above the counter lists the different meals available, and on a separate list you'll find the choice of meats, which includes molé chicken, chile verde pork or chicken, chile Colorado beef or chicken, and carne asada. Watch for the Maya-style murals on the walls out front. **Santa Fe Taqueria** at 831 NW 23rd Ave. (tel. 220-0406) is run by the same folks and serves equally delicious food.

BREAKFAST/BRUNCH

ATWATER'S RESTAURANT AND LOUNGE, U.S. Bancorp Tower, 111 SW Fifth Ave. Tel. 275-3600.

Cuisine: NORTHWEST/CONTINENTAL. **Reservations:** Required.

$ Prices: $17–$21.50. AE, CB, DC, MC, V.

Open: Sun 10am–3pm.

You just can't beat the brunch views from this 30th-floor restaurant. See "Dining with a View," above, for a description of the restaurant.

BIJOU CAFE, 132 SW Third Ave. Tel. 222-3187.

Cuisine: INTERNATIONAL/NATURAL. **Reservations:** Not accepted.

$ Prices: $3.50–$6.60. No credit cards.

Open: Daily 7am–3pm.

Although open only for breakfast and lunch, the Bijou is still one of the most popular restaurants in Portland, and the lines can be long, especially on weekends. The folks here take both food and health seriously. They'll let you know that the eggs are from Chris's Egg Farm in Hubbard, Oregon, and they'll serve you a bowl of steamed brown rice for breakfast. However, the real hits here are the hash browns and the muffins. Don't leave without trying these two. At lunch, there are plenty of salads, which are made with organic produce whenever possible. Even the meats are natural. If you're concerned about how you eat, drop by the Bijou. Your body will be happy that you did.

BREAD & INK CAFE, 3610 SE Hawthorne Blvd. Tel. 239-4756.

Cuisine: NORTHWEST. **Reservations:** Required.

$ Prices: $12.50. MC, V.

Open: Sun 9am–2pm.

This casual café in southeastern Portland serves up an unbelievably filling four-course Yiddish brunch. (See "Southeast Portland," above, for a description of the restaurant.)

THE LONDON GRILL, The Benson Hotel, 309 SW Broadway. Tel. 228-2000.

Cuisine: CONTINENTAL. **Reservations:** Essential.

$ Prices: $19.50. AE, CB, DC, DISC, ER, JCB, MC, V.

Open: Sun 9:30am–2pm.

This is the ritziest and most lavish Sunday brunch in Portland. You'll feel as though you have been admitted to a private club when you cross the marble-floored hotel lobby and descend to the elegantly appointed vaults of the London Grill. (See "Hotel Dining," above, for a description of the restaurant.)

AFTERNOON TEA

THE HEATHMAN HOTEL, SW Broadway at Salmon St. Tel. 241-4100.

Cuisine: TEA. **Reservations:** Recommended.

$ Prices: $6.50–$16. AE, CB, DC, DISC, MC, V.

Open: Daily 2–4:30pm.

Once again I must send you back to The Heathman Hotel. (See "Downtown Hotels," in Chapter 14, for a description of the hotel.) In the hotel's lobby lounge, tea hostesses in lace aprons serve pâtés, finger sandwiches, scones, pastries, and of course excellent tea (blended especially for the hotel). The service is on Royal Doulton's "Twilight Rose" bone china at marble-topped tables. A pianist plays gentle melodies, and on chilly afternoons a fire crackles in the fireplace. An elegant affair, tea at the Heathman is a welcome respite from shopping or business meetings.

LATE NIGHT

GARBANZO's, NW 21st Ave. and NW Lovejoy St. Tel. 227-4196.
    Cuisine: MIDDLE EASTERN. **Reservations:** Not accepted.
$ Prices: Salads $2–$4.50; sandwiches $3.50–$4.50; dinners $5.75–$6.75. AE, DISC, MC, V.
    Open: Sun–Thurs 11:30am–1:30am, Fri–Sat 11:30am–3am.

Calling itself a felafel bar, this casual little place next door to the Cajun Café & Bistro has become very popular, especially late at night. The menu includes all the usual Middle Eastern offerings, most of which also happen to be American Heart Association approved. You can eat at one of the tiny café tables or get your order to go. They even serve beer and wine. Another Garbanzo's is at 3433 SE Hawthorne Blvd. (tel. 239-6087).

WHAT TO SEE & DO IN PORTLAND

Portland does not have very many museums, and those that it does have are rather small. This isn't to say that there isn't much for the visitor to see or do. Portlanders are active folks and they prefer snow skiing on Mount Hood to museum-going. They prefer gardening over old-homes tours, and consequently there are numerous world-class public gardens and parks within the city. You can easily see all of Portland's tourist attractions in one or two days. No visit to Portland would be complete, however, without venturing out into the Oregon countryside. This is the city's real attraction. Within an hour and a half you can be skiing on Mount Hood or swimming in the chilly waters of the Pacific Ocean. However, for those who prefer more urban and urbane activities, the museums and parks listed below should satisfy.

SUGGESTED ITINERARIES

IF YOU HAVE 1 DAY

Day 1 Start your day at Skidmore Fountain and walk around Old Town. If it's a Saturday or Sunday, you can visit Portland Saturday Market underneath Burnside Bridge. While in this area, you can also stroll through Chinatown and visit the American Advertising Museum. Walk south through downtown after lunch and visit the Oregon Historical Center and the Portland Art Museum. Finish your day at the Japanese and International Rose Test gardens in Washington Park.

IF YOU HAVE 2 DAYS

Day 1 Spend your first day as outlined above, except for visiting the Japanese and International Rose Test gardens.
Day 2 After visiting the Japanese and International Rose Test gardens in the morning, take the miniature train over to Metro Washington Park Zoo. In the afternoon, visit the World Forestry

Center across the street from the zoo, and finish the day at the Oregon Museum of Science and Industry, on the east bank of the Willamette River.

IF YOU HAVE 3 DAYS

Days 1–2 Follow the 2-day strategy as outlined above.
Day 3 On your third day, do the Mount Hood Loop, as described on p. 246.

IF YOU HAVE 5 DAYS OR MORE

Days 1–3 Follow the 3-day strategy as outlined above.
Day 4 In the morning, visit Pittock Mansion and perhaps stroll through Hoyt Arboretum or Forest Park. In the afternoon, visit Fort Vancouver across the Columbia River in Washington State.
Day 5 Drive to the coast or tour through the wine country.

1. THE TOP ATTRACTIONS

AMERICAN ADVERTISING MUSEUM, 9 NW Second Ave. Tel. 226-0000.

✪ I long ago gave up watching television and listening to commercial radio because I have no tolerance for advertising. That this is my favorite Portland museum should tell you something about the exhibits. Not only will you learn about the history of advertising in America, but you'll be able to see old favorite TV commercials. One exhibit shows the changes in advertising over several centuries, while another displays the all-time best advertising campaigns. Test your familiarity with different logos. There's even a complete series of Burma Shave roadside signs.

Admission: $3 adults, $1.50 senior citizens and ages 6–12, under age 6 free.

Open: Wed–Fri 11am–5pm, Sat–Sun noon–5pm. **MAX:** Skidmore Fountain Station.

PORTLAND ART MUSEUM, 1219 SW Park Ave. Tel. 226-2811.

Although this small museum has a respectable collection of European and American art, it is the Northwest Coast Native American exhibit that requires a special visit. Particularly fascinating are the transformation masks. Worn during ritual dances, the masks are transformed from one face into a completely different visage by pulling several strings. A totem pole and many other wood carvings show the amazing creative imagination of Northwest Indians. There are also exhibits of Pre-Columbian art, Asian antiquities, African art from Cameroon, and a large hall for temporary exhibits. If you happen to be in town on the first Thursday of any month, you can save the admission by coming between 4 and 9pm; this free admission

FROMMER'S FAVORITE PORTLAND EXPERIENCES

Shopping and Eating at Portland Saturday Market This large arts-and-crafts market is an outdoor showcase of the best of the Northwest's creative artisans. There are food stalls selling delicious and unusual meals.

Quaffing a Microbrew at Mission Theater Portland is the microbrewery capital of America, and at this combination movie theater and brew pub you can taste the city's best beers while watching recently released movies.

Strolling the Grounds of the Japanese Gardens These are the best Japanese gardens in the United States, perhaps the best anywhere outside of Japan. They look particularly stunning in June, when the irises are in bloom, but any time of year they are beautiful and tranquil. There's no better place in the city to relax.

First Thursday Art Walk On the first Thursday of every month, Portlanders get dressed up and go gallery hopping. There are openings that often include live music, hors d'oeuvres, and wine, as well as plenty of new artworks. The galleries stay open until 9pm, and there are even special shuttle buses to carry people from one gallery district to the next.

Peanut Butter & Jam Sessions At noon on summer Tuesdays and Thursdays, Pioneer Courthouse Square is packed with people who come to hear local musicians jam. The free concerts last an hour, and over the summer virtually every type of music has its day. An added bonus of the noon hour is the daily weather forecast by the *Weather Machine* sculpture.

Hiking and Skiing on Mount Hood Less than an hour from Portland, Mount Hood offers year-round skiing and hiking. Timberline Lodge, high on the extinct volcano's slopes, was built by the Works Project Administration during the Great Depression and is a showcase of craftsmanship.

is part of the First Thursday program of art-gallery openings throughout Portland. On Wednesday nights (except in summer), the Museum After Hours program presents live music.

Admission: $4.50 adults, $2.50 ages 12–18, $1.50 ages 6–12; under age 6 free, senior citizens free every Thurs. Free 4–9pm on first Thurs of each month.

Open: Tues–Sat 11am–5pm, Sun 1–5pm; first Thurs of each month 11am–9pm. **Bus:** 57.

OREGON HISTORICAL CENTER, 1230 SW Park Ave. Tel. 222-1741.

Oregon Territory was a land of promise and plenty. Thousands

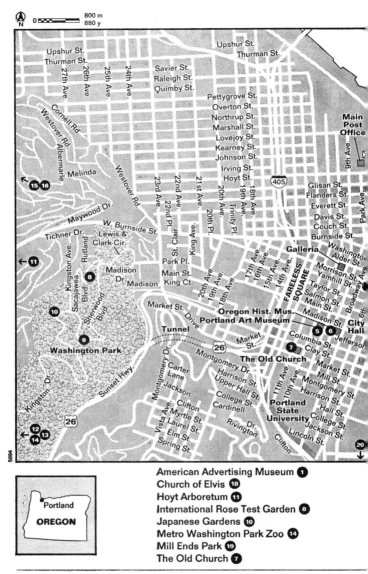

Scale: 0 — 800 m / 880 y

Main Post Office

(405)

(26)

Galleria
FARELESS SQUARE
Oregon Hist. Mus.
Portland Art Museum
City Hall
The Old Church
Portland State University

Tunnel

Washington Park

American Advertising Museum ❶
Church of Elvis ⓲
Hoyt Arboretum ⓫
International Rose Test Garden ❽
Japanese Gardens ⓾
Metro Washington Park Zoo ⓮
Mill Ends Park ⓳
The Old Church ❼

Portland
OREGON

of hardy individuals set out along the Oregon Trail, crossing a vast and rugged country to reach the fertile valleys of Oregon's rivers. Others came by ship around the Horn. Today the state of Oregon is still luring immigrants with its bountiful natural resources, and those who wish to learn about the people who discovered Oregon before them should visit this well-designed museum. Oregon history from before the arrival of the first white men to well into this century is chronicled in an educational and fascinating exhibit. The displays incorporate parts of old buildings; objects

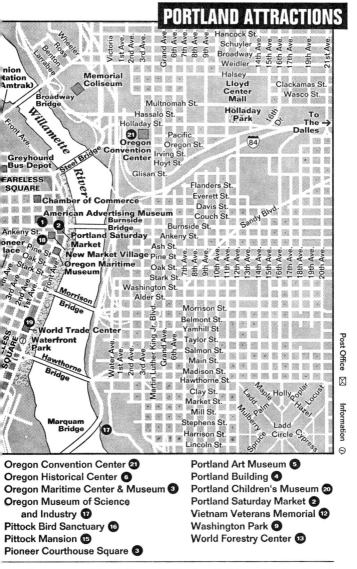

PORTLAND ATTRACTIONS

Oregon Convention Center ㉑	Portland Art Museum ❺
Oregon Historical Center ❻	Portland Building ❹
Oregon Maritime Center & Museum ❸	Portland Children's Museum ⓴
Oregon Museum of Science	Portland Saturday Market ❷
and Industry ⑰	Vietnam Veterans Memorial ⑫
Pittock Bird Sanctuary ⑯	Washington Park ❾
Pittock Mansion ⑮	World Forestry Center ⑬
Pioneer Courthouse Square ❸	

---

such as snow skis, dolls, and bicycles; fashions; Native American artifacts; nautical and surveying instruments; even a covered wagon. Museum docents, with roots stretching back to the days of the Oregon Trail, are often on hand to answer questions. There is also a research library that includes many journals from early pioneers.

Admission: \$3 adults and senior citizens, \$1 students and children ages 5–18, free to members and children under age 5.

Open: Mon–Sat 10am–5pm, Sun noon–5pm. **Bus:** 57.

DID YOU KNOW . . . ?

- Mill Ends Park is the world's smallest dedicated park, measuring 24 inches in diameter.
- Portland is the only city in America with an extinct volcano within its city limits—Mount Tabor.
- Portland has been called the politest U.S. city.
- There are more restaurants per capita in Portland than in any other West Coast city.
- Matt Groenig, creator of the hit TV series "The Simpsons," got his start in Portland. Giant wall murals of the Simpsons can be seen on buildings around town.
- Jean Auel, author of *The Clan of the Cave Bear* and subsequent sequels, is from Portland and studied winter survival techniques on Mount Hood.

OREGON MUSEUM OF SCIENCE AND INDUSTRY (OMSI), 1945 SW Water Ave. Tel. 797-4000 or toll free 800/955-6674.

Formerly located in Washington Park, OMSI moved to a large and impressive new building on the east bank of the Willamette River in late 1992. Six huge halls have given the museum lots of space to play with, and kids and adults are finding the new exhibits both fun and fascinating. Two of the most exciting exhibits allow visitors to touch a tornado or ride an earthquake. This is a hands-on museum and everyone is urged to get involved with displays. There's plenty of pure entertainment as well with Oregon's first OMNIMAX theater and the Murdock Sky Theater, which features laser light shows and astronomy presentations.

Admission: Museum, $6.50 adults, $5.50 senior citizens, $4 children ages 3–17; OMNIMAX, $6.50 adults, $5.50 senior citizens, $4 children ages 3–17; Sky Theater, $4 adults, $3.50 senior citizens, $3 children ages 3–17; Light Show—Evening, $6 adults, senior citizens, and children. Combination tickets also available at considerable discount.

Open: Sat–Wed 9:30am–5:30pm, Thurs–Fri 9:30am–9pm. **Closed:** Dec 25. **Bus:** 6.

PITTOCK MANSION, 3229 NW Pittock Dr. Tel. 823-3624.

At nearly the highest point in the West Hills, 1,000 feet above sea level, stands the most impressive mansion in Portland. Once slated to be torn down to make way for new housing, this grand château built by the founder of Portland's *Oregonian* newspaper has been fully restored and is open to the public. Built in 1914 in a French Renaissance style, the mansion featured many innovations, including a built-in vacuum system and amazing multiple showerheads in the baths. Today it is furnished with 18th- and 19th-century antiques, much as it might have been at the time the Pittocks occupied the building. Lunch and afternoon tea are available in the Gate Lodge, the former caretaker's cottage.

Admission: $3.50 adults, $3 senior citizens, $1.50 ages 6–18.

Open: Daily noon–4pm. **Closed:** Three days in November, most major holidays, and the first three weeks in January. **Bus:** 20 to Burnside and Barnes. Half-mile walk.

PORTLAND SATURDAY MARKET, underneath Burnside Bridge between SW First Ave. and SW Ankeny St. Tel. 222-6072.

★ Portland Saturday Market (held on both Saturday and Sunday) is arguably the city's single most important and best-loved event. For years the Northwest has attracted artists and craftspeople, and every Saturday and Sunday nearly 300 of them can be found selling their exquisite creations here. In addition to the dozens of craftspeople's stalls, you'll find flowers, fresh produce, ethnic and unusual foods, and lots of free entertainment. This is the single best place in Portland to shop for one-of-a-kind gifts. The atmosphere is always cheerful and the crowds colorful. At the heart of the Skidmore District, Portland Saturday Market makes an excellent starting or finishing point for a walk around Portland's most historic neighborhood. Don't miss this unique market. On Sunday, on-street parking is free.

Admission: Free.
Open: Mar–Christmas, Sat 10am–5pm and Sun 11am–4:30pm.
MAX: Skidmore Fountain Station.

WORLD FORESTRY CENTER, 4033 SW Canyon Rd. Tel. 228-1367.
Although with each passing year Oregon depends less and less on the timber industry, the World Forestry Center is still busy educating visitors about the importance of our forest resources. Step inside the huge wooden main hall and you come face to bark with a very large and very lifelike tree. Press a button at its base and it will tell you the story of how trees live and grow. In other rooms you can see exhibits on early forest homesteads, forests of the world, and a collection of woods from every type of tree grown in America. In summer, a vintage carousel is on the grounds.

Admission: $3 adults, $2 senior citizens and ages 2–18, under age 2 free.
Open: Daily 9am–5pm (10am–5pm in winter). **Closed:** Christmas Day. **Bus:** 63.

2. MORE ATTRACTIONS

LANDMARK

THE OLD CHURCH, 1422 SW 11th Ave. Tel. 222-2031.
Built in 1883, this wooden Carpenter Gothic church is a Portland landmark. It incorporates a grand traditional design, but is constructed with spare ornamentation. An active church until 1967, the deteriorating building was to be torn down; however, preservationists stepped in to save it. Today it's a community facility, and every Wednesday there's a free lunchtime classical music concert.

Admission: Free.
Open: Mon–Fri 11am–3pm. **Bus:** 57, 59, 88, or 89.

MUSEUM

OREGON MARITIME CENTER & MUSEUM, 113 SW Front Ave. Tel. 224-7724.
Inside the museum, you'll find models of ships that once plied the Columbia and Willamette. Also on display are early navigation instruments, artifacts from the battleship *Oregon*, old ship hardware,

and other maritime memorabilia. The stern-wheeler *Portland,* moored across Waterfront Park from the museum, is also open to the public. Inside this old vessel, you'll see operating steam-driven machinery and more displays on maritime history.

Admission: $3 adults, $2 senior citizens and students, free for children under age 8.

Open: Summer, Wed–Sun 11am–4pm; winter, Fri–Sun 11am–4pm. **MAX:** To Portland Saturday Market.

OUTDOOR ART/PLAZAS/ARCHITECTURAL HIGHLIGHTS

CHURCH OF ELVIS, 219 Ankeny St.

Two blocks from Portland Saturday Market on narrow little Ankeny Street is Portland's most bizarre attraction: the first 24-hour video psychic and church of Elvis. A window full of kitschy contraptions bearing the visage of the King never fails to stop people in their tracks as they stroll past. What is it? Well, for a quarter, you can find out. Care to have Elvis hear your confession? No problem. The King will absolve you of sin, unless, of course, you have committed the unforgivable sin of believing that Elvis is dead. Great fun if you are a fan of Elvis, tabloids, or the unusual.

Admission: 25¢.

Open: 24 hours. **MAX:** Skidmore Fountain Station.

OREGON CONVENTION CENTER, 777 NE Martin Luther King Jr. Blvd. Tel. 235-7575.

As you approach downtown Portland from the direction of the airport, it is impossible to miss this unusual architectural bauble on the city skyline. Christened "Twin Peaks" even before it opened in the summer of 1990, the center is worth a visit even if you don't happen to be in town for a convention. Its "twin peaks" are two tapering glass towers that channel light into the center of this huge complex. Outside the main entrance are two Asian temple bells. Inside are paintings on a scale to match the building, a dragon boat hanging from the ceiling, and a brass pendulum swinging slowly through the hours. Small plaques on the outside wall of the main lobby spotlight telling quotes about life in Oregon.

Admission: Free for self-guided tours.

Open: Daily. **MAX:** To Convention Center.

PIONEER COURTHOUSE SQUARE, bounded by Broadway, Sixth Ave., Yamhill St., and Morrison St.

Today it is the heart of downtown Portland and acts as an outdoor stage for everything from flower displays to concerts to protest rallies, but not too many years ago this beautiful brick-paved square was nothing but a parking lot. The parking lot itself had been created by the controversial razing in 1951 of the Portland Hotel, an architectural gem of a Queen Anne–style château. Today the square, with its tumbling waterfall fountain and free-standing columns, is Portland's favorite gathering spot, especially at noon, when the *Weather Machine,* a mechanical sculpture, forecasts the upcoming 24 hours. Amid a fanfare of music and flashing lights, the *Weather Machine* sends up clouds of mist and then raises either a sun (clear weather), a dragon (stormy weather), or a blue heron (clouds and drizzle). Keep your eyes on the square's brick pavement.

Every brick contains a name (or names) or statement, and some are rather curious.

MAX: To Pioneer Courthouse Square stop. **Bus:** Any downtown bus that goes to the Transit Mall.

PORTLANDIA and THE PORTLAND BUILDING, 1120 SW Fifth Ave.

Portlandia is the symbol of the city, and this hammered bronze statue of her is the second-largest such statue in the country. The largest, of course, is New York City's Statue of Liberty. The massive kneeling figure holds a trident in one hand and with the other reaches toward the street. Strangely enough, this classically designed figure reminiscent of a Greek goddess perches above the entrance to Portland's most controversial building: The Portland Building, considered the first postmodern structure in the country. Today anyone familiar with the bizarre constructions of Los Angeles architect Frank Gearhy would find it difficult to understand how such an innocuous and attractive building could have ever raised such a fuss, but it did.

PARKS & GARDENS

FOREST PARK, bounded by W. Burnside St., Newberry Rd., St. Helens Rd., and Skyline Rd. Tel. 823-4492.

With 4,800 acres of wilderness, this is the largest forested city park in the United States. There are 50 miles of trails and old fire roads for hiking and jogging. More than 100 species of birds call these forests home, making this park a birdwatcher's paradise.

Admission: Free.

Open: Daily dawn to dusk. **Bus:** 15, 17, 20, or 63.

INTERNATIONAL ROSE TEST GARDEN, 400 SW Kingston Ave., Washington Park. Tel. 823-3636.

Covering 4½ acres of hillside in the West Hills above downtown Portland, these are the largest and oldest rose test gardens in the United States. They were established in 1917 by the American Rose Society, itself founded in Portland. Though you will likely see some familiar roses in the Gold Medal Garden, most of the 400 varieties on display here are new hybrids being tested before marketing. Among the roses in bloom from late spring to early winter, you'll find a separate garden of miniature roses. There is also a Shakespearean Garden that includes flowers mentioned in the works of William Shakespeare. After seeing these acres of roses, you will certainly understand why Portland is known as the City of Roses and why the Rose Festival in June is the city's biggest annual celebration.

Admission: Free.

Open: Daily, dawn to dusk. **Bus:** 63.

JAPANESE GARDEN SOCIETY OF OREGON, off Kingston Ave. in Washington Park. Tel. 223-4070.

I have always loved Japanese gardens and have visited them all over the world. Outside of those in Japan, this is still my favorite. What makes it so special is not only the design, plantings, and tranquillity, but the view. From the Japanese-style wooden house in the center of the garden, you have a view over Portland to Mount Hood on a clear day. This perfectly shaped volcanic peak is so reminiscent of Mount Fuji that it seems almost as if it were placed there just for the sake of this garden.

Admission: $4.50 adults, $2.50 students and senior citizens, under age 6 free. **Bus:** 63.

Open: Apr 1–May 31 and Sept 1–Sept 30, daily 10am–6pm; June 1–Aug 31, daily 9am–8pm; Oct 1–Mar 31, daily 10am–4pm. **Closed:** Thanksgiving, Christmas, and New Year's Day. **Bus:** 63.

MILL ENDS PARK, SW Taylor St. and SW Front Ave.

Pay attention as you cross the median strip on Front Avenue or you might walk right past this famous Portland park. The smallest public park in the world, it contains a whopping 452.16 square inches of land. It was the whimsical creation of Dick Fagen, a local journalist who used to gaze down from his office at a hole left after a telephone pole was removed from the middle of Front Avenue. He dubbed the park Mill Ends (the name of his column) and peopled it with leprechauns. On St. Patrick's Day of 1976, it was officially designated a Portland city park. Despite the diminutive size of the park, it has been the site of several weddings.

ZOO

METRO WASHINGTON PARK ZOO, 4001 SW Caynon Rd., Washington Park. Tel. 226-1561.

This zoo has been successfully breeding elephant for many years and has the largest breeding herd of elephant in captivity. The Africa exhibit, which displays zebras, rhinos, giraffes, and a few other animals, is the most lifelike habitat I have ever seen in a zoo—and it's giving the elephants a lot of competition. In 1991 the zoo added a new rain-forest exhibit to this already impressive African section. Equally impressive is the Alaskan-tundra exhibit, with grizzly bears, wolves, and musk oxen. Throughout the Cascade Exhibit, the trees and shrubbery are labeled. There's an outdoor pond with birds, and you'll see otters and beavers. This is also where you'll find the trout on view.

For the younger set, there's a children's petting zoo filled with farm animals and a center where many of the zoo's new babies are kept. Be sure to check in the flyer you get at the front gate to find out what special programs are being held on the day of your visit.

The Washington Park and Zoo Railway travels between the zoo and the International Rose Test and Japanese gardens. Tickets for the miniature railway are $2.50 for adults, $1.75 for senior citizens and children 3 to 11. In the summer, there are jazz concerts on Wednesday nights and bluegrass on Thursday nights from 6:30 to 8:30pm. Concerts are free with zoo admission.

Admission: $5 adults, $3.50 senior citizens, $3 ages 3–11, under age 2 free; free second Tues of each month from 3pm to closing.

Open: May–Oct, daily 9:30am–6pm; Oct–May, daily 9:30am–4pm. **Bus:** 63.

3. COOL FOR KIDS

The **Oregon Museum of Science and Industry** is primarily for kids, with lots of hands-on exhibits, classes, an astronaut-training program, and laser shows in its planetarium. At the **World Forestry Center,** there is a carousel operating during the summer months.

The **Metro Washington Park Zoo** is one of the best in the country, and is particularly well known for its elephant-breeding program. From inside the zoo, it's possible to take a small train through Washington Park to the International Rose Test Garden. In addition to these attractions, described earlier in this chapter, there are two other attractions in Portland of particular interest to kids:

PORTLAND CHILDREN'S MUSEUM, 3037 SW Second Ave. Tel. 823-2227.

Although this museum is small, it's loads of fun. Visitors can shop in a kid-size grocery store or play waiter or diner in a restaurant. Clayshop is frequently open for families who want to build with clay. In H2 Oh! kids can blow giant bubbles and pump water.

On the second floor a miniature version of Portland's own MAX light-rail system goes round and round in circles, making more noise than the real thing. Listening to seashells, sculpting clay, blowing bubbles—there's plenty to entertain kids at this big little museum.

Admission: $3.50 adults, $3 children, under 1 year free.

Open: Daily 9am–5pm. **Closed:** National holidays. **Bus:** 1, 12, 40, 41, 43, 45, or 55.

OAKS PARK, east end of the Sellwood Bridge. Tel. 233-5777.

What would summer be without the screams of happy thrillseekers risking their lives on a roller coaster? Pretty boring, right? Just ask the kids. They'll tell you that the real Portland excitement is at Oaks Park. Covering more than 44 acres, this amusement park first opened in 1905 to coincide with the Lewis and Clark Exposition. Beneath the shady oaks for which the park is named, you'll find waterfront picnic sites, miniature golf, music, and plenty of thrilling rides. The largest roller-skating rink in the Northwest is also here.

Admission: Free (all activities are on individual tickets).

Open: Mar–June 18, Sat–Sun 12–5pm; June 18–Labor Day, Tues–Thurs noon–9pm, Fri–Sat noon–10pm, Sun noon–7pm.

4. SPECIAL-INTEREST SIGHTSEEING

FOR THE TROLLEY BUFF

WILLAMETTE SHORE TROLLEY, 2511 SW Moody Ave., Portland, and intersection of State St. and A St., Lake Oswego. Tel. 222-2226.

If you like to reminisce about the good old days of well-planned public transportation systems or long to ride an old-fashioned trolley but can't make it to San Francisco, book a trip on the historic Willamette Shore Trolley. Two fully restored trolleys dating from the early part of this century operate on a 7-mile line connecting Portland with the prestigious southern suburb of Lake Oswego. The trip takes 45 minutes each way, and along the route you can enjoy the scenery and admire the craftsmanship that went into the old trolleys. Reservations required.

Fare: $7.75 adults, $5.75 seniors and children.

Open: Mar–May, mid-Sept–Dec Fri–Sun; June–mid-Sept Tues–Sun.

5. ORGANIZED TOURS

BUS TOURS

Gray Line (tel. 285-9845) offers quite a few half-day and full-day tours. One tour visits the International Rose Test Garden and the World Forestry Center, another stops at the Japanese Gardens and the grounds of Pittock Mansion. Either tour is priced at $16 for adults and $8 for children. You can combine the two trips for $28 for adults and $14 for children. However, the trip I most highly recommend is the full-day Mount Hood loop ($32 for adults, $16 for children). By taking this tour rather than driving it yourself, you can enjoy the scenery instead of keeping your eyes on the road. There's also a Columbia Gorge excursion that includes a ride on a stern-wheeler, and another tour that goes to the northern Oregon coast— either of these is priced at $40 for adults and $20 for children.

RIVER CRUISES

For those wishing to get out on the mighty Columbia River or the less thrilling but equally important Willamette River, there are quite a few possibilities. A century ago it was paddle wheelers similar to those used on the Mississippi River that helped open up the Oregon Territory to settlers. Today paddle wheelers are once again cruising the rivers.

The stern-wheeler **Columbia Gorge** (tel. 223-3928) cruises the Columbia River between mid-June and early October and the Willamette River between October and mid-June. The trip up the Columbia, with its towering cliffs, is a spectacular and memorable excursion. This trip includes stops at the Cascade Locks and Bonneville Dam. There are lunch, brunch, dinner, and dance cruises (call for information and reservations). The basic 2-hour day trips are priced at $11.95 for adults and $5.95 for children. Ticket prices range all the way up to $75.95 for the annual 5-hour cruise back down the Columbia to Portland at the end of the summer season.

Rose City Riverboat Cruises and Charters (tel. 234-6665), offers cruises on a modern catamaran power yacht. It cruises the Willamette River on a regular basis from mid-April through October. There are dinner, moonlight, Sunday brunch, Portland Harbor, and Willamette River tours, with ticket prices ranging from $9 to $30.95 for adults.

CARRIAGE TOURS

Another way to see Portland is by horse-drawn carriage. These tours are operated by the **John Palmer House,** a bed-and-breakfast (tel. 284-5893), and are best combined with a stay at this magnificently restored Victorian painted lady. An hour's tour is $60. These prices are per carriage, which will hold four adults. June through August, carriage rides are given daily from 6 to 10pm. In April, May, September, and October, they are given on Friday and Saturday from 6 to 10pm and on Sunday from noon to 6pm.

OTHER TOURS

If you'd like to learn more about downtown Portland and the city's history, try the **Portland on Foot** tour, 1611 SE Nehalem St. #5, Portland, OR 97202 (tel. 235-4742). This tour costs only $2.50.

Outdoor activities are one of the best reasons to visit Portland and the reason so many Portlanders choose to live in this rainy neck of the woods. If you'd like to explore this part of the Northwest's great outdoors, you can do so with several tour companies offering interesting trips. **Downhill Bike Tours,** 3890 NW 169th Ave., Portland, OR 97006 (tel. 629-2023), offers a 20-mile mountain-bike excursion for $49. This trip is almost completely downhill and takes you through the scenic Columbia River Gorge. **The Wild Side,** P.O. Box 973, Hood River, OR 97031 (tel. 503/354-3112), also offers mountain-biking trips, as well as fishing, hiking, and cross-country skiing trips. Rates range from $45 to $100. **EcoTours of Oregon,** 1906 SW Iowa St., Portland, OR 97201 (tel. 245-1428), offers hikes through an ancient forest, as well as trips to the Oregon coast and through the wine country. Rates range from $45 to $60.

6. SPORTS & RECREATION

SPECTATOR SPORTS

AUTO RACING   **Portland International Raceway,** 1940 N. Victory Blvd. (tel. 285-6635), operated by the Portland Bureau of Parks and Recreation, is home to road races, drag races, motocross and other motorcycle races, go-kart races, and even vintage-car races. February to October are the busiest months here. Admission is $5.50 to $67.50.

BASEBALL   The **Portland Beavers Baseball Club** plays class AAA minor-league ball at Civic Stadium, SW 20th Avenue and Morrison Street (tel. 2-BEAVER). The box office is open Monday through Saturday from 10am to 5pm. Admission is $5 to $7 for adults, $2.50 for ages 14 and under.

BASKETBALL   The **Portland Trail Blazers,** one of the hottest NBA teams in recent years, pound the boards at Memorial Coliseum, 1401 N. Wheeler St. (tel. 231-8000), between fall and spring. Call for current schedule and ticket information. Tickets are $10 to $46.50.

IMPRESSIONS

While the people of Portland are not mercurial or exciteable—and by Californians or people "east of the mountains" are even accused of being lymphatic, if not somnolent—they are much given . . . to recreation and public amusements.
—HARVEY SCOTT, EDITOR OF THE *OREGONIAN*, 1890

GREYHOUND RACING The race season at the **Multnomah Greyhound Track,** NE 223rd Avenue, Wood Village (tel. 667-7700), runs from April to September. Post time is 7:30pm Wednesday through Saturday, with Saturday and Sunday matinees at 1pm. In July and August, there are also Tuesday night races. You must be 18 to bet on the greyhounds, and if you've never bet on dog races before, they'll gladly give you a quick course. To reach the track, take I-84 east to the 181st Street exit south and then turn left on Glisan Street. It's also easy to reach the park by public transit. Take the MAX light-rail system to the Gresham City Hall or Central Station and transfer to bus no. 82, which goes directly to the racetrack. Admission is $1 to $3.50.

HORSE RACING **The New Portland Meadows,** 1001 N. Schmeer Rd. (tel. 285-9144), is the place to go if you want a little horse-racing action. The race season runs from October to April, with post time at 7pm on Friday and 12:30pm on Saturday and Sunday. By car, take I-5 north to the Delta Park exit. Admission is $2 to $3.

ICE HOCKEY The **Portland Winter Hawks,** a minor-league hockey team, carve up the ice at Memorial Coliseum, 1401 N. Wheeler St. (tel. 238-6366), from October to March. Call for schedule and ticket information. Admission is $8.50–$12.

MARATHON The **Portland Marathon** is held in September. For further information, call 226-1111.

PARTICIPATORY ACTIVITIES

BEACHES The nearest ocean beach to Portland is **Cannon Beach,** about 90 miles to the west. See Section 2 of Chapter 20 for more information.

There are a couple freshwater beaches on the Columbia River within 45 minutes of Portland. **Rooster Rock State Park,** just off I-84 east of Portland, includes several miles of sandy beach as does **Sauvie Island,** off Oregon Hwy. 30 northwest of Portland. You'll need to obtain a parking permit for Sauvie Island; it's available at the convenience store located just after you cross the bridge onto the island. Both beaches include sections that are clothing optional.

BICYCLING You'll notice many bicyclists on Portland streets. If you want to get rolling with everyone else, head over to **Agape Cycle & Sports,** 2314 SE Division St. (tel. 230-0317), where you can rent road or mountain bikes for $15 to $25 per day. They're open Monday to Saturday from 10am to 6pm. Once you have your bike, you can head for **Waterfront Park,** where there's a 2-mile bike path. The **Terwilliger Path** starts at the south end of Portland State University and travels for 10 miles up into the hills to Tryon Creek State Park. The views from the top are breathtaking. Stop by a bookstore to pick up a copy of the "From Here to There by Bike" map.

FISHING The Portland area is salmon, steelhead, sturgeon, and trout country. You can find out about licenses and seasons from the **Oregon Department of Fish and Wildlife,** P.O. Box 59, Portland, OR 97207 (tel. 503/229-5403). If you prefer to have a guide take you where the big ones are always biting, contact **Oregon Guides & Packers Association,** P.O. Box 10841, Eugene, OR

97440 (tel. 503/683-9552), for a copy of their annual directory. A day of fishing will cost you around $100.

GOLF If you're a golfer, don't forget to bring your clubs along on a trip to Portland. There are plenty of public courses around the area, and greens fees are only $12 for 18 holes on a weekday and $14 on weekends and holidays. Public golf courses operated by the Portland Bureau of Parks and Recreation include **Eastmoreland Golf Course,** 2425 SE Bybee Blvd. (tel. 775-2900); **Heron Lakes Golf Course,** 3500 N. Victory Blvd. (tel. 289-1818); **Rose City Golf Course,** 2200 NE 71st Ave. (tel. 253-4744); and **Double Eagle Golf Center Progress Downs Golf Course,** 8200 SW Scholls Ferry Rd., Beaverton (tel. 646-5166).

HIKING Hiking opportunities in the Portland area are almost unlimited. In fact, if you head over to Mount Hood National Forest, you can get on the **Pacific Crest Trail** and hike all the way to Mexico. Of course, there are also plenty of other shorter hikes in this region. For details, contact the **U.S. Forest Service,** 70220 E. Hwy. 26, Zig Zag, OR 97049 (tel. 503/666-3191).

If you are interested in a more strenuous mountain experience, Mount Hood offers plenty of mountain- and rock-climbing opportunities. **Timberline Mountain Guides,** Timberline Ski Area, Timberline Lodge, OR 97028 (tel. 503/272-3717), leads summit climbs from May to August, with ski descents during these same months. They also offer climbing courses between May and September. If you're an experienced mountain climber, you can rent equipment here also. You can also buy or rent camping and climbing equipment from **REI Co-op,** 1798 Jantzen Beach Center (tel. 283-1300) or at 7410 SW Bridgeport Rd., Tualatin (tel. 624-8600). This huge outdoor recreation-supply store also sells books on hiking in the area.

For shorter hikes, you need not leave the city. Bordered by West Burnside Street on the south, Newberry Road on the north, St. Helens Road on the east, and Skyline Road on the west, **Forest Park** is the largest forested city park in the country. You'll find more than 50 miles of trails through this urban wilderness.

If you have been keeping up with the controversy over saving the remaining old-growth forests of the Northwest, you might want to go see an ancient forest for yourself. Though there isn't much publicly accessible ancient forest right in Portland, you can find plenty within an hour-and-a-half's drive. Along the coast, Ecola State Park, Oswald West State Park, Cape Meares State Park, and Cape Lookout State Park all have trails through stands of old-growth trees. If you are heading to Mount Hood, you can detour to Oxbow Park in Sandy to see a small grove of old-growth trees.

SAILBOARDING Serious enthusiasts already know about the sailboarding mecca at the town of **Hood River** on the Columbia River. The winds come howling down the gorge with enough force to send sailboards airborne.

SKIING Skiing is probably Portland's favorite sports activity after jogging. This is because the city has several ski resorts within about an hour's drive. One of them even boasts skiing all summer. To help you get to the slopes, there is the **Mount Hood Express** (tel. 250-4379 in Portland or 622-5554 in the Mount Hood area). This van service from the Portland area to the ski resorts of Mount Hood costs from $54 for one person and $6 for each additional passenger—that's up to $84 for six people—from the airport to Timberline Lodge. They have airport pick ups that can whisk you directly from the baggage area to the slopes in less than an hour.

Timberline Ski Area (tel. 231-7979 in Portland or 272-3311 outside Portland; 222-2211 for snow report), high on the slopes of Mount Hood, offers skiing all the way through to Labor Day. Six chair lifts carry skiers for miles of tree-lined runs. After dark, three lifts continue running for those diehards who just can't get enough of the slopes. In addition to the excellent skiing here, there is the stunning **Timberline Lodge,** which was built during the depression by the WPA. (See Section 1 of Chapter 20 for details.) The ski area is open November to September, daily from 9am to 10pm in winter and from 7am to 1:30pm in summer. Lift rates in winter, for day and night, are $24 for adults, $15 for children (lift tickets for shorter hours are cheaper); in summer, $22 for all ages.

Mount Hood Meadows (tel. 337-2222 in Portland; 227-7669 for snow report) is the largest ski resort on Mount Hood, with more than 2,000 skiable acres. There are nine chair lifts that can carry 14,400 skiers per hour. With 2,777 vertical feet and a wide variety of terrains, Mount Hood Meadows is ideal for everyone from beginner to expert. In the day lodge, you can sit and watch the action on the slopes through a 120-foot-long wall of glass. When you're ready to hit the slopes yourself, there are rentals and plenty of instructors to help you improve your form. The resort even offers direct bus service to and from Portland (tel. 287-5438). Lift tickets are $29 for adults and $17 for children 11 and under (tickets for night skiing and shorter hours are less expensive). The ski area is open from mid-November to mid-May: Monday and Tuesday from 9am to 4:30pm, Wednesday through Saturday from 9am to 10pm, and on Sunday from 9am to 7pm.

Mt. Hood SkiBowl (tel. 272-3206; 222-2695 for snow report) is the closest ski area to Portland and offers 65 runs to challenge skiers of all levels of ability. There are four double-chair lifts and five surface tows. With 1,500 vertical feet, SkiBowl has more expert slopes than any other ski area on the mountain. This also happens to be the largest lighted ski area in the United States. In summer there's an Alpine Slide for exhilarating runs down warm grassy slopes. Mt. Hood SkiBowl is open from Thanksgiving to April: on Monday through Thursday from 9am to 10pm, on Friday from 9am to 11pm, and on Saturday and Sunday from 8:30am to 11pm. Lift rates are $20 for adults for day skiing, $12 at night; children aged 11 and under are charged $14 for day skiing, $10 at night.

TENNIS The Portland Bureau of Parks and Recreation operates more than 120 tennis courts, both indoor and out, all over the city. Outdoor courts are generally free and available on a first-come, first-served basis. My personal favorites are those in Washington Park just behind the International Rose Test Garden. Some of these courts can be reserved by contacting the **Portland Tennis Center,** 324 NE 12th Ave. (tel. 823-3189). Rates are $2 per hour. If the weather isn't cooperating, head for the Portland Tennis Center itself. They have indoor courts and charge $4 to $5.25 per person per hour for singles matches and $2.50 to $3.50 per person per hour for doubles. The hours here are 6:30am to 11:15pm.

WHITE-WATER RAFTING The Cascade Range produces some

of the best white-water rafting in the country and Deschutes River, White Salmon River, and Clackamas River offer plenty of opportunities to shoot the rapids from early spring to early fall. **River Drifters,** 13570 NW Lakeview Dr., Portland, OR 97229 (tel. 645-6264 or toll free 800/972-0430), leads trips on both of these rivers for $60 (with lunch included). **Carrol White-Water Rafting,** P.O. Box 130, Maupin, OR 97037 (tel. 503/395-2404), and **Ewings' Whitewater,** P.O. Box 427, Maupin, OR 97037 (tel. 503/395-2697), offer similar trips on the Deschutes and other rivers. A 4-hour trip costs $60. Longer trips are also possible.

CHAPTER 17

STROLLING AROUND PORTLAND

• WALKING
TOUR—OLD TOWN

Portland's compactness makes it an ideal city to explore on foot. In fact, the local government is doing all it can to convince Portland's citizens to leave their cars behind when they come downtown. There's no better way to gain a feel for Portland than to stroll through the Skidmore Historic District and down along Tom McCall Waterfront Park. If it happens to be a weekend, you'll also be able to visit the intriguing Portland Saturday Market. No matter where you walk in Portland, you're never far from a public work of art. Keep your eyes peeled. *Note:* For additional information on several stops, see Chapter 16.

WALKING TOUR — OLD TOWN

Start: Skidmore Fountain.
Finish: Skidmore Fountain.
Time: Allow approximately 1½ hours, not including museum and shopping stops.
Best Times: Saturday and Sunday, when the Portland Saturday Market is open (except January and February).
Worst Times: After dark, when this neighborhood is not as safe as in daylight.

Although Portland was founded in 1843, most of the buildings in Old Town date only from the 1880s. A fire in 1872 razed much of the town, which afterward was rebuilt with new vigor. Ornate pilasters, pediments, and cornices grace these brick buildings, one of the largest collections of such structures in the country. However, their most notable features are their cast-iron facades.

Begin your exploration of this 20-block historic neighborhood at the corner of SW First Avenue and Ankeny Street at:

1. **Skidmore Fountain,** the heart of Old Town. Erected in 1888, the fountain was intended to provide refreshment for "horses, men, and dogs," and it did that for many years. Today, however, the bronze-and-granite fountain is purely decorative. Across SW First Avenue is the:

2. **New Market Block,** constructed in 1872 to house the unlikely combination of a produce market and a theater. The New Market Block now contains popular shops and restaurants, as do many of the restored historic buildings in this area. The

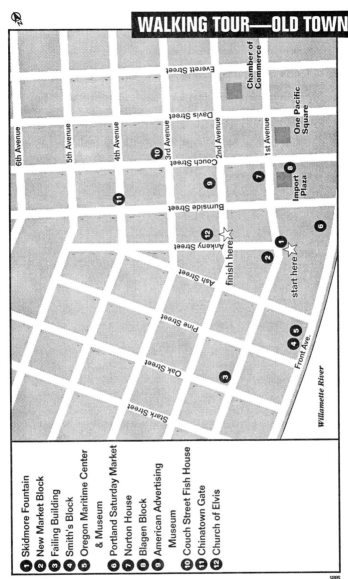

Map labels: Everett Street, Davis Street, Couch Street, Burnside Street, Ankeny Street, Ash Street, Pine Street, Oak Street, Stark Street

6th Avenue, 5th Avenue, 4th Avenue, 3rd Avenue, 2nd Avenue, 1st Avenue, Front Ave.

Chamber of Commerce, One Pacific Square, Import Plaza

finish here, start here

Willamette River

① Skidmore Fountain
② New Market Block
③ Failing Building
④ Smith's Block
⑤ Oregon Maritime Center & Museum
⑥ Portland Saturday Market
⑦ Norton House
⑧ Blagen Block
⑨ American Advertising Museum
⑩ Couch Street Fish House
⑪ Chinatown Gate
⑫ Church of Elvis

9895

freestanding wall of archways extending out from the New Market Building was salvaged from another Old Town structure that didn't survive the urban renewal craze of the 1960s. Two blocks south is the:

3. Failing Building, 235 SW First Ave. Built in 1886, this attractive structure integrates French and Italian influences. Turn left on SW Oak Street and left again on SW Front Avenue and you'll pass by:

4. Smith's Block, containing some of the most beautifully restored buildings in Old Town. At one time this whole district was filled with elegant structures such as these. The cast-iron filigree appears both solid and airy at the same time. This building houses the:

5. **Oregon Maritime Center & Museum,** 113 SW Front Ave., which is dedicated to Oregon's shipping history. If it's a Saturday or Sunday from March through December, you will no doubt have noticed the crowds under the bridge ahead of you. This is the:

6. **Portland Saturday Market,** where you'll find the best of Northwest crafts being sold by their makers. There typically are more than 250 booths plus entertainers and food vendors.

REFUELING STOP Portland Saturday Market makes an excellent refueling stop in this neighborhood. In the market's **food court** you can get all manner of delicious, healthful, and fun foods. Stalls sell everything from "dragon toast" to over-stuffed fajitas to pad thai to barbecued ribs.

At the MAX tram stop, cross First Avenue and turn right. Just as you leave the shadow of Burnside Bridge, you will be walking along the covered sidewalk of:

7. **Norton House.** Though this is not the original covered sidewalk, it is characteristic of Portland buildings 100 years ago. Across First Avenue toward the river is:

8. **Blagen Block,** another excellent example of the ornate cast-iron facades that appeared on nearly all the buildings in this area at one time. Note the cast-iron figures of women wearing spiked crowns. They are reminiscent of the Statue of Liberty, which had been erected two years before this building opened in 1888. Turn left up NW Couch (pronounced Kooch) Street to the corner of NW Second Avenue. Just around the corner to your left on the opposite side of the street is the:

9. **American Advertising Museum,** 9 NW Second Ave. This is the only museum in the United States dedicated to the history of advertising. Back in the late 1800s the building housed the very popular Erickson's Saloon, with a 684-foot-long bar, card rooms, and a brothel. If you return to NW Couch Street and continue to the corner of NW Third Avenue, you will see on the northwest corner:

10. **Couch Street Fish House,** an excellent example of using innovative methods to renovate Old Town. This excellent and highly recommended restaurant incorporates two historic structures into its design. One houses the restaurant itself, the inside of which is very modern. The other is merely an ornate brick facade behind which you'll find the restaurant's parking lot. Continue up NW Couch Street to Fourth Avenue and turn left. Directly ahead of you is:

11. **Chinatown Gate.** Since you are already in Chinatown, you will have to cross to the opposite side of the brightly painted three-tiered gateway to appreciate its ornateness, including two huge flanking bronze Chinese lions. After passing through this gate, cross Burnside Street and turn left on narrow, little Ankeny Street. In two blocks you will see on your left:

12. **The Church of Elvis:** 219 Ankeny St. This unusual little altar

to kitsch is the world's only 24-hour coin-operated video psychic and church of Elvis. For a quarter you can have one of the interactive videos in the window hear your confession. For $1 you can be "married" by the King himself. It's all very tongue-in-cheek and great fun. From here it's only a block and a half to Skidmore Fountain.

CHAPTER 18

PORTLAND SHOPPING

1. THE SHOPPING SCENE

2. SHOPPING A TO Z

Perhaps the single most important fact about shopping in Portland, and all of Oregon for that matter, is that there is no sales tax. The price on the tag is the price you pay. If you come from a state with a high sales tax, you might want to save your shopping for your visit to Portland.

1. THE SHOPPING SCENE

Over the past few years Portland has managed to preserve and restore a good deal of its historic architecture, and many of these late 19th-century and early 20th-century buildings have been turned into unusual and very attractive shopping centers. New Market Village (50 SW Second Ave.), Morgan's Alley (515 SW Broadway), and Skidmore Fountain Square (28 SW First Ave.) are all outstanding examples of how Portland has preserved its historic buildings and kept its downtown area filled with happy shoppers. Yamhill Market (SW First Avenue and Yamhill Street), although in a new building, was designed to fit in with the classic architecture of the neighborhood surrounding it.

Portland's most "happening" area for shopping is the Nob Hill district of northwestern Portland. Northwest 23rd Avenue beginning at West Burnside Street is the heart of Nob Hill. Along this stretch of road, and on adjoining streets, you'll find antiques stores, boutiques, card shops, design studios, ethnic restaurants, florists, galleries, home furnishings stores, interior decorators, pubs, and all the other necessities of a bohemian neighborhood gone upscale.

Hours Most small stores in Portland are open Monday through Saturday from 9 or 10am to 5 or 6pm. Shopping malls are usually open Monday through Friday from 9 or 10am to 9pm, on Saturday from 9 or 10am to 6pm, and on Sunday from noon until 5pm. Most art galleries and antiques stores are closed on Monday. Department stores stay open on Friday night until 9pm.

2. SHOPPING A TO Z

ANTIQUES

OLD SELLWOOD ANTIQUE ROW, at east end of Sellwood Bridge on SE 13th St.

With its old Victorian homes and turn-of-the-century architecture, Sellwood is Portland's main antiques district. You'll find **13** blocks with more than 30 antiques dealers and restaurants.

ART GALLERIES

If you're in the market for art, try to arrange your visit to coincide with the first Thursday of a month. On these days galleries in downtown Portland schedule coordinated openings in the evening. Stroll from one gallery to the next, meeting artists and perhaps buying an original work of art. As an added bonus, the **Portland Art Museum,** 1219 SW Park Ave. (tel. 226-2811), offers free admission from 4 to 9:30pm on these nights.

An art-gallery guide listing more than 50 Portland galleries is available from the **Portland/Oregon Visitors Association,** Three World Trade Center, 26 SW Salmon St., Portland, OR 97204-3299 (tel. 222-2223 or toll free 800/962-3700).

QUINTANA GALLERIES-OLD TOWN, 139 NW Second Ave. Tel. 223-1729.

Virtually a small museum of Native American art, this Old Town store sells everything from baskets and rugs to contemporary painting and sculpture by various Indians. The jewelry selection is outstanding. Prices are not cheap.

Quintana's grew so big that it had to split off its Northwest Coastal Indian and Inuit art offerings, as well as Edward S. Curtis photogravures. These can now be found at the downtown gallery, 818 SW First Ave. (tel. 228-6855). Masks, soapstone carvings, and prints fill the smaller gallery.

RAINDANCE GALLERY, 1115 NW Glisan St. Tel. 224-4020.

Located in the Pearl District, a former shipping center that now houses galleries and living lofts, Raindance features works by established Northwest artists. There are several rooms of ceramics, painting, sculpture, jewelry, and hand-blown glass from the Pilchuck School in Washington State.

BOOKS

POWELL'S "CITY OF BOOKS," 1005 W. Burnside St. Tel. 228-4651.

This is one of the largest bookstores in the United States selling new and used books, and no visit to Portland would be complete without a stop here. You'll find nearly a million volumes in this massive store. To help you locate subjects, there's a handy map of the store available at the front door. Just so you don't starve while wandering the aisles, they also have a coffee shop. You should actually try to make this one of your first stops in town so you can pick up a copy of their excellent free map of downtown Portland. Open Monday to Saturday 9am to 11pm, Sunday 9am to 9pm.

If you are looking for a technical book, try **Powell's Technical Books,** 33 NW 11th St. (tel. 228-3906), a block away.

POWELL'S TRAVEL STORE, 701 SW Sixth Ave. Tel. 228-1108.

Located beneath Pioneer Courthouse Square at the corner of SW Sixth Avenue and Yamhill Street, this travel bookstore has plenty of

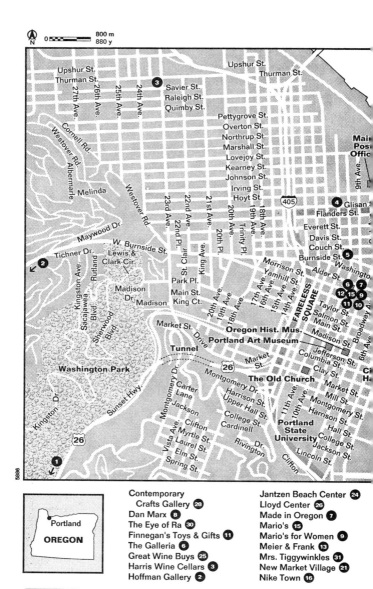

Contemporary		Jantzen Beach Center 24
Crafts Gallery 28		Lloyd Center 26
Dan Marx 8		Made in Oregon 7
The Eye of Ra 30		Mario's 15
Finnegan's Toys & Gifts 11		Mario's for Women 9
The Galleria 6		Meier & Frank 13
Great Wine Buys 25		Mrs. Tiggywinkles 31
Harris Wine Cellars 3		New Market Village 21
Hoffman Gallery 2		Nike Town 16

books and maps on Portland, the Northwest, and every other part of
the world. The map collection is one of the region's largest, and if you
ask at the front counter, you can pick up a free Portland walking tour
map. Open Monday to Saturday 9am to 7pm, Sunday 10am to 5pm.

CRAFTS

For the largest selection of local crafts, visit Portland Saturday
Market (see below). This entertaining outdoor market is a show-

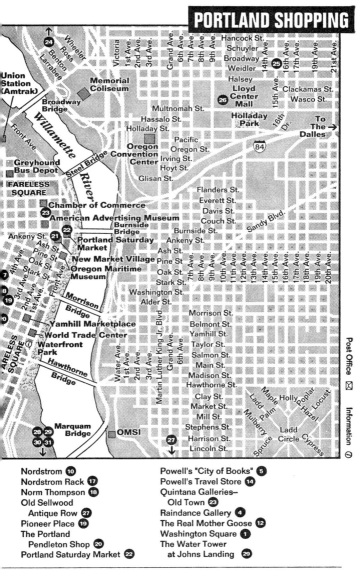

case for the high-quality crafts that are created in this part of the country.

CONTEMPORARY CRAFTS GALLERY, 3934 SW Corbett Ave. Tel. 223-2654.

In business since 1937, this is the nation's oldest nonprofit art gallery showing exclusively artwork in clay, glass, fiber, metal, and wood. It's located in a residential neighborhood between downtown and the John's Landing neighborhood, and has a spectacular tree-shaded porch overlooking the Willamette River. The bulk of the gallery is taken up by glass and ceramic pieces, with several cabinets of designer jewelry. Open Tuesday to Saturday 10am to 5pm, Sunday 1 to 5pm.

HOFFMAN GALLERY, 8245 SW Barnes Rd. Tel. 297-5544.

Hoffman Gallery is located on the campus of Oregon School of Arts and Crafts, which has been one of the nation's foremost crafts education centers since 1906. The gallery offers installations and group shows by local, national, and international artists. The adjacent gift shop has an outstanding selection of handcrafted items.

THE REAL MOTHER GOOSE, 901 SW Yamhill St. Tel. 223-9510.

This is Portland's premier crafts shop. They showcase only the very finest contemporary American crafts, including imaginative ceramics, colorful art glass, intricate jewelry, exquisite wooden furniture, handmade fashions, and sculptural works. Hundreds of craftspeople and artists from all over the United States are represented here, and even if you're not buying, you should stop by to see the best of American craftsmanship.

Other locations include Washington Square; Tigard (tel. 620-2243); and Portland International Airport, Main Terminal (tel. 284-9929).

DEPARTMENT STORES

MEIER & FRANK, 621 SW Fifth Ave. Tel. 223-0512.

Meier & Frank is a Portland institution. They have been doing business here for more than 100 years. Their flagship store on Pioneer Courthouse Square was built in 1898 and, with 10 stories, was at one time the tallest store in the Northwest. Today those 10 stories of consumer goods still attract crowds of shoppers. The store is open daily, with Monday and Friday usually the late nights. Other locations include 1100 Lloyd Center (tel. 281-4797) and 9300 SW Washington Square Rd. in Tigard (tel. 620-3311).

NORDSTROM, 701 SW Broadway. Tel. 224-6666.

Directly across the street from Pioneer Courthouse Square and a block away from Meier & Frank, Nordstrom is a top-of-the-line department store that originated in the Northwest and takes great pride in its personal service and friendliness. This pride is well founded—the store has devoutly loyal customers who would never dream of shopping anywhere else. Although Nordstrom's legendary service is primarily aimed at repeat customers, visitors should not let that dissuade them from shopping here.

DISCOUNT STORE

NORDSTROM RACK, 401 SW Morrison St. Tel. 299-1815.

Nordstrom is the premier Northwest department store and this is their merchandise clearance store. You'll find discontinued lines, end-of-the-season overstock, and much more packed into a crowded underground shop. Before heading to the main store, be sure to stop by the Rack. You might make your shopping dollars go a lot further.

FASHION

NIKE TOWN, 930 SW Sixth Ave. Tel. 221-6453.

★ This superglitzy, ultracontempo showcase for Nike products blasted onto the Portland shopping scene with all the subtlety of a Super Bowl celebration. Matte black decor, George Segal–style plaster statues of athletes, and videos everywhere give NIKE TOWN the feel of a sports museum or disco. A true shopping experience. Open Monday to Thursday 10am to 7:01pm, Friday 10am to 8pm, Saturday 10am to 6:52pm, Sunday 11:25am to 6:23pm.

NORDSTROM, 701 SW Broadway. Tel. 224-6666.
For fashions for the whole family, I must once again send you to this incomparable department store. Their personal service is second to none, and they have a wide selection of fashions at competitive prices. They also offer wardrobe consultations and an alteration service.

NORM THOMPSON, 420 SW Morrison St. Tel. 243-2680.
Known throughout the rest of the country from its mail-order catalogs, Norm Thompson is a mainstay of the well-to-do in Portland. Classic styling for men and women is the name of the game here. A second store is at Portland International Airport (tel. 249-0170).

THE PORTLAND PENDLETON SHOP, 900 SW Fourth Ave. (between Salmon and Taylor). Tel. 242-0037.
Pendleton wool is as much a part of life in the Northwest as forests and salmon. This company's fine wool fashions for men and women define the country-club look in the Northwest and in many other parts of the country. Pleated skirts and tweed jackets are de rigueur here, as are the colorful blankets that have helped keep generations of northwesterners warm through long chilly winters.

CHILDREN'S FASHION

MRS. TIGGYWINKLES, 5331 SW Macadam Ave. Tel. 227-7084.
Located in The Water Tower at Johns Landing shopping center, Mrs. Tiggywinkles sells classic handmade children's clothing, and custom designs and special orders are welcome. They also have a great selection of costumes for Halloween or dress up. This is a good place to shop for wooden toys and puzzles by Northwest craftspeople.

MEN'S FASHION

MARIO'S, 921 SW Morrison St. Tel. 227-3477.
Located inside the Galleria, Mario's sells self-consciously stylish European men's fashions straight off the pages of *GQ* and *M*. Prices are as high as you would expect. If you long to be European, but your birth certificate says otherwise, here you can at least adopt the look.

WOMEN'S FASHION

THE EYE OF RA, 5331 SW Macadam Ave. Tel. 224-4292.
★ Women with sophisticated tastes in ethnic fashions will want to visit this pricey shop in The Water Tower at John's Landing shopping center. Silks and rayons predominate, and there is plenty of ethnic jewelry by creative designers to accompany any ensemble you might put together here. Ethnic furniture and home decor are also for sale.

MARIO'S FOR WOMEN, 811 SW Morrison St. Tel. 241-8111.

Flip through the pages of a European edition of *Vogue* magazine and you'll get an idea of the fashions you can find at the women's version of fashionable Mario's. Up-to-the-minute and back-to-the-future European fashions fill the racks.

FOOD

The Made in Oregon shops offer the best selection of local food products such as hazelnuts, marion berry and raspberry jam, and smoked salmon. See "Gifts/Souvenirs," below, for details.

GIFTS/SOUVENIRS

For unique handmade souvenirs, your best bet is Portland Saturday Market (see "Market," below, for details).

MADE IN OREGON, 921 SW Morrison St. (in the Galleria). Tel. 241-3630.

This is your one-stop shop for all manner of made-in-Oregon gifts, food products, and clothing, every product they sell is either grown, caught, or made in Oregon. This is the place to visit for salmon, filberts, jams and jellies, Pendleton woolens, and Oregon wines. If you forgot to pick up a salmon or any of their other popular products while you were in town, give them a call at their toll-free number (tel. 800/828-9673).

Other Portland area branches can be found in Portland International Airport's Main Terminal (tel. 282-7827); in Lloyd Center, SE Multnomah St. and SE Broadway (tel. 282-7636); at Clackamas Town Center, 12000 SE 82nd Ave. (tel. 659-3155); in Old Town at 10 NW First Ave. (tel. 273-8354); and at Washington Square, off Oregon Hwy. 217 in Tigard (tel. 620-4670). All branches are open daily, but hours vary from store to store.

JEWELRY

DAN MARX, 511 SW Broadway. Tel. 228-5090.

For almost as long as Portland has existed, Dan Marx has been selling the city's better-off citizens fine jewelry. Everything sparkles and shines inside this store, and the helpful staff will be happy to educate you on the fine points of buying precious stones.

MALLS/SHOPPING CENTERS

THE GALLERIA, 921 SW Morrison St. Tel. 228-2748.

Located in the heart of downtown Portland, The Galleria is a three-story atrium shopping mall with more than 50 specialty shops and restaurants, including a Made in Oregon store where you can stock up on Oregon-made gifts. Before being restored and turned into its present incarnation, this building was one of Portland's earliest department stores. Parking validation available at adjacent parking garage.

JANTZEN BEACH CENTER, 1405 Jantzen Beach Center. Tel. 289-5555.

This large shopping mall is located on the site of a former amusement park, and the old carousel still operates. There are four major department stores and more than 80 other shops. You'll also find the R.E.I. co-op recreational-equipment store here. This mall has long been popular with residents of Washington State, who come to shop where there is no sales tax.

LLOYD CENTER, bounded by SE Multnomah St., SE Broadway, SE 16th Ave., and SE Ninth Ave. Tel. 282-2511.

Lloyd Center was the largest shopping mall on the West Coast when it opened in 1960. In 1991 an extensive renovation was completed to bring it up to current standards. There are now more than 165 shops here, including a Nordstrom and a Meier & Frank. A food court, ice-skating rink, and eight-screen cinema complete the mall's facilities.

NEW MARKET VILLAGE, 50 SW Second Ave. Tel. 228-2392.

Housed in a brick building built in 1872, this small shopping center is listed in the National Register of Historic Places. You'll find it directly across the street from the Skidmore Fountain and the Portland Saturday Market. A long row of freestanding archways salvaged from a demolished building creates a courtyard on one side of the New Market Village building. Also on this side are several open-air restaurants.

PIONEER PLACE, 700 SW Fifth Ave. Tel. 228-5800.

Located only a block from Pioneer Courthouse Square, Portland's newest downtown shopping center is also its most upscale. Anchored by a Saks Fifth Avenue, Pioneer Place is where the elite shop when looking for high fashions and expensive gifts. You'll also find Portland's branch of the Nature Company and the city's only Godiva *chocolatier* here.

WASHINGTON SQUARE, off Oregon Hwy. 217 in Tigard. Tel. 639-8860.

This is the only shopping mall in the Northwest with five major department stores, plus more than 120 specialty shops and eating establishments. It's the main shopping center for Portland's western suburbs. Lots of free parking.

THE WATER TOWER AT JOHNS LANDING, 5331 SW Macadam Ave. Tel. 228-9431.

As you're driving south from downtown Portland on Macadam Avenue, you can't miss the old wooden water tower for which this unusual shopping mall is named. Standing high above the roof of the mall, it was once used as a storage tank for fire-fighting water. The building, originally a furniture factory, was converted to a shopping and office complex in 1973. Hardwood floors, huge overhead beams, and a tree-shaded courtyard paved with Belgian cobblestones from Portland's first paved streets give this place plenty of character. There are about 40 specialty shops and restaurants here.

MARKET

PORTLAND SATURDAY MARKET, underneath Burnside Bridge (between SW First Ave. and SW Ankeny St.). Tel. 222-6072.

Portland Saturday Market (held on both Saturday and Sunday) is arguably the city's single most important and best-loved event. For years the Northwest has attracted artists and craftspeople, and every Saturday and Sunday nearly 300 of them can be found selling their exquisite creations here. In addition to the dozens of craftspeople's stalls, you'll find flowers, fresh produce, ethnic and unusual foods, and lots of free entertainment. This is the single best place to shop for one-of-a-kind gifts in Portland. The atmosphere is always cheerful and the crowds are always colorful. At the heart of the Skidmore District, Portland Saturday Market makes an excellent starting or finishing point for a walk around Portland's most historic neighborhood. Don't miss this unique market. On Sunday, on-street parking is free. Open March through December, Saturday 10am to 5pm, Sunday 11am to 4:30pm. MAX: Skidmore Fountain station. Closed: January and February.

TOYS

FINNEGAN'S TOYS & GIFTS, 922 SW Yamhill St. Tel. 221-0306.

We all harbor a bit of child within ourselves, and this is the sort of place that has that inner child kicking and screaming in the aisles if you don't buy that silly little toy you never got when you were young. Kids love this place too. It's the largest toy store in downtown Portland. Open Monday to Saturday 10am to 6pm, Sunday noon to 5pm.

WINE

An excellent selection of Oregon wine can be found at any Made in Oregon shop. They're located in the Lloyd Center shopping mall, the Galleria, Washington Square, and Portland Airport. See "Gifts/Souvenirs," above, for details.

There are a number of wineries within easy driving distance of Portland where you can taste and buy wine. See Section 3 of Chapter 20 for details.

GREAT WINE BUYS, 1515 NE Broadway. Tel. 287-BUYS.

Oenophiles who have developed a taste for Oregon wines will want to stock up here before heading home. This is one of the best wine shops in Portland. The staff is helpful and all of them make wine. Wine tastings are on Friday and Saturday nights. Open Monday to Thursday 10:30am to 6:30pm, Friday 10:30am to 8pm, Saturday 10:30am to 5pm, Sunday noon to 5pm.

HARRIS WINE CELLARS LTD, 2300 NW Thurman St. Tel. 223-2222.

Located at the northern and less fashionable end of NW 23rd Avenue, Harris Wine Cellars caters to serious wine connoisseurs, and has been doing so for many years. It isn't glamorous, but the folks here know their wine. Hearty lunches are also available. Open daily 10am to 6pm.

CHAPTER 19

PORTLAND NIGHTS

1. **THE PERFORMING ARTS**
- **MAJOR CONCERT HALLS & ALL-PURPOSE AUDITORIUMS**
2. **THE CLUB & MUSIC SCENE**
3. **THE BAR SCENE**
4. **MORE ENTERTAINMENT**

Portland has become the Northwest's second cultural center. Its symphony orchestra, ballet, and opera are all well regarded, and the many theater companies offer classic and contemporary plays. If you are a jazz fan, you'll feel right at home—there's always a lot of live jazz being played around town. In summer, festivals move the city's cultural activities outdoors.

To find out what's going on during your visit, pick up a copy of **Willamette Week,** Portland's weekly arts-and-entertainment newspaper. You can also check the Friday and Sunday editions of The **Oregonian,** the city's daily newspaper.

Many theaters and performance halls in Portland offer discounts to students and senior citizens. You can often save money by buying your ticket on the day of a performance or within a half hour of curtain time.

Anyone who wants can pick up half-price day-of-show tickets to theater performances at **PDX TIX,** 921 SW Morrison St. (tel. 241-4903). This phone number is for information only, since they don't take telephone reservations. The small ticket counter is located inside the Galleria shopping center and is open October through June on Thursday to Saturday from noon to 6pm and on Sunday from noon to 5pm.

1. THE PERFORMING ARTS

MAJOR PERFORMING ARTS COMPANIES

OPERA & CLASSICAL MUSIC

THE OREGON SYMPHONY, Arlene Schnitzer Concert Hall, 1111 SW Broadway, at SW Main St. Tel. 228-1353.

Founded in 1896, this is the oldest symphony orchestra on the West Coast. Under the expert baton of conductor James De Preist, it has achieved national recognition and status. Four series are held each season, including classical, pops, Sunday matinees, and children's concerts. The season runs from September to June.

Prices: $9.50–$45. Sun matinees are the least expensive. Senior citizens and students may purchase half-price tickets 1 hour before a classical concert.

PORTLAND OPERA, Portland Civic Auditorium, SW Third Ave., at SW Clay St. Tel. 241-1802.

The Portland Opera offers five different productions of grand opera and musical theater. The season runs from September to May.
Prices: $19.50–$81. Senior citizens and students may attend dress rehearsals for a nominal charge.

THEATER

OREGON SHAKESPEARE FESTIVAL PORTLAND, Portland Center for the Performing Arts, 1111 SW Broadway, at SW Main St. Tel. 274-6588.

The immensely popular Oregon Shakespeare Festival, which takes place every summer in Ashland, way down near the California state line, became so popular a few years back that they brought the whole program to Portland for the winter season. The season, which runs from November to April, includes five productions of classic and modern plays.
Prices: $8–$29. Student and senior-citizen rush tickets available 1 hour before a show for half price.

PORTLAND REPERTORY THEATER, World Trade Center, 25 SW Salmon St. Tel. 224-4491.

Portland's oldest Equity theater offers consistently excellent productions, which have such a reputation that it is almost impossible to get individual tickets to performances. The Rep does reliable plays, nothing too avant-garde and no classics (who can compete with the Oregon Shakespeare Festival Portland?).
Prices: $23–$26.

TYGRES HEART SHAKESPEARE CO., Dolores Winningstad Theatre, 1111 SW Broadway, at SW Main St. Tel. 222-9220.

The play's the thing at Tygres Heart and old Will would be proud. While the Oregon Shakespeare Festival has broadened its thespian horizons, Tygres Heart remains true to its name and stages only works by the bard himself.
Prices: $7.50–$19.50.

DANCE

OREGON BALLET THEATRE, Portland Civic Auditorium, SW Third Ave., at SW Clay St. Tel. 227-6867.

This company was formed in late 1989 from two popular Portland ballet companies, and is now much stronger than either of its two predecessors ever were. Programs range from traditional ballets such as *The Nutcracker* and *Romeo and Juliet* to new works. Each season includes a guest performance by a visiting nationally acclaimed company.
Prices: $8–$55.

MAJOR CONCERT HALLS & ALL-PURPOSE AUDITORIUMS

The **Portland Center for the Performing Arts,** has helped spur a renaissance along SW Broadway, once the heart of Portland's dining and entertainment district. The center includes four units.

ARLENE SCHNITZER CONCERT HALL, 1111 SW Broadway, at SW Main St. Tel. 248-4496.

Formerly a 1920s movie palace, the Schnitz, as it is known locally, still displays the original Portland theater sign and marquee out front. Inside, you'll be thrilled by the immaculate restoration of this stately old theater. It is home to the Oregon Symphony, and also hosts popular music bands, lecturers, a travel-film series, and many other special performances.

Tours: Wed 11am and Sat 11am, noon, and 1pm; free.
Prices: $7–$50.

NEW THEATRE BUILDING, 1111 SW Broadway, at SW Main St. Tel. 248-4496.

Across the street from the Schnitz is the beautiful New Theatre Building, which houses two smaller theaters—the **Intermediate** and the **Winningstad.** A brilliant contrast to the art deco Schnitz, this building is a sparkling glass jewel box. The Intermediate Theatre is home to the Oregon Shakespeare Festival Portland, while the two theaters together host stage productions by local and visiting companies.

Tours: Wed 11am and Sat 11am, noon, and 1pm; free.
Prices: $3.25–$55. Student and senior-citizen discounts sometimes available.

PORTLAND CIVIC AUDITORIUM, SW Third Ave., at SW Clay St. Tel. 248-4496.

The Civic Auditorium is a few blocks from the three theaters mentioned above. It was constructed shortly after World War I and completely remodeled in the 1960s. Touring Broadway musicals perform in this large hall. This is also the home of both Oregon Ballet Theatre and the Portland Opera.

Prices: $15–$85.

2. THE CLUB & MUSIC SCENE

CABARET

DARCELLE XV, 208 NW Third Ave. Tel. 222-5338.

This campy Portland institution with a transvestite show has been a huge hit with the natives for years. Darcelle, a one-time transvestite beauty-contest winner, is so much a part of the Portland scene that he shows up on floats in official city parades.

Showtimes: Wed–Thurs 8:30pm, Fri–Sat 8:30 and 10:30pm.
Admission: $8. Reservations required Fri–Sat.

COMEDY CLUB

THE LAST LAUGH, 1130 SW Main St. Tel. 295-2844.

This is Portland's grandest and most popular comedy club, where local and nationally known comedians perform. You'll think you're in Las Vegas when you see the interior of this place. Dinner and drinks are available.

Open: Nightly 4pm to 12:30am.

Showtimes: Sun–Thurs 8pm; Fri–Sat 7:45 and 10:30pm. Reservations required.

Admission: Sun–Thurs $6; Fri–Sat $8.

FOLK & ROCK

KEY LARGO, 31 NW First Ave. Tel. 223-9919.

One of Portland's most popular nightclubs, Key Largo has been packing in music fans for more than a decade. A tropical atmosphere prevails at this spacious club and Cajun food is served. Rock, reggae, blues, and jazz performers all find their way to the stage here, with local R&B bands a mainstay. A nationally known act occasionally shows up here. Open nightly.

Admission: $3–$7 (higher for national acts).

ROSELAND THEATER, 8 NW Sixth Ave. Tel. 227-4418.

Roseland Theater is only a couple blocks from Key Largo. The same diversity of popular musical styles prevails. A couple of heavy-metal nights each week attract a rougher crowd than you're likely to find at Key Largo, but other nights you might encounter the likes of John Mayall or the latest Seattle grunge band. Open nightly.

Admission: $5–$15.

SATYRICON, 125 NW Sixth Ave. Tel. 243-2380.

A block away from Roseland Theater, Satyricon leans heavily toward heavy metal, grunge rock, and neopsychedelia. Though most bands playing here are local, the occasional national act also appears. Crowds are young and rowdy. Open nightly.

Admission: $3–$5 (higher for national acts). No cover charge until 11pm on weeknights.

JAZZ & BLUES

Portland is well known as a jazz town. You'll find that lots of restaurants and bars feature live or recorded jazz nightly. Because of this reputation, you're likely to encounter jazz greats performing here at any time of year. In summer, there are numerous jazz festivals and special jazz concert series in the area. Below are some of the more popular jazz clubs.

BRASSERIE MONTMARTRE, 626 SW Park Ave. Tel. 224-5552.

There's live jazz music from 8:30pm on Monday to Thursday and Sunday and from 9pm on Friday and Saturday at this French restaurant. Both food and music are popular with a primarily middle-aged clientele that likes to dress up when it goes on the town. Dress the part and expect a line at the door at any hour of day or night. This is the place to see and be seen if you're part of the Portland social scene. Open nightly 5:30pm to 1am.

Admission: Free.

PARCHMAN FARM, 1204 SE Clay St. Tel. 235-7831.

If you're into jazz, Parchman Farm is where you hang out in Portland. This club features a music library of more than 1,000 jazz albums, and there's live music Monday through Saturday starting between 8 and 9:30pm. A quiet, casual spot in which to dine and listen to great jazz, Parchman Farm attracts the sort of audience that gets up onstage and starts jamming with the evening's main act. The place also serves "American-style Italian food with a nouvelle flair."

Admission: Free most nights.

DANCE CLUBS/DISCOS

EMBERS AVENUE, 110 NW Broadway. Tel. 222-3082.

Though this is still primarily a gay disco, straights have discovered its great dance music and have started making the scene as well. Lots of flashing lights and sweaty bodies until the early morning. On Saturday nights, there are drag shows.

Admission: Thurs–Sun $2.

MAXI'S LOUNGE, Red Lion/Lloyd Center, 1000 NE Multnomah St. Tel. 281-6111.

For an evening of dancing to live or recorded Top 40 music, head for this or any of the other Red Lions in the Portland area. They all offer elegant settings for dancing the night away, though this lounge is the most spectacular. A long corridor of quilted dusty-rose velvet trimmed with red neon leads to a dark and sparkling disco with glowing etched-glass pillars, two dance floors, and lots of comfortable seating and live music nightly.

Brickstone's, Red Lion/Columbia River, 1401 N. Hayden Island Dr. (tel. 283-2111), attracts a similar upscale crowd.

Admission: Free.

3. THE BAR SCENE

PUBS

If you are a beer connoisseur, you'll probably find yourself with little time out from your brew tasting to see any other of Portland's sights. This is the heart of the Northwest microbrewery explosion and has more microbreweries than any other city in the United States. They're brewing beers up here the likes of which you won't taste anywhere else this side of the Atlantic. Although many of these beers—as well as ales, stouts, and bitters—are available in restaurants, you owe it to yourself to go directly to the source. At any of these pubs, you can pick up a guide and map to Portland's microbreweries and brew pubs.

BRIDGEPORT BREWERY & BREW PUB, 1313 NW Marshall St. Tel. 241-7179.

Portland's oldest microbrewery was founded in 1984, and is housed in the city's oldest industrial building. Windows behind the bar let you watch the brewers. It has four to seven of its brews on tap on any given night, and live music on Saturday night.

HILLSDALE BREWERY & PUBLIC HOUSE, 1505 SW Sunset Blvd. Tel. 246-3938.

This was the cornerstone of the McMenamin brothers' microbrewery empire, which now includes more than 20 pubs in the greater Portland metropolitan area. The McMenamins pride themselves in crafting flavorful and unusual ales with bizarre names like Terminator stout and Purple Haze.

Some of their other pubs include **Cornelius Pass Roadhouse,** Sunset Hwy. and Cornelius Pass Road, Hillsboro (tel. 640-6174), in an old farmhouse; **Blue Moon Tavern,** 432 NW 21st St. (tel. 223-3184), on a newly fashionable street in northwest Portland; and **The Ram's Head,** 2282 NW Hoyt St. (tel. 221-0098), between 21st and 22nd avenues.

SPECIALTY BARS
BAR WITH A VIEW

ATWATER'S RESTAURANT AND LOUNGE, 111 SW Fifth Ave. Tel. 275-3600.

Up on the 30th floor of the pale-pink U.S. Bancorp Tower is one of Portland's most expensive restaurants and certainly the one with the best view. However, if you'd just like to sit back and sip a martini while gazing out at the city lights below, they have a splendid little bar. Perfect for a romantic nightcap. On the weekend there is live jazz from 8:30pm to 12:30am. The lounge menu here is the most creative in Portland.

SPORTS BAR

CHAMPIONS, Portland Marriott Hotel, 1401 SW Front Ave. Tel. 274-2470.

Portland's premier sports bar boasts "good food, good times, and good sports." If sports are your forte, this is the bar for you. There is also a small dance floor here, with dancing nightly to Top 40 tunes.

4. MORE ENTERTAINMENT

MOVIES

BAGDAD THEATER & PUB, 3702 SE Hawthorne Blvd. Tel. 230-0895.

In a reversal of recent cinematic trends, the ever-inspired McMenamin brothers restored a classic Arabian Nights movie palace to its original size after it had been split up into a multiplex theater. They now show second-run films and pull more than 20 microbrew drafts at the bar. There's good pizza by the slice to go with your brew and a separate non-theater pub.
Admission: $1.

CINEMA 21, 616 NW 21st Ave. Tel. 223-4515.

Located on the edge of Nob Hill, one of Portland's most fashionable neighborhoods, Cinema 21 is a reliable art-film house. This is also where you can catch animation festivals and the occasional revival of an obscure classic.
Admission: $2-$5.

MISSION THEATER & PUB, 1624 NW Glisan St. Tel. 223-4031.

This was the McMenamin brothers' first theater pub. Movies are recent releases that have played the main theaters already but not yet made it onto video.
Admission: $1.

NORTHWEST FILM & VIDEO CENTER, 1219 SW Park Ave. Tel. 221-1156.

Affiliated with the Portland Art Museum, this repertory cinema schedules an eclectic blend of classics, foreign films, daring avant-garde films, documentaries, visiting artist programs, and thematic series. There's no telling what might turn up on a given night.

Admission: $4–$6.

CHAPTER 20

EASY EXCURSIONS FROM PORTLAND

1. MOUNT HOOD LOOP
2. OREGON COAST
3. WINERY TOUR

Portland likes to boast about how close it is to both mountains and ocean, and no visit would be complete without a trip or two into the countryside. In an hour and a half you can be swimming in the icy Pacific Ocean or skiing in the Cascade Range. In fact, you'll even have this latter choice in the middle of summer, when there is still snow skiing on Mount Hood. A drive through the Columbia River Gorge is an absolute must. If wine is your interest, you can spend a day visiting wineries and driving through the rolling farmland that enticed pioneers to travel the Oregon Trail beginning in the 1840s.

1. MOUNT HOOD LOOP

If you have time for only one excursion from Portland, I strongly urge you to do the Mount Hood Loop. This is a long trip, so start your day as early as possible.

To begin your trip, take I-84 east out of Portland. Sixteen miles from downtown, take the second Troutdale exit onto the **Columbia River Scenic Highway** (U.S. 30), which was opened in 1915. The highway is an engineering marvel, but it is dwarfed by the spectacular vistas that present themselves whenever the scenic road emerges from the dark forest. To learn more about the road and how it was built, stop at **Vista House,** 733 feet above the river on **Crown Point.** There are informative displays with old photos and a spectacular view of the gorge, including **Beacon Rock,** an 800-foot-tall monolith on the far side of the river.

Between Troutdale and Ainsworth State Park, 22 miles east, the road passes nine **waterfalls** and six state parks. Latourelle, Shepperds Dell, Bridal Veil, Wahkeena, Horsetail, Oneonta, Multnomah—the names of the falls evoke the Native American and pioneer heritage of this region. Of all the falls, **Multnomah** is the most famous. At 620 feet from the lip to the pool, it's the tallest waterfall in Oregon. An arched bridge stands directly in front of the falls and is a favorite of photographers.

The next stop on your tour should be the **Bonneville Lock and Dam.** One of the dam's most important features, and the attraction drawing thousands of visitors each year, is the fish ladders. These ladders allow salmon and other anadromous fish (fish that are spawned in freshwater, mature in saltwater, and return to freshwater to spawn) to migrate upstream. Underwater windows permit visitors to see fish as they pass through the ladders. Visit the adjacent fish hatchery to see how trout, salmon, and sturgeon are raised before they are released into the river.

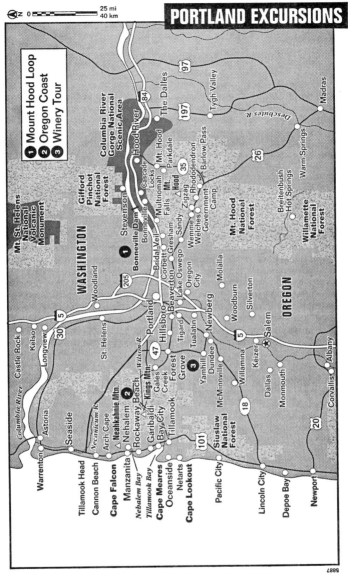

PORTLAND EXCURSIONS

1 Mount Hood Loop
2 Oregon Coast
3 Winery Tour

    Not far past the dam is **Bridge of the Gods,** which connects
Oregon to Washington at the site where an old Indian legend says a
natural bridge once stood. Because of the unusual formation of rocks
in the river at this site, as well as the frequent volcanic activity here in
the past, geologists tend to believe the legend.
    Just beyond Bridge of the Gods are the **Cascade Locks.** These
navigational locks were built to enable river traffic to avoid the
treacherous passage through the cascades here. In earlier years many
boats were portaged around the cascades instead of attempting the

dangerous trip. When the locks were opened in 1896, they made traveling between the Dalles and Portland much easier. But the completion of the Columbia River Scenic Highway in 1915 made the trip even easier by land. With the construction of the Bonneville Dam, the cascades were flooded and the locks became superfluous. There are two small museums here at the locks, one of which also holds the ticket office for the stern-wheeler **Columbia Gorge** (tel. 503/223-3928), which makes regular trips on the river all summer.

Anyone who sailboards has heard of the town of **Hood River.** This section of the Columbia River is one of the most popular sailboarding spots in the world because of the strong winds that come rushing down the gorge. Almost every other car in this once-sleepy little town has a sailboard on the roof. If you want to try this thrilling sport yourself, stop by **Sailboards Hood River,** 202 Cascade St. (tel. 503/386-5363). They offer sales, rentals, and lessons for beginners and advanced sailors. In the winter (and summer for that matter) they rent and sell skis and snowboards.

If you are staying overnight on the Loop, you might want to consider getting out of your car and riding the rails. The **Mount Hood Railroad,** 110 Railroad Ave. (tel. 503/386-3556), operates its Fruit Blossom Special from mid-April to early December. The cars that carry you up the Hood River are vintage Pullman coaches, and the Mount Hood Railroad Depot is a National Historic Site. Departures are at 10am and 3pm. The trip lasts four hours and costs $18.95 for adults, $16.95 for senior citizens, and $11.95 for children 2 to 11. In summer the train runs daily except Monday, and in late spring and early fall it runs Wednesday through Sunday, changing to weekends only in the colder months.

From Hood River, turn south on Oregon Hwy. 35, passing through thousands of acres of apple and pear **orchards.** Every fall, roadside stands in this area sell fresh fruit, butter, and juice. The orchards are especially beautiful in the spring, when the trees are in bloom. No matter what time of year, you will have the snow-covered peak of Mount Hood in view as you drive through the orchards, making them all the more spectacular.

About 10 miles off Oregon Hwy. 35, just south of Parkdale, is the **Cooper Spur Ski Area,** a day-use area. (In summer, there is camping hereabouts at Cloud Cap Saddle Campground and Tilly Jane Campground.) **Mount Hood Meadows** (tel. 503/337-2222), the largest ski area on Mount Hood with nine chair lifts, can transport 14,400 skiers per hour to more than 2,000 acres of ski slopes.

Beyond Mount Hood Meadows, you reach **Barlow Pass.** At 4,157 feet, it's the highest point on the Loop. This is where the Pacific Crest Trail crosses the highway on its 2,000-mile journey between Canada and Mexico.

Just after Hwy. 35 merges into U.S. 26, turn right onto the road to Timberline Lodge. At the top of this road, you'll be as close to the peak of Mount Hood as it's possible to drive. The peak looms directly in front of you with no obstructing trees or hills to block the view. As the name implies this is the timberline, and a walk on one of the trails in the vicinity will lead you through wildflower-filled meadows in summer. Surprisingly you can also ski here all summer on a glacier above Timberline Lodge. Needless to say, there's also plenty of winter skiing.

Back down on U.S. 26 heading west toward Portland, there is

another popular ski area, the **Mt. Hood SkiBowl** (tel. 503/ 243-3937). It's also open in summer, with an Alpine Slide and go-kart racing. The SkiBowl, the closest ski area to Portland, is located near the town of Government Camp, which has many small lodges and restaurants that cater primarily to winter skiers.

Between Government Camp and the Resort at the Mountain, watch for the marker beside the road showing where the end of the **Barlow Trail toll road** (a section of the Oregon Trail) around Mount Hood was located. There is a reproduction of the gate that once stood on this spot, and you can still see the trail itself.

It's a lot easier to cover the last 40 miles to Portland now than it was 150 years ago. Just stay on Oregon Hwy. 26 all the way back to town or follow the signs for I-84.

WHERE TO STAY

HOOD RIVER

Very Expensive

COLUMBIA GORGE HOTEL, 4000 Westcliff Dr., Hood River, OR 97031. Tel. 503/386-5566 or toll free 800/345-1921. Fax 503/386-3359. 42 rms. TV TEL

$ Rates (including five-course breakfast): $135 single; $190 double, $145 special weekday rate. AE, DC, DISC, MC, V. **Parking:** Free.

Located just west of the town of Hood River off I-84, and opened shortly after the Columbia River Scenic Highway was completed in 1915, the Columbia Gorge Hotel has long attracted celebrities and the well-heeled. This little oasis of luxury in the wilderness was completely restored in 1989 and today offers the same genteel atmosphere that was once enjoyed by the likes of Rudolph Valentino and Clara Bow. With its yellow stucco walls and red-tile roofs, this hotel would be right at home in Beverly Hills or Santa Barbara, and the gardens surrounding the hotel could hold their own in Victoria, British Columbia. Inside, however, the decor is strictly Old World, with deep forest greens and salmon pinks reflecting a Northwest palette. Louis XIV and Colonial America furnishings are tastefully intermingled throughout the lobby and lounge. Despite the attractive furnishings and gardens, it is almost impossible to notice anything but the view out the windows. The hotel is perched more than 200 feet above the river on a steep cliff, and the stream that meanders through the gardens suddenly cascades over the precipice.

Guest rooms are all a little different, with a mixture of antique and classic furnishings. There are canopy beds, brass beds, and even some hand-carved wooden beds. Unfortunately, many of the rooms are rather cramped, as are the bathrooms, most of which have older fixtures and some exposed pipes. Also unfortunate is the fact that the original architect didn't design larger windows in the guest rooms. If you're room is too small for you, the lounge is a delightful place to while away an afternoon.

Dining/Entertainment: The Columbia River Court Dining Room is one of the best restaurants in the Northwest, well known for a four-course farm breakfast. The breakfast nearly requires you to fast beforehand and diet after. Evening meals are rather pricey but feature Northwest cuisine with an emphasis on salmon, lamb, and venison.

Services: Limited room service, complimentary shuttle to Hood River.

Moderate

HOOD RIVER HOTEL, 102 Oak St., Hood River, OR 97031. Tel. 503/386-1900. Fax 503/386-6090. 32 rms, 9 suites. TV TEL

$ Rates: $64–$92 single; $75–$103 double; $85–$157 suite. DC, DISC, MC, V. **Parking:** On street.

Though the location isn't as nice, the atmosphere of the Hood River Hotel is very similar to that at the Columbia Gorge Hotel, and at a fraction of the price. Built in 1913 and located in the heart of downtown Hood River, this hotel was recently restored and boasts the casual elegance of a vintage hotel. You're greeted by brass rails, a streetside patio, and beveled-glass French doors as you arrive, and huge paned windows inside flood the high-ceilinged lobby with light. On winter nights a fire crackles in the fireplace. Guest rooms are all different and are furnished almost identically to the guest rooms at the Columbia Gorge Hotel. Canopy beds, ceiling fans, and oval floor mirrors capture a mood of elegance. Most third-floor rooms have skylit bathrooms, which makes them my favorites. Suites have full kitchens, and of course, river-view rooms are the most expensive.

Dining/Entertainment: Italian cuisine is featured in the hotel's casual dining room, which spans the front patio, the lobby, and the mezzanine.

Services: Complimentary newspaper, valet/laundry service.

Facilities: No-smoking rooms.

ON & NEAR MOUNT HOOD

Expensive

THE RESORT AT THE MOUNTAIN, 68010 E. Fairway, Welches, OR 97067. Tel. 503/622-3101 or toll free 800/669-7666. Fax 503/622-5227. 160 rms and suites. A/C TV TEL

$ Rates: Oct–mid-June, $105–$145 single or double, $155–$185 suite; mid-June–Sept, $118–$170 single or double, $170–$205 suite. Children under 18 free in parents' room. Special packages available. AE, CB, DC, DISC, MC, V. **Parking:** Free.

Calling the surrounding area "the Highlands of Oregon," the Resort at the Mountain has adopted a Scottish theme that emphasizes the resort's 27-hole golf course. When the fog hangs low in the valley, it is indeed easy to imagine oneself in the Scottish Highlands, except for the towering fir trees and nearby peak of Mount Hood. Beautifully landscaped grounds that incorporate concepts from Japanese gardens hide the resort's many low-rise buildings. Guest rooms are large and all have either a balcony or patio. Coffee makers and special closets for ski gear are just two features of these rooms.

Dining/Entertainment: The Tartans Inn and Pub is a casual dining room decked out in plenty of tartan and overlooking the golf course. The Highlands Restaurant and Bar is the resort's premier dining room and serves a combination of Northwest, Scottish, and continental dishes at surprisingly reasonable prices.

Services: Room service, valet/laundry service.

Facilities: 27-hole golf course, 6 tennis courts, indoor and outdoor swimming pools, whirlpool tub, fitness center, horseshoes, hiking and nature trails, volleyball, badminton, croquet, basketball, gift shops, pro shop, Scottish shop.

Moderate

TIMBERLINE LODGE, Timberline, OR 97028. Tel. 503/ 231-7979 or toll free 800/547-1406. Fax 503/272-3710. 59 rms (49 with private bath).

$ Rates: $55 single or double without bath; $90–$150 single or double with bath. AE, DC, DISC, MC, V. **Parking:** Free.

Constructed during the Great Depression of the 1930s as a WPA project, this classic Alpine ski lodge overflows with craftsmanship. The grand stone fireplace, huge exposed beams, and wide plank floors of the lobby impress every first-time visitor. Details are not overlooked either. Wood carvings, imaginative wrought-iron fixtures, hand-hooked rugs, and handmade furniture complete the rustic picture. An exhibit in the lower lobby presents the history of the hotel and its restoration a few years ago. There are also tours of the hotel.

Rooms vary in size considerably, with the smallest rooms lacking private bathrooms. However, no matter which room you stay in, you'll be surrounded by the same rustic furnishings. Unfortunately room windows are not very large, but you can always retire to the Ram's Head lounge for a better view of Mount Hood.

Dining/Entertainment: The Cascade Dining Room enjoys a nearly legendary reputation. Some people come to stay at the lodge just to have dinner here. The tables are rustic and the windows are small (which limits views), but the food is superb, if a bit pricey. There is also a casual snack bar in the Wy'East Day Lodge across the parking lot. The Blue Ox Bar is a dark dungeon of a place that shouldn't be missed. The Ram's Head Bar, a more open and airy place, is on the mezzanine.

Services: Firestarters for rooms with fireplaces, guided hotel tours.

Facilities: Ski lifts, ski school and rentals, outdoor swimming pool, hiking trails, gift shop, no-smoking rooms, wheelchair accommodations, coin laundry.

2. OREGON COAST

With so much water around Portland, it is often difficult to believe that it's 90 miles to the coast. Still, the miles go by quickly as you drive, and before long you are thrilled by spectacular vistas, crashing surf, and long quiet beaches. There are more than 400 miles of coastline in Oregon, but I'll concentrate on the section that's most accessible to Portland.

The quickest route from Portland to the Oregon coast is via U.S. Hwy. 26, also called Sunset Highway. From downtown to the beach takes less than two hours. Just before reaching the junction with U.S. Hwy. 101, watch for a sign marking the **world's largest Sitka spruce tree.** This giant is located in a small park just off the highway. Trees of this size were once common throughout the Coast Range, but almost all have now been cut down. The fight to preserve the remaining big trees is a bitter one that has divided the citizens of Oregon.

At the junction with U.S. Hwy. 101, turn south and watch for the turnoff to **Ecola Beach State Park.** Located just north of the town of Cannon Beach, this park provides some of the most spectacular views on the coast. Just offshore is **Haystack Rock,** a massive rock island 235 feet tall that is the most photographed rock on the coast. And stretching out to the south is Cannon Beach. There are stands of old-growth spruce, hemlock, and Douglas fir in the park, and a number of trails offer a chance to walk through this lush forest. The trail down to the beach is steep, but you can still get a good view of sea lions basking in the sun even if you don't go all the way down.

Cannon Beach, known as the Provincetown or Carmel of the Northwest, depending on which coast you hail from, is named for the cannon and capstan of the USS *Shark,* which washed ashore here after the ship sank in 1849. Haystack Rock, only a few feet out from the beach, is popular with beachcombers and tide-pool explorers. In town, there are many art galleries and interesting shops, even a popular little theater (the Coaster Theater), that stages performances year-round. Every summer the **Cannon Beach Sandcastle Contest** attracts sand sculptors and thousands of appreciative viewers. Any time of year, you'll find the winds here ideal for kite flying.

Heading south out of Cannon Beach will bring you to the rugged and remote **Oswald West State Park,** named for the governor who promoted legislation to preserve all beaches as public property. The beach is in a cove that can only be reached by walking a few hundred yards through dense rain forest; once you are there, all you will hear is the crashing of the surf. The beach is strewn with huge driftwood logs that give it a wild look. High bluffs rise up at both ends of the cove and it is possible to hike to the top of them. There are plenty of picnic tables and a campground for tent campers only.

Highway 101 continues south from Oswald West State Park and climbs up over **Neahkahnie Mountain.** Legend has it that at the base of this oceanside mountain, the survivors of a wrecked Spanish galleon buried a fortune in gold. Keep your eyes open for elk, which frequently graze on the meadows here at the top of Neahkahnie Mountain.

Just below this windswept mountain is the quiet resort village of **Manzanita.** Tucked under the fir, spruce, and hemlock trees are the summer homes of some of Portland's wealthiest residents. There is also a long stretch of sandy beach at the foot of the village.

Tillamook Bay is one of the largest bays on the Oregon coast and at its north end is the small town of Garibaldi, which is a popular sportfishing spot. If you aren't an angler, you can still go for a cruise either around the bay or to look for whales.

Just before reaching the busy town of **Tillamook,** you will come to the **Tillamook Cheese Factory.** This region is one of Oregon's main dairy-farming areas, and much of the milk is turned into cheddar cheese and butter. The first cheese factory opened here in 1894. Today you can watch the sophisticated cheese-making process through large windows. The cheese-factory store is a busy place, but the lines move quickly and you can be on your way to the next picnic area with an assortment of tasty cheeses.

From Tillamook the **Three Capes Scenic Route** leads to Cape Meares, Cape Lookout, and Cape Kiwanda, all of which provide stunning vistas of rocky cliffs, misty mountains, and booming surf. As the name implies, this is a very scenic stretch of road, and there are plenty of places to stop and enjoy the views and the beaches.

Cape Meares State Park perches high atop the cape, with the Cape Meares lighthouse just a short walk from the parking lot. This lighthouse, 200 feet above the water, was built in 1890. Today it has been replaced by an automated light a few feet away. Be sure to visit the **octopus tree** here in the park. This Sitka spruce has been twisted and sculpted by harsh weather.

As you come down from the cape, you will come to the village of **Oceanside,** which clings to the steep mountainsides of a small cove. One tavern and one restaurant are the only commercial establishments, and that's the way folks here like it. After seeing the overdevelopment in other coastal towns, you'll understand why.

South of Oceanside the road runs along a flat stretch of beach before reaching **Cape Lookout State Park.** Cape Lookout, a steep forested ridge jutting out into the Pacific, is an excellent place for whale watching in the spring. A trail leads from either the main (lower) parking area or the parking area at the top of the ridge out to the end of the point. From the upper parking lot it is a 5-mile round trip to the point.

At Sandlake Junction, about 14 miles south of Oceanside, turn left and you will return to U.S. Hwy. 101. Head north to Tillamook, where Oregon Hwy. 6 heads east toward Portland. This road is subject to landslides and is sometimes closed so be sure to ask in Tillamook before heading east. Oregon Hwy. 6 joins U.S. Hwy. 26 about 25 miles west of Portland. Allow about 2½ hours to get back from Tillamook.

3. WINERY TOUR

In recent years Oregon wine has been winning many awards for outstanding quality. This isn't surprising when you realize that Oregon is on the same latitude as France's wine-growing regions. The climate is also very similar—cool, wet winters and springs and long, dry summers with warm days and cool nights. These are ideal conditions for growing wine grapes, and local vineyards are making the most of a good situation.

A "Discover Oregon Wineries" brochure describing more than 50 Oregon wineries is available from the **Oregon Winegrowers' Association,** 1200 NW Front Ave., Suite 400, Portland, OR 97209 (tel. 503/228-8403). Almost all wineries are within an hour or two of Portland, and consequently a day of driving from one winery to another makes for a pleasant outing. I suggest picking four or five that sound interesting and then mapping out the best routes among them. A trip through wine country is a chance to see the fertile valleys that lured pioneers across the Oregon Trail. For more information about the Oregon wine scene, including a calendar of winery events, pick up a copy of **Oregon Wine,** a monthly newspaper, in any local wineshop, or contact the **Oregon Wine Press,** 644 SE 20th Ave., Portland, OR 97214 (tel. 503/232-7607). With summer festivals a big part of the Oregon winery scene, you can enjoy picnics while listening to live jazz bands at many vineyards.

The trip outlined below takes in some of the region's best wineries and most beautiful countryside. Allow yourself at least half a day for a winery tour. I recommend taking along a picnic lunch, which you can supplement with a wine purchase. Most wineries have picnic tables.

To begin your winery tour, head west out of Portland on U.S. Hwy. 26 (Sunset Highway) and then take Oregon Hwy. 6 toward Tillamook. After a few miles on this two-lane highway, watch for signs indicating a left turn onto Oregon Hwy. 8 toward Forest Grove. Heading back east on this road, watch for a sign to **Laurel Ridge Winery,** 255 David Hill Rd. (tel. 503/359-5436). This is one of the oldest wineries in Oregon. The first grapes were planted here in the late 1800s, but Prohibition interrupted wine production and the vineyard was slow to return to wine making. However, today, Laurel Hill produces excellent Pinot Noir, gewürztraminer, Semillon, Sylvaner, and Riesling. Laurel Ridge also produces excellent sparkling wine by the *méthode champagnoise.* The winery is open daily from noon to 5pm.

Continue into Forest Grove on Oregon Hwy. 8 and then turn right onto Oregon Hwy. 47 toward Yamhill. Just south of town, you'll see signs for **Montinore Vineyards,** 3663 SW Dilley Rd. (tel. 503/359-5012). This is the largest wine producer in the state and enjoys an enviable location with sweeping views across the Tualatin Valley to the Cascade Range. A tree-lined drive leads up to a Victorian mansion that seems to have been transported from a Southern plantation. With 14 wines and a large tasting room and gift shop, Montinore is popular with tour groups. Landscaped grounds invite a stroll or picnic after tasting a few wines. Pinot Noir, Pinot Gris, chardonnay, and white Riesling are among the more popular wines produced here. The winery is open daily from noon to 5pm from May to October; the rest of the year it is open weekends only.

Back on Oregon Hwy. 47, continue south to the small town of Yamhill where you turn east on Oregon Hwy. 240. After a few miles watch for signs to **Knudsen Erath Winery,** Worden Hill Road (tel. 503/538-3318). Situated on 45 acres above the town of Dundee, this winery has one of the most spectacular settings in the region. The cedar-shingled buildings of the winery are set between forest and vineyard, and the views are stunning. Wines produced here include Pinot Noir, Riesling, gewürztraminer, chardonnay, cabernet sauvignon, and a brut. The winery is open daily from noon to 5pm.

At the bottom of the Knudsen Erath driveway, you'll find a shady little park that makes a good picnic spot if you haven't already eaten at one of the wineries.

Head downhill into the valley from Knudsen Erath and you will soon see a sign for **Lange Winery,** 18380 NE Buena Vista Rd. (tel. 503/538-6476). This is a tiny winery with only a few acres of its own grapes, and the tasting room is the basement of the owners' home. However, the wines produced here are some of the best in the state. Pinot Noir, chardonnay, and Pinot Gris are specialties. The winery is open weekends from noon to 5pm.

Continuing down into the valley again, you will come to the town of Dundee and U.S. Hwy. 99W. Turn right on the highway and a few miles out of town you will see the sign for **Sokol Blosser Winery,** 5000 NE Sokol Blosser Lane (tel. 503/864-2282), which sits high on a hill overlooking the valley. This is one of the larger wineries in Oregon and maintains a spacious tasting room and gift shop. On any given day, three wines will be available for tasting. These might include Pinot Noir, chardonnay, gewürztraminer, Riesling, or Muller-Thurgau. The winery is open daily from 11am to 5pm.

Directly across the street from Sokol Blosser's driveway, you'll see **Laube Orchards.** This former roadside fruit stand is now a full-fledged specialty foods shop featuring Oregon products. Stop in and stock up on boysenberry jam or roasted hazelnuts. If it is late in the day, you might want to stop for dinner in Dundee, which has several excellent restaurants. **Tina's,** 760 Hwy. 99W (tel. 503/538-8880), is a tiny place with a menu that is limited to about half a dozen well-prepared dishes. **Alfie's Wayside Country Inn,** 1111 Hwy. 99W (tel. 503/538-9407), is a much larger place. You just can't help but notice the pink Dutch colonial home that houses Alfie's. Both restaurants serve a mixture of continental and Northwest cuisine and reservations are highly recommended. Should you wish to spend the night, there are also quite a few bed-and-breakfast inns nearby. I suggest contacting **Yamhill County Bed and Breakfast Association,** P.O. Box 656, McMinnville, OR 97128. There are also motels in McMinnville and Newberg. To return to Portland, just head east on U.S. Hwy. 99W.

FOR FOREIGN VISITORS

Although American facts, fads, and fashions have spread across Europe and other parts of the world, so that America may seem like familiar territory before your arrival, there are still many peculiarities and uniquely American situations that any foreign visitor will encounter.

1. PREPARING FOR YOUR TRIP

TOURIST INFORMATION

Tourist information on Seattle is available by writing to the **Seattle–King County Convention & Visitors Bureau,** 520 Pike Street, Suite 1300, Seattle, WA 98101-9927 (tel. 206/461-5840). You can stop by their office located at the Washington State Convention & Trade Center, 800 Convention Place, Galleria Level, at the corner of Eighth Avenue and Pike Street. For information on the rest of Washington State, contact the **Washington State Tourism Office,** P.O. Box 42500, Olympia, WA 98504-2500 (tel. 206/586-2102 or 206/586-2088 or toll free 800/544-1800).

For information about Portland and the state of Oregon contact the **Portland/Oregon Visitors Association,** Three World Trade Center, 26 SW Salmon St., Portland, OR 97204-3299 (tel. 503/222-2223 or toll free 800/962-3700). For further information on Oregon State, contact the **Oregon Tourism Division,** 775 Summer St. NE, Salem, OR 97310 (tel. 503/373-1200 or toll free 800/547-7842).

ENTRY REQUIREMENTS

DOCUMENTS   Canadian nationals need only proof of Canadian residence to visit the United States. Citizens of Great Britain and Japan need only a current passport. Citizens of other countries, including Australia and New Zealand, usually need two documents: (1) a valid **passport** with an expiration date at least six months later than the scheduled end of their visit to the United States and (2) a **tourist visa,** available at no charge from a U.S. embassy or consulate.

To obtain a tourist or business visa to enter the United States, contact the nearest American embassy or consulate in your country. If there is none, you will have to apply in person in a country where there is a U.S. embassy or consulate. Present your passport, a passport-size photo of yourself, and a completed application, which is available through the embassy or consulate.

You may be asked to provide information about how you plan to finance your trip or show a letter of invitation from a friend with whom you plan to stay. Those applying for a business visa may be asked to show evidence that they will not receive a salary in the United States.

Be sure to check the length of stay on your visa; usually it is six months. If you want to stay longer, you may file for an extension with the Immigration and Naturalization Service once you are in the United States. If permission to stay is granted, a new visa is not required unless you leave the United States and want to reenter.

The visitor arriving by air, no matter what the port of entry—San Francisco, Los Angeles, New York, Anchorage, Honolulu, or any other—should cultivate patience and resignation before setting foot on U.S. soil. Getting through immigration control may take as long as two hours on some days, especially summer weekends; and then it takes additional time to clear Customs. When planning connections between international and domestic flights, you should allow an average of two to three hours at least for any delays.

In contrast, for the traveler arriving by car or by rail from Canada, the border-crossing formalities have been streamlined to the vanishing point. And for the traveler by air from Canada, you can sometimes go through Customs and Immigration at the point of departure, which is much quicker. If arriving in Seattle by ferry from Victoria, you will go through Customs at the ferry terminal in Seattle.

MEDICAL   No inoculations are needed to enter the United States unless you are coming from, or have stopped over in, areas known to be suffering from epidemics, especially of cholera or yellow fever. Applicants for immigrants' visas (and only they) must undergo a screening for AIDS under a law passed in 1987.

If you have a disease requiring treatment with medications containing narcotics or drugs, or requiring injections with syringes, carry a valid signed prescription from your physician to allay any suspicions that you are smuggling drugs.

CUSTOMS   Every adult visitor may bring in, free of duty: 1 liter of wine or hard liquor; 200 cigarettes or 50 cigars (but no cigars from Cuba) or 2 kilograms of smoking tobacco; $100 worth of gifts. These exemptions are offered to travelers who will spend at least 72 hours in the United States and who have not claimed these exemptions within the preceding six months. It is altogether forbidden to bring into the country foodstuffs (particularly cheese, fruit, cooked meats, and canned goods) and plants (vegetables, seeds, tropical plants, etc.). Foreign tourists may bring in or take out up to $10,000 in U.S. or foreign currency with no formalities; larger sums must be declared to Customs on entering or leaving.

INSURANCE

Unlike most other countries, the United States has no national health-care system. Because the cost of medical care is extremely high, we strongly advise every traveler to secure health coverage before setting out. In addition, you may want to take out a travel policy that covers (for a relatively low premium) loss or theft of your baggage; trip-cancellation costs; guarantee of bail in case you are arrested; sickness or injury cost (medical, surgical, and hospital); cost of accident, repatriation, or death. Such packages (for example, "Europe Assistance" in Europe) are sold by automobile clubs at attractive rates, as well as by insurance companies and travel agencies.

MONEY

CURRENCY & EXCHANGE The U.S. monetary system has a decimal base: 1 American dollar ($1) = 100 cents (100¢).

Dollar bills commonly come in $1 ("a buck"), $5, $10, $20, $50, and $100 denominations (the last two are not welcome when paying for small purchases and are not accepted in taxis). There are also $2 bills (seldom encountered).

There are six denominations of coins: 1¢ (one cent, or "penny"); 5¢ (five cents, or "nickel"); 10¢ (ten cents, or "dime"); 25¢ (twenty-five cents, or "quarter"); 50¢ (fifty cents, or "half dollar"); and the $1 piece (this includes the older, larger silver dollars and the newer, small Susan B. Anthony coin). *Note:* Outside of Las Vegas, NV, and Atlantic City, NJ, you will rarely encounter a $1 piece.

For currency exchange in Seattle, go to **American Express Travel Agency,** 600 Stewart St. (tel. 441-8622), or **Thomas Cook,** 906 Third Ave. (tel. 623-6203). Both are open Monday through Friday from 9am to 5pm.

In Portland, go to **American Express,** 1100 SW Sixth Ave. (tel. 226-2961). It is open Monday through Friday from 9am to 5pm.

TRAVELER'S CHECKS Traveler's checks in U.S. dollar denominations are readily accepted at most hotels, motels, restaurants, and large stores. Traveler's checks in other than U.S. dollars will almost always have to be changed at a bank or currency-exchange office, with the possible exception of those in Canadian dollars. Because of the proximity of the Canadian border, many hotels, restaurants, and shops will accept Canadian currency.

CREDIT CARDS The method of payment most widely used for paying hotel and restaurant bills and for making major purchases is the credit card. The following are the major credit cards listed in roughly descending order of acceptance: **VISA** (BarclayCard in Britain), **MasterCard** (EuroCard in Europe, Access in Britain, Diamond in Japan), **American Express, Discover Card, Diners Club,** and **Carte Blanche.** You can save yourself trouble by using "plastic money," rather than cash or traveler's checks, in 95% of all hotels, motels, restaurants, and retail stores (except for those selling food or liquor). A credit card can serve as a deposit for renting a car, as proof of identity (often carrying more weight than a passport), or as a "cash card," enabling you to draw money from banks that accept them.

Note: The "foreign-exchange bureaus" so common in Europe are rare even at airports in the United States; these exchange bureaus do not exist outside major cities. Try to avoid changing foreign money or traveler's checks not denominated in U.S. dollars; in fact, leave any currency other than U.S. dollars at home—it may prove to be more of a nuisance to you than it's worth.

SAFETY

While tourist areas usually are safe, crime is on the increase everywhere, and U.S. urban areas tend to be less safe than those in Europe or Japan. Visitors should always be alert, especially in large U.S. cities. It is wise to ask a city or regional tourist office if you are in doubt about which neighborhoods are safe. Avoid deserted areas, especially at night. Don't enter a city park at night unless there is an occasion that attracts crowds. Generally speaking, you can feel safe in areas where there are many people and many open establishments.

Avoid carrying valuables with you on the street and don't display expensive cameras or electronic equipment. Hold on to your pocketbook and place your billfold in an inside pocket. In restaurants, theaters, and other public places, keep your possessions in sight.

Remember also that hotels are open to the public, and in a large hotel, security personnel may not screen everyone entering. Always lock your room door; don't assume that once inside your hotel you are automatically safe and need no longer be aware of your surroundings.

DRIVING Safety while driving is particularly important. Question your car-rental agency about personal safety, or ask for a traveler safety tips brochure when you pick up your car. Obtain written directions, or a map with the route marked in red, from the agency showing how to reach your destination. And, if possible, arrive and depart during daylight hours.

Recently, more and more crime has involved cars and drivers. If you drive off a highway into a neighborhood that seems threatening, leave the area as quickly as possible. If you have an accident, even on a highway, remain inside your car with doors locked until you assess the situation, or until the police arrive. If you are bumped from behind on the street or are involved in a minor accident with no injuries and the situation appears to be suspicious, motion to the other driver to follow you. *Never* leave your car in such situations. You can also keep a premade sign in your car reading, "PLEASE FOLLOW THIS VEHICLE TO REPORT THE ACCIDENT." Show the sign to the other driver and go directly to the nearest police precinct, well-lighted service station, or open store.

If you see someone on the road who indicates a need for help, do not stop. Take note of the location, drive on to a well-lighted area, and telephone the police by dialing 911.

Park in well-lighted, well-traveled areas if possible. Always keep your car doors locked, whether attended or unattended. Look around before you get in or out of your car, and never leave packages or valuables in sight. If someone attempts to rob you or steal your car, do not try to resist and report the incident to the police immediately.

2. GETTING TO & AROUND THE USA

Air travelers from overseas can take advantage of **APEX (Advance Purchase Excursion)** fares offered by all major U.S. and European carriers. Aside from these, attractive values are offered by **Icelandair** on flights from Luxembourg to New York and by **Virgin Atlantic** from London to New York/Newark.

Some large airlines—for example, **TWA, American, Northwest, United,** and **Delta**—offer transatlantic and transpacific travelers special discount tickets under the name **Visit USA,** allowing travel between any U.S. destinations at minimum rates. These tickets are not on sale in the United States and must therefore be purchased before you leave your foreign point of departure. This system is the easiest and fastest way of seeing the country at low cost. You should obtain information well in advance from your travel agent or the office of the airline concerned, since the conditions attached to these discount tickets can be changed without advance notice.

Visitors should also be aware of the limitations of long-distance railroad travel in the United States. With notable exceptions (for instance, the Northeast Corridor between Boston and Washington, D.C.), service is rarely up to European standards: Delays are common, routes are limited and often infrequently served, and fares are rarely significantly lower than discount airfares.

For further information about travel to and around Seattle and Portland, see "Getting There" in Chapters 2 and 12, and "Getting Around" in Chapters 3 and 13.

FAST FACTS / FOR THE FOREIGN TRAVELER

Accommodations   It is always a good idea to make hotel reservations as soon as you know your trip dates. Reservations require a deposit of one night's payment. Seattle and Portland are particularly busy during summer months, and hotels book up in advance—especially on weekends when there is a festival on. If you do not have reservations, it is best to look for a room in the midafternoon. If you wait until evening, you run the risk that hotels will be filled.

In the United States, major downtown hotels, which cater primarily to business travelers, commonly offer weekend discounts of as much as 50% to entice vacationers to fill empty rooms. Note that rates in Seattle and Portland tend to go up in the summer, when there is a greater demand. If you wish to save money and don't mind cloudy or rainy weather, consider visiting sometime other than summer, though these cities really are at their best when the sun is shining.

Auto Organizations   If you are planning to drive a car while in the United States and you are a member of an automobile organization in your home country, check before leaving to see if they have a reciprocal agreement with one of the large U.S. automobile clubs, such as **AAA.** However, if you plan to drive a rented car, the rental company should provide free breakdown service.

Business Hours   **Banks** are open weekdays from 9am to 3pm, and usually have later hours on Friday; many banks are now open on Saturday also. There is also 24-hour access to banks through automatic teller machines. Most **offices** are open weekdays from 9am to 5pm. Most **post offices** are open weekdays from 8am to 5pm. In general, **stores** open between 9 and 10am and close between 5 and 6pm, Monday through Saturday; some **department**

stores stay open till 9pm on Thursday and Friday evening; and many stores are open on Sunday from 11am to 5 or 6pm.

Climate   See "Climate" in Section 2 of Chapters 2 and 12.

Currency & Exchange   See "Money" in Section 1 of this chapter for an explanation of U.S. currency. To exchange money in Seattle, go to **American Express,** 600 Stewart St. (tel. 441-8622), or **Thomas Cook,** 906 Third Ave. (tel. 623-6203). To exchange money in Portland, go to **American Express,** 1100 SW Sixth Ave. (tel. 226-2961).

Customs & Immigration   See "Entry Requirements" in Section 1 of this chapter.

Drinking Laws   The legal drinking age in both Washington and Oregon is 21. The penalties for driving under the influence of alcohol are stiff.

Electricity   U.S. wall outlets give power at 110 to 120 volts, 60 cycles, compared to 220 to 240 volts, 50 cycles, in most of Europe. Besides a 110-volt converter, small appliances of non-American manufacture, such as hair dryers or shavers, will require a plug adapter with two flat, parallel pins.

Embassies & Consulates   Almost all embassies are located in the national capital, Washington, D.C. Some consulates are located in major cities, and most nations have a mission to the United Nations in New York City. Listed here are embassies and consulates of some major English-speaking countries. If you are from another country, you can obtain the telephone number of your embassy by calling **Information** in Washington, DC (tel. 202/555-1212).

- **Australia** The **embassy** is at 1601 Massachusetts Ave. NW, Washington, DC 20036 (tel. 202/797-3000). The nearest **consulate** is in San Francisco at 1 Bush St., San Francisco, CA 94104-4413 (tel. 415/362-6160).
- **Canada** The **embassy** is at 501 Pennsylvania Ave. NW, Washington, DC 20001 (tel. 202/682-1740). The regional **consulate** is at 600 Stewart St., Seattle, WA 98101 (tel. 206/443-1777).
- **Ireland** The **embassy** is at 2234 Massachusetts Ave. NW, Washington, DC 20008 (tel. 202/462-3939). The nearest **consulate** is in San Francisco at 655 Montgomery St., Suite 930, San Francisco, CA 94111 (tel. 415/392-4214).
- **New Zealand** The **embassy** is at 37 Observatory Circle NW, Washington, DC 20008 (tel. 202/328-4800). The nearest **consulate** is in Los Angeles at Tishman Bldg., 10960 Wilshire Blvd., Suite 1530, Westwood, CA 90024 (tel. 310/477-8241).
- **United Kingdom** The **embassy** is at 3100 Massachusetts Ave. NW, Washington, DC 20008 (tel. 202/462-1340). There is a **consulate** in Seattle at 999 Third Ave., Seattle, WA 98101 (tel. 206/622-9255).

Emergencies   Call **911** for fire, police, ambulance. If you encounter such problems as sickness, accident, or lost or stolen baggage, it will pay you to call **Travelers Aid,** an organization that specializes in helping distressed travelers, whether American or foreign. In Seattle, phone 206/461-3888.

Gasoline [Petrol]   Most cars in the United States now use unleaded gasoline (gas) only, and leaded gasoline is not available in many parts of the country. However, it is available in both Washington and Oregon. In Oregon you are not allowed to pump your own gasoline, but in Washington "self-service" gas stations are common and usually are less expensive than full-service stations.

Holidays   On the following legal national holidays, most banks, government offices, post offices, and many stores, restaurants, and museums are closed:

January 1 (New Year's Day)
Third Monday in January (Martin Luther King, Jr. Day)
Third Monday in February (Presidents' Day, Washington's Birthday)
Last Monday in May (Memorial Day)
July 4 (Independence Day)
First Monday in September (Labor Day)
Second Monday in October (Columbus Day)
November 11 (Veterans Day/Armistice Day)
Fourth Thursday in November (Thanksgiving Day)
December 25 (Christmas Day)

The Tuesday following the first Monday in November is Election Day. It's a legal holiday in presidential-election years (1996, 2000).

Information   Information on Seattle is available by writing to the **Seattle–King County Convention & Visitors Bureau,** 520 Pike Street, Suite 1300, Seattle, WA 98101-9927 (tel. 206/461-5840). You can stop by their office located at the Washington State Convention & Trade Center, 800 Convention Place, Galleria Level, at the corner of Eighth Avenue and Pike Street. For information on the rest of Washington State, contact the **Washington State Tourism Office,** P.O. Box 42500, Olympia, WA 98504-2500 (tel. 206/586-2102 or 206/586-2088 or toll free 800/544-1800).

For information about Portland and the state of Oregon contact the **Portland/Oregon Visitors Association,** Three World Trade Center, 26 SW Salmon St., Portland, OR 97204-3299 (tel. 503/222-2223 or toll free 800/962-3700). For further information on Oregon State, contact the **Oregon Tourism Division,** 775 Summer St. NE, Salem, OR 97310 (tel. 503/373-1200 or toll free 800/547-7842).

Legal Aid   The foreign tourist, unless positively identified as a member of the Mafia or a drug ring, will probably never become involved with the American legal system. If you are stopped for a minor driving infraction (for example, of the highway code, such as speeding), never attempt to pay the fine directly to the police officer; you may wind up arrested on the much more serious charge of attempted bribery. Pay fines by mail, or directly into the hands of the clerk of the court. If accused of a more serious offense, it is wise to say and do nothing before consulting a lawyer. Under U.S. law, an arrested person is allowed one telephone call to a party of his or her choice. Call your embassy or consulate.

Liquor Laws   See "Drinking Laws," above.

Mail   Mailboxes are blue with a red-and-white logo and carry the inscription "U.S. Mail." The international postage rates at the time of publication are 40¢ for a 1-ounce letter and 30¢ for a postcard mailed to Canada. All other countries cost 50¢ for a ½-ounce letter and 40¢ for a postcard.

Medical Emergencies   Dial **911** for an ambulance.

Post Office   In Seattle the main post office is at the intersection of Third Avenue and Union Street (tel. 206/442-6340). In Portland the main post office is at 715 NW Hoyt St. (tel. 503/294-2424).

Radio & Television   Audiovisual media—with four coast-to-coast commercial networks (ABC, CBS, NBC, and Fox), along with the Public Broadcasting System (PBS) and a growing network of cable channels—play a major part in American life. In Seattle there are six over-the-air channels, most of which broadcast 24 hours a day, and in Portland there are seven. In addition, there are pay-TV channels showing sports events or recent movies. Both Seattle and Portland have more than 30 local radio stations, most broadcasting a particular type of music—classical, country, jazz, Top 40, oldies—along with news and frequent commercials.

Safety   See "Safety" in Section 1 of this chapter.

Taxes   In the United States there is no VAT (value-added tax) or other indirect tax at a national level. But every state, and each city in it, can levy a local tax on all purchases, including hotel and restaurant checks, bills and airline tickets. In Seattle and King County the **sales tax rate** is 8.2%. In Portland and the rest of Oregon, there is no sales tax.

Telephone, Telex & Fax   The telephone area code is **206** for Seattle and **503** for Portland. Pay phones can be found at street corners and in bars, restaurants, hotels, public buildings, stores, and service stations. **Local calls** cost 25¢.

For **long-distance** or **international calls,** stock up with a supply of 25¢ coins (quarters); the pay phones will instruct you when, and in what quantity, you should put them into the slot. For direct overseas calls, first dial 011, followed by the country code (Australia, 61; Republic of Ireland, 353; New Zealand, 64; United Kingdom, 44; and so on), and then by the city code (for example, 71 or 81 for London, 21 for Birmingham) and the number of the person you wish to call. For long-distance calls in Canada and the United States, dial 1, followed by the area code and number you want.

Before calling from a hotel room, always ask if there are any telephone surcharges. These are best avoided by using a public phone, calling collect, or using a charge card.

For **reverse-charge** or **collect calls,** and for **person-to-person calls,** dial 0 (zero, not the letter "O"), followed by the area code and number you want; an operator will then come on the line and you should specify that you are calling collect or person-to-person or both. If your operator-assisted call is international, ask for the overseas operator.

For local **directory assistance ("information"),** dial 555-1212; for long-distance information, dial 1, then the appropriate area code and 555-1212.

Like the telephone system, **telegraph** and **telex** services are provided by private corporations like ITT, MCI, and, above all, Western Union. You can bring your telegram to the nearest Western Union office (there are hundreds across the country), or dictate it over the phone (a toll-free call, 800/325-6000). You can also telegraph money, or have it telegraphed to you very quickly over the Western Union system.

Time   The United States is divided into six time zones. From east to west these are: **Eastern Time (ET), Central Time (CT), Mountain Time (MT), Pacific Time (PT), Alaska Time (AT),** and **Hawaii Time (HT).** Always keep in mind the different time zones when traveling (or even telephoning) long distances. For example, noon in Seattle (PT) is 1pm in Denver (MT), 2pm in Chicago (CT), 3pm in New York City (ET), 11am in Anchorage (AT), and 10am in Honolulu (HT). **Daylight Saving Time** is in effect from 1am on the first Sunday in April until 2am on the last Sunday in October except in Arizona, Hawaii, part of Indiana, and Puerto Rico.

Tipping   If restaurant service has been good, tip 15 to 20% of the bill. Taxi drivers expect about 10% of the fare. Airport porters and bellhops should be tipped about 50¢ per bag. For chambermaids, $1 per night is an appropriate tip.

Toilets   Often euphemistically referred to as restrooms, public toilets can be found in bars, restaurants, hotel lobbies, museums, department stores, and service stations—and will probably be clean (although those at service stations sometimes leave much to be desired). Note, however, that some restaurants and bars display a notice that "Toilets Are for the Use of Patrons Only." You can ignore this sign, or better yet, avoid arguments by ordering a cup of coffee or a soft drink, which will qualify you as a patron. The cleanliness of toilets at railroad stations and bus depots may be questionable; some public places are equipped with pay toilets, which require you to insert one or two 10¢ coins (dimes) into a slot on the door before it will open.

White Pages & Yellow Pages   There are two kinds of telephone directories. The general directory, called the **White Pages,** lists subscribers (business and personal residences) in alphabetical order. The inside front cover lists emergency numbers for police, fire, and ambulance, as well as other vital numbers (Coast Guard, poison control center, crime-victims hot line). The first few pages are devoted to community-service numbers, including a guide to long-distance and international calling, complete with country codes and area codes.

The second directory, the **Yellow Pages,** lists local services, businesses, and industries by type, with an index at the back. The listings cover not only such obvious items as automobile repair services by make of car, or drugstores (pharmacies)—often by geographical location—but also restaurants by type of cuisine and geographical location, bookstores by special subject, places of worship by religious denomination, and other information that the tourist might otherwise not readily find. The Yellow Pages also include city plans or detailed area maps, often showing postal Zip Codes and public transportation.

AMERICAN SYSTEM OF MEASUREMENT
LENGTH

1 inch (in.)	=	2.54cm				
1 foot (ft.)	=	12 in.	=	30.48cm	=	0.305m
1 yard (yd.)	=	3 ft.	=	0.915m		
1 mile	=	5,280 ft.	=	1.609 km		

To convert miles to kilometers, multiply the number of miles by 1.61. Also use to convert miles per hour (mph) to kilometers per hour (kmph). **To convert kilometers to miles,** multiply the number of kilometers by 0.62. Also use to convert kmph to mph.

CAPACITY

1 fluid ounce (fl. oz.)	=	0.03 liters			
1 pint	=	16 fl. oz.	=	0.47 liters	
1 quart	=	2 pints	=	0.94 liters	
1 gallon (gal.)	=	4 quarts	=	3.79 liters	=
		0.83 Imperial gal.			

To convert U.S. gallons to liters, multiply the number of gallons by 3.79. **To convert liters to U.S. gallons,** multiply the number of liters by 0.26. **To convert U.S. gallons to Imperial gallons,** multiply the number of U.S. gallons by 0.83. **To convert Imperial gallons to U.S. gallons,** multiply the number of Imperial gallons by 1.2.

WEIGHT

1 ounce (oz.)	=	28.35g				
1 pound (lb.)	=	16 oz.	=	453.6g	=	0.45kg
1 ton	=	2,000 lb.	=	907kg	=	0.91 metric tons

To convert pounds to kilograms, multiply the number of pounds by 0.45. **To convert kilograms to pounds,** multiply the number of kilograms by 2.2.

TEMPERATURE

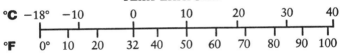

To convert degrees Fahrenheit to degrees Celsius, subtract 32 from °F, multiply by 5, then divide by 9 (example: 85°F − 32 × 5/9 = 29.4°C). **To convert degrees Celsius to degrees Fahrenheit,** multiply °C by 9, then divide by 5, and add 32 (example: 20°C × 9/5 + 32 = 68°F).

INDEX

SEATTLE

SEATTLE GENERAL INFORMATION

SEATTLE SIGHTS & ATTRACTIONS

EXCURSION AREAS

Note An asterisk * indicates an Author's Favorite.

SEATTLE ACCOMMODATIONS

Key to Abbreviations * = Author's Favorite; *$* = Super-Special Value; *B&B* = Bed & Breakfast; *E* = Expensive; *I* = Inexpensive; *M* = Moderate; *VE* = Very Expensive.

EXCURSION AREAS

SEATTLE RESTAURANTS

Key to Abbreviations * = Author's Favorite; *$* = Super-Special Value; *E* = Expensive; *I* = Inexpensive; *M* = Moderate; *VE* = Very Expensive.

PORTLAND

PORTLAND GENERAL INFORMATION

PORTLAND SIGHTS & ATTRACTIONS

EXCURSION AREAS

Note An asterisk * indicates an Author's Favorite.

PORTLAND ACCOMMODATIONS

EXCURSION AREA

Key to Abbreviations * = Author's Favorite; $ = Super-Special Value; B&B = Bed & Breakfast; E = Expensive; Hs = Hostel; I = Inexpensive; M = Moderate; VE = Very Expensive.

PORTLAND RESTAURANTS

Key to Abbreviations * = Author's Favorite; $ = Super-Special Value; E = Expensive; I = Inexpensive; M = Moderate; VE = Very Expensive.

Please Send Me the Books Checked Below:

FROMMER'S COMPREHENSIVE GUIDES
(Guides listing facilities from budget to deluxe,
with emphasis on the medium-priced)

	Retail Price	Code		Retail Price	Code
☐ Acapulco/Ixtapa/Taxco 1993–94	$15.00	C120	☐ Jamaica/Barbados 1993–94	$15.00	C105
☐ Alaska 1994–95	$17.00	C130	☐ Japan 1992–93	$19.00	C020
☐ Arizona 1993–94	$18.00	C101	☐ Morocco 1992–93	$18.00	C021
☐ Australia 1992–93	$18.00	C002	☐ Nepal 1994–95	$18.00	C126
☐ Austria 1993–94	$19.00	C119	☐ New England 1993	$17.00	C114
☐ Belgium/Holland/ Luxembourg 1993–94	$18.00	C106	☐ New Mexico 1993–94	$15.00	C117
☐ Bahamas 1994–95	$17.00	C121	☐ New York State 1994–95	$19.00	C132
☐ Bermuda 1994–95	$15.00	C122	☐ Northwest 1991–92	$17.00	C026
☐ Brazil 1993–94	$20.00	C111	☐ Portugal 1992–93	$16.00	C027
☐ California 1993	$18.00	C112	☐ Puerto Rico 1993–94	$15.00	C103
☐ Canada 1992–93	$18.00	C009	☐ Puerto Vallarta/ Manzanillo/Guadalajara 1992–93	$14.00	C028
☐ Caribbean 1994	$18.00	C123	☐ Scandinavia 1993–94	$19.00	C118
☐ Carolinas/Georgia 1994–95	$17.00	C128	☐ Scotland 1992–93	$16.00	C040
☐ Colorado 1993–94	$16.00	C100	☐ Skiing Europe 1989–90	$15.00	C030
☐ Cruises 1993–94	$19.00	C107	☐ South Pacific 1992–93	$20.00	C031
☐ DE/MD/PA & NJ Shore 1992–93	$19.00	C012	☐ Spain 1993–94	$19.00	C115
☐ Egypt 1990–91	$17.00	C013	☐ Switzerland/ Liechtenstein 1992–93	$19.00	C032
☐ England 1994	$18.00	C129	☐ Thailand 1992–93	$20.00	C033
☐ Florida 1994	$18.00	C124	☐ U.S.A. 1993–94	$19.00	C116
☐ France 1994–95	$20.00	C131	☐ Virgin Islands 1994–95	$13.00	C127
☐ Germany 1994	$19.00	C125	☐ Virginia 1992–93	$14.00	C037
☐ Italy 1994	$19.00	C130	☐ Yucatán 1993–94	$18.00	C110

FROMMER'S $-A-DAY GUIDES
(Guides to low-cost tourist accommodations and facilities)

	Retail Price	Code		Retail Price	Code
☐ Australia on $45 1993–94	$18.00	D102	☐ Israel on $45 1993–94	$18.00	D101
☐ Costa Rica/Guatemala/ Belize on $35 1993–94	$17.00	D108	☐ Mexico on $45 1994	$19.00	D116
☐ Eastern Europe on $30 1993–94	$18.00	D110	☐ New York on $70 1992–93	$16.00	D016
☐ England on $60 1994	$18.00	D112	☐ New Zealand on $45 1993–94	$18.00	D103
☐ Europe on $50 1994	$19.00	D115	☐ Scotland/Wales on $50 1992–93	$18.00	D019
☐ Greece on $45 1993–94	$19.00	D100	☐ South America on $40 1993–94	$19.00	D109
☐ Hawaii on $75 1994	$19.00	D113	☐ Turkey on $40 1992–93	$22.00	D023
☐ India on $40 1992–93	$20.00	D010	☐ Washington, D.C. on $40 1992–93	$17.00	D024
☐ Ireland on $40 1992–93	$17.00	D011			

FROMMER'S CITY $-A-DAY GUIDES
(Pocket-size guides with an emphasis on low-cost tourist accommodations and facilities)

	Retail Price	Code		Retail Price	Code
☐ Berlin on $40 1994–95	$12.00	D111	☐ Madrid on $50 1992–93	$13.00	D014
☐ Copenhagen on $50 1992–93	$12.00	D003	☐ Paris on $45 1994–95	$12.00	D117
☐ London on $45 1994–95	$12.00	D114	☐ Stockholm on $50 1992–93	$13.00	D022

FROMMER'S WALKING TOURS
(With routes and detailed maps, these companion guides point out the places and pleasures that make a city unique)

	Retail Price	Code		Retail Price	Code
☐ Berlin	$12.00	W100	☐ Paris	$12.00	W103
☐ London	$12.00	W101	☐ San Francisco	$12.00	W104
☐ New York	$12.00	W102	☐ Washington, D.C.	$12.00	W105

FROMMER'S TOURING GUIDES
(Color-illustrated guides that include walking tours, cultural and historic sights, and practical information)

	Retail Price	Code		Retail Price	Code
☐ Amsterdam	$11.00	T001	☐ New York	$11.00	T008
☐ Barcelona	$14.00	T015	☐ Rome	$11.00	T010
☐ Brazil	$11.00	T003	☐ Scotland	$10.00	T011
☐ Florence	$ 9.00	T005	☐ Sicily	$15.00	T017
☐ Hong Kong/Singapore/			☐ Tokyo	$15.00	T016
Macau	$11.00	T006	☐ Turkey	$11.00	T013
☐ Kenya	$14.00	T018	☐ Venice	$ 9.00	T014
☐ London	$13.00	T007			

FROMMER'S FAMILY GUIDES

	Retail Price	Code		Retail Price	Code
☐ California with Kids	$18.00	F100	☐ San Francisco with Kids	$17.00	F004
☐ Los Angeles with Kids	$17.00	F002			
☐ New York City with Kids	$18.00	F003	☐ Washington, D.C. with Kids	$17.00	F005

FROMMER'S CITY GUIDES
(Pocket-size guides to sightseeing and tourist accommodations and facilities in all price ranges)

	Retail Price	Code		Retail Price	Code
☐ Amsterdam 1993–94	$13.00	S110	☐ Montreál/Québec City 1993–94	$13.00	S125
☐ Athens 1993–94	$13.00	S114	☐ New Orleans 1993–94	$13.00	S103
☐ Atlanta 1993–94	$13.00	S112	☐ New York 1993	$13.00	S120
☐ Atlantic City/Cape May 1993–94	$13.00	S130	☐ Orlando 1994	$13.00	S135
☐ Bangkok 1992–93	$13.00	S005	☐ Paris 1993–94	$13.00	S109
☐ Barcelona/Majorca/ Minorca/Ibiza 1993–94	$13.00	S115	☐ Philadelphia 1993–94	$13.00	S113
☐ Berlin 1993–94	$13.00	S116	☐ Rio 1991–92	$ 9.00	S029
☐ Boston 1993–94	$13.00	S117	☐ Rome 1993–94	$13.00	S111
☐ Cancún/ Cozumel 1991–92	$ 9.00	S010	☐ Salt Lake City 1991–92	$ 9.00	S031
☐ Chicago 1993–94	$13.00	S122	☐ San Diego 1993–94	$13.00	S107
☐ Denver/Boulder/ Colorado Springs 1993–94	$13.00	S131	☐ San Francisco 1994	$13.00	S133
☐ Dublin 1993–94	$13.00	S128	☐ Santa Fe/Taos/ Albuquerque 1993–94	$13.00	S108
☐ Hawaii 1992	$12.00	S014	☐ Seattle/ Portland 1992–93	$12.00	S035
☐ Hong Kong 1992–93	$12.00	S015	☐ St. Louis/Kansas City 1993–94	$13.00	S127
☐ Honolulu/Oahu 1994	$13.00	S134	☐ Sydney 1993–94	$13.00	S129
☐ Las Vegas 1993–94	$13.00	S121	☐ Tampa/St. Petersburg 1993–94	$13.00	S105
☐ London 1994	$13.00	S132	☐ Tokyo 1992–93	$13.00	S039
☐ Los Angeles 1993–94	$13.00	S123	☐ Toronto 1993–94	$13.00	S126
☐ Madrid/Costa del Sol 1993–94	$13.00	S124	☐ Vancouver/ Victoria 1990–91	$ 8.00	S041
☐ Miami 1993–94	$13.00	S118	☐ Washington, D.C. 1993	$13.00	S102
☐ Minneapolis/St. Paul 1993–94	$13.00	S119			

Other Titles Available at Membership Prices

SPECIAL EDITIONS

	Retail Price	Code		Retail Price	Code
☐ Bed & Breakfast North America	$15.00	P002	☐ Marilyn Wood's Wonderful Weekends (within a 250-mile radius of NYC)	$12.00	P017
☐ Bed & Breakfast Southwest	$16.00	P100	☐ National Park Guide 1993	$15.00	P101
☐ Caribbean Hideaways	$16.00	P103	☐ Where to Stay U.S.A.	$15.00	P102

GAULT MILLAU'S "BEST OF" GUIDES
(The only guides that distinguish the truly superlative from the merely overrated)

	Retail Price	Code		Retail Price	Code
☐ Chicago	$16.00	G002	☐ New England	$16.00	G010
☐ Florida	$17.00	G003	☐ New Orleans	$17.00	G011
☐ France	$17.00	G004	☐ New York	$17.00	G012
☐ Germany	$18.00	G018	☐ Paris	$17.00	G013
☐ Hawaii	$17.00	G006	☐ San Francisco	$17.00	G014
☐ Hong Kong	$17.00	G007	☐ Thailand	$18.00	G019
☐ London	$17.00	G009	☐ Toronto	$17.00	G020
☐ Los Angeles	$17.00	G005	☐ Washington, D.C.	$17.00	G017

THE REAL GUIDES
(Opinionated, politically aware guides for youthful budget-minded travelers)

	Retail Price	Code		Retail Price	Code
☐ Able to Travel	$20.00	R112	☐ Kenya	$12.95	R015
☐ Amsterdam	$13.00	R100	☐ Mexico	$11.95	R128
☐ Barcelona	$13.00	R101	☐ Morocco	$14.00	R129
☐ Belgium/Holland/Luxembourg	$16.00	R031	☐ Nepal	$14.00	R018
☐ Berlin	$13.00	R123	☐ New York	$13.00	R019
☐ Brazil	$13.95	R003	☐ Paris	$13.00	R130
☐ California & the West Coast	$17.00	R121	☐ Peru	$12.95	R021
☐ Canada	$15.00	R103	☐ Poland	$13.95	R131
☐ Czechoslovakia	$15.00	R124	☐ Portugal	$16.00	R126
☐ Egypt	$19.00	R105	☐ Prague	$15.00	R113
☐ Europe	$18.00	R122	☐ San Francisco & the Bay Area	$11.95	R024
☐ Florida	$14.00	R006	☐ Scandinavia	$14.95	R025
☐ France	$18.00	R106	☐ Spain	$16.00	R026
☐ Germany	$18.00	R107	☐ Thailand	$17.00	R119
☐ Greece	$18.00	R108	☐ Tunisia	$17.00	R115
☐ Guatemala/Belize	$14.00	R127	☐ Turkey	$13.95	R027
☐ Hong Kong/Macau	$11.95	R011	☐ U.S.A.	$18.00	R117
☐ Hungary	$14.95	R118	☐ Venice	$11.95	R028
☐ Ireland	$17.00	R120	☐ Women Travel	$12.95	R029
☐ Italy	$18.00	R125	☐ Yugoslavia	$12.95	R030